UNFETTERED
GLOBALIZATION

UNFETTERED GLOBALIZATION

A New Economic Orthodoxy

C-RENÉ DOMINIQUE

Westport, Connecticut
London

Library of Congress Cataloging-in-Publication Data

Dominique, C-René.
    Unfettered globalization : a new economic orthodoxy / C-René
Dominique.
        p.   cm.
    Includes bibliographical references and index.
    ISBN 0–275–96378–0 (alk. paper)
    1. Economics.   I. Title.
    HB75.D458   1999
    330—dc21   98–25615

British Library Cataloguing in Publication Data is available.

Library of Congress Catalog Card Number: 98–25615
ISBN: 0–275–96378–0

First published in 1999

Praeger Publishers, 88 Post Road West, Westport, CT 06881
An imprint of Greenwood Publishing Group, Inc.

Printed in the United States of America

The paper used in this book complies with the
Permanent Paper Standard issued by the National
Information Standards Organization (Z39.48–1984).

10 9 8 7 6 5 4 3 2 1

Copyright Acknowledgments

The author and publisher gratefully acknowledge permission for use of the following material:

Excerpts from an article by Anita Chan, *The Guardian Weekly*, November 17, 1996.

Excerpts from "Les economistes en guerre contre les salaires," by Serge Halimi, *Le monde diplomatique*, July 1996.

Excerpts from "Excellents indices economiques . . . ," by Richard Farnelli, *Le monde diplomatique*, February 1997.

Excerpts from *World Economic Outlook*, May 1997, p. 45. The International Monetary Fund is the original source of the material.

Excerpts from *The World Within the World*, by John D. Barrow (Oxford: Clarendon Press, 1988), 10–12 passim, 24. Used by permission of Oxford University Press.

Excerpts from *The Invisible Hand*, by Bruna Ingrao and Giorgio Israel (Cambridge, MA: The MIT Press, 1990), pp. 361–362.

Excerpts from *The Growth Illusion*, by Richard Douthwaite (Tulsa: Council Oak Books, 1993), pp. 6–7, 16, 66. Used by permission of Green Books Ltd.

Every reasonable effort has been made to trace the owners of copyright materials in this book, but in some instances this has proven impossible. The author and publisher will be glad to receive information leading to more complete acknowledgments in subsequent printings of the book and in the meantime extend their apologies for any omissions.

To my son, Cristian

CONTENTS

Figures and Tables ix

Acknowledgments xiii

Abbreviations xv

Introduction xvii

I. Science, Mathematics, and Economics 1
   1 On Science and the Scientific Status of Economics 3
   2 The Scientific Theory of Economics 31
   3 The Operation of a Simple Economy 61

II. The New Orthodoxy 85
   4 The Emerging Economic Orthodoxy 87
   5 The Impacts of the New Orthodoxy 121

III. Poverty, Growth, and Distribution 161
   6 Unemployment and Social Security in the Age of
     Deconstruction 163
   7 Growing Economies in a Finite Ecosystem 191
   8 Poverty and Income Distribution 215

Summary and Conclusions 235

Notes 247

Bibliography 251

Index 259

FIGURES AND TABLES

FIGURES

1.1	The Scientific Process	12
1.2	The Organizational Scale of Matter, Forces, and Sciences	25
2.1	Linear and Partial Orderings of the Consumption Set X	44
2.2	The Conjectural Nature of Preference and Utility	47
A2.1	A Bundle in $\Re^3$	53
3.1	Plot of Variable: X_{pn}	76
3.2	Plot of Variable: X_{os}	76
5.1	Indices of Percent Change from a Year Earlier in the Wage, Unit Labor Costs, and the GNP/GDP Deflator in G7 Countries: 1973 = 100	124
5.2	Real GDP Growth Rates of Industrial Countries	126
5.3	OPEP Nominal Reference Price Index: 1973–1993	130
5.4	Indices of Domestic Investment as a Percent of GDP and Capacity Utilization: Industrial Countries	132
5.5	Operations of the Foreign Exchange Market	136
6.1	Employment Index by Technology Level in 17 Industrial Countries: 1970–1992	176
7.1	Optimal Level of Exploitation of a Renewable Resource	206
7.2	Daly's Depletion Quota Scheme	208
A7.1	The Production Process	213
8.1	The Distribution of World GDP Among the World Population by Region: 1970–1997	221
8.2	Inequality in Three Growing Economic Blocs: 1993	223

TABLES

4.1	The Productivity Slowdown in the G7 Countries	108
4.2	The Debt to GDP Ratio in the G7 Countries: 1980–1998	113
4.3	Cross-Border Transactions in Bonds and Equities: 1980–1996	115
5.1	The Link Between Inflation and Economic Growth	128
5.2	Testing the Transition to Market Against Economic Performance	149
5.3	Testing the Level of Sovereign Debt Against Economic Performance	151
5.4	Testing the Level of Inflation Against Economic Performance	152
A5.1	Factor Productivity Growth Outlook in Industrial Market Economies	153
A5.2	Consumer Price Index in Industrialized Market Economies: 1972–1996	153
A5.3	Levels of Unemployment in Selected Developed Market Economies: 1967–1996	154
A5.4	Real GDP Growth Rates in Countries Under the New Orthodoxy for More than 5 Years: 1976–1995	154
A5.5	Real Rates of Change in the Money Supply in G7 Countries: 1979–1980	155
A5.6	Loan Rates, Nominal and Real, in G7 Countries: 1978–1981	155
A5.7	Real Total Domestic Demand Growth in G7 Countries: 1971–1983	155
A5.8	Net Transfer of Financial Resources to Developing Economies: 1980–1991	156
A5.9	Net Transfer of Resources to Developing Economies: 1982–1992	156
A5.10	World Trade Pattern: 1980–1991	157
A5.11	Current Account Balance of Developed and Developing Market Economies: 1982–1992	157
A5.12	Foreign Debt of 122 Developing Economies: 1982–1992	158
A5.13	GDP Growth Rates of Countries in Transition: 1983–1996	158
A5.14	Military Expenditures in G7 Countries: 1980–1993	159
A5.15	Market Capitalization of Firms in G7 Countries: 1985–1993	159
A5.16	World Real Rates of GDP Growth: 1981–1997	160
A6.1	Labor Force Growth in Developed Market Economies: 1961–1993	187
A6.2	Employment, Unemployment, and Inactivity in Selected Countries: 1973–1992	187
A6.3	The Anatomy of Unemployment in Selected Developed Market Economies	188
A6.4	Life Expectancy of 60-Year-Old Men and Women in Selected Countries: 1950 and 1990	188
A6.5	Proportions of Dependents in the Total World Population: 1970–2025	189

A7.1   Estimation of the NRB by Region: 1994   211
8.1   Economic Growth, Pollution, and Poverty   224
8.2   Income Distribution in the United States: 1980–1994   225
8.3   The Share Ratio of Real GDP per Capita of the Richest
        20% to that of the Poorest 20% in Selected Countries and
        Regions over the 1980–1994 Period   228

ACKNOWLEDGMENTS

This book could not have been written without the help and encouragement of friends and colleagues. They have encouraged me to undertake the project. On numerous occasions, they have forced me to explain my ideas more clearly, and their generous advice has helped me in shaping up the manuscript. I owe them a huge debt of gratitude. They are, of course, too numerous to be enumerated by name; but a few deserve special mention.

I am heavily indebted to my colleagues Drs. François des Rosiers and Antonio Lagana. Beside steadfast encouragement, both were often subjected to my untidy elocution over dinner without ever complaining. Both gentlemen offered me comments and suggestions that have ended up by giving me greater confidence in my own argumentation.

For comprehension, I have tested my technical jargons on a number of noneconomists. For this, professors Michèle and Jacques Bernier, Owen Masters, Dr. Souren Teghrarian, and Dr. Viana Muller deserve special accolades. For helpful comments and special organizational services, I owe a great debt to Professor Stanley C. W. Salvary, Dr. Muller, and Colleen Bilodeau. They generously read the manuscript from one end to the other, while straightening up my syntax; in this sense they acted as public defenders of the general nonscientific reader. I should mention the people who acted out the role of the general public: Arturo Rodriguez Muller, Marianne R. Wickmann, Maidi Elliot, Eugenia and Gustavo Rojas. They have always patiently listened to my cogitation before pointing out to me unclear passages.

I would also like to take this opportunity to thank two groups of scholars who have indirectly helped me. The works of John L. Casti, John D. Barrow, Herman E. Daly, Richard Douthwaite, Jean-François Gautier, Bruno Ingrao and Giorgio Israel, among others, have stimulated me and sharpened my reasoning.

The ideas of scholars, extant and long gone, such as Hubert Reeves, Léon Walras and Henri Poincaré, just to name a few, generated my interests and shaped up my intellect. I thank them all, for their works have helped me in countless ways.

This is also a good place to acknowledge the people at the Greenwood Publishing Group, Inc., in particular Dr. James T. Sabin, as well as Ms. Deborah Whitford of Publishing Support Associates, for their efforts in attending to the many details needed to bring this book to completion; they deserve special mention for their expert editorial guidance.

Finally, I thank the students in my 1997 course on policy analysis who suffered through a good part of the first version, and made many elucidating comments. If I had the patience to incorporate all the suggestions that I have received, I would have written a better book. However, whatever shortcomings that remain are due to my own obstinacy.

ABBREVIATIONS

ADC	Arrow-Debreu Commodity
CER	corrected exchange rate
CPI	consumer price index
D&R	downsizing and restructuring
EDP	excessive deficit procedure
EMU	European monetary union
EPI	externalies, public goods, increasing returns to scale
EU	European Union
G7	Group of Seven (Canada, France, Germany, Italy, Japan, United Kingdom, United States)
GDP	gross domestic product
GD&R	globalization, downsizing and restructuring
GNP	gross national product
ILO	International Labor Organization
IMF	International Monetary Fund
IOSCO	International Organization of Securities Commission
MER	monetary exchange rate
MEW	measure of economic welfare
MIT	Massachusetts Institute of Technology
NAIRU	non-accelerating inflationary rate of unemployment
NMAD	von Neumann-Morgenstern-Arrow-Debreu
NRB	natural resource base
OECD	Organization for Economic Cooperation and Development
PPP	purchasing power parity
SRF	stimulus-response framework
UK	United Kingdom

UN	United Nations
UNCTAD	United Nations Conference on Trade and Development
UNDP	United Nations Development Programme
WEO	*World Economic Outlook*
WHS	Walras-Hicks-Samuelson

INTRODUCTION

For quite some time now, I have been toying with the desire to write a scholarly book on economics that would be as easy to read as a newspaper. This is exactly what I have tried to do here. Before going any further, however, I would like to tell the reader about the hurdle of such a project. Economics is now a quantified subject matter. It is therefore difficult to tackle its technicalities without the help of a few graphs, tables, and some simple equations. I tried to surmount this difficulty in the following way. As is well known, graphs have their usefulness as pictures that economize on words; I keep them in the text. Occasionally the parameters of an equation require comments, in which case an explanation in words is placed right above the equation. There is one extended mathematical derivation in Chapter 3, but it is confined to an appendix to the chapter. The same is true for all long tables, which are kept in chapter appendices where only the curious need venture. Finally, whenever appropriate, I indicate my guiding sources, but the reflection is mine. The reader will therefore not be bothered with a justifying citation every other line or with an interruptive footnote per page.

In writing this book, I have two objectives that are cast as two principal questions. Is the dominant economic orthodoxy of the 1980s a trustworthy scientific program, or the holy writ of a new god of deconstruction? What should the general public know about economics before it can fully participate in the process of economic policy formulation? Put somewhat differently, I first sketch a coherent overview of the prevailing economic orthodoxy in light of the scientific theory of free markets and society's economic well-being. Second, I address the unsung need to display the essentials of economic science in a less pedantic fashion so as to foster a greater understanding of economic policy.

By now, most people know that the 1980–1982 recession was triggered by a monetarist overreaction to the oil shocks inflation of the late 1970s. What they might not realize is that the consequences of the recession that followed it are still with us and will continue to be for many years to come. Because it has spurred the development of a new orthodoxy in the economic arena, known as GD&R, globalization, downsizing, and restructuring. GD&R is a new perspective on economic organization, which found its first faithful adherents in England and the United States. After some quick field tests in Pinochet's Chile and New Zealand, GD&R was extended to Latin America and Africa. By 1990, it had surfaced in the rest of Asia and in the former planned economies of Eastern Europe. By 1994, that is, in less than a decade, it had swept the world.[1]

The rapidity with which a untested doctrine such as GD&R has spread is not my primary concern. I am above all leery of the attempt to present it as a series of statements thrown off by *the* scientific theory of free markets as a solution to virtually all known economic ills, such as high debt levels, productivity growth slowdown, inflation, and unemployment. The tacit understanding behind that attempt is that GD&R describes a legitimate rule of economic behavior because its statements are grounded in a scientific theory. Why should that be so? Because under normal conditions the scientific theory of a discipline, by virtue of the simple fact that it has endured the test of time, is more credible than the numerous ad hoc theories that aspire to inclusion in the scientific theory. Ad hoc theories, on the other hand, are just that – they do not always make it. More importantly, as I make clear, the meaning of the adjective *scientific*, when applied to social sciences, is contextual. Prudence is, therefore, in order for a number of reasons. On one hand, to say that a statement is grounded in the scientific theory of an experimental discipline is to say that it is meaningful. Hence, it stands to be as credible as the scientific theory itself. But even so, society should still proceed with prudence, as any scientific theory may be inconsistent and/or incomplete. If, on the other hand, a statement is thrown off by an ad hoc theory, then even greater prudence is necessary, as such a theory may be completely unreliable. And when it comes to a social discipline, a double dose of prudence is required at each level, for these and for a host of additional reasons to be discussed shortly.

Unfortunately, GD&R has been uncritically embraced by the financial establishment, headed by the World Trade Organization, International Monetary Fund, and the World Bank. It has already captivated executives of central and private banks, brokerage firms, multinational firms, and other international economic organizations, think-tank economists, and national media. The problem is that it is not clear whether it is a bold new interpretation of the scientific theory, an amalgamation of defunct ad hoc theories such as monetarism, supply side theory, among others, or the new thinking of some invisible college. Yet, its prescriptions are presented with an air of conviction and inevitability. Indeed, not since the heyday of the free trade debate in the last century has an economic doctrine evoked such certainty. But in the social sciences in particular, wide acceptance means only that. It does not imply reliability as in the experimental sciences, and it never implies truth in any science.

The big question now is: How much trust should be placed in the recommendations of GD&R? The question is obviously pregnant with implications. For better guidance, therefore, we must map out a methodical approach to assessing GD&R. Economics is a science that is more statistical in character than purely experimental. This means that its pronouncements are more fragile, as they are plagued with uncertainty. To some extent, this applies to any science. Therefore, in order to see clearly through the panoply of meanings conjured by the term *scientific*, we must begin by stressing the difference between a science, a scientific theory, ad hoc theories of a science, and even the difference between normal and social sciences. Next, we must somehow ensure that the basic tenets of GD&R are meaningful before deciding on the degree of confidence that may be placed in its recommendations.

However, this is not all. A second question looms large over this assessment. What is at stake? Whether legitimate or not, what are the actual and potential impacts of GD&R on society's well-being? Sheer common sense would dictate that we pay greater attention to an untested orthodoxy that requires almost irreversible changes in economic structures. Then there seems to be no alternative to a serious inquiry into the nature of the underlying theory to see if in fact it can confer the supposed legitimacy. Even if it can, we must still balance the benefits and costs of compliance.

I have said that my second objective is a by-product of addressing these theoretical issues. Actually, it is embedded in the second question. In order to implement the major policy shift demanded by GD&R, I believe that public debate and support are needed. However, in this case, the general public has no information other than being told that future growth is necessarily mediated by present-day austerity. What is not said, but is obvious in the data, is that the austerity is for the bottom 80% of income earners, while the benefits are for the top twenty. Yet, the same economic theory invoked for legitimacy also requires that the benefit of a decision be accrued to those that bear the cost of that decision. There is thus an urgent need for the bottom 80% to become familiar with the rudiments of economic policy. Indeed, a better idea of the working of economic theory is necessary for assessing beforehand whether this policy shift and its concomitant sacrifices are capable of furthering the greatest good or instead promoting the quest for capital accumulation of the top 20%. But, that is where things get complicated. I doubt whether or not the bottom 80% can effectively carry out such an assessment without a clearer understanding of economic science.

In every market-based modern society, most individuals practice economics on a daily basis. Yet, few seem able to see market mechanisms through the lens of economic theory. The consequences of this problem are worrisome. In the December 2, 1996, issue of the *New Yorker*, John Cassidy published an article that quite accurately describes the image problem of economics even among professional economists, not to mention the uneasiness of the general public with economic prescriptions. Is it because economics is a strange, difficult, or complex subject matter? Is it poorly taught? I am inclined to believe that it is both. Let us begin with teaching economics. More often than not, the teaching of economics consists of throwing at students hundreds of two-dimensional graphs and lots of "double speaks," such as: "On the one hand this, on the other that." Students often leave with the impression that economic explanations are either fuzzy or very complex. It is reasonable to suppose that students that fail to grasp the workings of market mechanisms will go on to become poor economic agents. Maybe yes, maybe no. If yes, how can economics be made intelligible to the general public, even for the fun of it? Metaphorically put: Is there a key capable of releasing economic understanding from the scientific theory, and thereby turning these millions of practicing economists into knowledgeable economic agents?

In the same vein, I know of the effort of those before me who have quite successfully brought science to the general public. The question is how did they do it? Professor Stephen Hawking must have faced the very same question before writing *A Brief History of Time.* In his case, the problem was partially resolved by leaving out equations. In my case, however, leaving out all equations may create an additional problem, as economic discourses are more controversial than those of astrophysics. Anyway, no one, to my knowledge, has successfully done so in economics; this, by itself, may be indicative of the difficulty of the task ahead. But at the same time, I also realize that there is a sincere desire on the part of the general public to understand natural as well as social sciences. It is this desire, combined with the ingenuity of a number of scientists, that seem to be fueling the present explosion in the diffusion of scientific knowledge. Take the case of the late Professor Carl Sagan. Sagan has managed to make a mathematical subject like astronomy intelligible to millions of people from very different backgrounds. Many others have done the same thing in other areas of science. The most familiar names that come to mind are David Attenborough in zoology, Stephen Jay Gould in paleontology, Steven Rose in neuroscience, Steve Jones in genetics, Paul Davies and George Smooth in astrophysics, among others. These exceptional individuals have somehow found the keys that open the door of apparently very complex scientific activities to the general public. The case of Hawking discussing the evaporation of black holes is perhaps the most astounding of them all.[2] If these individuals can bring arcane subjects such as astronomy and advanced physics to the general public, why can the same be done for economics? After all, economics is a subject people interface with every day in their lives.

Much to their credit, some economists such as John Kenneth Galbraith and Lester Thurow have tried to talk to the general public.[3] However, they have restricted themselves to clarifying certain facets of economics for certain groups. My ambition here is to demystify the gist of market operations for those called on to bear the brunt of the new orthodoxy. These stakeholders may safely be divided into two main groups. Those believing that economics is an art form best left to the artist, and those believing that economics is akin to politics, a device for deceiving others. Such beliefs obviously make them either uninformed economic agents or easy prey. The task is to make economic discourse intelligible to everyone and at the same time portray economics as a rigorous subject on par with all the known sciences. Indeed, a science that affects the public's welfare perhaps more frequently than any other, including the political and medical sciences.

This is a big challenge, because to seriously discuss a science the most appropriate language is mathematics. Yet according to the conventional wisdom, the general public is unable to understand or, even worse, is prejudiced against mathematics. There is another pitfall to worry about. I still recall with real sadness my experience in teaching a course in market operations to Ph.D. students in finance. Their reaction was, of course, varied. However, one student with a good mind but a mechanical approach to learning, became particularly upset with conjectures, thought experiments, and alternate explanations of what he had learned previously. Such persons, found anywhere and at any time, must be borne in mind. It is my firm belief, however, that without mathematics as a backup, a multitude of economic interpretations become likely. And in general, each interpretation favors the position of the interpreter, leading to a *capharnarum.* In order to avoid this sort of thing, I have decided not to completely shy away from mathematics. My language, mostly in the first three chapters, is definitely mathematical, but without the symbolic display that may instill fear. Chapter 2 is written in mathematical language, but it is only a reference. Chapter 3 describes the workings of a simple economy, but the potentially troublesome equations are confined to an appendix, where only hard-to-convince types such as the finance student and the curious need venture. I remain confident that the general public will understand that there will always be the curious few eager to check the main assertions and to ascertain that the storyteller is not forcing on them a private interpretation of some sort. The mathematical language should make all of this easier. The level of mathematical rigor adopted is designed to make my conclusions as robust as necessary. In discussing and clarifying the subtleties of the scientific theory, I also draw parallels with physics wherever possible and appropriate. Even those that are not interested in double-checking may still find the scientific anecdotes used to convey the economic story intellectually stimulating.

I suppose that by making economic theory more intelligible, I will be in a better position to address my second objective. One of the most troublesome aspects of the new orthodoxy is its demand to deconstruct the social contract that has enhanced the well-being of the citizens of the Northern countries (Western Europe, North America, among others) over the last 40 years or so. The same social contract, I surmise, would have brought the same benefits to the South (the rest of the world) had it been more honestly enforced, and had the South have a more enlightened leadership. This being so, and powerless to arrest the momentum behind the policy shift, I would like nevertheless to accompany the general public on a journey to uncover the theoretical basis, if any, for such massive deconstruction.

This book is divided into three parts. The first part consists of three chapters in which I demystify the general scientific discourse by balancing the strength and limitations of both science and mathematics. The first chapter deals with scientific issues in general and clarifies the scientific status of the activity known as economics. The second chapter, my reference chapter, briefly reviews the evolution of the mathematization of the theory of free markets, and attempts to shed more light on its strength and limitations. The main elements of the theory are in the appendix. As I have already stressed, the appendix may be of interest to curious individuals with some economic and mathematical background. The average reader may skip over it and move directly to Chapter 4, since the third chapter is an exercise designed to show how economic knowledge is produced. Hence, Chapters 2 and 3 may then be skipped without loss of continuity.

The second part, consisting of Chapters 4 and 5, is devoted to the new orthodoxy and to the preliminary results from its implementation. The promised benefits of GD&R are outlined in Chapter 4, so Chapter 5 focusses mainly on the known and potential costs of implementation.

The third part is devoted to policy matter and society's well-being. Chapter 6 looks at unemployment and social security. Chapter 7 reviews the process of economic growth and its associated environmental impacts. Chapter 8 tackles the unspoken, that is, income distribution. Throughout, I try to shy away from the conventional benefit-cost analysis to focus on the hidden consequences of deconstruction. The selected topics covered reflect the areas where I feel the policy shift is likely to have the greatest impact. Whenever appropriate, I also point out the limitations of underlying ad hoc theories and the hazard of un-reliability in policy formulation.

Obviously, it is not for me to judge whether or not I have achieved my stated objectives; in particular the second objective which is to explain the formulation of economic policy. However, I was encouraged to try. The response of the general public, over the last two decades or so, enlightened with regard to both natural and social, has not ceased to surprise me. I sincerely hope that this book will be seen as further encouragement for others, better qualified perhaps, to take us further along.

I

SCIENCE, MATHEMATICS, AND ECONOMICS

1

ON SCIENCE AND THE SCIENTIFIC
STATUS OF ECONOMICS

INTRODUCTION

The practice of economics is as old as human society itself. It could not have
been otherwise since economics essentially concerns the satisfying of human
wants. Here, however, I am not interested in its origin as a human activity but
rather in its status as a science. For that purpose, we need to go back no farther
than the mid-eighteenth century, because prior to that time economics proper did
not exist as a separate field of inquiry. In earlier periods, there was something
that we could charitably call economic thought, but no more. Scholars who
wanted an idea of what economic thought was all about had to extract it from the
writings of priests, lawmakers, and philosophers. What was in fact extracted
whenever someone dared to tackle such a difficult task was a series of unrelated
observations and moral pronouncements on production, consumption, and
exchanges, expounded in religious, ethical, and political terms. A more succinct
way of putting it is that economic thought was not only unsystematic, but
dominated by religious beliefs and the like.

However, as the nature and scope of economic activities began to increase,
the religious and ethical beliefs shaping the prevailing attitudes toward the
acquisition of wealth began to abate. Hence, man's speculations about economic
phenomena became more and more systematized. It was then that the field came
to be known as political economy.[1]

In the hands of the physiocrats, that is, those reformers in the France of the
post Louis XIV era, economic thought took a significant turn. The physiocrats,
it will be recalled, were the first to equate the notion of an *ideal society* with the
natural order. The physiocratic ideas were essentiel for the eventual thrust of
economic thought toward an analytical expression. It must be remembered that

they constituted a very influential group whose main argument was that the natural order was to be discovered through the intellect, and brought to fruition through some form of enlightened dirigism so as to instruct society in the enjoyment of the freedom consistent with self-interest.

For Adam Smith, a close observer of the reform movement initiated by the physiocrats, the natural order could only reach its optimal expression through individual liberty, a liberty anchored in the morality of sympathy and in the influence of the social experience. This seems to have totally escaped the understanding of the present captains of industry whose patron saint is none other than Adam Smith. Smith is mainly known for two pieces of work, *The Theory of Moral Sentiments* (1759) and *The Wealth of Nations* (1776). In the former, he recognizes the selfish nature of human beings. However, Smith thought that human nature involved some principles which interested people in the fortune of others and made their happiness necessary to them, though they may derive nothing from it except the pleasure of seeing it.[2] Thus, the desire of individuals for the approval of society and the censure of their own conscience should keep them compassionate moral beings. As long as they are moral in their actions, they and society as a whole move toward the same goal, and mankind prospers to the extent that individuals are permitted to exercise freedom of action.

Some Smithian scholars claim that there is a divergence between the first and the second work, precisely on this moral question. I am, of course, not in complete agreement with this assessment. While it is true that the moral philosophy underlying the economic principles set forth in *The Wealth of Nations* is not explicitly mentioned, it nevertheless pervades the entire work.[3]

It should be recalled that in the first work, Smith outlines his profound belief in individual morality, shaped through individual introspective psychology. Claiming that the imagination of even mean individuals will prompt them at times to sacrifice their own interest to the greater interests of society. On this score, the manufacturers and traders who selectively worship the Smith of *The Wealth of Nations*, receive his most pungent criticisms whenever they cease to be moral beings. This is the underlying message of the second work to which I now turn.

Following Smith's encounter with the physiocrats, pure political economy took another turn toward systematization. *The Wealth of Nations* attests to that. However, I have no intention of reviewing that work here. Suffice it to note that Smith describes pure political economy as the process by which a man can both employ his capital in the support of domestic industry, and so to direct that industry that its produce may be of the greatest value. In so doing, he continues: he intends only his own gain, and he is in this, as in many other cases, led by an "invisible hand" to promote an end which was no part of his intention. (Smith 1776, Bk. IV, Ch. 2). This, in essence, is the task of the moral entrepreneur working under the censure of his or her conscience.

In order to make sense of Smith's emphasis on morality, it should be pointed out that besides physiocratic thoughts he also drew on the works of Bernard de

Mandeville, a Dutch doctor living in England at that time. The latter shook the intellectual establishment with the publication in 1705 of a work entitled *The Grumbling Hives: Or Knaves Turn'd Honest.* That work was republished in 1714 under the title of *The Fable of the Bees.* In it, he essentially argued that great social achievements resulted from human vices, and that vices and self-interest produce the public good. Smith, as many other English intellectuals, was appalled by the immorality of the tale of the *Fable.* He then tried to debunk it by writing *The Theory of Moral Sentiments.* However, the force of de Mandeville's argument was too compelling to be easily debunked.[4] So in *The Wealth of Nations,* Smith tried a different approach; that is, on the belief that man is a moral being, in pursuing his self-interest, he or she will be led by an invisible hand to promote the public good. This is not to take anything away from Smith, not even the concept of the division of labor that he also got from de Mandeville. But when markets are perfect, that is, when agents are very small, the question of morality does not come into play; it arises when markets are imperfect. As I show in later chapters, when economic agents are not "small," in particular when producers have market power and are not required to pay the full costs of the resources they use, it is hard to pursue the profit imperative embedded in markets on high moral ground. No matter how distasteful de Mandeville's arguments appeared to Smith, they nevertheless accurately reflect our nature. What indeed appears immoral to me is to pretend otherwise. For the moment though, I am only interested in the scientificity of economics. Throughout this chapter, I digress a little to show that, in general, morality and the practice of science are not outright incompatible. In economics, or in any other science, we should collectively see to that.

From Smith onward, pure political economy has emerged as Economic Analysis, a separate field of inquiry into the satisfaction of human needs. Many years after the complete "formalization" of economics, Kenneth J. Arrow and Frank H. Hahn provide us with a modern definition. According to Arrow and Hahn, modern economics is: A social system moved by independent actions in pursuit of different values which are consistent with a final state of balance, meaning a state in which every participant in the game ends up a happy winner.[5]

This modern definition of economics is incomplete, as I will show. For the moment though, it is nevertheless a very useful point of departure for an eclectic inquiry into the scientific status of this activity, that is, the main purpose of this chapter. Also, I should stress right away that throughout the book, I will often refer to *natural* sciences (sciences that are concerned with nature) and to *social* sciences (those that deal with human societies). However, at this juncture I am not yet ready to formally distinguish between the two. The need to begin with the scientificity of economics is motivated by the fact that modern economic discourse elicits a variety of interpretations and even differing opinions about economics itself. For example, the majority of economists are indeed very proud of their subject matter. There is absolutely no doubt, it seems, that economics is a science, if not the most advanced of the so-called social sciences. On the other hand, judging by the poor track record of economics in explaining and predicting economic phenomena, the claim that economics is a science brings a polite smile to the faces of natural scientists. Whereas for the average noneconomist or nonscientist, whether economics is a science or an art is really immaterial. She or he is more familiar with the impacts of economics. A case in point is that over the last decade or so, the only thing the uninitiated have experienced in this regard is bad news, such as higher taxes (but lower benefits from the government) and lower taxes on the rich at the same time, and lower wages and employment that result in a loss of income share for the bottom 80% and significant gains for the top 5%. Never before has the average wage earner been confronted with so many austerity measures pushing her or him toward greater inequality, so many seemingly contradictory explanations of falling living standards, and so many erroneous predictions by economists. Hence for the individual, economics is unintelligible beyond the vague notions of supply and demand. The individual's inability to grasp the workings of the game makes her or him easy prey for some cleaver operators. Time and again these clever operators have managed to further confuse her or him with an ever increasing array of buzzwords enticing her or him to either part with savings or purchase what may not even be needed.

While I may have something of interest to say to the economist or the smiling science practitioner, this book is mainly addressed to a third category of individuals; individuals who have had no serious training in economics and who, by the sheer dint of circumstance, find themselves caught in the melee of actors jockeying for higher economic ground. I hasten to add that I have no intention of unduly raising their expectations. As I explain later, there is as yet no way of making individual predictions in the game of economics. I have some suggestions to make in Chapter 2, but for now I suppose that such predictions can not be made for reasons I will elaborate on in the forth section. My modest aim is simply to increase their understanding of the so-called rules of this vital game. In so doing, I hope to be able to help them better decode economic discourse, discern emerging trends, and therefore make better decisions about their economic future.

I shall begin with the status of economics in the chain of human activities. There are many reasons for this choice. They will become increasingly clear as we proceed, but the main reason is encapsulated in the following story. Recently, a Delphi experiment was conducted (see Klein 1994), in which a number of high profile economists (two of them Nobel Laureates) were asked to answer two questions. What is the role of economic theory? How should the theory be defined so that it is meaningful to economists? If you find these questions a bit strange, rest assured that the answers were not only incoherent but outright bizarre. This prompts me to believe that the existing confusion about the scientificity of economics is the root cause of much of the misunderstanding regarding this activity.

The general confusion about the nature of science is not confined to the economic arena. Indeed, it is not difficult to find even natural scientists who equate science with truth. In order to see how this could come about, let us step back in time to show how misleading this posture could be.

ON PRIORS OR VIEWPOINTS OF SCIENCE

The average economic actor may not have a definite viewpoint, but certainly some sort of an idea of what science is. What might it be? If by any chance he or she, or anyone else for that matter, believes that science is an infallible enterprise, practiced by objective (nonbiased) practitioners holding a monopoly on truths spelled out as precise prescriptions, then he or she is a prime candidate for being duped by manipulations and buzzwords. As it turns out, the practitioners of science operate with some sort of viewpoint. As will be discussed at some length, the difference between scientists and others is that scientists attempt to control for their viewpoints, but they are in no way value-free. In fact, such viewpoints, which I simply term priors, are so solidly embedded in their consciousness that practicing scientists no longer dwell on them, whether they choose to call them viewpoints, priors, or values. If pressed on such niceties, they would probably say that they are only after what works.

To illustrate this point more forcefully, let me quote from two individuals who have long ago examined this matter closely. In the *Adventures of Ideas* (1933), A. N. Whitehead summarizes his reflections this way: "The common interpretation of the world, in every age, is controlled by some scheme of unchallenged and even unsuspected presupposition" (emphasis is mine). Michael Polanyi makes essentially the same point in *Personal Knowledge* (1960), but more explicitly: "The metaphysical presuppositions of science... are never explicitly defended or even considered by themselves by inquiring scientists. They arise as aspects of the given activity of inquiry as its structurally implicit presuppositions, not as consciously held axioms preceding it.... [W]e think *with them and not of them.*"[6]

These underlying presuppositions, so uncritically referred to by these two authors, are what I call priors or miniparadigms.[7] They are unavoidable due to the simple fact that scientists can neither divorce themselves from their mental constitution nor isolate themselves from the commonly held values of their environment. To further complicate matters, nature itself is not revealed in an open book; in many regards, it is very subtle. Priors may even be a sort of defense against the ignorance of and/or the subtleties of nature itself. Obviously, this has nothing to do with being dishonest or immoral. It simply reminds us that scientists are only human.

Everyone, carries with him or her a baggage of priors. The problem is that the practitioner of science does not explicitly acknowledge such priors, hence they are not easily refuted; they may, therefore, survive a long life of practice. At the level of the layperson, on the other hand, they mainly blur understanding and drive the extrascientific interpretations of the prescriptions of science.

For the time being, I will not discuss whether priors are a good or bad thing to carry around. However, I want to show that they do have an impact on the practice of science. Before I can probe this matter I should clarify two related points. First, although I have not made a clear distinction between social and natural sciences, the two are not treated on an equal footing. The point here is that natural sciences are often considered as synonymous with the "laws" of nature. In this section, I use the two terms science and laws interchangeably at times. Second, these priors may also manifest themselves in the way scientists perceive the laws of the universe. It might be useful, therefore, to briefly review some traditional viewpoints about natural laws in order to see how they have shaped our understanding while evolving into what they might be now before trying to assess their impact on today's science.

Over the years, we have seen the world of science practitioners subdivided mainly into three large and distinct families: empiricism (and its close relatives, positivism, operationalism, and instrumentalism) followed by idealism and rationalism, just to name the main ones.[8] I now briefly review the respective position of each, then examine the impact they might have had on science.

According to the empiricist, all meaningful concepts about nature (or for that matter, the laws thereof), were to be reducible to sense data, and individual observers could exert absolutely no influence on them. For a positivist, the meaning of a scientific statement (or a law) was defined by the very procedure designed to verify the statement as well as by the logical relationship between the words or concepts we use in talking about them. The operationalist, on the other hand, argued that a scientific statement was meaningful only if it could be reduced to a sequence of practical steps called operations. The instrumentalist, for his part, stressed the notion that scientific theories and laws of the universe were to be viewed as mere instruments for learning about the universe. Thus, for the latter group the laws of nature were nothing but particulars having no universal existence. Obviously these different labelings suggest minor differences in viewpoints. They are of no real interest for us at this point, except perhaps to show that differences can surface even within a given family.

The idealist and the realist, belonged to two families with unreconciliable views. To wit, the idealist believed in an external world that was, in fact, unknowable. What we consider its properties are really disorderly glimpses on which our brain imposes meaning. There was an even more extreme version of this viewpoint known as solipsism according to which the external world was the product of our imagination, pure and simple. For the realist there was actually a big external world out there, but it was independent of its observers. At this point, one is tempted to ask where the difference was? The answer is attitude. As the astute observer may have already gauged, for the former there was only a fabricated image; for the latter there was something real, but to know about it we had to deal directly with *it* rather than with an *image* of it.

From the foregoing, we can therefore easily see how priors could have impinged on our theories and, in turn, on our observations of the universe. But there is more to this disheartening result. No matter how sophisticated a prior might be, if it is rigid and unidimensional, it will sooner or later be found wanting in its ability to increase our understanding of a subtle universe. Imagine a world populated by instrumentalists. There would be no theories or laws of nature in such a world since both are useful only for the collection of facts. However, before long that world would be without facts as well, because a fact is per force defined by a theory. If that world was populated by operationalists instead, all theories would be ad hoc, that is, they would simply be devices for constructing bigger and bigger ad hoc theories so as to manipulate nature to the advantage of the inhabitants, and not to learn about its ways; the danger here is quite obvious. Likewise, in a world of strict positivists it would be impossible to have any knowledge about things that cannot directly be observed. No thought experiments would be allowed and no one could plan for the future since the laws of nature are convenient particulars guaranteeing absolutely nothing. In a world populated by the empiricist family, science itself would not make strides. Indeed, if scientific theories were mere aggregates of facts, Albert Einstein probably would have been unemployed all his life. Remember that the general relativity theory was first conceived as a thought experiment before it was upheld by observations. Likewise, elementary particle physicists would have been out in the cold. For, there too, the existence of many of these particles were first postulated from the compelling concept of symmetry, about which I will have more to say, while other useful concepts such as quarks remain unobservable to this day.

Similarly, the other two viewpoints, namely idealism and realism, are subject to the same limitations. Clearly, if the laws of nature were only the products of our imagination, each culture would have ended up by producing its own version of them. On the other hand, the viewpoint of the realist is not entirely accurate either. The best way I can think of depicting the limitations of realism is to make (as we will do from time to time) a foray into physics, since it is often portrayed as the queen of the sciences. Establishing various parallels with physics whenever appropriate can only reinforce my argument. To wit, in 1924, the French physicist, Louis-Victor de Broglie showed us how to measure the correlation between observations of the external world and the kind of measurements being performed. Succinctly put, he postulated that all bodies display a wavelike property whose wavelength (L) is equal to the Planck constant, h (= 6.63×10^{-34} Joule-seconds) divided by the momentum (mass x velocity) of the body. This is a crude version of what is known as the quantum wave property character of all bodies. However, as the Planck constant is such a small number (the 6.63 is preceded by 33 zeros after the decimal), ordinary objects are far larger in size than their L values. Or equivalently, their L is insignificant relative to their body size. Hence it makes some sense to talk about observing the so-called real world. But once we leave the macro to enter the microscopic world, where body sizes are equal to or less than their L, the act of observing (e.g., shining light on) inevitably disturbs the state of what is being observed.

This intrinsic limitation on the meaning and the precision of observations was reaffirmed three years after de Broglie's finding in the celebrated uncertainty principle of Werner Heisenberg. The latter can be interpreted to mean that it is impossible to know exactly what the state of the world was before a measurement was performed. Here also we have bad news for our friend the realist. Remember, she or he has argued that observations constitute knowledge of the external reality. We have just seen that in a world of things of sizes equal to or smaller than their L, knowledge can not progress by observations alone due to our inability to observe without interfering.

To sum up, we have seen that the dominant priors of the past were rather diverse and split into subversions, some of which were quite extreme. All of them had something of substance to say, but none had captured the whole story. It is obvious that they have influenced our theories and observations. In that connection, think of the Aristotelian laws of motion or the status astrology used to have. However, as knowledge of ourselves and of the external world accumulates, our priors evolve but do not disappear. Most of the primitive species reviewed above, if they still exist, must be on the endangered list. Those which have evolved, on the other hand, constitute the gamut of present-day views of modern science. As I have hinted, they are not easily acknowledged or refuted. The only option then is to first submit to the fact that the practitioners of modern science have priors, and that these priors have great staying power, and second, to recognize that science is nonetheless a very useful activity, for it affords humanity with a minimum of knowledge. With this in mind, we can now ask a question which better suits our purpose, namely, how today's scientific activities are to be distinguished from those that are not?

ON SCIENTIFIC THEORIES AND SCIENCE

The above question is of central importance for the present inquiry because over the years science has made great strides in making our universe intelligible, so much so that science has become synonymous with respectability. As we well know, in our world respectability brings other kinds of rewards. More than anything else, these rewards lie behind the frantic efforts of the practitioners of various activities to claim scientific status for their subject matter.

In order to avoid multiplying viewpoints, modern scientists have sought a common ground. As a result, there is now a fairly high degree of consensus on a set of characteristics that can effectively separate genuine scientific activities from the pretenders. Before we examine them, however, we must first define a scientific theory. The reason for this will become clear in a moment.

A scientific theory is first and foremost a mathematical construct (not necessarily consistent or complete) which attempts to mimic some domain of the observable universe. Its purpose is to allow its adherents to formulate meaningful statements that are capable of broadening the scope of the scientific theory and therefore our understanding of the domain. I hasten to add that such statements are meaningful if they are reasonably well corroborated by observations on their explanations of how events have unfolded and/or on their predictions of events yet to unfold within the domain covered by the scientific theory.

There is another way of defining meaningfulness that we will get to later, but before going any farther two remarks are in order.

We must be careful about two things. First, when we say "not necessarily consistent or complete," this does not mean anything goes, but rather sooner or later these two properties will be found missing; I will return to that point in the final section of this chapter. Second, *the* scientific theory should not be confused with *a* theory. To illustrate this point consider a few examples borrowed from physics. The electromagnetic theory of James Clerk Maxwell, which describes the symbiotic relationship of electric and magnetic fields and, Einstein's special relativity theory that shows that the notion of simultaneity in time had no absolute meaning. Both are subtheories of physics, the scientific theory. When the term theory is used in this way, it generally refers to a specific law governing behavior in a part of the domain covered by the scientific theory. Sometimes such a theory is simply referred to as a model. There may be many of them around, but whatever their number, they are all subject to the same procedure of falsification (i.e., disproving) and they may not contradict the prescriptions of the scientific theory. Such theories may also open new vistas, subsume previous theories, or be quite encompassing. The best way of clarifying the latter point is to think of the following. Newton's theory of gravitation pictures actions at a distance in an elegant way indeed. However, Maxwell's not only describes the intertwined phenomena of electricity and magnetism but also describes many interesting phenomena beyond Newton's, which were never even suspected before. On the other hand, we have Einstein's theory of gravitation that is encompassing enough to describe some facets of the whole known universe. Interestingly enough, it can even predict the existence of other universes.[9] Even so, these theories do not in any way commit patricide. At their beginning, they were merely ad hoc theories. But over time, they were found to be quite reliable, and were included in and remain to this day useful components of the scientific theory. Despite my somewhat lax use of these terms, the reader should have no trouble distinguishing the difference between the theory and a theory according to the context.

A science, on the other hand, is a process by which the validity of statements thrown off by a scientific theory is checked through the application of an appropriate experimental design. Validity means ensuring that the statements possess two prerequisite characteristics, explicitness and publicness, and two final ones called objectivity and reliability. The four together define meaningfulness; from now on, validity and meaningfulness will be used synonymously.

Figure 1.1 shows the two criteria that define the scientificity of an activity, that is, a scientific theory that enlightens and generates potentially meaningful statements, and a procedure for checking the meaningfulness of such statements. Keeping this simplified picture in mind should make the ensuing discussion easier to follow.

I would like now to expound further on the characteristics of meaningfulness, but before let me say that the scientific theory is in fact a culture. It trains

Figure 1.1
The Scientific Process

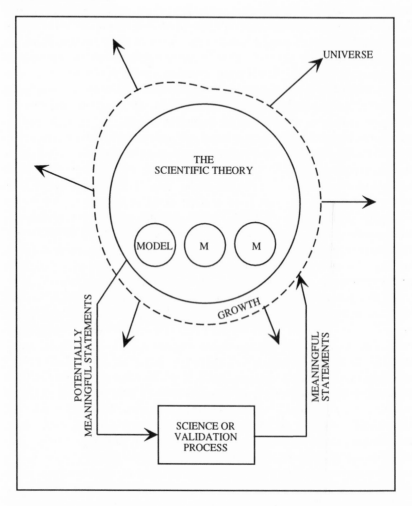

its adherents into thinking in a like manner, and it also defines *a priori* all the concepts that are used in making a statement. Given such a context, explicitness means that all the adherents of the scientific theory have no difficulty understanding the idea expounded in the statement. If you wondered why the construct must be mathematical, wonder no more. Among other things, the precision of the mathematical language leaves no room for the private interpretation of some invisible authority. By publicness, I mean that the statement is open to public scrutiny in the professional literature, hence it is accessible to anyone who is learned in the matter and who has the time, funding, and equipment necessary to scrutinize it. Reliability here means resisting various attempts at invalidation through repeatable experiments, or enduring the test of time; hence a reliable statement has the ability to guide the understanding of appropriate phenomena through time. This characteristic is perhaps the most important of the four because it is necessary. If the statement fails on this characteristic, it becomes automatically meaningless. If it holds through time, it stands a good chance of being elevated to the dignity of scientific law. However, such a law, if it ever comes to that, is never endowed with the property of infallibility. The point is that if actual evidence heavily weighs in its favor, it enjoys the status of law but only until new evidence overthrows it. Finally, by objectivity, one should understand that statements are falsifiable and that the validation process is supposed to be controlled as much as possible for investigators' biases. Obviously, it is rather difficult to control for unconsciously held priors. Nonetheless, it should be and is in fact easier to control for a bias for or against electrons than for one for or against certain social groupings. A good example of the fragility of objectivity is the case of William Shockley. His work on transistors was significant enough to be recognized by the Nobel Committee for Physics in 1956, when he was named the co-laureate. Subsequently, he left physics to make a foray into genetics and social theory, with disastrous consequences for both his reputation as a scientist and for social harmony, due to his difficulty controlling for his biases against some ethnic groups.

At this juncture, it is only fair, I believe, to warn the reader that the foregoing arguments reflect a particular assessment of modern science. Obviously, everyone might not agree with it. Every single point I have made thus far could either be questioned or expanded to become a book by philosophers of science. Some (e.g., trained under Karl Popper) may place greater emphasis on the failure of a statement to be meaningful. In the language of Popper (1959), a statement is meaningful simply if it is falsifiable. I believe that it is highly unlikely though that most practitioners of modern science that I know and work with would agree that their main task is falsification. At the same time, however, they might not be hostile to the idea itself as a criterion. Whether they accept the criterion of falsification or not, they would certainly agree that a statement is never checked in isolation. Tests are made for the correctness of an intertwined aggregate of assumptions and initial conditions. The experimental design might focus on a particular statement, but the scientist must ensure that other related statements have been properly verified in a sequence of other experiments as an additional insurance against errors. Such errors would be devastating to the reputation of the scientist in charge. Thus, the practice of science is carried out with an eye on the evolution of the scientific theory, and another on the prestige, honors, and rewards for its practitioners.

Stumbling Toward Maturity: The Case of Modern Cosmology

Before closing this section, let me emphasize once more that there is nothing infallible about the scientific activity. Assumptions can be wrong, initial conditions may change, instruments may be faulty, and some anomalies or pathologies may not be ripe for solutions but, by and large, the scientific process in the natural arena possesses self-correcting characteristics allowing it to attain a high degree of success in providing us with a number of useful regularities called laws, which in turn underlie our technologies and constitute the foundation of our present view of the universe. However, it may be found in error at any time. The case of modern cosmology is a remarkable illustration of this danger.

Cosmology is the dean or *primus inter pares* among the natural sciences. Its evolution has something to teach us, because its development was anything but smooth. In his book, *L'univers existe-t-il?* (1994), Jean-François Gautier tells, with particular rigor and fairness, how cosmology (the study of the laws of the universe) evolves from cosmography (the description of) to cosmology and to cosmogony (the origin of) and back to modern cosmology. Gautier's story illustrates my points so aptly that I will conclude this section likewise.

As is commonly known, human beings have been collecting bits and pieces of the ways of the universe since time immemorial. The need to know about the heavens probably arose in agriculture in Mesopotania and China. The Mesopotamians, for example, excelled in the observation of heavenly bodies. But, lacking a theory, they only succeeded in producing a body of ad hoc explanations, known as astrology. From what is now known, the Greek mathematician Pythagoras, who lived in the 6th century BC, may have been the first to give the world a primitive cosmography. Among other things, he deduced that the earth was a sphere, revolving on itself. By the 4th century BC, his disciples had extended his ideas to a full heliocentric universe. However, that construct was never accepted because it appeared counter-intuitive. Around the 3rd century BC, the great Aristarcus of Samos had again rightly argued that the earth was a rotating sphere in orbit around the sun. Although the heliocentric version of Aristarcus was very efficient in mimicking the real thing, it was not taken seriously by his contemporaries, despite his reputation as a scholar. Yet, when Claud Ptolemy presented his *Mathematical Composition*, or the *Almageste* (140 AD), in which he argued that the earth was fixed at the center of the universe, while the sun and the stars revolved around it, it was immediately accepted. Why then did the flawed cosmography of Ptolemy win over the more correct versions of earlier periods? The only reason that seems plausible is that the Ptolemaic version incorporated all the received views, such as man's place in the universe, perfect (circular) motion, among others. The contemporaries of Ptolemy were so happy to find their own beliefs in this geocentric construct that they accepted it without serious scrutiny. The world had to wait until Nicolas Copernicus (1473–1543) to begin reconsidering Aristarcus' construct, thanks largely to a simpler geometry and well after the Ptolemaic one had become too fuzzy and too clumsy. Soon afterwards though, Copernicus' contemporaries too began finding his version mechanically right but geometrically wrong in its details. Fortunately, Johannes Kepler (1571–1630) arrived just in time, armed with tedious but numerous observations compiled by Tycho Brahe, to add a final touch showing that planetary orbits are in fact elliptical rather than circular. This addition revolutionized and transformed cosmography into cosmology proper.

However, the cosmology of Kepler, Galilei, and others had not gotten rid of its metaphysical connection; its authors were more concerned with the "how" than with the "why." The observed order of the system was left in the hands of God. Even Isaac Newton (1642–1727), who gave cosmology greater depth by substituting laws as the direct guarantor of order, left the location of celestial bodies and their orbital stability in the hands of God. Any question as to the why had to be addressed to God. Then Pierre Simon Laplace (1749–1827) arrived to take cosmology to a higher level of generality.[10] He reworked the Newtonian construct and along the way postulated modern concepts such as scale invariance, and the formation of black holes, among others. However, his actual contributions were twofold. First, he described the origin of solar systems. Based on the observed quasicircularity and the quasicoplaneity of planetary orbits around the sun, Laplace deduced that a solar system such as ours (including planets with moons) evolved from the cooling down of initial nebulae. Next and perhaps the most ambitious of the Laplacian ideas was the realization that, time being completely reversible, the Newtonian laws are eternal. If only one could get a hold of a little demon, capable of making fast calculations, these laws could in principle take us back and principally forth to the end of time. God was thus removed from the picture. By then the Catholic Church had entered the debate. The error in its position, together with the new Laplacian ideas, liberated cosmology from metaphysics and moved it to cosmogony.

As I make clear in the appendix to this chapter, Einstein, Friedmann, Lemaitre, Hubble, and Gamow, among others, have turned the universe into an object of physics. Is it really? While podering the question, consider the advice of the German philosopher, Emmanuel Kant: One can not deduce the existence of anything. In other words, to scientifically study anything, one must begin by accepting its existence. To this, add the paradox of the British philosopher, Bertrand Russell: Form a super set as the set of all sets. Now is the super set itself a set? No, said Russell, otherwise it would be included in the super set. These considerations have led Gautier to ask the crucial question: Does the universe, as an object of study, really exist? In the following sections, I will show just how pertinent the question is and that even if the universe exists as an object of study, we can never fully understand it because we are a part of it.

The lesson here is that nothing has been definitely proven. In fact, if our universe exists, it is evolving. It is, therefore, quite likely that its laws are evolving as well. If so, what we now have may only be stopgaps which in no way imply truth. Nonetheless, until further notice and for the present purpose, we will take it that a scientific activity is characterized by two criteria, that is, a scientific theory and a process for determining the meaningfulness of the theory's statements (shown in Figure 1.1). We must therefore determine the scientificity of economics by them alone.

ON THE SCIENTIFIC STATUS OF ECONOMICS

As noted in the previous section, a scientific activity possesses a scientific theory and a process or method of verifying the meaningfulness of statements thrown off by the scientific theory. Then, by symmetry, the scientificity of economics must be judged solely by these attributes and not by some other vague criterion, for example, like the diversity or the inconsistency of solutions offered by economists for a given puzzle.

On the question as to whether economics possesses a scientific theory, I guess that even those who deride economic explanations and forecasts would not be so cavalier as to deny the existence of an economic theory. It was not always so, however. At first, what had passed for the theory was nothing but an assemblage of insights, correlations and lessons drawn from practical applications. The field of economics, until the 1930s, was even subdivided into two distinct and well delimited areas. That is, micro and macroeconomics, which could not function harmoniously as a whole to demonstrate the viability of the market system, although the building blocks required to transform economics into a formalized science (i.e., cast into a mathematical structure) had been in place since the 1860s.

In comparison with most of the natural sciences, the formalization of economics was rather late in coming, but when it finally did, it was a collective effort. The first serious step was taken by the French economist Léon Walras (1874). Significant refinements were subsequently introduced, among others, by the Austrian Abraham Wald (1932), the Hungarian John von Neumann (1937), the Britisher John Hicks (1939), and the American Paul Samuelson (1947). Following these refinements, a grand synthesis was jointly achieved by the American Kenneth Arrow and the French Gérard Debreu (1954).

The work of Arrow and Debreu, including the refined version presented by Debreu (1959), is mathematical, hence axiomatic, and constitutes the core of the scientific theory. By any standard, it is an elegant construct. Despite a few hiccups to be spelled out in the next chapter, Arrow-Debreu's construct succeeds in demonstrating (in theory, of course) the viability and efficiency of the market system under the premises of individual rationality, market clearing, and rational expectations. This theory will be referred to as the theory of general equilibrium or the theory of interdependent markets, because essentially that is what it is. It describes how a social system, driven by independent actions of individual agents in the pursuit of their different and selfish objectives, ends up producing a final state of balance, in line with Adam Smith's poetic metaphor of the invisible hand. In the appendix of the next chapter, I present a brief outline of that theory. Within the chapter, I only attempt to retrace the evolution of its mathematization, and I comment on its strength and weaknesses proper. According to the above criteria of scientificity, the reader will be able to check that we are dealing with a scientific theory. Because it outlines a mathematical construct that describes the behavior of economic agents while producing the market price vector. It has guided and no doubt will continue to guide economists in formulating a host of statements. Whether these statements meet all the characteristics of meaningfulness or not is another matter to be examined shortly. However, the previous argument suffices to establish that the activity called economics passes on the first criterion of scientificity.

A straightforward demonstration of how economics fares with regard to the second criterion is not easy at this juncture. This is due in part to the difficulty of examining the kinds of statements that have sprung out of the construct because I have not yet defined the needed concepts. I will, therefore, concentrate for now on the pitfalls of the characteristics of meaningfulness and leave the demonstration of compliance for Chapter 3.

Although I have yet to define the relevant concepts, it can nevertheless be taken for granted that economists have no problem understanding their meaning in view of the mathematical formulation and the standard training they have received. Thus, the statements in question are unambiguous statements often phrased in the affirmative form, that is, in the form of a proposition such as: "if...then....", that are next subject to statistical analyses. This way, statements are both explicit and public by virtue of the fact that they are unambiguously defined and are published in the professional literature. They can, therefore, be scrutinized with impunity by anyone who cares to do so.

When it comes to the characteristics of reliability and objectivity, it is an entirely different story. Let us look at reliability first. It is worth recalling that reliability essentially means upholding or following the repeated application of a well-known procedure, and withstanding the test of time. There are, however, a few caveats in the case of economics that are again best explained with a few examples taken from the natural sciences. First, nothing can be measured with 100% accuracy so uncertainty reigns supreme and can only be tamed with repeated measurements under similar conditions. Second, the ability to measure is not all. For example, in physics, there is a consensus on a value for the speed of light. But, the true value, if there is such a thing, is not as vital to physics as knowing that that speed (whatever it is) is the same for any observer, regardless of his state of motion, even though the lengths and time pieces used to measure it vary because of relativity. This means that beside the ability to measure, physics is far more interested in nature's laws of changes and symmetries. For one thing if changes are dictated by laws, then they can not be arbitrary, and since everything does not change, something must be conserved. Things that do not change are expressions of some sort of symmetry. A symmetry, or invariance, of the universe exists whenever the description of a law of physics (previous symmetries) remains unaffected by a change in the frame of reference. For example, a system of bodies behaves the same if translated to another place. This invariance or symmetry of space to translation implies the conservation of linear momentum (the product of mass and velocity). The rotation of a sphere about any of its axis, or the rotation of its observer, leaves the image of the sphere intact. This invariance of the rotation leads to the law of conservation of angular momentum; the invariance to the translation of time leads to the law of conservation of energy, and so on. Thus, for each natural symmetry, there exists a conserved quantity and hence a conservation law. Therefore, symmetries or invariances provide an economical representation of laws and, more interestingly, they also give rise to whole collections of laws.

Thus, armed with the possibility of making many measurements of single entities, invariance, and conservation laws, the natural scientist can easily extend the scope of the "if... then...." statements to explain and predict a wide variety of phenomena over a relatively long period of time. Under such circumstances, clearly reliability is easier to uphold as a characteristic. But because all it takes to falsify a law (i.e., to make it unreliable or meaningless), is a single unfavorable observation. Then even in the natural sciences, laws may be nothing but stopgaps.

This approach works well in the macroscopic world of everyday objects. In the microscopic world (or the world of the social sciences) it does not because there, things are statistical in character. To illustrate this point more forcefully, let me begin with John D. Barrow's characterization of thermodynamics in *The World Within the World* (1988), as the last great corner-stone of nineteenth-century science. There, Barrow argues, no "if... then...." statements about how individual particles will behave under the influence of particular forces are allowed. Instead, statements are made about the behavior of whole aggregates of particles. This is to say that no predictions whatsoever are allowed about the behavior of single entities, precisely because individual characteristics are independent of one another, apart from some flukes. Likewise, economic laws are framed in statistical terms, where repeated measurements can not be made on a sequence of events that changes in time and where there are few invariances. This is the first caveat, for, in dealing with statistical distributions, only "if... maybe...." statements are admitted. Another caveat arises from the fact that an "if... maybe...." statement cannot be falsified. There is a third one which is more specific to economics. In that arena, entities (or agents) are conscious. They react differently to information; a point that will be developed in Chapter 2. Due to the foregoing arguments, in the main, economic statements relative to the behavior of individual agents are not reliable.

Objectivity, on the other hand, is perhaps just as difficult to meet as reliability. However, the difficulty here is common to all the sciences. In this regard, I have said earlier that it is not possible for individual scientists to report on completely value-free observations due to their own priors. As was also made clear, a scientific theory is first and foremost a mental construct. In this sense, it already includes an element of subjectivity. When one looks at the evolution of scientific theories, one can not fail to see how relevant preoccupations seem to vary with the stock of accumulated knowledge and particularly with the passage of time. The kinds of statements that are made are therefore not neutral. Again, this is blatantly so in economics and in the formulation of public policy based on economic prescriptions. In that connection, we can hardly imagine tumbling on anyone who would claim with a straight face that public policies do have the same impact on all social classes. Then how can the economist, who belongs to or who is paid by a particular social class, be entirely free of class bias or vision? Real problems arise only when that person tries to camouflage his or her biases behind some neat little meaningless statements, such as: "The economist qua economist must concern himself or herself with what is and not with what there ought to be." The economist who does this ceases being a moral agent in the sense of Adam Smith.

In order to discuss the characteristic of objectivity in an honest fashion, it is necessary to first stress something that, due to commonly received views, many might find hard to believe. That is, in itself, a fact has no intrinsic meaning. It becomes intelligible in relation to the interpretation we give to it. Hence, facts and judgment are intertwined, but eventually one's priors quite naturally surface in one's judgment. The point here is that not being objective does not necessarily mean engaging in conscious distortions of experimental results. The problem arises from unconscious distortions or from the kind of spin put on the results so as to protect one's class interest or long held social values. I can make this point crystal clear with an example of two reportings on a study commissioned to evaluate a Tobin "tax" (see Chapter 8). Report #1: "A Tobin tax of only 1% on speculators in the financial market is sufficient to wipe out the deficits of the G7 governments without any significant impact on efficiency." Report #2: "The deficits of the G7 governments could in principle be wiped out, but for that a tax bringing $13 billion per day would have to be imposed on business, which would impair efficiency." Notice, nobody distorts any fact, but the two reports will certainly have dramatically different impacts on the public and on legislators. Here and elsewhere, I do not want to leave the impression that economists are engaged in conscious distortions of facts. This is far removed from my mind set. What I insist on is the awareness of the fact that objectivity in any science does not mean subjectivity-free. When it comes to the social sciences, we should even pause and wonder whether or not objectivity can exist independently of some form of moral judgment.

At any rate, if we were to rate all activities with a claim to scientificity, even physics would not score 100% although it would certainly come up with one of the highest scores. This explains why I have used so many examples from physics. Turning now to the economic arena, the first thing to observe is that the theory of economics is still incomplete. I will discuss that shortly. But more importantly for present purposes, we have seen that economic statements fail on two of the four characteristics of meaningfulness. They fail on reliability due mainly to its statistical character, and they fail on objectivity like all other sciences. Furthermore, as I will have an opportunity to show below, economics has not yet reached its goal, which is supposed to be the maximization of people's welfare. However, from the foregoing assessment, the only reasonable conclusion to be drawn at this point is that economics is as scientific as a social science can be for the moment. In saying this, I am of course well aware that two other relevant points are left pending. First, I said "can be for the moment" and not "can ever hope to be." I believe that there is room for improvement in the reliability arena. I will tackle this issue in the last section of this chapter.

Second, I may have left those who are looking for consistency, completeness, and truth in science on tenterhooks so I will address these issues immediately.

ON INCONSISTENCY, INCOMPLETENESS, AND TRUTH

Back in the third section, I stressed the fact that a scientific theory is a mathematical construct. This is a definite advantage in so far as mathematics yields an economy of words and the characteristic of explicitness at the same time. This is also a disadvantage to the extent that mathematics is nothing but a collection of axioms and rules for deriving new statements of mathematics. It is indeed disheartening news for those who place so much faith in mathematics to discover that it does not refer to anything concrete or external to it. We will see later that this weakness is carried over to all the sciences, but first let us take a closer look at how if affects mathematics itself.

The problem of mathematics is mainly due to the fact that mathematical statements can not be relied on to check the consistency of the axioms of mathematics because sooner or later these same axioms will produce some form of inconsistency. This surprising and negative result was first formalized in a theorem by a young mathematician then at the University of Vienna. It shook the world of mathematics, in particular the Formalist School, whose best known proponent was none other than David Hilbert.

The theorem, known as the First Incomplete Theorem of Kurt Gödel,[11] was a terrible blow to Hilbert and other leading mathematicians of his time who had hoped to complete the formalist program of putting all forms of mathematics under a single logical umbrella. The negative result was the abrupt realization that the formalist goal was unattainable. Succinctly put, the theorem asserts that: "No axiomatic construct, big enough to contain arithmetic, can ever be consistent." This means that: (1) There is no way to guarantee that some inconsistency will not eventually surface in any axiomatic structure, and; (2) If no inconsistency is found, then the construct must be incomplete, that is, some statements, derived from and using the symbols of the axiomatic construct, will remain undecidable. Let me add that a statement is termed undecidable when it appears to be accurate, yet there is no known way of demonstrating that it is so.

Evidently, this result is of powerful consequence not only for the ego of mathematicians but also for the general idea of what science is all about. On the other hand, something good flew out of this negative result. If anything, it helps us to formally define the notions of consistency and incompleteness. To wit, if using the rules of the construct we find that all statements are either true or false, or that some are true and some are false, the construct is then said to be consistent. If at least one statement is both true and false within the confines of the construct, the statement is meaningless and the construct is inconsistent. If, on the other hand, the statement is shown to be neither true nor false, then the construct itself is incomplete. In this regard, consider the so-called Goldbach's conjecture. Since the time it was first proposed in the mid-eighteenth century to this day, it remains undecidable. Simply put, the conjecture maintains that "every even number is the sum of two primes," where a prime is a number divisible by one or by itself. No counter example has ever been found. Hence, one is free either to assume it as an axiom, or to assume that it is false, as it can be neither proved nor disproved.

More astoundingly, the notions of inconsistency and incompleteness can demonstrate that it is impossible for a formalized construct to generate all possible truths. This point is well illustrated by an anecdote attributed to John Casti, in his book *Complexification* (1994), which I will only paraphrase here. Imagine a formal construct, represented by a universal truth machine (UTM), which is designed to print out only true statements fed to it orally. Now try to feed a statement like: "The UTM will never print out this statement," and call it statement *S*. If the UTM were to print out *S*, it would have put out a false statement (since the statement says the UTM will never print out untrue statements and it does). As the UTM is designed to print out only true statements, it is logical to suppose that it will not print out *S*. But we would *ipso facto* have another problem. The statement says that the UTM will not print untrue statements, so if the UTM does not, that would in fact make *S* true, although the UTM turns it down as a false. Thus, one way or another, the UTM is damned if it does and damned if it does not print out *S*.[12]

To appreciate the full impact of Casti's anecdote, let us consider another example closer to our subject matter. Take a statement like "Economics is a science" and call it statement *A*. Suppose now we want to show that *A* is true. We could then produce another, called statement *B*, which would go as follows: "Either this whole statement is false or *A* is true." The latter must either be true or false. If it is false, then *A* is true. If it is true, then both of its clauses must also be true, hence *A* is true. What we have done here is to show *A* to be true whenever and whatever we choose *A* to be.

Both of these anecdotes are variations on the famous Epimenides paradox, recounted by St. Paul in one of his letters to Titus: "All Cretans are liars. One of their own poets has said so." Notice that there are two statements in one. Taken separately, each one makes sense, but the minute they are combined, an inconsistency surfaces. How should truth then be defined? Or more appropriately, what is the lesson for builders of axiomatic structures?

The lesson is that truth is not describable within the construct that produces it. In other words, there exists neither a construct nor a set of rules broad enough to generate all possible truths without at the same time generating some inconsistency, as asserted by Gödel's theorem. Hence, despite it all, we are in this regard no farther ahead than the common man who said: "you cannot pull yourself up by your own bootstraps." This problem, which arises in any structure (be it mathematics, science, philosophy, or logic), leaves us wondering how such linguistic conundrums can be avoided.

A tentative solution was first proposed by the Polish mathematician Alfred Tarski back in 1941. He suggested that we distinguish between talking *of* the construct and talking *about* it. For any language in which a statement is written, there always exists a metalanguage which must be used to talk about that language. The failure to make that distinction produces linguistic inconsistencies. If, for example, we were to apply this rule to our second anecdote, we would quickly realize that statement *B* is inadmissible, for it mixes a statement of a language with a statement of a metalanguage. This kind of mixture produces meaningless statements, where one can show any statement is true, including its negation.

From the foregoing arguments, and to get around problems of the Gödel type, could we feed all mathematics and its rules of deduction to a super computer and ask it to check every possible statement of mathematics for consistency? Yes, we could in principle, but we would soon find that some statements are undecipherable. In fact, mathematics is full of what is called unperformable operations. That is, problems that can not be decided in a finite sequence of logical computations due to the existence of uncountably infinite sets. Is there another way of outwitting Gödel's theorem? One naive solution would be to add new axioms. Of course, new axioms could in principle make previously meaningless statements meaningful but would also produce new meaningless statements, as most economists already know. Why not develop a metamathematics, you say. Soon a metametamathematics would be needed, and so on until a hierarchy of metamathematics would exist.

To return to our main argument, it is now easier to see the pertinence of Gautier's question. How do we know whether or not the universe exists, if we can never step out of it? Albeit in different words, this is what I have tried to stress all along. The scientific theory of economics, built as it is on mathematics, must be plagued with inconsistencies and incompleteness as well. However, if that is an unacceptable weakness for some, they must be ready to admit that it is common to all scientific activities.

A final point before closing this section. If it is not advisable to build metastructures, what is a workable alternative to inconsistencies and incompleteness? Stop trying to make our universe intelligible to us! The practitioners of science have long ago realized that this would be worse. Consequently, they circumvent this dilemma by always choosing simple constructs and rules. This is what is called Occam's Razor, after the medieval philosopher William Occam who established the principle whereby entities are not to be unnecessarily multiplied. But again, we humans must decide on what is simple. Is this not tantamount to introducing subjectivity in the scientific enterprise, but by the back door this time?

ON THE DIFFERENCE BETWEEN NATURAL AND SOCIAL SCIENCES

Although I have yet to make an explicit distinction, I am sure that the reader has already noticed a real divide between natural and social sciences. The problems of inconsistency and incompleteness notwithstanding, we have seen that some kinds of science, termed *natural*, are held in high esteem. Because they have provided us with a number of useful laws, which in the end are extended by symmetry to the whole observable universe. Why are they successful, or why do they score so high on the characteristic of reliability? I believe that one reason is that they mimic the behavior of entities whose sizes are much bigger than their wavelength (L), and which are more or less concrete or external to the constructs themselves. When it comes to making observations, natural scientists can therefore rely on repeated measurements of single external entities and on the principles of invariance or the symmetries (also found in the external world). Observations on something external, discipline theoretical statements and make them more reliable.

I have also remarked that this approach does not work in sciences that are statistical in character such as thermodynamics, or the kinds of sciences that try to mimic social behavior, termed *social* sciences. In these areas, it is impossible either to describe the motion or the behavior of single entities. In addition, the objects of the social sciences do not possess a sufficiently concrete external existence to discipline axiomatic statements. In certain instances (e.g., thermodynamics), this limitation is handled by statistical distributions and the associated measures of central tendency; but in so doing valuable information is lost, as a cost of our inability to measure as well as that of the absence of invariances. In other instances (e.g., quantum physics), where reliability (prediction in particular) is deemed vital, a complete new approach is used. I now turn to that approach with the hope that it might be of some help to the social sciences too.

In the early part of this century, physicists discovered additional limitations in the microscopic world, where entities sizes are equal to or less than their L. These limitations arose from the unexpected behavior of these entities as well as from observers interference. A drastic change in our understanding of nature's behavior was therefore required. This new understanding came to fruition with the advent of the "quantum theory," which incidentally challenges all previous ideas about the nature of reality.[13] Clearly, this is not the place to discuss that theory. Suffice it to say that it describes a contextual reality in so far as the steps taken to observe seem to determine what will be observed. Such a situation produces a number of peculiarities that were captured in a single differential equation developed by the Austrian physicist and the 1933 Nobel Laureate Erwin Schrodinger. This equation, known as Schrodinger's equation, governs the behavior of the wave-function of these small entities.

Schrodinger's equation allows us to get around the statistical limitations of observations of small entities by giving the specification of the wave-function in space at a particular time. From there, it becomes possible in principle to compute its specification at all future time. Thus, if the wave-function could be observed directly, the microscopic world would then become as deterministic as the macroscopic one. But it cannot, so predictions are still confined to probabilistic discourses, although the theory still provides a new vista on the workings of nature. To place such a powerful vista into perspective, I return to the statement that all bodies display a wave-function. For an everyday object, the function is localized around its average value, allowing the object to be described using the approach described at the beginning of this section. When we come to a quantum object, that is, an object whose wavelength is equal to or less than its body size, the wave-function still describes its state, but it appears as a distribution of possible states. Though it cannot be observed directly, physicists have learned to detect it by its pattern. In other words, the squared magnitude of the detection pattern of the wave-function is equated with an intensity measure of the impact of the quantum entity. A useful way of interpreting this situation is that the quantum wave is really a wave of information, giving the probability of localizing the impact associated with the existence of a quantum entity. I have had a chance to analyze the effect of a wave of hysteria (Dominique 1990) on the behavior of illegal gamblers. The experience gained from this research leads me to believe that I could just as easily talk about a wave of luck hitting a particular area. Wherever the wave collapses, we should find a lottery winner.

I do not mean to imply that there are no symmetries in the quantum world. Indeed, there are group, internal, and discrete symmetries, but a detailed description will not serve the present purpose at this point. The important thing to stress is that they are not space-time symmetries. They are simply bold new concepts that enable the quantum theory to make predictions on single quantum entities instead of on a collection of entities. For example, the quantum theory predicts that a proton will decay into a pion and a positron after 10 billion trillion years, on the average. Because this is so much greater than the estimated age of the universe, proton decay should be unobservable. Yet, if a particle physicist could focus on some 150 tons of matter for two years, he would observe at least one proton decay. Thus, generally, although no one seems to understand that theory, the remarkable fact is that its predictions are extremely accurate.

What about the social sciences? We have seen that in these areas, the characteristic of reliability does not really obtain due to the absence of anything external and concrete, among other things. This then leaves room for private interpretations or judgments, which stand to affect the interest of the social scientist who is not dealing with something external to him or her. Consequently, it is more difficult to detect meaningless statements and therefore the realities of the social sciences become as contextual as the quantum realities. Statements in the social sciences will probably continue to always be unreliable, not because these sciences are not "good" sciences, but rather due to social scientists' insistence on making predictions on single statistical entities within the confines of an approach that is inappropriate. A "quantum theory of human behavior" is therefore needed before individual predictions of behavior can generally become meaningful. I do not pretend to know how that should be done, but in Chapter 3, I sketch a conjecture of how we might begin.

There is another reason why the normal sciences score high on reliability. Consider Figure 1.2. It shows the approximate domains covered by these sciences on the organizational scale of matter. The great achievement of the normal sciences can be gauged by how they have increased our understanding of

Figure 1.2
The Organizational Scale of Matter, Forces, and Sciences

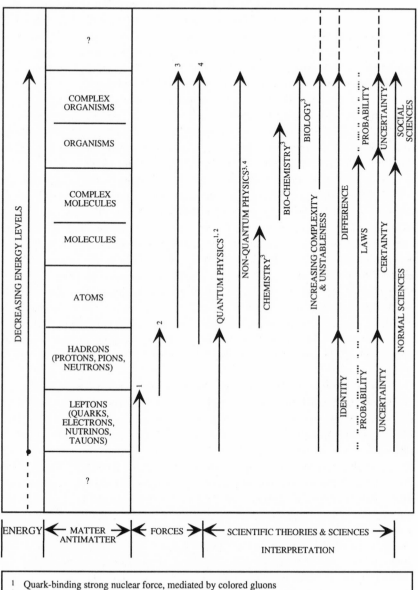

1 Quark-binding strong nuclear force, mediated by colored gluons
2 Weak nuclei-binding force, mediated by boson-gluons
3 Hydron-lepton binding electromagnetic force, mediated by photon-gluons
4 Large mass-binding gravity force, mediated by graviton-gluons

the four fundamental forces of nature. Quantum physics, for example, supplies us with seemingly reliable information about the strong and weak forces. That is, among other things, we know that the strong force operates over a range of 10^{-13} cm, with a strength that is 10^{39} times stronger than that of gravity. This means that within the appropriate range, the strong force overshadows all other forces; it binds the quarks together inside protons and neutrons by means of colored gluons to form nuclei without which no atom could ever have been formed. The weak force, on the other hand, operates over a range of 10^{-15}cm, is 10^{34} stronger than gravity, and is mediated by weak gluons. There would be no atomic bonds and no radioactivity without it. As it may be known, in the process of radioactivity, the flavor or structure of quarks inside hadrons changes. The weak force transforms a proton into a neutron, and an electron into a neutrino, among other things, and this produces heat. Other normal sciences such as atomic physics, condensed matter, and plasma physics, chemistry and biology have increased our understanding of the electromagnetic interaction. The latter is 10^{37} times stronger than the force of gravity and operates over an infinite range. That force is responsible for the attraction and the repulsion of like electric charges. Without it, the world would consist of gigantic nuclei but there would be no light, no diversity, and no beauty. Finally, cosmology has unraveled the gravitational interaction, whose strength is "1" over an infinite range. It also explains the shape of the cosmos, for it manifests itself as a long-range force of attraction between all heavenly bodies. The remarkable thing about all of this is that all of the above statements, and many more, have been found meaningful and reliable in countless experiments.

As shown also in Figure 1.2, the social sciences, in relation to the normal sciences, occupy a small portion of the organizational energy scale. In addition, they fall in the uncertainty region, but they are even less reliable than those in the quantum region. Moreover, concepts such as symmetry and identity (no difference between two photons) and laws (such as conservation of mass, momentum, baryon number, electric charge, and quark flavor) seem to be absent there. However, the point I want to stress is that the goal of each of the four forces, taken individually, is known. For example, the goal of gravity is to form black holes. Since we are fairly sure that it will always be so, statements thrown off by a normal science covering a domain in which gravity predominates have a good chance of being reliable; in this regard, think about the realibility of statements about the orbit of, for example, Halley's comet. The social sciences, on the other hand, fall in the portion of the scale (Figure 1.2) where the electromagnetic force predominates. A peculiarity of that force is its tendency to form fragile, diverse, and complex structures. Moreover, the products of this twin force are generally bipolar. As there are always two fields in interaction, complexities and reversals of polarity arise. Therefore, the characteristic of reliability does not as easily obtain in the social sciences. Put more simply, the very nature of the electromagnetic force makes statements in the social sciences more polemical.

APPENDIX 1: HOW SURE ARE WE?

In this chapter, I have remarked on the difficulties of getting the story right in cosmology. I have also said that at one time cosmogony was perceived as a higher level generalization. I would like to return to these two statements in order to pinpoint the need to be careful. I begin with cosmogony. To see what I mean by a higher level of generality, consider the following. It explained the coplaneity of planetary orbits; it explained the irregularity of planetary motions through the classical solution of the two-body problem and, in so doing, Laplace even discovered a superimposed cycle of perturbations in the orbital positions of Jupiter and Saturn. Moreover, cosmogony resolved the orbital instability that Newton so feared. It planted the seed of certainty in human knowledge and absolute faith in natural sciences. It is no exaggeration to say that it also planted the seed of a new science, thermodynamics. The idea that the Laplacian nebula could just cool down at its outer fringe to form the planets got Sadi Carnot (1796–1832) interested in understanding the process of heat flow. Out of his effort came the new field of study called thermodynamics. Later Rudolf Clausius (1822–1888) took thermodynamics to still a higher level with the introduction of the so-called Clausius inequality as a consequence of the second law of thermodynamics. This law, in turn, led to the concept of entropy, which is an extensive property of a system that allows us to quantitatively express the law. I will not dwell too much on entropy at this juncture, but in Chapter 7, I show how it can shed light on the production process.

In order to foster greater understanding, I should perhaps backtrack a little to clarify the concept of solar nebula. A solar nebula is simply an aggregation of matter. As it may be known, changes in the properties of matter and energy are always accompanied by thermal effects, then think of a solar nebular as a system. Once its boundaries are delimited, and its initial conditions are known, the path of its changing conditions is also determined. For the present purpose, we need only to focus on the path of changing states, which is the locus of the whole series of states through which the system must pass until it reaches its final state. The interesting thing about all of this is that only paths that conform to the first and second laws of thermodynamics are allowed. These laws were derived from common experience, but they are quite reliable. Laplace and his contemporaries had hoped that laws such as these could have helped in retracing the evolution of the system. However, it turned out to be not the case. There is no way back in time to find out what the laws were at the beginning.

Ironically, it is thermodynamics and the work of Poincaré that would pierce the armor of cosmogony. First, the fact that the flow of heat is an irreversible process exposed a major flaw in the Laplacian construct. In other words, we cannot go back in time through a nonlinear heat flow to find out how our universe began (i.e., to uncover the initial conditions); this is a way of saying that the present does not explain the past. But by then, Auguste Comte (1798–1857) had already picked on Laplacian hidden periodicities to suggest a periodic universe, the same idea which was to evolve into the bigbang–big-crunch theory of the twentieth century. Actually, there was more to it. The two-body solution that Laplace found easy and orderly was shown by Henri Poincaré (1854–1912) to be quite unstable with three bodies, and outright chaotic with more than three. This then dealt a mortal blow to the Laplacian determinism. Incidentally, let me remind the reader that Poincaré is not only the discoverer of chaos, but also the father of the Relativity Theory. To make a long story short, in a paper presented at the First International Meeting of Mathematicians, held at the Polytechnicum of Zurich in 1896, Poincaré demonstrated that space-time is not absolute, and that a non-Euclidean geometry was needed to decipher it. This new geometry, when used with tensors, argued Poincaré, explains why a massive body deforms its surrounding space. Later, in 1905, he drew on Lorentz's work on electromagnetism and on the notion of inertia to suggest that the speed of light would constitute a speed barrier in this universe. Albert Einstein was probably in the audience when Poincaré presented his paper in 1896, since by then he was a student at the Polytechnicum, and we know that by 1902 Einstein was a passionate reader of Poincaré (see Gautier 1994, 44–48).

More explicitly, Poincaré was the first to notice that the initial properties of matter determine the principle of inertia of energy states, but are in turn determined by the total energy content. If E is the total energy content, m_o is the rest mass of a piece of matter, and c is the speed of light, the mass-energy relation, argued Poincaré in 1900, is $E = m_0 c^2$. Einstein arrived at the same conclusion, but in 1905. Even the space-time transformation equations and their associated equations for the electromagnetic field quantities of Lorenz had to be completed and extended by Poincaré in 1905. These relations, known today as the Lorenz-Poincaré equations, are the same as those advanced by Einstein in his special relativity theory, although he arrived at them within a different underlying conceptual framework.

In the hands of Einstein, however, the relativity of things was preserved, but the relativistic universe of Poincaré became static and closed. It was now Einstein's turn to be questioned. In 1924, Aleksander Friedmann argued that the relativeness of Einstein's equations leads to a dynamic universe, and that universe is either expanding uniformly or has a periodic existence alternating between expansion and contraction. In 1927, the Belgian mathematician Georges Lemaitre proposed a closed and homogeneous universe with an increasing radius and with a purposeful existence. Cosmogony then reached a peak. Next, the expanding universe of Lemaitre found support in the findings of Edwin Hubble in 1929. The redshift of distant galaxies, discovered by Hubble, was presented as definite proof of an expanding universe. The British physicist, Arthur Eddington, made this viewpoint even more acceptable when he provided a theoretical support to Lemaitre's conjecture.

All of these efforts arose from the dilemma produced by the different solutions to Einstein's equations. Each solution describes a different universe. We may have an expanding or a contracting one, a static or a dynamic one, a rotating or irregular one expanding in all directions, but at different rates. By the time of Eddington, we had settled on a uniform and expanding universe that will eventually come to a stop if it contains enough matter. Under Eddington, cosmography, cosmology, and cosmogony merged into one field of study: modern cosmology. There are 100 billion stars in each galaxy and there are 100 billion galaxies, according to Eddington. The universe became an object of physics, subject to measurement and study. In 1948, a former student of Friedmann, George Gamow, went even farther by stating that the expanding universe was born out of a primitive explosion.

Subsequently, a few theoreticians suggested another interpretation of Hubble's redshift. Could it mean a loss of photon's energy due to the distance traveled, argued Zwicky and Bogorodski? No, said the establishment. Besides, how does one interpret the background radiation (of 2.7 degrees Kelvin in all directions), discovered by Robert Wilson and Arno Panzias? It can only mean the cooling down of a primitive and hot universe, born of an explosion at the beginning of time. The expanding universe arising out of a primitive explosion, enters the collective consciousness as a fact.

Troubling questions still remained. Measurements from the earth's surface pointed to a homogeneous universe, true, but homogeneity does not lead to the formation of galaxies. To answer this crucial question, the COBE satellite was launched in 1989. Fortunately, COBE detected some heterogeneity in temperature. The project director, George Smoot, presented this as the final proof of a bigbang. But there is a catch. Is there enough matter to stop the expansion? Because some 90% of the matter of the observable universe, it is said, can not be seen. Obviously, nonluminous objets can not be seen. However, the universe does not seem to be full of black holes either, for they would have deformed the shape of the galaxies. Even if we add planets, black holes, and white dwarfs about 60% of the missing matter would still not be accounted for. Should we throw in neutrinos? Where do elementary particles come from? What is next? Massive nutrinos or a black hole in every galaxy?

To recapitulate: According to Ptolemy, the universe is geocentric. According to Aristark and Copernicus, it is heliocentric. For Brahe, Kepler and Newton, the universe is governed by imperturbable laws. Laplace went further, by declaring determinism always and forever to be his main argument. Poincaré said no to Laplace with a multibody universe, the future is not knowable. Carnot and Clausius told us that all isolated systems, such as the observed universe, always run down. Prigogine, by introducing the concept of dissipative structures, assured us that nonisolated (or open) systems, instead of running down, evolve toward greater complexity. Finally, Einstein and Friedmann opened up the possibility that the observed universe might not be isolated. Now then, if there is one isolated universe, it is running down, and until then it may be unknowable. If there are many of them, then they are open, evolving, and, at the same time, each one is unknowable from within. These are the big problems.

On a more mundane level, let me say that those who criticize economics for its lack of precision and reliability should realize that in cosmology things are no better. Cosmologists are neither sure of the distance of the stars nor of their age. In fact, calculations from some of the best models show that some of the stars are older than the universe itself. As this is clearly impossible, it means that cosmologists are neither sure of the age nor of the rate of expansion or contraction of the universe, yet no one questions the scientificity of cosmology.

2

THE SCIENTIFIC THEORY OF ECONOMICS

INTRODUCTION

This chapter deals with the core of what I called the scientific theory of economics in Chapter 1. The main elements of the theory, that is, its objects, hypotheses, and so on, appear in the appendix. Here, I confine myself to a brief historical outline of its mathematization, and I also offer some brief comments on its strength and weaknesses. My purpose is somewhat twofold. First, I hope that the chapter, including the appendix, gives the interested reader a bird's-eye view of the theory, and particularly its primary objective and limitations. Second, I hope that it is useful for expository purposes, as well as the ultimate frame of reference for the rest of the discussion.

The path followed by the theory toward its definitive formalization is the normal one, in the sense that it was the same followed by all the sciences, notwithstanding sporadic disagreements and competing claims. The first step toward formalization, it will be recalled, was taken by Léon Walras. However, as any first step, it was not an easy one. He struggled with what is now referred to as the Walrasian system for more than 15 years, and consulted widely, in particular with renowned natural scientists like Henri Poincaré, Paul Piccard, among others, before he felt sufficiently confident to publish it. Of course, by today's standard, the Walrasian effort to mathematically determine market prices appears pristine. It was nonetheless an important step forward although (I should perhaps emphasize) Walras did not start from scratch. He made use of previous bits and pieces developed by others, and his successors have improved on it as well. Obviously, this is not the place to review every individual contribution. I can only mention what I consider to be the most significant inputs to the mathematization of the theory, beginning with Walras's initial effort.

As I have already indicated, the initial Walrasian system was rather clumsy and obviously incomplete. It was Abraham Wald and in particular John Hicks, in his *Value and Capital* (1946), who brought sufficient eclecticism to bear in order to make way for the partial acceptance of the Walrasian effort. Almost ten years after the publication of Hicks's book, Paul Samuelson, in another widely disseminated book, *Foundations of Economic Analysis* (1947), made a second but more ambitious attempt to tidy up the Walrasian system. I will, therefore, call this developmental line the Walras-Hicks-Samuelson's (WHS) connection. There might not be complete agreement on this, but I believe that it is no exaggeration to say that this connection had two main goals: (1) To provide greater rigor for WHS's mathematical structure, on the one hand; and (2) to bring about more realism so as to counter charges of excessive abstraction and empirical irrelevance, on the other.

At about the same time that Hicks and Samuelson were busy at work, another approach began to take shape, that is, a novel formulation using hypotheses and axioms cast in rigorous mathematical language too, but aiming mainly at greater theoretical freedom instead of realism. This approach was first associated with the names of John von Neumann and Oscar Morgenstern, and it is generally considered the first impulse toward axiomatization. To put things in their proper context, it should be emphasized that both von Neumann and Morgenstern started out with some radical criticisms of the WHS approach before calling for a complete break with it on the grounds that it was outdated and still lacked the necessary rigor to be a scientific theory. As it turns out, both gentlemen were excessively well trained in mathematical formalism, and as the saying goes, one cannot escape one's own past. They, therefore, pushed things in the direction with which they were most familiar. It is the same path that Arrow and Debreu (two other formalists) followed to arrive at the complete formalization of the theory in the early 1950s. In contrast to the WHS, this alternative will be called the von Neumann-Morgenstern-Arrow-Debreu (NMAD) connection, about which I will have much more to say in the remaining sections of this chapter.[1]

Stepping back in time a little, we see that the 1930–1960 period was indeed a tumultuous one in the field of economics. Most nonmathematical economists were stacked in what was called the Interpretative School, and the rest belonged to a Mathematical School split into the WHS and the NMAD variants. More specifically, the Interpretative School saw economics as a simple heuristic model of competition. The WHS connection was more in keeping with the empirical sciences, that is, those that put greater emphasis on the measurement of external manifestations in line with the Western cultural tradition; in this case, what was to be measured was manifested behavior. The NMAD connection, on the other hand, in a complete break with the obsession for measuring things, put more emphasis on axioms in line with its formalist origins.

As it was to be expected, the WHS approach, being more empirical in character, made no significant headway as a research programme. The NMAD approach, on the other hand, with its lack of concern for experimentation, offered a bigger field for theorizing. In line with the modern definition of a scientific theory, given in Chapter 1, it appears normal that the NMAD approach would have won over the WHS framework. Throughout this chapter, I will mainly comment the NMAD version, but whenever appropriate, I will also make passing references to the WHS variant. But beforehand, let us meet the main characters of the story.

THE MAIN CHARACTERS AND THEIR CONTRIBUTIONS

Léon Walras was born in the city of Evreux, the capital of the Department of Eure (Northern France), on December 16, 1834. He studied at the College of Caen from 1844 to 1850, then on to the Lycée of Douai from where he graduated three years later. After failing twice to gain admittance to the Ecole Polytechnique, he succeeded in entering the Ecole des Mines in Paris to study engineering. Once there, he quickly realized that engineering was not to his liking. He then dropped out to devote his time to reading literary criticisms, political economy, and social studies. The mathematical training he got at the lycée and at l'Ecole des Mines was going to be crucial to his lifetime work, but his scientific training was, shall we say, at best superficial.

Walras's father, Auguste, was a school teacher and an amateur economist with a "big project" in mind, that is, to create a social science in mathematical form. Upon realizing, by 1858, that his goal was out of reach, he extracted from the young Léon the promise that his son would devote himself to the study of pure political economy so as to bring the project to completion.

Young Léon did not disappoint his father. While working at a number of odd jobs, he devoted time to reading Augustin Cournot's *Recherches sur les principes mathématiques de la théorie de la richesses* (1838), Isnard's *Traité des richesses* (1781), and principally Louis Poinsot's *Éléments de statistique* (1803). Most of all, Walras wanted to turn pure political economy into a physicomathematical science, built on the model of classical mechanics and astronomy. He was fascinated by the Newtonian model, augmented by Laplace. We know this because in his writings and correspondences, one finds numerous passages in which he kept on comparing his approach to utility maximization and price determination to the Roman Balance and to Newton's system of gravity, respectively.

Obviously, Walras's place was in academia. But sadly enough, he had no respectable credentials to secure a position. But despite his lack of credentials, he did manage to often get himself invited to lecture on social topics. He also wrote many articles for the press. In the midst of all these side activities, he kept on working on the big project. In 1860, he participated in an international congress on taxation in Lausanne. There, he attracted the attention of a Swiss politician, Louis Ruchonnet, who first befriended and later recommended him for a post at the University of Lausanne.

When he landed in Lausanne in 1870, his system was still underdeveloped, although his theory of exchange, for example, correctly posited a structure based on traders' preferences and initial endowments and abstracted from the use of money. The reason was simply that his system had fewer independent equations than variables. The system could not yield a determinate solution unless one of the goods becomes the numéraire, because, by definition, the price of the numéraire is set equal to "1"; this also means reducing thus the number of unknowns by one. On the assumption that a trader's demand for a particular good exists, Walras argued that the price of any good, times the number of units the trader wants to buy, represents the value of the supply of the trader. Thus, the supply of the latter good can be expressed as a function of the former. In addition, Walras was already well aware of the concept of utility, but he was still operating on the assumption that traders' utilities were independent and additive; although the variation of utility with respect to the quantity purchased (marginal utility) was already known to be a decreasing function. Actually, the Walrasian system can be solved without appealing to utility at all. But he wanted to show that traders get the maximum satisfaction from the market. Hence, the utility function of the trader had to be somehow maximized, except that he just did not know how to show that. Paul Piccard, a professor of industrial mechanics at Lausanne, came to his rescue by showing him how one can get the desired results from utility maximization. After that, Walras was ready to send to press his magnum opus: *Éléments d'économie politique pure* (1874).

The Walrasian formulation of the process of pure exchange begins with utility maximization, leading to the demand curve of a trader for a particular good. In economics, contrarily to layperson language, we make a distinction between the quantity demanded at a particular price and a demand curve. That curve is a relation showing what quantity the buyer would take at any given price; that is, the higher is the price, the fewer the quantity demanded at that price. We call this an *inverse relation* between price and quantity variables, and we try not to confuse the curve with the quantity that would be demanded at a given price. Within the Walrasian system, if a trader has a demand, then he is supposed to possess some endowment with which to pay his way; the same requirement applies to every trader. The summing up of all traders' demand curves gives the total market demand for a particular good, this operation is repeated for every good offered for trade. On the assumption that a trader has at least one good that he wants to trade for several others, the amounts he brings to all other markets become a function of the price of every other commodity. Thus, the total market demand for every commodity is a function of the price of every good offered for trade. Consequently, the demand and supply quantities, as well as the price in any market, are dependent in part on the prices in all other markets. This is so because a particular trader's demand for any good implies the offer of goods in exchange for it. The total value of every trader's planned purchases must be equal to the total value of his planned sales. This being so for every trader, then on the budget equation (see Appendix 2), total demand must equal total supply.

Overall, Walras displayed an intuitive feel for how a market operates. For example, he remarked: If wheat and silver have any value at all, it is because they are scarce; that is, they are useful but limited in quantity. Elsewhere, he said: The market is a place where individual desires are freely expressed in supply and demand. The price is determined on the market regardless of individual wishes as a result of *objective facts* connected with the scarcity of the goods exchanged. These remarks are essentially true, but only as far as the mathematical theory is concerned. The problem lies elsewhere. For example, it is true that wheat and silver have value because they are scarce, but this is also true because consumers have subjective preferences for them. What he should have said is that a single consumer, among millions, can not influence the result. Beside that, what is so objective about a result that is, in part, based on subjective preferences? The above reference to objective facts shows that Walras, instead of accounting for subjective preferences, was indeed working on the erroneous assumption that economics could be modeled on the deterministic suppositions of classical mechanics.[2] Even today, there are many people who still believe that market prices are objective values; this is not all. When supply is equal to demand, we are already in equilibrium (i.e., the rest point where motion stops). Walras has not demonstrated how we get there. Put differently, he failed to explain the dynamics of his system. To cut through his explanation, we must first imagine the situation just before trading begins. Traders are permitted to make pledges, but not to trade. A trader must first look at the aggregate of pledges to buy and to sell, and then moves from trader to trader to make further pledges, but does not actually spend a penny. Meanwhile, other sellers continue on offering their wares, but do not sell. In Walras's language, this process is termed *tâtonnement* (or groping), but it is highly unreasonable.[3] As a theorist has aptly observed, the whole system goes through a costless process of information acquisition and changes, without a single actual transaction until traders get a signal from a market manager. The role of the latter is to first change prices in the direction of what we call excess demand (i.e., the difference between quantities demanded and supplied), and then to give the permission to trade.

In the Walrasian system, at a given price cried, the total quantities demanded and supplied may not be equal. If the difference is positive, the market manager raises the price cried. If the difference is negative, he lowers it until the excess demand vanishes in the particular market in question. While attempting to follow Walras's reasoning, one is left with many troublesome questions. If the excess demand is positive in a given market and at a particular price, that price is adjusted upward. But this may perturb other markets that were previously in equilibrium, since all markets are linked through prices. When the manager adjusts prices elsewhere, then the equilibrium in the initial market may be perturbed again, and so on. In reality, Walras's answer was to explain how the equilibrium in all markets may be reached, but he failed to prove that the system has a determinate solution. Moreover, a decentralized system is supposed to move to its equilibrium on its own power. One is amply justified in asking why do we then need a market manager?

Clearly, a sound system is one with a correct dynamic structure; I will show exactly what this means in Appendix 3. For the moment, however, let us take the concept of *correct dynamics* to mean the ability of a system to show that the price vector is well determined, meaning that a solution exists and it is unique and stable. Walras showed none of these; instead, he confined himself to counting equations and unknowns, and left the whole problem to his successor at Lausanne, Vilfredo Pareto. The latter tried his best, but in a speech he delivered at the University of Lausanne in 1917, he admitted defeat: "At a certain stage of my studies of political economy, I found myself in a dead end. I could see the experimental truth, but could not reach it. I was blocked by numerous obstacles, among others, by the mutual dependence of social phenomena." (Ingrao and Israel [1990], quoting from Busimo, *Scritti sociologici di Vilfredo Pareto*, UTET, 1966). Pareto died in 1923 leaving the problem to his successors.

Abraham Wald (1902–1950) tackled only one aspect of the problem left unresolved by Walras and Pareto. That is, the existence of a solution. Wald, who was born in Cluj (Romania), arrived in Vienna in 1927 to study mathematics with the geometrician Karl Menger, himself the son of a well-known economist, Carl Menger. By that time, many scholars had already tried their hands at the Walrasian system, but without much success. So when Wald became a tutor in economics, given his mathematical background, it was natural that he would have tackled a problem that other great names, such as Cassel, Schlesinger, among others, did not managed to solve. He was successful somehow. His proof of existence was rather clumsy, but it nevertheless laid the groundwork for Lionel McKenzie, Arrow, and Debreu to work on.

John Hicks, on the other hand, turned his attention toward the dynamics of the Walrasian system, that he found a bit sterile. Hicks was from a different school. Born in Warwick in 1904, he studied at Oxford for four years, and moved on to the London School of Economics where he taught from 1926 to 1935. From there, he went to the University of Manchester, where he stayed for almost 11 years before returning to Oxford. But the work I am concerned with here, *Value and Capital* (1939, 1946), was done at the London School of Economics. In that book, Hicks sought out to combine the static theory of price determination, trade cycle, and capital theory. Perhaps he attempted too much. To his great surprise, however, the book was immensely successful in the economics profession, although the economic dynamics is incomplete and fuzzy.

For Hicks, the most important problem facing economics at the time was the development of the proper tools for the study of market interrelations. It is mainly for this reason that he wanted to improve on the foundations laid by Walras and Pareto. Consequently, a major part of the book is devoted to the foundations of economics dynamics, and another is devoted to the workings of the Walrasian system. However, it seems that Hicks underestimated the difficulty of unifying the static equilibrium and the dynamic theory. He put lots of energy into the manipulation of what he called the law of change in a general equilibrium system. He succeeded in developing certain conditions of stability, but failed to come up with the necessary and sufficient conditions for the economic system to be stable. This was at least one of the problems that Samuelson sought to remedy.

Paul Samuelson was born in Gary, Indiana in 1915. He did his undergraduate studies at the University of Chicago, and moved to Harvard in 1935 for graduate studies. He taught there for a while and then moved to the MIT in 1940. Samuelson had, of course, read *Value and Capital,* but had found Hick's treatment of stability unsatisfactory. He then put forward an alternative that was viewed in some circles as the first rigorous formalization of the concept of *tâtonnement* employed by Walras. That alternative was also seen as the first serious step toward the mathematization of economic theory. For Samuelson, theoretical physics represented the most mature example of scientific deduction. Therefore, it provided him with the ideal point of departure for the construction of the scientific theory of economics.

In his *Foundations of Economic Analysis* (1947), Samuelson tries to identify from various area of economics what he calls *meaningful theorems.* According to him, a meaningful theorem is simply a hypothesis about empirical data that could conceivably be refuted under ideal conditions. In other words, a proper analysis, employing the methods of scientific deduction, must lead to the formulation of refutable statements. But there was a catch. In economics, it is not always possible to put concepts in equation form, and probability statements are not refutable. Samuelson welcomed this restriction and saw it as a means of achieving somehow wider generality. To do so, he then placed emphasis on two types of restrictions that he thought were applicable to the mathematical economic model, so as to arrive at meaningful theorems. That is, those that could be derived from the maximum principle, and those that are derived from stability conditions. Therefore, from the hypothesis of the maximizing behavior of the economic agent, it is possible to obtain theorems of comparative statics as well as the restrictions to be imposed on the demand functions.[4] However, this was wishful thinking, because it was to be demonstrated later that it is not generally possible to derive meaningful theorems of comparative statics based solely on these restrictions. The second class of restrictions was to be derived from the so-called correspondence principle. That principle states that the hypothesis of dynamic stability of a system yields all the restrictions that made it possible to address comparative equilibrium questions. In other words, it is possible to specify the stability conditions of such generality and plausibility as to be assumed among the very hypotheses of comparative statics.

Despite the greater sophistication though, Samuelson's definition of comparative statics followed Hicks's, since he started by postulating the existence of the equilibrium, while the correspondence principle in reality just removes the problem of stability by implicit hypotheses. However, his contributions must still be seen as the first decisive step forward in regard to the question of equilibrium stability since Walras. He also impressed on the profession the need to keep economics grounded in the empirical reality. This is the main message that I retain from Samuelson. It is not necessary for the reader to go through Samuelson contributions in detail at this juncture or later. The important thing to remember, I believe, is that he made many of the vague notions of his predecessors constructive and got the whole economics profession to think in mathematical terms. He was among the first to realize the need for a scientific theory to be cast in mathematical terms. He will, I think, be remembered for that and, most of all, for his penchant for the discipline of the data. His successors have not followed the path he laid out, nor have they paid heed to his concern in this regard. Instead, they turned toward pure axiomatization. I do not mean to say that modern economists do not perform empirical studies. Regression analysis, for example, in which one attempts to estimate and test a presupposed and axiomatic relationship among variables, is their favorite passtime. But, when the relationship is not upheld by the data, they attempt to explain the discrepancy away by appealing to a dose of imagined causes. They rarely question the underlying axiom. This may turn out to be their undoing, for I believe that a scientific theory that divorces itself from the reality that it purports to explain is well on its way to becoming a parlor game.

Oscar Morgenstern was born in Goerlitz (Silesia) in 1902. He studied and spent a good part of his life in Vienna. While in Vienna, he became a disciple of the economists Eugen Bohm-Barek and Karl Menger. Upon receiving his doctorate from the University of Vienna in 1925, he immediately became a professor at the same institution, and later, the Director of the Austrian Institute for Business Cycle Research, a post he held until his emigration to America. Though his early works were mainly in the area of forecasting, Morgenstern was deep down a mathematical formalist, as was his teacher Karl Menger.

Jansci (John) von Neumann, on the other hand, was born in Budapest in 1903. He studied at the University there for a while, moved to Berlin to study with Erhard Schmidt, and then to the *Eidgenossische Technische Hochschule* in Zurich to work under Herman Weyl and George Polya, before returning to Budapest to complete his doctorate in 1926. It is well known that von Neumann was a gifted mathematician, but his main interest laid mainly in mathematical formalism. It is said that while he was in Berlin, he often made the six-hour round trip by train to Gottingen just to discuss mathematics with David Hilbert. The latter was at that time considered to be the foremost mathematical formalist of the Germanic world.

To give the reader a preview of the direction in which Morgenstern and von Neumann were about to take economics, let me make a small digression into mathematical formalism. At the turn of this century, mathematicians had uncovered a number of paradoxes regarding the properties of infinite collections of objects. Their existence was well established by mathematical proofs, but they could not be constructed in a finite number of steps. The formalist mathematical school grew out of the debate on the existence of, and the rules that were to be applied to such infinite sets. The goal of Hilbert, a prominent member of that school, was to develop a programme in which all of mathematics would have been confined to the manipulations of symbols according to specified rules. In other words, and as I have already stressed in Chapter 1, the goal of all of mathematics would be confined to the construction of self-consistent axioms. Under the Hilbertian programme, mathematics would have been once and for all liberated from the obligation of finding meaning in abstract objects such as infinite sets.

When Morgenstern met von Neumann at Princeton, they quickly realized that their common interest laid in the Hilbertian formalism. In addition, both were critical of everything that went on in economics before, from Walras to Samuelson. After von Neumann had developed the fixed-point theorems (see appendix) that were going to play a significant role in establishing the existence of a solution, the two men decided to break away from previous trends. Put differently, they agreed that the Hilbertian axiomatic method was applicable to any science as long as that science is sufficiently advanced in its development. According to Morgenstern, economics was one such science, hence it was ready to be axiomatized; von Neumann agreed. Their common effort came to fruition in their book, *The Theory of Games and Economic Behavior* (1944). Both Kenneth Arrow and Gérard Debreu were to follow along the path laid out by Morgenstern and von Neumann, marking a complete break with earlier frameworks of analysis.

Kenneth Arrow and Gérard Debreu. I have much to say about the work of these two gentlemen in the appendix. For now, suffice it to say that both were also convinced formalist. Arrow was influenced by Morgenstern's work, and even more so by that of von Neumann as regards the mathematical object previously referred to as convex set. In addition, quite early on while a student at Columbia University Arrow became interested in the question of existence, which by then relied completely on the fixed-point theorems for a solution, and in the optimality of competitive equilibrium. Debreu, on the other hand, trained in Bourbakism, a mathematical school that took the Hilbertian formalism to an extreme, was interested in problems of efficiency and optimality. They began their collaboration in the 1950s with a joint proof of the theorem of existence. This was followed by their work on general equilibrium, to which I return in the appendix. In 1959, Debreu published the *Theory of Value: An Axiomatic Analysis of Economic Equilibrium,* in which he outlines the final method of mathematical economics.

To recapitulate a little, we have seen that Walras has developed the initial mathematical structure, but has not shown whether or not its solution was well determined. Wald, McKenzie, Arrow, and Debreu, among others, resolved the existence problem. Hicks, and Samuelson, among others, tackled the problem of the stability of the solution, but as we will see later in the chapter, this problem is still with us. Finally, von Neumann, Morgenstern, Arrow, and Debreu contributed the present axiomatic structure of the theory, but again left the problem of uniqueness and stability largely unresolved.

THE THEORY'S STRENGTHS

The scientific theory of economics, presented in Appendix 2, has a number of weaknesses and is obviously incomplete, however, it also has strength. Even after more than 40 years, it remains the underpinning of all advanced works in the analysis of interrelated markets. In other areas, it receives either direct or indirect deferential references, or else, it provides their language and their axiomatic orientation. This alone is a testimony to some kind of strength that I will now try to bring to the fore.

One of the obvious strong points of the construct lies in its definition of a commodity physically, spatially, and temporally. Defined in this way, the commodity is referred to as an Arrow-Debreu Commodity (ADC), and in the market, only ADCs are traded. More specifically, an ADC is a given quantity of a commodity to be delivered at a particular place and at a particular time. The subtle idea behind this definition is that the more vague the descriptions of an ADC, the more those interested in it stand to miss out on the satisfaction it may bring to them. It is, therefore, when the description of the commodity can no longer be improved on that it becomes an ADC. By giving the place of delivery, the construct eliminates in one stroke the burden of having to add transportation costs to prices. Furthermore, exchanges are not carried out over different time periods. Processes like saving and lending money, or exchanges of financial assets, are not explicitly considered. The definition then limits the number of ADCs made available at any one moment without however specifying a time when exchanges will end. Defining the commodity according to its state of nature also allows the theory to incorporate the framework for analyzing the optimal allocation of risk. As indicated in the appendix, the characteristics of an ADC are compressed into a point on a straight line of real numbers, making it possible to define the analytical space of commodities.

As the reader can verify, all the objects of the theory, such as the commodity space, consumption and production sets, the economic agent, and so on, are defined with a similar precision. There are many items that are not explicitly addressed, but they are implicit either within another definition or *ex hypothesi*. A good example is the survival of the consumer which is not explicitly addressed. However, the fact that the vector of initial endowments, $w^i \in X^i \subset \mathfrak{R}^n$ means that the consumer can ensure his own survival even if he does not participate in exchanges. Likewise, the notion of price with which everyone is familiar, is not a property of an ADC. It is instead a real number, indicating the quantity that must be given out in exchange for a given quantity of another ADC; it is therefore an exchange ratio. Since the economic agent can not get something for nothing, a price is always a positive value in the market.

The hypotheses, on the other hand, are explicitly designed to avoid pathologies. Although I do not intend to repeat here what is in the appendix, it is worth commenting on the subtleness behind the hypotheses. For example, the convexity of consumption and production sets ensures that ADCs are perfectly divisible. This rules out certain phenomena that the construct is not prepared to handle, such as returns to scale, gains from specialization, and so on. The properties of the preference relation do the same thing. Connectedness rules out ignorance on the part of the agent. Transitivity rules out inconsistencies. Continuity forbids discontinuous behavior, while strong monotonicity and convexity lead directly to maximizing behavior in the consumption of infinitely divisible ADCs.

We also see in the appendix that the modern theory preserves intact two strong premises coming all the way from the physiocrats and Adam Smith, the pursuit of self-interest and competition. The fact that, on the average, agents know their interests and that they always want more rather than less, compels them to move on the demand and supply hypersurfaces in response to price changes if they are consumers or suppliers, respectively. On the other hand, it is competition among them (because the number of agents m and firms K are large numbers) which is the force driving down excess demand in each market. In the next chapter, I use the term *arbitrage opportunities* or *unrealized gains* to describe the origin of the driving force. Meanwhile, let us just suppose that there is a positive excess demand in market j at a given price. (Remember, an excess demand is the difference between the quantity demanded and the quantity supplied.) As consumers want more j at that price than producers are willing to offer, there will always be some consumers willing to compete with one another by offering a higher price. As consumers compete, the price will continue moving upward until the excess demand vanishes. Similarly, if the excess demand is negative, producers will compete with one another by lowering the price in order to sell more. This then puts pressure on the price to fall until the excess demand is reduced to zero. This is why we say that if excess demand is positive (negative), price will be moving upward (downward); as it can be seen, there is no need for a market manager. Additionally, agents that are driven by self-interest need no monitoring. They need no additional incentives to either seek or go after opportunities to trade. Putting all of these together gives us the maxim: the market delivers the goods, and at the lowest prices possible on top.

Of course, it would be useful to know what is behind demand and supply. The reader should also understand that when the price in one market changes, prices in other markets may be affected. These notions are explained in the appendix for those that are interested. Short of that, the reader can get from the foregoing explanation all he needs to understand the basic functioning of a market.

Before looking into the major limitations, there are a few more mundane ones worth mentioning at this point. Let us return to the strict convexity assumption. It is recalled that it implies that agents will always prefer averages of any two ADCs to any single one of them; imagine an agent preferring a mixture of wine and whiskey to either wine or whiskey alone. Likewise, according to free disposal, another customary assumption of the theory, if some good is still in excess supply at the equilibrium price, it must be free. Or if at the equilibrium price vector, p^*, the excess demand vector for that good is negative, then its equilibrium price must be zero. Clearly, some good like nuclear waste or PCBs can not be freely disposed of, nor does the agent need a mixture of wine and whiskey. However, the strict convexity defines the direction of motion in utility space and, as we will see shortly, it also defines the contour of equivalence. The mixture of wine and whiskey is a worse case scenario. The consumer may still be better off with one half glass of each. Even so, strict convexity may indeed become pathologic in markets with few agents, but the theory is careful in stating that the numbers of both consumers (m) and firms (K) are large. In the case of free disposal, on the other hand, the construct has the option of admitting negative prices or weakening the monotonicity assumption; it chooses the second option. Other areas that are likely to be of interest to the general public are the inability of the theory to handle exchanges in firms' shares or incomplete asset markets, bankruptcies, and asymmetric information. However, these can easily be dispensed with by simply including them in the research programme of the proponents of the theory.

There are also a few other hurdles, three in particular that I will define. In economics, an *externality*, whether positive or negative, is a market impact that cannot be accounted for by the theory. An example of a positive externality is the economic service performed by a beekeeper to an apple grower, and for which the beekeeper cannot be compensated. Beside externalities, there are certain goods that we call *public goods*. A good is public if it does not possess the characteristics of ADCs, in the sense that many agents can consume it without reducing the quantity available (e.g., street lighting). Finally, there is a very troublesome notion encountered mainly in the production process that we call *increasing returns to scale* that characterizes regions of production where outputs increase proportionally more than increases in all the inputs that brought about the increases in outputs. When increasing returns to scale are present, they prevent the solution of the economic model from being well determined. Externalities, public goods, and increasing returns to scale are, therefore, three limitations of the Arrow-Debreu theory.

As of now, the construct can not account for any of these three phenomena. Hence, potentially meaningful statements can be formulated around them. Consider one such statement: "If ADCs are distinguished by who ultimately consume them, then externalities and public goods are ADCs." In line with our discussion in the fifth section of Chapter 1, if after verification this statement is found to be both true and false, or if it turns out to be neither true nor false, then we would say that the construct is inconsistent or incomplete. Other examples of likely statements are: "The more finely ADCs are defined, the less competitive markets are"; or "if the rationality of agents is "bounded," then the burden of rational calculations imposed on them will be halved." These are good candidate statements for verification. The attempt to do so should normally keep the adherents of the theory busy in the sense of Thomas Kuhn (*The Structure of Scientific Revolutions* [1970]). In other words, what is presently considered as limitations may also be seen as incentives or spurs to develop ad hoc theories.

The above hurdles have been known for some time, and economists have already attempted to address them in a number of ad hoc models. Let me mention in passing though that a new and more formidable one looms large over the theory. The fact that the theory does not cover the financial market was never perceived as a major limitation. However, with the new phenomenon called globalization, the international Arrow-Debreu market is fast becoming insignificant in relation to the international financial market. There is then a reason for alarm. It is quite possible that the Arrow-Debreu market might become completely overshadowed as is the case of Newtonian physics. I will not dwell on this point now, however, because there are more worrisome limitations to consider first. I examine them forthwith.

SERIOUS LIMITATIONS

Theoretical limitations may be divided into three categories. (1) the Gödel type, which happens to be common to all scientific theories and against which nothing can really be done; (2) the mundane type of limitations already discussed above; and finally, (3) logical flaws that must be addressed if the theory is to evolve. The theory has a few limitations falling in the third category. I now focus on them.

As emphasized in the appendix, the first serious limitation concerns the preference or P-relation of consumer i. As explained in the Appendix 2, it gives rise to a utility function u: $u^i : X^i \rightarrow \Re$ such that if $xPy)i$ (consumer i prefers bundles of goods x to y), then $u(x)i \geq u(y)i$, where X^i is the consumption set, defined in the appendix. The P-relation is also involved in the definition of the equivalence class, defined over X^i. Suppose we divide X^i into subsets, each of which is composed of all and only those elements that are equivalent to one another. These classes of equivalence lead to what is known as *indifference curves*. Take two distinct vector bundles x and y in a given equivalent class. All the points on the line joining x and y (excluding the end points) are points that are preferred to either x or y. The indifference curve is then immediately defined; it must lie below that line and therefore must be convex. This concept, derived from the indifference subrelation (I), allows us to say that if a class A is composed of vectors of ADCs preferred to vectors in another class B, then the real number assigned to A must be higher than that assigned to B. By the same token, if the consumer is indifferent to both, $xIy)i$, then $u(x)i = u(y)i$. Hence u is the utility index of i, or a representation of his preferences for goods in the market.

In actual markets, however, producers have an incentive to change the characteristics of their wares. Consumer i often faces a consumption set $X^i = V \cup W$, composed of two subsets V and W, representing known and unknown goods. She may have enough knowledge to rank the elements of V but not those of W. Hence at best X^i is not connected and can therefore only be partially ordered. In that case, the transitivity of both the P and I relations does not obtain as a consequence of asymmetry and connectedness. To make this situation very clear, I have depicted it in the von Wright (1987) diagram below (Figure 2.1). *Asymmetry* here means that if i prefers x to y, she or he cannot at the same time prefer y to x. *Connectedness* implies that if x is preferred to y, then x is preferred to any third object z, or z is preferred to y. *Irreflexivity* means that x, for example, cannot be preferred to x. Given *H1* and *H2*, *C1* may obtain and, if

Figure 2.1
Linear and Partial Orderings of the Consumption Set X

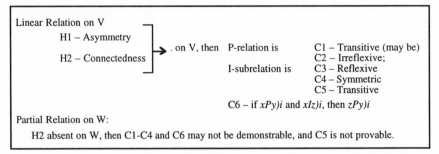

so, then *C2* to *C6* follow. If *P* satisfies *H1*, *H2*, and *C1*, then the ordering is complete. If *P* satisfies only *H1* and *C1*, then *P* is a partial ordering. In that case, the *I* relation is not provably transitive. We should note, however, that *C6* only refers to the possible interchangeability of objects of equal worth, while *H2* is a strong assumption, which is rarely met.

Not surprisingly, in many experimental designs, consumers are often observed making irrational choices. This type of irrationality, coined *preference reversals*, is said to occur when economic agents place a lower selling price on their preferred option.[5] As preferences are supposed to be monotone, the initial intuition was that preference reversals can only arise from a violation of the axioms of transitivity, or perhaps from *procedural invariance*, which requires that the same ordering emerges from equivalent methods of elicitation. But, as just shown, preference reversal may arise simply due to the absence of *H2*. I will return to this question in a moment, but already it can be seen that the axiomatic rationality assigned to the representative consumer in the Arrow-Debreu construct is suspect, because, if the consumption set does not possess the property of connectedness, what is perceived as irrational choices may not be irrational at all.

When we move to the utility arena, we encounter another problem. The neoclassical notion of marginal utility is carried intact to the modern version. Accordingly, the additional utility of consuming greater amounts of a given ADC diminishes until it corresponds to the market price of the ADC, presupposing a concave function. In other words, the rate at which the consumer is willing to substitute a good *j* for another good *k* changes relative to the amounts bought of the two, given her or his income. Thus, the marginal rate of substitution is equal to the ratio of the marginal utility of the two goods. The same marginal rate of substitution is then translated into quantities and set equal to the price ratio in equilibrium. While this may be correct in some way, the relation nonetheless supposes that the consumer values *j* and *k* in a ratio corresponding to their prices. One is immediately prompted to ask: How can she do that unless she or he already knows or owns the two goods? Or perhaps, she or he is using past known market prices to assess the two goods. In which case she is not at all maximizing utility, because she knows neither the utility function nor equilibrium prices. Or maybe, just maybe, the representation is incorrect. This last point gives a glimpse of the difficulties involved in utility maximization. It also prompts me to make the following conjecture about the true nature of preference and utility.

A Conjecture on Consumer Rationality

The Arrow-Debreu construct attempts to give greater substance to the notion of utility maximization, but remains very faithful to the neoclassical tradition in this regard. Indeed, in the next chapter, I show that the Walrasian system does not have to appeal to utility maximization for a solution. This makes it even more plausible that it is tradition that lies behind the rationality described above. In the present conjecture, I do not hesitate to break away from tradition to propose an alternative based on more modern theories of mental processes.

Here, however, is not the place to review all such theories. I will only focus on the two that are directly relevant to the present purpose, that is, cognitivism and the stimulus-response framework (SRF). The basic tenet of cognitivism is that mental particulars may actually be non-neurophysiological. Compared to the so-called central-identity theory, which rules out any property of the brain not directly involving neurons, cognitivism assumes instead that most, if not all, behavior patterns are driven by some sort of software. This theory is perhaps the latest vintage of a long line of developments starting with the Cartesian dualist interpretation to the various forms of behaviorism that mushroomed during the 1920–1960 period. What makes cognitivism attractive for economic theory is its recognition that mental states arise from disembodied processes, even though an important role is still assigned to neuronal activities.

Cognitivism is also the abstract equivalent of the earlier and more familiar SRF, which is rich in empirical content and also more amenable to the analysis of choice at the same time. Dominique (1992) has developed a cognitivist model cast in SRF language and concepts. For lack of space and perhaps interest, it will not be reproduced here, although it is available on request. Suffice it to say that the model essentially extends Beltrami's theory (1987) to human beings viewed as electromagnetic fields in which mental processes are observable as electro and magneto-encephalograms. Maxwell's equations are used to describe the fields, where preferences and dispreferences are represented as energy flows in the form of a vector with two components: e and m. The basic equations are:

$$\dot{e} = (I/b) - (a/b)e - (c/b)(m+\bar{z})m$$
$$\dot{m} = (d/g)(m+\bar{z})e - (h/g)m;$$

where the dot refers to differentiation of the state variables with respect to time; a, b, c, d, g, and h are constants greater than zero applicable to the individual; I is the constant energy input, including the income level and $\bar{z}$ is an informational sequence with zero mean in $\bar{z} \in (-1,1)$. The main idea is the sequence $\bar{z}$ is first subjectively interpreted within the interval $(-1,1)$ before being encoded in the system.

As such, the above system extends the SRF in two ways. First, it makes it more constructive by putting it in circuitry format rather than preserving the matrix or polynomial forms. Second, it allows one of the independent input channels into the state space to originate from the limbic system, beaming emotional signals such as fear, pain, basic tastes, and so on. They are treated as genuine signals rather than just noise. This way, there is no limit to the number of input channels that can be accommodated. Finally, the intensity of preference or dispreference, or attraction and repulsion if you will, is measured by the intensity of the flow vector.

To solve the system, we first multiply $\dot{m} = 0$ by (a/b), substitute in $\dot{e} = 0$ and set $e = m$. To eliminate the squared term m^2, we apply the smooth transformation $m = x - 2\bar{z}/3$ to write down the equilibrium manifold. Three solutions emerge when the mean of the external informational sequence is zero; that is, the information is judged neutral $\bar{z} = 0$. Two of these solutions are stable, one is a saddle. Whenever $\bar{z} \neq 0$, either x^* (attraction) or x^{**} (repulsion) is observed. The way to interpret this is as follows. At any given moment, the system is at or near an equilibrium state, which can be interpreted as attraction or repulsion for a good j, for example. Depending on the assessment of any incoming signal relative to good j, the attraction (repulsion) for j may increase or decrease to a lower valued equilibrium, or even be reversed completely if the mean of $\bar{z}$ is negative. To make this assertion clearer, I graph the equilibrium manifold in Figure 2.2. It consists of a linear term given by $\phi = (dI\,\bar{z}) + (dI - ha)x$, and a cubic term $\psi = dc(x + \bar{z})^2 x$. Equilibria are given by the intersection of ϕ and ψ. Assuming that $dI > ha$, then for $\bar{z} = 0$, both relations pass through the origin and we have one positive (x^*) and one negative (x^{**}) equilibria. For $\bar{z} > 0 (<0)$, there is a fold near the origin on the left (right) of zero.

As shown in Figure 2.2, the equilibrium values of x^* and $F(x^*)$ are plotted in the fourth quadrant, and x^{**} and $-F(x^{**})$ are in the third, showing what utility and disutility functions, respectively, may look like for the individual in question. It also follows from preference that the intensity of utility or disutility may go up or down, or utility may reverse to disutility, depending on how the incoming informational sequence is interpreted.

The solutions of this nonlinear system are broad enough to explain the nature of choices, love or hate, political dirty tricks, competitive advertising, among others. It also gives substance to a remark made by the pioneers (Grether and Plott) of the preference reversal research program. They asked themselves whether the notion of tastes (preferences) did not significantly differ from what is portrayed in standard economic theory. From the above conjecture, the answer is yes.

Which Agent Is the Representative One?

In Chapter 1 (forth section), I said that until the 1930s, economics was divided into two distinct subareas: micro and macroeconomics, which could not

Figure 2.2
The Conjectural Nature of Preference and Utility

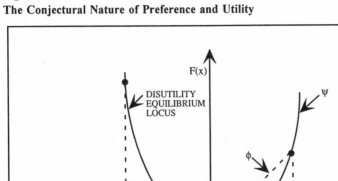

be unified into a single theory. It is indeed charitable to put it in the past tense. The truth is that a grand unification is still out of sight. The Arrow-Debreu theory is, as I have alluded to throughout, microeconomics, which essentially describes the behavior of a single utility maximizer, whereas macroeconomics refers to the aggregate behavior of extremely heterogeneous individuals. From the 1930s to the 1970s, macroeconomics, principally under the impetus of John Maynard Keynes, was transformed into a more or less formal collection of heuristics (i.e., behaviorism at its best) having nothing to do with the prescriptions of the theory. When predictions went wrong, no one knew why, and explanations were nothing but spins. In addition, from the 1970s onward, for some strange and paradoxical reason, macroeconomists took to the bad habit of aggregating the choices of some mysterious representative agents. In other words, the behavior of a single entity is summarily extended to the behavior of a collection, to use the language of the first chapter. This is indeed paradoxical since the basic premises of the scientific theory are that agents are diverse and that they are pursuing their own divergent and selfish interests. The problem here, as Alan P. Kirman (1992) has rightly observed, is that macroeconomists have been pressured into committing the sin of induction by generalizing from the representative individual of Arrow-Debreu in order to answer the plea for some microfoundations for macroeconomics.

I certainly agree with the observation, but I suspect that there is more to it. If economic agents were identical, and I am not the first to say this, there would either be no trade at all or goods would be exchanged in a precise one to one ratio (see Appendix 3 in Chapter 3), mostly if identical means that they have identical preference distributions, identical initial endowment distributions, and identical interests. How could they then be involved in the search for arbitrage opportunities, which I shall show in the next chapter is precisely the missing law of motion of the Walrasian system? In fact, it suffices for agents to have identical preference distributions (but different everything else) to completely change the structure of the economy. I will examine just such a model in the next chapter. More importantly, I will show that the focus on a single entity is one of the most serious limitations of the Arrow-Debreu theory. At any rate, regardless of the reason or reasons why macroeconomists would begin with a representative utility maximizer to end up with individuals whose very differences are responsible for the equilibrium, the approach is flawed. In Chapter 1, I dealt with the danger of inferring aggregate behavior from single entities in activities that are statistical in character. In addition, the above conjecture shows clearly that the role of individual parameters in the logic of choice is such to forbid the practice.

Market Clearing and Perfect Foresight

As I stressed in Chapter 1, theories must be distinguished from the scientific theory. A theory is drawn from the scientific theory for a particular purpose. For example, certain assumptions of the parent theory may be questioned at any time. Then a theory may be formulated under what is believed to be more realistic assumptions. This point can be illustrated by three important examples taken right from economics itself, that is, the Keynesian theory, rational expectations, and game theory.

Keynes, no doubt, disagreed with many basic assumptions of the Classical economics of A. C. Pigou. This is not the place to review them all, except to say that Keynes must have had a particularly strong objection to the assumption that markets always clear, that is, supply always equals demand. He then constructed a theory in which prices do not quickly adjust. In other words, many markets, including the labor market, may remain out of equilibrium for very long periods, in which case, effective demand is below available supply. If so, the only way of reestablishing balance is for the public sector to stimulate demand by either cutting taxes or increasing spending or both. Another important element of the theory was the negative correlation between inflation and unemployment. This latter idea gave rise to a straight falsifiable proposition:

"The rate of increase in prices [inflation] will fall as the rate of unemployment rises." As it turns out, this proposition was found to be meaningless in the late 1970s. Just that one negative result was enough to discredit the whole theory in the eyes of the New Classicals.

The New Classicals, led by Robert E. Lucas, recommended that we turn away from Keynesianism and instead embrace the theory of rational expectations monetarism.[6] That theory returned to the assumptions of market clearing and perfect foresight (i.e., every agent knows what to do). Consequently, monetary authorities should give up attempts to fine tune the economy. If agents are rational and have perfect foresight, they will anticipate and quickly discount any change in policy. Therefore, such policies shall have no lasting impacts on employment and output. Moreover, if the same authorities attempt to surprise agents with their policies, they will only destabilize the economy. Here again, we have statements that are falsifiable. Almost all empirical studies have since found that monetary policies do have lasting effects, whether anticipated or not. Also, when following the dramatic rise in interest rates from 10% to 19% in the late 1970s, the American economy went into the 1980–1982 recession, it was the turn of the New Classicals to see their theory discredited.

Likewise, the proponents of game theory, developed by von Neumann and Morgenstern, tried to replace the Arrow-Debreu theory. Game theory too lost its credibility when it was found that when the number of players is greater than two or less than infinite, or when games can be replayed, either there are more than one solutions or none at all.

What can be learned from these examples? Game theory's outcomes are not reliable, and market clearing and perfect foresight are not valid assumptions. Hence, to strengthen the scientific theory, these assumptions must simply be replaced.

Returning now to Kirman's observations, it seems that the search for the elusive properties of uniqueness and global stability might just be the real reason why macroeconomists have settled for the flawed concept of the representative agent. Let me now turn to these last two major limitations.

Uniqueness and Global Stability

I said earlier that one of the would-be major achievements of the theory is the demonstration that p^* is well determined. In the next chapter, I show precisely that with the Walrasian system. However, the Walrasian system is criticized for its lack of a law of motion. The Arrow-Debreu solution is in the meantime offered as an improvement over Walras's suggestion that p^* could be approached *à tatons* in a process whose continuous analogue is the system of differential equations given in the appendix. It is instructive, though, that both the Arrow-Debreu (1954) and Debreu's (1959) versions are silent on the questions of uniqueness and stability. It is no exaggeration to say that since then no general theorems of uniqueness have been presented. Instead, there have been some works on local uniqueness, showing that individual equilibria are isolated. Some commentators have argued that such works should offer a minimum condition guaranteeing the system a simile of stability for comparative static analyses. Clearly, this is not enough to make the price vector well determined.

I discuss stability within the context of uniqueness in the appendix. Here I only want to stress the importance of both for a satisfactory interpretation of the theory. The property of global stability, for example, is much more important for the theory than it appears at first sight. As Ingrao and Israel more or less put it, in their work *The Invisible Hand* (1990, 330–331), in order to make sense of Adam Smith's idea of an invisible hand, the construct must be self-propelled, that is, it must demonstrate the existence of an inherent market force which, whatever the initial value of the state variable (i.e., the prices), is capable of adjustment so as to arrive at the equilibrium price vector. Failure to do so would be a singular weakness. This also must be seen in light of one of the strong assertions of the theory to the effect that the competitive system is capable of achieving an efficient allocation of resources on its own power. If that state were to be imposed instead, as it was in centrally planned economies, then the claim that the market possesses all the wonderful properties attributed to it would have to be dropped.

Sadly enough, after reviewing all the efforts to demonstrate global stability, Ingrao and Israel conclude: "While no agreement has yet been reached as to the implications of the results concerning uniqueness, those concerning global stability... are unquestionably negative." Because of this result, they argue that: "The classical hypotheses as codified by [Arrow]-Debreu's axiomatization have led to one clear result. There is a contradiction between the theory's aims and the consequences derived from the system of hypotheses constituting its structure" (Ingrao and Israel 1990, 361).

This is a good place to recall our discussion of axiomatization in Chapter 1. Precisely because it is axiomatic, Arrow-Debreu's, and in particular Debreu's, construct is under no obligation of defending the interpretative notion of economic reality. Debreu himself has commented on this situation with an astoundingly clear understanding of the limitations of formalist structures. In a speech delivered at the University of Bonn in 1977, he says: "axiomatization facilitates the detection of logical errors within the model, and perhaps more importantly, it facilitates the detection of conceptual errors in the formulation of the theory and in its interpretation."[7] As such, one can not disagree with the statement. However, it should be pointed out that he only referred to the detection of errors and not to the safeguard against whimsicalities, inconsistencies, or incompleteness.

Despite the psychological pain criticisms of the theory seem to inflict on its more fanatical adherents, they must come to grips with the realization that it is the axiomatic formulation itself that brings out these criticisms; here like anywhere else, they cannot have it both ways. An axiomatic construct, however elegantly built, cannot escape Gödel's trap. At the same time though, the critics of the theory must also realize that inconsistency and incompleteness are not valid criteria by which the scientificity of an activity should be judged.

On the Welfare of Society

As was shown in Chapter 1, the goal of natural sciences is to discover whether or not there are laws of nature that we must abide by. The goal of social sciences is to discover the rules of behavior of man-made societies. As such, the goal must carry an ethical or a moral dimension (embedded in policies and in the social setting); this explains why the French Academy used to refer to them as the moral sciences. In that connection, economics claims that its ultimate goal is the maximization of society's welfare. So far we have examined the technical prowess of the scientific theory of economics, but not the ethical dimension that would make the claim constructive. The way that the theory hopes to handle the philosophical concept of welfare is summarized in three theorems, known as the first, second, and third theorems of welfare economics. It is indeed tempting to critically examine their assertions for the desired ethical dimension at this point, but I shall resist the temptation until Chapter 4, where I will take up the question of policy implications. Suffice it to say for now that the efficiency and fairness claims made on behalf of market mechanisms are not demonstrable. I show in Chapter 4 that in the end, economics may have to settle on a more modest goal.

After having seen the basis for all the wonderful claims made on behalf of the free market, I hope that the noneconomist has a clearer bearing. At the same time, I am well aware that I have not yet examined the attendant consequences of market operations. To do so, I will have to return to Walras's formulation in the next chapter. After that I will briefly look at the crucial role played by the social and political institutions in which markets are embedded. Also, the production process, as handled now by the theory, comes close to being arbitrary, for the technology of firms is simply given and not explained. In addition, as I will demonstrate in Chapter 3, exchange is studied as a continuous process leading to an equilibrium point called a "sink," whereas production is a periodic phenomenon subject to noneconomic laws (in particular the laws of thermodynamics). It is not easy to juxtapose the two processes. However, since this is not crucial to our point, I will therefore draw our main inferences from the pure market exchange process.

APPENDIX 2: THE SCIENTIFIC THEORY

The Concepts

A scientific theory must always begin by defining, mostly for its own purposes, a number of concepts. Obviously I cannot cover them all here, and this is hardly necessary. But in order to make subsequent discussions more intelligible, we must at least go through the basic ones. However, to promote greater understanding, I will use laypersons' definitions wherever precision is not called for. The basic definitions, sometimes also called objects, needed to adequately describe economic behavior within the theory are the following:

Arrow-Debreu Commodity (ADC). This is an object specified by a numerical index of quantity, made available in a particular location at a particular time. Examples of ADCs are, for example, one kilogram of Sunkist oranges made available in New York City on July 4, 1996, or a one hour lecture delivered at New York University (New York City) on October 10, 1996. It follows from that definition that the same lecture, delivered by the same professor at the same university but on October 11, 1996, is a different ADC. These characteristics are now compressed into a point on a straight line of real numbers ($\Re$) into which the Cartesian system of coordinates is then introduced. Thus, on the right of zero on the abscissa, the construct represents ADCs made available to someone by others, while ADCs made available by someone to others are on the left of zero. Such amounts may, therefore, be mathematically written as $x \in \Re_+$ or $x \in \Re_-$.

Commodity Space. This refers to the coordinate system in its entirety, representing the number of commodities available for exchange as its dimensions. For three distinct ADCs, for example, the space is $\Re^3$; for n distinct ADCs, the space is $\Re^n$.

Bundle of ADCs. This refers to a number of different ADCs grouped together for a particular purpose. Such a grouping is a vector in the commodity space. The negative components of the vector are goods to be given away in exchange for goods to be consumed; these are represented as the positive components of the vector. Thus, a bundle of three distinct ADCs is a vector x of three elements in $\Re x \Re x \Re$ or $\Re^3$ as shown in Figure A2.1 for a bundle of (2,2,3), that is, a vector with its tail at the origin and its head at the coordinates 2,2,3. Similarly a bundle of n distinct ADCs is representable by an *n-ple* in the commodity space. Compactly written, we have $x \in \Re^n$.

Consumption and Production Plans. These are programs of consumption and production, respectively, decided on by an economic agent at a particular instant, and so for all future times.

Economic Agents. Agents are divided into two categories. On the one hand, the agent is a consumer if she or he formulates a consumption plan, that is, when she or he specifies the quantities of ADCs she or he plans to transfer to others and the quantities she or he plans to obtain from them, now and for all future.

Figure A2.1
A Bundle in $\Re^3$

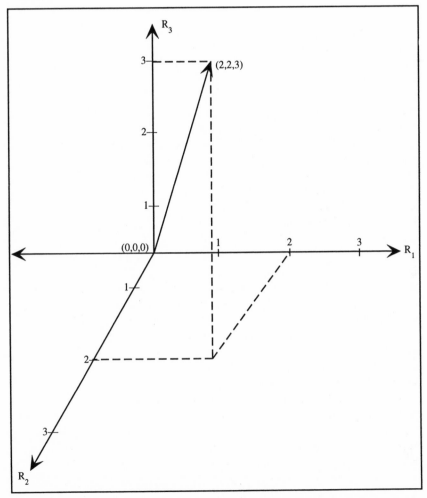

Consumption and Production Sets. A consumption set X is the set of all possible consumption plans of a consumer. Since it is reasonable to suppose that the consumer does not consume all the goods available, X is a subset of the commodity space. Likewise, the producer selects her or his inputs and a technology to produce a vector y of ADCs; the negative components of y are the inputs, positive components are the outputs. The production set Y is therefore the set of all productible y; however, as she or he does not produce all the ADCs, $y \in \Re^n$.

Initial Endowments. These are consumer's wealth at the beginning of her or his economic activity, allowing her or him to enter into exchanges. Such endowments are expressed in terms of physical resources. The theory does not allow for money as we know it, so the initial resources vector w of the consumer represents her or his claims on any combination or subset of ADCs actually not in her or his possession. Nothing prevents the consumer from owning shares in each of the firms (to be defined).

Price. The price of an ADC is a real number indicating what must actually be given in order to obtain a unit of the ADC. Instead of being a property of the ADC, the price is rather an exchange ratio, or the value of the ADC in terms of a numéraire good. The numéraire is an ADC whose price is 1. Then it plays the role of money. Thus, the price vector is an n-1-ple (p_1, p_2,..., p_{n-1}) of individual relative prices. As the price of good j indicates its value, it follows that if $p_j = 0$, good j is a free good; if $p_j < 0$, good j may be harmful, and; if good j is scarce, $p_j > 0$.

Budget Set. If both bundle and prices are vectors in the same commodity space, then their Euclidean inner product is the scalar value of the ADCs included in any bundles. The budget set of a consumer is, therefore, the set of bundles whose value (at a given price vector) does not exceed the scalar value of her or his initial endowments vector. In the language of the theory, the set of all permissible choices of the consumer is then constrained by the hyperplane (an n-dimensional plane), $px = pw$, in the positive orthant of the commodity space.

Firm. This is an entity characterized by the distribution of the owners of its shares, and by its technological capacity to transform commodities. Each consumer may own a fraction of the firm's value or shares, which is then added to his or her initial endowments. Stock certificates are not ADCs, for their possession would entitle their owners to ADCs outside the process of exchange. In equilibrium, the ownership of the firm and the money that would be needed to purchase it are equivalent.

The Hypotheses

Mostly for mathematical reasons, the construct makes a number of very strong hypotheses. The most basic ones for the present purpose may be summarized as follows:

Properties of Consumption and Production Sets. The consumption set, X, is said to be connected, meaning that it can not be expressed as the union of disjoint non empty open subsets of it. In other words, it can not be composed of separate pieces. X, therefore, is also said to be convex, which means that if x and z are any two bundles in X, then any weighted average of x and z is also in X. Likewise, the production set, Y, is assumed closed and convex, containing zero. These properties are routinely assumed and their definitions are standard. However, I use a slightly different definition of connectedness in the following discussion of preference.

The Number of Consumers and ADCs. There are m consumers, indexed by i ($=1,2,...$, m) with consumption plans x lying in some consumption set X. It is crucial for the main assertions of the theory that m be a large number; I will return to this point later. There are n ADCs, indexed by j ($=1,2,...$, n); that is, a list of the quantities given by some vector in the commodity space. It is also important that n be a large number, for the same reason, to be discussed later.

Consumers' Preferences. Each consumer has a well-defined preference ordering given by a P-relation over every pair (x, y) in $X^i \times X^i$. The P-relation may be expressed as $xPy)i$, meaning that i prefers x to y. $P)i$ is assumed *asymmetric*, ruling out nonsense like $xPy)i$ and $yPx)i$. It is *connected*, implying that given, for example, three vector bundles x, y and z in X, then $xPy)i$ implies $xPz)i$ or $zPy)i$. It also follows that if $xPy)i$ and $yPz)i$, then $xPz)i$, that is, the P-relation is *transitive*. Finally, if $yPz)i$ and if x is a bundle that is sufficiently close to y, then $xPz)i$; if this holds, the P-relation is said to be *continuous*. The properties of connectedness (which may imply transitivity) and continuity embody the neoclassical notion of *rational choice*. Asymmetry and connectedness also imply that there exists a subrelation, I, representing an equivalence class, which is *reflexive* $(xIx)i)$, *symmetric* $(xIy)i$ and $yIx)i)$, and *transitive*. The theory makes two additional strong assumptions. They are *strong monotonicity*, inferring essentially that i will always prefer more to less, and *strict convexity*, which means that i prefers weighted averages to boundary points.

Utility and Profit Functions. A connected consumption set and the properties of the P-relation imply the existence of a utility function for consumer i. That function encapsulates i's behavior in the process of consumption. Some may object, on the grounds that such a function is unobservable. As remarked in the previous chapter, most sciences possess unobservable entities. The eventual weakness is not unobservability per se, but rather the absence of something concrete to discipline speculations. The utility function, observable or not, is a crucial notion on the consumption side of the theory, although it can be shown that the same conclusions obtain without having to directly invoke the maximization of that function. Let us wait until the next chapter to see how. The counterpart of the utility function on the production side is the profit function of firm k (=1,2,..., K). It is given by the inner product of the price (p) and output (y^k) vectors.

Efficiency of Decentralization. The individual consumer, exercising free choices and pursuing a maximization objective among many, cannot in the end do better than she has. There is no point asking about the future, for she or he can forecast all future prices until the end of time. This perfect foresight is what is known in economics as rational expectations. Likewise, each firm or producer, struggling among many, must in the end come up with the optimal production plan, guaranteeing the highest profit to be had. Thus, the agents themselves know better that anyone else what they want and they know best how their environment is changing. Hence, decentralizable decision-making is efficient and therefore desirable.

The foregoing objects and hypotheses lead to a number of intermediate concepts on which the theory operates. For example, the market demand for good j is the summation of the optimal quantities that the m consumers would select at various price levels. The optimal quantity of good j that the K firms would offer at various price levels is the market supply of good j. There is a market demand and a market supply for each good $j = 1, 2,..., n$. As we will see in the next chapter, consumers are constrained to move on the demand hypersurface, while firms are constrained to move on the supply hypersurface. At any given price level, the difference between quantities demanded and quantities supplied of good j is the excess demand of good j. Excess demand, whether positive or negative, is therefore a function of the price level (p). These are the important notions needed to define a market as the confrontation of demand and supply for each good. While *the* market equilibrium is a state that any market may attain, or a particular price vector p^* that drives excess demand in each market down to zero. Put differently, the equilibrium price vector is the one at which all markets clear.

One of the fundamental objective of the scientific theory is to demonstrate that p^* is well determined, meaning that it exists, and it is unique and stable. The questions of existence and uniqueness seem straightforward enough at this point, mostly if we assume that the excess demand vector is homogeneous of degree zero. This means that the budget set remains unchanged if all prices are multiplied by a positive constant. But it is quite understandable that the astute observer would want more explanation on stability. The main reason is that as we are not dealing with a dynamical system, where would the force pushing the system toward a stable equilibrium come from? This very complex question will be critically examined in the last section. For now, however, let us suppose that such a force exists. It is precisely the existence of a well-determined p^* that provides the adherents of the theory the basis for unashamedly claiming that an appropriate price system must always exist, and that the invisible hand can guide diverse and independent agents to make mutually compatible choices. I now take a brief look at the workings of the theory in order to gain a deeper understanding of how this could come about.

The Economy

There are m consumers and K producers. The economy therefore consists of $m + K$ agents. For each consumer i, the constraint on her or his choices, X^i, her preference relation, $P)i$ (including her $I)i$), and her vector of initial endowments, w^i, are defined and given. Similarly, for each producer k, the constraints on her actions, Y^k, are also defined and given. Both sets of agents are compelled by their own interests to behave so as to maximize their satisfaction and profits, respectively.

The market demand for each good j can be compactly written as $X_j = \sum x_j^i$. Likewise, the market supply of good j is $\overline{X}_j = \sum y_j^k$. The excess demand for j is therefore $\xi_j(p) = X_j - \overline{X}_j - \sum w_j^i$. A similar equation is of course written for all j as a function of prices with coefficients standing for consumers' choice (α) and initial endowments (w). For more details, the reader should turn to the Appendix of Chapter 3, where I develop a complete system under two different sets of assumptions.

Taking the price level as the state variable, the excess demand function of good j may be simplified to $\varsigma_j(p)=f_j(p;\alpha,w)$, for all j. Here we abstract from firms' activity without any impairment to either clarity or the essential characteristics of the market economy. It makes sense then to view such an economy as a single pseudovector of excess demand, whose components are the excess demand in each market. That is, $\varsigma_j(p)=\varsigma_1..\varsigma_2,...,\varsigma_n)$. In compact form, the pseudovector is:

$$\varsigma(p) = \dot{p} = f(p;\alpha,w)$$

I now suppose, to simplify, that $\varsigma(p)$ is a single-valued function, in which case, the two questions of existence and uniqueness collapse into one. That is, . does there exist a p^* such that $\varsigma(p) = 0$? If the answer is yes, then both the existence and uniqueness requirements of the equilibrium are satisfied.

In the pristine Walrasian framework, similar to the above, a solution is brought about by a force, but that force is activated by a market manager. The role of the force is to push the price p_j upward if the excess demand for j is positive or downward if negative, or even to keep it unchanged if excess demand for j is zero. This operation, of course, appears contradictory, but it is brought about by the dynamic necessity of an otherwise static system. If this is not clear, ask yourself how can one justify the presence of a market manager, endowed with an unspecified behavioral and centralizing rule, in a system that is supposed to be self-regulating and self-piloting toward p^*? I will have more to say about this apparent contradiction in the next chapter. For now, however, let us just accept this simple law of motion driving excess demand down to zero, for all j. And knowing that the budget set remains unchanged under the assumption of homogeneity, each consumer demand (hence the excess demand function) is homogeneous of degree zero in prices. Then we choose a particular good as the numéraire, and the pseudo-system of differential equations given above converges to a *n-1-ple* of prices which is unique and stable.

Arrow and Debreu, taking advantage of the freedom given by axiomatization, propose a different solution concept. I have no intention of going deep into mathematical demonstrations at this point. However, we have now come to a passage where the subsequent discussion might not at all be clear without some mathematical precisions. First, to get to the gist of the Arrow-Debreu solution, I begin by defining a mathematical object called a unit simplex, Δ, while letting $\Omega = \Re^n_+$ stands for the positive orthant of the commodity space. Then we have $p^* \in \Delta = \{p \in \Omega \bot \sum_j p_j = 1\}$. This is a normalization of the price vector so it falls in Δ. This by the way also implies that $p^* \cdot \varsigma(p^*) \le 0$, that is, if $p \ne 0$, the set $\varsigma(p)$ is below the hyperplane passing through the null vector, 0, and is orthogonal to Δ, or at most has some points on it. To put it more simply, the pseudovector of excess demand and the price vector form an obtuse angle.

Second, I have not said much about the power of the fixed point theorem needed to guarantee existence, nor have I given an answer to the often raised question as to whether or not the Arrow-Debreu solution is applicable to the Walrasian system. The answer to the question is yes, but it might take two successive normalizations. Suppose we start with n absolute prices. In the first normalization, the price of good j, for example, is set to 1 and n-1 relative prices are established. In the second, each one of the n-1 relative prices is normalized by their sum so the p^* belongs to an n-1 dimensional simplex. Now the Fixed Point Theorem applies to a unit interval $p = [0,1]$ or to a continuous function from the unit simplex to itself, that is, $f: \Delta^{n-1} \to \Delta^{n-1}$. The fixed point of the mapping f is just a p^* in $[0,1]$ such that $p^*= f(p^*)$. Since f is continuous, the intermediate value theorem can be applied to conclude that there exists a p^* in $[0,1]$. Then each component of p^* can now be rescaled back by multiplying by the sum of n-1 relative prices.

This is also a good place to point out the difference between a function and a correspondence. A function is a point-point mapping in which an element of a set is associated with a single element of another set. A correspondence, on the other hand, is a point-set mapping where an element of a set is associated with a nonempty subset of another set and where at least one such subset contains more than one elements. The fixed point in $f: p = [0,1] \to p = [0,1]$, where $p \cap p \neq 0$, is a point $p^* \in f(p^*)$. Above, I have made reference to Brouwer's fixed point theorem which applies to functions, whereas Kakutani's is a generalization to correspondences. As I did assume that the excess demand vector to be single valued, the reference to Brouwer's should not cause any confusion.

The main departure from the Walrasian solution is to invoke $p^*.\varsigma(p^*) = 0$, called Walras's Law, to interpret the pseudovector of excess demand originating at some initial $p > 0$ as a vector tangent to the surface of the unit simplex and pointing inward. Actually, the mathematically trained has probably realized already that in equilibrium, $\varsigma(p^*)$ and p^* are perpendicular, hence their dot product is necessarily zero. However, Oscar Lange incorrectly called it Walras's Law and the name stuck. Be that as it may, within the solution concept, the pseudovector of excess demand is thereby assigned the role of defining a continuous and general vector field on the nonnegative orthant of the unit simplex. If all the coordinates of p are nonnegative, mathematicians say that p^* is a 0 of the field (i.e., a rest point). Brouwer's Fixed Point Theorem, or Kakutani's also asserts the existence of a p^*. In addition, Herbert Scarf, in his *The Computation of Economic Equilibrium* (1973), uses what is called the simplicial technique to make the assertion of the Fixed Point Theorem constructive by developing an algorithm for approximating the fixed point. All I know is that it does when the algorithm is not too large, of course, implying that the number of goods and agents cannot be infinite.

In the early 1970s, Debreu initiated another line of research on what is now known as *regular economies*. The main conclusion from this effort, among others, is that this particular class of economies has finite sets of equilibria. So much then for uniqueness and stability. However, as regards this disappointing result, it should be borne in mind the sad fact that the difficulty of demonstrating these properties is not to be underestimated. This is partly the reason why above I have decided to consider pure exchange where it is relatively simple to do so, because the minute one adds production, things get nasty, as the production process seems to be responsible for all the observed fluctuations in output and prices.

3

THE OPERATION OF A SIMPLE ECONOMY

INTRODUCTION

In the previous chapter, I presented a broad outline of the scientific theory of economics; following that I discussed, albeit briefly, what I surmised to be its main strength and limitations. What I saw as major limitations were, it is recalled, the preference ordering and the assumption of utility maximization, the notion of the representative agent, and the approach to the determination of the equilibrium price vector. Although I consider these limitations particularly troublesome, I have not abandoned the hope of circumventing them. Since it was appropriate at that time, I then proposed a conjecture that, if taken seriously, may shed more light on the mechanism of choice. In this chapter, I go further into the discussion of potential remedies for the remaining limitations.

Arrow and Debreu's attempt to give greater substance to the utility function of the representative agent is seen as a noteworthy effort that, I surmise, was driven by tradition and the state of knowledge at the time. However, in the 1950s, when the two authors embarked on the task of modernizing the theory, they certainly did not have the new theories of mental states at their disposal. Consequently, they never imagined human preferences as equilibrium states rather than primitive characteristics. Arrow and Debreu then turned toward the preference ordering, discussed in Chapter 2, just as Newton turned toward his ad hoc explanation of the universal acceleration of different masses in a given gravitational field. It is easy to see how we have come to confuse an equilibrium manifold (a dynamic representation) with a simple utility function. In this regard, the conjecture presented in Chapter 2 shows that the difficulty of further modernizing the logic of choice is not insurmountable after all. Why not attempt to do the same for other troublesome points?

Let us begin with the determination of the equilibrium price vector within the Arrow-Debreu construct; it differs from the Walrasian one in terms of its solution concept. But remember, the Arrow-Debreu solution concept makes use of the Fixed-Point Theorem in its attempt to demonstrate the existence of the equilibrium price vector. In order to see how additional problems surface in the overall solution, I must briefly return to the fixed point. The Arrow-Debreu solution begins by saying that a continuous function, f, maps an interval $[0,1]$ into another $[0,1]$. To see what this implies more clearly, I will restrict myself to two dimensions. If I have a continuous f, mapping $[0,1]$ in one dimension into $[0,1]$ in another, sooner or later it will cross the diagonal of the unit square. The point at which f crosses the diagonal is by definition the equilibrium point sought. Then we can say that the existence of the equilibrium is now asserted by one of the most important theorems of all of mathematics. In this sense at least, most observers would agree on this being an improvement over Walras's counting of equations and variables to prove existence.

Problems arise when one asks the troublesome question: What do we know about f? We at once find ourselves facing what another group of economists subsequently discovered. That is, the so-called Sonnenschein-Mantel-Debreu pitfall which reveals a very sad fact indeed; we do not know much about f. Succinctly put, this line of research, initiated by Sonnenschein, shows that the excess demand pseudovector derived from utility maximization is arbitrary. All the Fixed-Point Theorem tells us, despite its awesome power, is that f, whatever its nature, must cross the diagonal of the unit square at least once. It does not rule out multiple crossings, which leaves open the possibility that f may be nonlinear.[1] This opens a Pandora's box, for if f is nonlinear, the number of crossings and the place at which f crosses matter. Indeed, crossings at certain regions of the diagonal produce fixed-points of many periods; that is, many unstable equilibria. Fixed-points of many periods range from *aperiodic* points all the way to chaotic ones. Under these circumstances, and for reasons that I have already discussed, economists cannot claim with a straight face that the equilibrium price vector is well determined. To put it more mildly, as long as we do not have sufficient information on f, nothing serious can be said about uniqueness and stability.[2] Thus, the effort of Arrow and Debreu to place the theory on a high level of generality somehow becomes one of its most serious limitations.

As was to be expected, the followers of Arrow and Debreu recognized very early on that Walras's market manager had to be replaced but, at the same time, the above difficulties also had to be addressed. They tried very steadfastly to locate the missing properties of the solution, which would have completed the axiomatization program. However, as Ingrao and Israel so aptly remarked, the results of that effort remain to this day unconvincing. As a consequence, and instead of facing up to these difficulties, the large majority of economists have given in to their priors and have gotten into the habit of making claims that the theory cannot fully support. This is an area which, I believe, requires our full attention, as modern societies are fast moving toward the belief that the market is a panacea for all socially difficult problems.

In this chapter, I return to the Walrasian solution concept of a simple pure exchange problem. Note, however, that we are not switching to a different theory but instead to a different solution concept of the same problem; except that this time around, I will introduce an important modification to the Walrasian solution, namely the missing law of motion. In other words, the first task of this chapter is to show that the basic initial intuition of most economists is right after all. The equilibrium price vector is indeed well determined, but of course not via the route chosen by Arrow and Debreu. Following that we will be in a position to simulate various scenarios and even infer what can be expected from the operations of real markets.

THE MISSING LAW OF MOTION OF THE WALRASIAN SYSTEM

Pure Exchange

On the average, if consumers are driven by self-interest to always seek more rather than less, they will be observed on their hyperplane, described by $px = pw$ (see Appendix 2). The pursuit of their self-interests dictates that they be there, where their behavior can also be observed. Being there also implies that the equilibrium market value of good j is a share (a) of the budget (B) of each consumer. In other words, for consumer i, and for good j, we have $p_j x_j^i = a_j^i B^i$, where $i = 1,2,...,m$, $j = 1,2,...,n$. As the a's sum up to 1, summing up both sides of this last equation overall j gives the equation of the hyperplane budget constraint of i. Hence, without having to claim that i maximizes his utility function, this last relation can be written as:

$$x_j^i = a_j^i B^i / p_j$$

This equation is a representation of the demand curve of i for good j. Of course, in two dimensions it is a curve; in n dimensions, it is a hypersurface, stating unequivocally that price and quantity are inversely related. This relation between price and quantity is one of the most reliable ones in economics. As it is usually the case, it is referred to as the *law of demand*. Similarly, we could show how price is positively related to quantity on the supply side. This is the *law of supply*. Since we are concerned with pure exchange, we may imagine the supply curve of good j to be a vertical line located at the total quantity of j brought to the market by those who want to trade good j.

Allow me here to digress a little to remark that the above equation is perfectly consistent with the result of utility maximization under the constraint of the budget of the consumer. I will not go into details because it is not necessary for the purpose. However, the easiest way to show this, is to assume that the utility function of the *ith* consumer is described by a Cobb-Douglas type of function. It can immediately be seen that budget shares (a's) are measures of the sensitivity or the elasticities of the utility function with respect to good j and, for all j. The process of maximizing utility gives the same result as the procedure advocated in Appendix 3. What this means is that there seems to be more than one approach to the derivation of meaningful statements, such as the shape of the demand hypersurface, the final price level, and so on. However, the maximization of utility explanation does not seem to be the most intuitive; the reason being, in utility maximization, consumers do not know their utility functions. They know even less about the final price vector or about the magnitude of their marginal utility with respect to a given good. On the other hand, they might have a good idea about their budget, principally when their incomes are derived from their labor effort. In the approach used in the appendix, they only need to know their budget shares and initial endowments. Why then was utility maximization chosen? I do not know. However, since Walras was one of the principal architects of the so-called marginalist revolution I suspect that it was perhaps quite natural for him to revert to utility maximization in order to satisfy the maximum principle in the area of consumer satisfaction.

Another important point to stress is that in pure exchange, goods are indistinguishable from initial endowments. Thus, i's demand for good j, given by equation (A3) in Appendix 3, accounts for this. Another important assumption behind the equation is that i may own each one of the n endowments available for trade. Since $x^i_j = w^i_j, X_j = \sum_i x^i_j$ and $\overline{X}_j = \sum_i w^i_j$, substituting and collecting like terms give the market demand equation for good j given in (A4). The removal of total supply from (A4) gives the excess demand equation for good j shown in (A5).

We also know from Chapter 2 that if the excess demand for j is positive at a given price, competition among consumers should push the price upward. If it is negative, competition among producers should push it downward. To put it more simply, a nonzero excess demand is an indication of the existence of an unrealized gain θ (or an arbitrage opportunity) ready to be captured by some agents. The gain is captured when excess demand is brought down to zero either from above or from below. Mathematically, θ is a dissipative and differentiable scalar potential that must be minimized.[3] Earlier on, I posited that: $\varsigma_j(p) = \partial p_j / \partial t = \dot{p}_j$. This relation was known to Walras, but he was unable to give an adequate explanation as to why it was so. This is exactly what I call the missing link in the relation between excess demand for a good j and a price (p) that varies over time. In Appendix 3, I develop a simple explanation for it, which results in equation (A8). Incidentally, it seems to me that it would have made better sense to define Walras's law as the force that minimizes the dissipative scalar potential θ. It should also be clear at this point that that force is mediated by self-interest and competition.

The main advantage of this solution concept is that its mathematics are well developed. There are a number of well-known theorems governing the flow of dissipative scalar potentials. Their main assertions may be summarized as follows: $\theta(p)$ is an n-dimensional object. Its derivative at p, evaluated at any

$p \in \mathfrak{R}^n$, gives the inner product of the pseudovector $\varsigma(p)$ and p. By the chain rule of differentiation, it can be shown that at any nonzero point of the pseudovector repels, while any minimum attracts. This is the law of motion that moves excess demand to its minima. In system dynamics' parlance, we call $p(t)$ an orbit or a trajectory that takes the system somewhere. Where exactly? Again in the same technical jargon, we say that the orbit converges to a zero of the gradient vector field. Put differently, $\dot{p}(t) \leq 0$ for all p in some open set; and $\dot{p} = 0$ if and only if p^* is a zero of the field. Furthermore, the vector field is orthogonal to all level surfaces of the gradient. An immediate consequence of this is that there can not be closed orbits (circular orbits) in such a vector field. This can be extended to a much more general sets of assertions. In gradient dynamics, equilibria are hyperbolic; mathematically, this means that no eigenvalue of the Jacobian of the system has zero real parts. In other words, there can only be saddle point equilibria, or isolated sinks. If I were to state these results in the fancy language made familiar to economists by Debreu, I would put it like this: In a gradient vector field: (1) the set of locally stable equilibria is discrete; (2) the set of saddle point equilibria is nonempty, and (3) the set of completely unstable equilibria has "zero Lebesgue measure," meaning none. I will not dwell too much on the language for now. I only wanted to establish a parallel with Debreu's results on regular economies, with which economists are already familiar, and gradient dynamics, which is applicable to pure exchange.

I can now surmise that the Walrasian system, starting at any non equilibrium initial price vector, will quickly approach p^* under the assumptions of self-interest and competition. And that, in general, p^* is either a saddle point or a locally stable equilibrium. If p^* is locally stable and unique, it is therefore asymptotically stable. The reader who wishes to check these assertions should turn to Appendix 3.

MARKET OPERATIONS

Scenario 1A

In order to keep things tractable, imagine a market of three consumers and three goods. Suppose further that consumers are identical in terms of their equilibrium market shares, but not in initial endowments distributions, as shown in the next page.

Plugging these values in (A8) in Appendix 3, we get (A9) whose solution is $p^* = (2, 4/3, 1)'$, if good 3 is the numéraire. I next prove that the system is a pure gradient when consumers are identical in terms of equilibrium budget shares distributions in (A9'). Again, I will not enter into the nitty-gritty of jacobian matrices, except to state a few facts that the curious can easily check. If (A9') is symmetric, the system is a pure gradient, and the matrix is symmetric if it remains unchanged when its orderly columns become its orderly line; this form of symmetry was discussed in Chapter 1. What else can be gauged from (A9')?

Equilibrium Budget Shares (a)   Initial Endowments (w)

j \ i	1	2	3	sum
1	.5	.5	.5	1.5
2	.3	.3	.3	.9
3	.2	.2	.2	.6
sum	1	1	1	

j \ i	1	2	3	total
1	50	40	10	100
2	20	25	45	90
3	30	15	35	80
total	100	80	90	

Observe that its main diagonal is negative and every off-diagonal value is positive; also the main diagonal elements are greater than the off-diagonal ones for all j. A matrix with this property is called a Hadamar matrix, which is stable, or we may call it a *Metzler matrix*, and it also has the property of being *stable* if the initial price vector $p_0 > 0$. This means that starting from any positive non equilibrium initial price vector, the system will preserve the positivity of the price vector until equilibrium. Therefore, p^* exists, and it is unique and stable.

It can also be observed from (A9') that the a's and the w's constitute the structure (the parameters) of the system, and p^*'s value depends on the structure. If it is modified, the value of p^* changes. In the present case, the price of good 1 is 2, that of good 2 is 4/3, and the price of the numéraire is 1. Hence, $p_1 > p_2 > p_3$ since there is a direct relationship between the sum of budget shares devoted to a good and the relative price of that good. Each one of the 3 consumers devotes 1/2 of their budget to good 1. This means that good 1 is in greater demand than the other 2 goods for a given supply. Note finally that if consumers were identical everywhere, the three goods would each have a price of 1, but this remains to be demonstrated.

There is obviously more to be said about the determination of prices in the market, but I will postpone further discussion until I can make the situation a bit more realistic. For example, I do not expect consumers to be identical in terms of budget share distributions. A pure exchange model with only three consumers and three goods is a thought experiment specifically designed to foster understanding. I will try to preserve that simplicity, including the endowments' distribution of Scenario 1A, but this time around I will suppose that consumers are not identical in terms of their market choices.

Scenario 1B

Imagine now that we are on an island whose surface area is unevenly divided among three inhabitants. The inhabitants live from celestial mannas that fall on their property each night. Mannas are of three types: 1, 2, and 3, which we now call goods. The inhabitants have come to the conclusion that it is in their interest to vary the combination of mannas bequeathed to them by nature. They have decided to open up a market in which mannas are freely traded each day prior to dinner. If each morning, their initial wealth and the way they want to see it traded are as shown below, trade will result.

Budget Shares

$_j\backslash^i$	1	2	3
1	.5	.3	.4
2	.3	.5	.3
3	.2	.2	.3

Initial Wealth

$_j\backslash^i$	1	2	3	total supply
1	50	40	10	100
2	20	25	45	90
3	30	15	35	80

Note that each morning consumer 1 receives 50 pounds of type 1 manna, 20 pounds of type 2 and 30 pounds of type 3. Consumer 2 receives 80 pounds of the three types, and consumer 3 gets 90 pounds. Summing up by lines, we see that the market receives a fixed supply of 100 pounds of manna of type 1, 90 pounds of type 2, and 80 pounds of type 3. Therefore, the numbers of Arrow-Debreu commodities are fixed by nature, but the demands are in the hands of the consumers. We could suppose also that the consumers want more rather than less, and that they are happier still if they decide for themselves the right combination of mannas they consume. Under these circumstances, we have all the prerequisites for exchange to take place. I then ask the fateful question: Can the system predict the equilibrium ratios or the prices of various types of mannas on the island? The answer is yes, and it is obviously not trivial.

In order to show how the answer is found, I plug the above values in (A8) or directly in (A10) in Appendix 3 to get (A11). The unique solution is $p^* = (1.39, 1.38, 1.00)'$. We now note that the Jacobian of this system, given in (A11'), remains a Metzler matrix with the same attendant consequences for stability. However, there is now a major difference. The matrix has lost its symmetry; it will always be so. When both budget shares and initial endowments are asymmetrically distributed, the Jacobian matrix is also asymmetrical, but the price vector remains well-determined.

We are now in a position to simulate various situations and determine their impacts on the price level. To do so, I take Scenario 1B above as the reference scenario. Then I ask:

(1) What would happen to the price of a particular type of manna if the demand for it were to fall, while its supply remains unchanged? Let us say, consumer no 1 loses interest in type 1 manna. He, therefore, intends to redistribute his budget between types 2 and 3, in the proportions .5: .5, respectively, while all else remains the same. Substituting the new values in (A8), the new price vector is now $p^* = (.55, 1.10, 1.00)'$. Thus, for a given supply, if the quantity demanded falls, the equilibrium price of the ADC must also fall. By the same token, we can infer that if the quantity demanded of manna of any type increases, for a given supply, its price must increase in equilibrium.

(2) Suppose now that the supply of, for example, manna type 2 increases, while all else remains the same. For example, $w_2^1 = 30, w_2^2 = 30, w_2^3 = 50$. The equilibrium price vector is now $p^* = (1.42, 1.14, 1.00)'$. Compared with Scenario 1B, output in the economy increases by some 7.4% (in real terms); the price level (the weighted average) falls to 1.19 instead of 1.27 found initially. Deflation causes the value of total trade (or the gross national product) to show a meager 1% increase. We may then infer that relative price movements in the economy can camouflage real change in welfare.

Using this example, I can easily show how weak the assumption of identical consumers actually is and, by extension, that of the representative agent. To do so, I ask: What would happen if the inhabitants were identical in every respect? An example of this would be: budget shares distribution of .5: .3: .2; initial wealth distribution of 50: 50: 50. The result from (A8) or (A10) would show that mannas are exchanged in a 1:1 ratio, that is, $p^* = (1.00, 1.00, 1.00)'$. Even if we were to introduce some variations such as: share distribution .5: .3: .2; wealth distribution 50: 30: 20, the same result would obtain, $p^* = (1.00, 1.00, 1.00)'$. Perhaps trade would not cease entirely, but all prices would be known in advance. Such a situation has never been observed in the real world, so we can therefore infer that the identical consumer hypothesis is false.

(3) What would happen if the supply of manna type 3, the numéraire, were to increase and all else were to remain the same? Consequently, the only change from Scenario 1B would be to increase the quantity of manna type 3 from 80 pounds to, say, 100 pounds. In equilibrium, we would have: $p^* = (1.78, 1.75, 1.00)'$. As it can be seen, the supply of the numéraire increases while the demand for it remains unchanged. Its price falls, but as all other prices are normalized by the price of the numéraire, the price level shows a marked increase. This is what we call inflation. However, if there were an increase in the demand of the numéraire as well, its price might not have fallen, and there would not have been any inflation. The clear lesson here is, in a real economy, the government or the central bank can not simply increase the money supply without a concomitant increase in the demand for money without creating some inflation.

(4) What would happen if each consumer receives only one type of manna? (e.g., Mr. 1 were to get 100 pounds of type 1, Mr. 2 90 pounds of type 2, and Mr. 3 would end up with all the 80 pounds numéraire). Then a monopoly situation would develop. The price vector would be $p^* = (1.5, 1.45, 1.00)'$, compared with Scenario 1B, that is, prices on the island would be higher as a result. The lesson here too is clear. The lack of competition prevents the equilibrium price vector from being as low as that of Scenario 1B. Notice also that a monopoly may arise from any number of traders pooling their preferences and endowments in some sort of coalition.

I could go on simulating all kinds of scenarios, but the above situations are sufficient to establish the main guiding principles governing the interaction of supply and demand. In summary, for a given supply to the market, an increase (decrease) in demand will bring about an increase (decrease) in prices. For a given demand, that is, distributions of budget shares and endowments, an increase (decrease) in supply of goods other than the numéraire will push the price level downward (upward). Therefore, (1) on the average, the interaction of demand and supply determines the direction of price movements in the Walrasian system, and; (2) the usual assertions of financial operators on TV, consisting mainly of saying: "The market will do this and that," is somewhat misleading. The market is not an external system operating under immutable laws like the solar system. True, the actions of a single agent may be specific and imperceptible, but overall the market only responds to our collective behavior.

What about production? The supposition that mannas fall from heaven rather than being produced is a simplification whose purpose is twofold, that is, to keep the algebra tractable, and to face the sad fact that we do not know much about the production process. To be more explicit about the latter point, consider the following. To talk about production, we ordinarily suppose an S-shaped production (i.e., cubic) function, Q, using capital (K) and labor (L), or a Cobb-Douglas type of function $Q = Q(K, L; A)$, where A is a exogenous shifting factor. We also claim that factor productivities determine the nature of production costs; and that a firm maximizes profits by continuously equating marginal factor costs and product price, under the assumption of constant factor prices. If the function is cubic, an increase (decrease) in output, in response to a rise (fall) in product price, requires a proportional decrease (increase) in the marginal product of each of the factor inputs. This means that the firm must balance two things that are not under its control. Some might argue that, the firm being so small, a change in its input mix should not affect factor prices. But there are problems with this view. If, for a given firm, factor productivities fall and factor prices remain the same, the firm would not be in an optimal situation. Moreover, when all firms adjust, factor prices can not remain the same unless factor productivities are constant. Then the production function cannot be cubic. If it is, what is more likely to happen is that the firm will leave things exactly as they were and sell the same output at a higher (lower) price; therefore, it is not maximizing profits.

Assume now a Cobb-Douglas function, with constant returns to scale (meaning that output changes in the same proportion as changes in all input quantities). Then the marginal product of each factor is more or less constant and proportional to the ratio of output to factor quantity. An increase, say, in output requires a concomitant increase in costs, and the profit function has no finite maximum or minimum. That is, if the difference between revenue and costs is positive (negative), there is no limit to profits (losses). Factor productivities cannot change by much. Then higher product prices must exactly be balanced by increases in factor prices. Otherwise, we must assume unlimited supplies of factors that are being exploited. Or else, argue that output changes depend on the shift factor A, about which we know next to nothing. If, on the other hand, the Cobb-Douglas function exhibits increasing returns to scale, then the maximum profit solution is not well characterized in terms of existence and stability.

These problems seem to originate from the axiomatic representation of the process of production as a simple real-valued, onto and one-to-one map F, mapping from a set of variables into a point. I believe that if economists had the obligation of confronting this representation to the economic "reality," they would have quickly realized that they are dealing with a periodic phenomenon. This means that F is a set of periodic functionals, where each element maps a set of functions into a finite set of states. If so, they would not have put so much emphasis on concepts such as input substitution, factor marginal productivity, and so on. They would also have realized that the second principle of thermodynamics calls for bifurcation points in state space.

Because of these unresolved issues, it is easier to suppose those mannas are somehow converted into consumption goods if they are not readily edible. Then, we must allow for downtime, delays, variations in the technique of transforming goods, transportation problems, among others. Any or all of these may cause both supply and budgets to fluctuate. These variations in the data of the economy are called *demand* and *supply shocks*. Furthermore, the number of the inhabitants on our hypothetical island, as well as the types of mannas may vary over time. An increase or decrease in the number of consumers is reflected in the parameters of system (A8), but will leave the dimensions of the matrix unchanged. On the other hand, each new good entering the market adds one line and one column to (A8). Thus, the market for mannas will respond to changes in i, j, new distributions, new information, and so on. These changes are necessarily reflected in the structure of the gradient. Because of these uncertainties, p^* will always appear as a wobbling point through time. Hence, price fluctuations through time are inevitable. If this is so evident in this oversimplified thought experiment, imagine what it would be like in actual markets where technological breakthroughs, the weather, resource scarcity, and governments regulations, among others, figure prominently.

In keeping with the principle of Occam's razor, I have developed an exceedingly simple Walrasian system. Obviously its goal was not to explain every possible detail. However, in theory at least, it should be sufficiently robust to guide the adherents of the theory to whatever explanation is required. This is what we must next try to corroborate through experiments. In the next section, I use the principle of Occam's razor and statements from the theory to uncover the logic behind observed market behavior.

THE OPERATIONS OF REAL MARKETS

Limited Number of Consumers and Producers

In tackling the operations of real markets, one of the first things to consider is that competition never reaches the point where the number of consumers (m) and the number of producers (K) are infinite. This is the limit where, if reached, competition becomes perfect competition. While it is true there are millions of both types of agents, only a limited number of them operate in a given market at a given time. In addition, individual consumers do not own every initial endowment; individual producers do not attempt to supply every good in the market. However, in each market, the lower is m, the weaker is the force applied to positive excess demands. The fewer the producers, the weaker the downward push on negative excess demands. Hence, markets may fail to clear in any given trading period, or there is no guarantee that the p^* at which markets clear is the lowest possible one.

Asymmetry of Information

As producers concentrate on the production of specific goods, they necessarily become specialized. On the other hand, many consumers only possess their own labor as initial endowment. The more developed the markets, the more specialized the agents, and the more asymmetric their market information sets. The more asymmetric the information sets, the more dependent the agents are on each other. In a real market with production and exchange, a producer is more likely to be better informed about her or his ware than a consumer. At the same time, a consumer is always seeking more information to improve her or his decision-making process, while a producer always appears to be willing to share information. Bear in mind, however, that a producer has a compelling advantage to bias and exaggerate the information she or he gives out, and the more information a consumer accepts, the more dependent on a producer she or he becomes. In the process, some producers acquire what is called market power, which drives their size upward. We have already stressed that a seller has an incentive to sell as dearly as possible. The excess of price over cost is what economists call monopoly power or rent, which is converted into monopoly profits at the expense of consumers. But repeated purchases, or the frequency with which the consumer uses a product, tend to increase his information set relative to the product. In order then to preserve his or her monopoly power and its concomitant monopoly profit, the seller frequently changes the appearance of the product. In so doing, she or he also distances her or his product from similar ones sold by other sellers. The idea here is to maintain the imbalance in information sets. It is not farfetched to say that the fear of losing monopoly or market power is the driving force behind product differentiation, innovations, and the introduction of new products. These activities must be financed by monopoly profits reaped from past sales.

The Impact of Demand Price Elasticity

Equation (A4) in Appendix 3 describes the market demand of good j (X). I will refer to this equation in order to define the price elasticity of demand (e) as the ratio of the logarithm of the quantity demanded over that of price at a given price. The price elasticity is consequently a dimensionless number that reflects the sensitivity of the demand curve to price changes. If the modulus of the demand price elasticity is less (more) than one, the seller gains more than she loses from a price rise (fall). Around the equilibrium, in the present case, (A12) shows that the direct price elasticity (i.e., the relation between the quantity demanded of good j and its own price) is shown to be less than one. While the cross-elasticity of the demand for j with respect to the price of another good k (e_{jk}) is positive. This means that if the price of good k were to rise, some consumers would decrease their consumption of k and increase that of j, because the positive value indicates that there is a degree of substitution between goods j and k. The quantity demanded of j would show an increase. Using the equilibrium values of Scenario 1B, $e_{11} = -.59$ and $e_{12} = +.35$, approximately. Note that the modulus of the direct price elasticity of individual demand is also less than one. This means that each seller would rather withhold goods from the market so as to command a higher price. In real markets, sellers most likely do not know the price elasticity of consumers' demands, but they may proceed by trial and error. These calculated values simply indicate what the seller is inclined to do the minute an opportunity arises. It is not difficult either to see how the low elasticity of the demand curve, the asymmetry of information, and the lack of competition could combine to engender monopoly rents or profits.

The Role of Belief in Value Determination

Returning to Scenario 1B, it can be seen that in terms of physical quantities, the consumer ranking, in descending order of wealth, is: Mr. 1, Mr. 3, and Mr. 2. After trade, and because the equilibrium market price vector is $p^* = (1.39, 1.38, 1.00)'$, the ranking is now Mr. 2, Mr. 1, and Mr. 3. The richest person before trade is not the richest after trade. In other words, the market is the final arbiter of wealth. Suppose now we perform another thought experiment which consists of introducing advertising in the market. Instead of treating advertising as another good, we can just as easily suppose that Mr. 1 spends one pound of manna type 1 and one pound of type 2 to convince the other two traders that manna type 1 improves health, for example. Whether this is true or false, as long as the message is favorably received, it may affect the distributions if both traders 2 and 3 increase their budget shares of good 1 as follows:

Budget Shares

$_j \diagdown ^i$	1	2	3
1	.6	.6	.6
2	.3	.2	.2
3	.2	.2	.2

Initial Endowment Distribution

$_j \diagdown ^i$	1	2	3	total	p^*
1	49	40	10	99	2.26
2	19	25	45	89	1.08
3	30	15	35	80	1.00

The ranking, in terms of market value, changes compared to Scenario 1B. Now Mr. 1 is by far the richest person in that society. In the previous market period, his wealth was second to that of Mr. 2, with \$107.1 compared with \$107.3. Because he was able to convince the other two that manna type 1 possesses a desirable characteristic, he indirectly influenced the market to assign a greater value to type 1. As a result, he becomes the richest individual with a consumption income of $161.26, compared with $132.4 for Mr. 2 and $106.2 for Mr. 3. Notice that the same quantities of mannas are being consumed. In fact, a smaller quantity passes through the market. The inhabitants nevertheless believe that they are better off. The new wealth of some $88 is first and foremost created in their mind. Mr. 1, however, gets 61.5% of it; Mr. 2 gets 28.5%; and Mr. 3 picks up the remaining 10%, although the last two did not advertise. The lesson from this thought experiment seems clear. First, the apparent wealth due to advertising is created in the mind of the agents. Second, the additional wealth is not equitably distributed. The agent who took the initiative, the risk, and put up the investment benefits most. This is a fact in real markets. The wealth created is never equitably distributed. Finally, advertising, if credible, whether truthful or not, works as shown in Figure 2.2 of Chapter 2.

Government Regulations and Institutional Impacts

We have shown above that the advantages of monopoly power are compelling. But the creation of monopoly power calls for entrepreneurship, up front investments and, more importantly, risk taking. What is less obvious, however, is that the easiest ways of creating monopoly power, that is, with a minimum of risk, are collusion, blocked entry into the market, untruthful advertising, and even strong-arm tactics. It can be seen that if our hypothetical island had a government making market policies, Mr. 1 could easily have figured out that it was easier to buy a policy favorable to manna type 1 rather than making the effort of convincing the others through advertising. Much more could be said about the multiple ways that government policy can deform the structure of the market opportunity gradient in favor of some individuals or groups. However, I believe that the results of this hypothetical case are sufficient to convey the logic behind attempts to buy political influence, either to prevent the enactment of or to influence the scope of policies consumers may deem necessary. In the absence of an enlightened and honest government, designing policies capable of making exchanges efficient, truthful and safe, Murphy's Law asserts that abusive behavior will be displayed in the market. Why? Because the structure of the gradient can be whatever we want it to be, and a given structure may confer market power.

Finally, real markets are also small social systems that are embedded in larger social and political institution which, in turn, further shape the overall structure of the opportunity gradient. As mannas do not actually fall from the heavens, there is no exchange without production. Then, the social institutions perform three important functions. They regulate in order to prevent the kind of unfair competition and fraud discussed above. They define the control instruments that smooth out price fluctuations arising out of changes in supply and expectations. And they legitimize market outcomes that are usually socially unfair, as real markets tend to distribute risks and rewards according to the market power of the participants.

THE PROFILE OF PRICES IN REAL MARKETS

I have argued that each market in the economy is subject to demand and supply shocks. Equation (A10) describes the procedure for calculating price movements in the economy due to such shocks. The price profile in each market, denoted $X(t, T)$, is a time series; a record of how the price of any good fluctuates at different points in time. The values of the equilibrium price or any other magnitude may be recorded at discrete intervals or continuously. Here, I will be referring to discrete time series of prices and output, where the observations at time t are real-valued, recorded over a length of time T.

Most individuals are already accustomed to seeing these irregular profiles of various market magnitudes. What might not be obvious to most is that the information contained in these series cannot be read of directly. These series are in general contaminated by seasonal variations, inflationary changes, trends, and random factors. To reveal the informational content of a series, economists must first eliminate the influence of these factors.

In the present case, I wish to draw attention to a market in which one would not normally expect to encounter many fluctuations, the housing market in Canada. My associates and I (Dominique, des Rosiers, and Kiss 1996) derive the housing price profile from two CANSIM-Statistics Canada series nos. P700078 and P700082, linked with interval weights supplied by Statistics Canada, to form the series labeled X_p. The latter represents the price movements of all types of residential housings (individual detached family units, semi-detached, condominiums, plex, row, and rental units). The values are monthly rental price equivalents from 1949–01 to 1995–01, that is, 553 monthly observations. In this case there was no evident seasonal influence present, but the series was highly influenced by inflation. We, therefore, detrended it with the consumer price index (series no. D484000) to obtain the series labeled X_{pn}. On further examination, the series was found to be slightly nonlinear.

The theory described above explains irregular fluctuations, but not nonlinearity. Where does this nonlinearity come from? The best explanation that I can offer is that in real economies nonlinearity may be due to the presence of production, consumption, and investment. Production involves the use of physical resources, labor, and capital. As I show in Chapter 7, physical resources are changed into artifacts that become waste in the end. Capital and labor act as two catalytic agents that are in conflict to appropriate the output of artifacts. To explain this nonlinearity, let us first divide agents into two classes: workers and capitalists. The output realized (endowments), at any time t, belongs to these two classes, the owners of raw materials included. Let us simplify by supposing that workers consume their share, and capitalists invest theirs. During periods of high profits and high investment, the demand for labor (hence the budget shares of capitalists devoted to workers' endowments) is increasing, as well as their prices (wages). However, as workers consume their increasing share, while capitalists have less to invest, sooner or later the supply of goods to the market will start falling too. With a shrinking capitalists' share, preferences for labor services shrink even faster, hence their prices too. As labor's share begins to fall, that of capitalists begin to recover. A new cycle begins. Put differently, suppose that the relationship between the growth of real wage and the employment ratio is positive, profits are reinvested, and all wages are consumed. Then it may be inferred that a high profit rate leads to the growth of employment, output and real wages. But higher wages squeezes profits and eventually lower employment until profits are restored.

Therefore, labor's share of output behaves as if it preys on the employment ratio. In other words, employment growth is depressed by labor's share, and the latter is enhanced by the growth of employment. This prey-predator relationship produces a nonlinear system whose outcome is cyclic, but without the property of orbital stability. Such systems are described in great details in Goodwin (1967), and Dominique (1991), among others. Thus, with production, consumption, and investment, the equilibrium point may wander from closed orbits to closed orbits due to changes in initial conditions and/or shocks. Whereas, in pure exchange models, the equilibrium point is a sink that wanders in economic space due to changes in the parameters.

Returning now to our analysis of the housing market, we deliberately neglect the nonlinearity for two reasons. First, the nonlinearity is small. Second, my main point was to show that the price of residential housing in Canada (Figure 3.1) fluctuates widely over the 46-year period.

Such fluctuations are not confined to prices alone. The supply of residential housing is subject to the same irregularities. Except that this time, each observation is the quantity of housing unit equivalent offered on the market in a given month. These raw values are represented in CANSIM series no. D2783, which gives the supply in terms of residential housing starts in all regions of Canada in communities of 10,000 inhabitants or more, from 1949–01 to 1995–01. These values were largely influenced by seasonality and trend. We smoothed out the seasonality with a 12-month centered moving average to yield a deseasonalized series. We next removed the linear trend to arrive at the stationary series labeled X_{os} shown in Figure 3.2.

The residential housing market was deliberately chosen to depict the kind of obstacles that must be surmounted when economists wish to trace the behavior of real market, compared with values obtained from thought experiments. Enormous expertise has been developed and can now be brought to bear on real data so as to obtain a true picture of market behavior. Figure 3.1 presents a vivid picture of the interactions of demand and supply in the actual world. Figure 3.2 confirms what we have said above as regards price fluctuations brought about by changes in the data of the economy. Once these fluctuations are accounted for, observations are indeed well explained by the scientific theory of economics.

Figure 3.1
Plot of Variable: X_{pn}

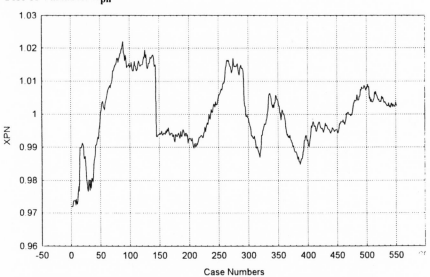

Case Numbers

Figure 3.2
Plot of Variable: X_{os}

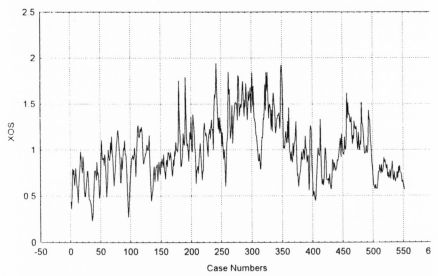

Case Numbers

ON THE QUESTION OF RESPECTABILITY

One clear lesson emerges from the above thought experiments. To predict the value of the equilibrium price vector, one needs three pieces of information. (1) the number of agents and goods; (2) the equilibrium distribution of budget shares desired by the agents; and (3) the distribution of their initial endowments. If this information was readily available, (A10) could be written forthwith, the price vector could be predicted, and economics (as a science) would enjoy the same deference afforded to physics and astronomy. Unfortunately, such information is available only ex post. Yet, economists are unceasingly prompted to do exactly what cannot be done. Such a pressure to know the economic future has given rise, it seems, to three problems, which in turn have come to further undermine credibility as regards predictions in economics. Let me briefly examine each in turn.

One of the problems stems from the deeds of those economists who never accepted or who have lost faith in the power of the Arrow-Debreu theory to provide a reasonable explanation of economic behavior. Consequently, they first distinguish the theory from its close relatives or other ad hoc models by labeling it orthodox economics. Next, they seem to thrive on the erroneous explanations and predictions of international economic institutions such as the International Monetary Fund (IMF), the Organization for Economic Cooperation and Development (OECD), among others. However, given the urge to do better, the same people do not hesitate to offer what they surmise to be the correct explanation of various phenomena. Such cases are simply too numerous to enumerate, but the recent book by Paul Ormerod, *The Death of Economics* (1994) is a typical one. Ormerod picks out a rich set of errors from these institutions and skillfully uses them as a springboard to proclaim the death of economics. But he assures us that a new theory, to be developed in collaboration with other social scientists, will rise from the ashes of orthodox economics.

However, without waiting for the new theory, Ormerod decides to offer a few theoretic explanations of his own vintage. For example, in *Le monde diplomatique* (July 1996, 12) he argues: "The refusal of the French Government to abandon the "gold standard" and its concomitant high rates of interest in the 1930s caused production level in that country to remain inferior to its 1929 level." What should be understood from this kind of pronouncement? From 1816 to 1914, most industrial countries were on the gold standard. From 1914 to 1934, they were on some sort of gold exchange standard. From 1934 to 1944, they moved to the gold bullion standard. From 1944 to 1971, they were again on the gold exchange standard but with capital control, fixed exchange rates, and stabilization policy to maintain full employment. The key role of the gold standard was to maintain the convertibility of national currencies into gold. Because a credible commitment to gold meant capital mobility and fixed exchange rates but, of course, not monetary policy independence. With the outbreak of World War I, the gold standard came to an end when the Bank of England suspended payments in gold, and exchange rate controls were imposed.

After the war, although the standard was not really reinstated, there was free capital mobility nevertheless but combined with tariff protection. With the onset of the great depression, countries began to restrict capital movements in an attempt to shelter their economies from deflation and depression. With plummeting agricultural prices, a number of countries raised tariffs further in 1929. In June 1930, the United States passed the Smooth-Hawley Tariff Act which raised duties on imports by 23%. Most countries retaliated with tariffs and quantitative restrictions. The United States, England, and countries in the sterling zone dropped the gold standard so as to devalue their currencies. Countries such as France, Italy, Belgium, the Netherlands, Switzerland, among others, stayed on gold but raised tariffs. A third group – Germany, Austria, and so on – instituted exchange controls. Until 1934, when the United States began to reduce tariff protection under the Reciprocal Trade Agreement, both international trade and world output plummeted.

The way Omerod puts it, one gets the impression that output fell in France because that country alone remained on the gold standard, while growth was explosive in countries that dropped it. The truth is that growth was rather low in France in the mid-1930s, but it was sluggish in every other industrial country. Take the case of the United States, for example. The United States abandoned the standard in 1934, yet the gross national product, the index of industrial production, the consumer price index, personal saving, undistributed corporate profits, among other things, remained well below their 1929 level until 1940. More importantly, according to U.S. Department of Commerce figures, the rates of growth of gross national product (GNP) of most industrial countries during the 1870–1913 period, when they were on the gold standard, were almost twice as high as those of the 1929–1950 period. It is much more plausible, therefore, that the low level of production in France is explained by the tariff war and the policy package instituted by the government in 1936. I am not the only one that offers this interpretation. For other points of views, the reader is referred to Bairoch and White (1996), Eichengreen (1996), among others.

The second problem arises from noneconomists. From time to time, a group of individuals emerges from nowhere to say to economists: Move over and let me show you, as John Field and Ralph Pressel did in their *Our Economy* (1993). These two authors assemble a number of heuristics to create a system called econodynamics, which we are told is an engineering system. According to the authors, the U.S. economy is in trouble due to the incompetence of conventional economists and to some 33,000 legislative assistants in Washington. These assistants, as a group, are apparently biased against free enterprise and ambitious to micromanage the private economy. Field and Pressel assemble a series of heuristics, taken from the same incompetent economists, to create their engineering system designed to put some order in the economic house. Needless to say, their explanations and predictions border on sheer nonsense.

The third and last problem resides in the way economic forecasts are delivered to the public. Apparently, in the late 1989, the investment house of Drexel Burnham Lambert had forecasted various alternative outcomes for the U.S.

economy in 1990. The outcomes ranged from a recession to an inflationary boom. John Casti (1994, 11) takes issue with the presentation and claims that: "It is predictions like this that give economics a bad name, preventing the field from being taken seriously as a science even by many of its practitioners." But sadly enough, it is Casti who needs to familiarize himself with the complex nature of economics.

Following the argument of Chapter 1, one would be inclined to think that all it takes to fix the Drexell Burnham Lambert's forecast is the probability values of various outcomes, but, I am not optimistic about our ability to do so. Macroeconomic phenomena do not occur and reoccur with the same frequencies. Perhaps this is just what to expect from an activity governed by the electromagnetic force. Our ignorance about these probability values used to be reflected in the multiplicity of macroeconomic schools of thought, such as Classical, Walrasian, Monetarist, and New Classical. Some time ago, a notable macroeconomist, Arthur Okun, told us that we need better theories of how markets really work; the response was the creation additional schools. We now have the New Keynesian, Neo-Keynesian, New Neo-Keynesian, Post-Keynesian, and still another school being formed that will be referred to as Post-Walrasian (Colander 1996). These new labels are telling us one thing: We have not deciphered the nonlinear macroeconomic environment.

Thus, as it can be seen, the grouch, the self-appointed economist, and all of those who fail to understand the complex nature of economics further compound an already formidable data problem and tend to reduce the import of economics in the eye of the public. Economics is now grappling with an even bigger problem; the tendency to hide one's ideology behind economic prescriptions. This additional problem is discussed in the next chapter.

APPENDIX 3: THE DERIVATION OF THE DEMAND OF CONSUMER i

Consumer i ($=1, 2, ..., m$) is driven by self-interest to always want more rather than less. On the market, he or she reaches an equilibrium point when the market value of his vector of initial endowments (w^i) is equal to that of the bundle of goods (x^i) purchased. Hence in equilibrium, the market value of good j ($=1, 2, ..., n$) to consumer i is:

(A1)
$$p_j x_j^i = a_j^i B^i$$

where a_j^i is a share of i's budget (B) devoted to good j. Therefore, the demand of i for good j is:

(A2)
$$x_j^i = a_j^i B^i / p_j$$

In pure exchange, $x_j^i = w_j^i$. (A2) can be written as:

(A3)
$$x_j^i = \frac{a_j^i}{p_j}\left(p_1 w_1^i + p_2 w_2^i + ... + p_n w_n^i\right)$$

Summing up the demand of all i, gives the market demand for good j. That is, $\sum_i x_j^i = X_j$. Collecting like terms, we have:

(A4)
$$X_j = \frac{1}{p_j}\Big[\left(a_1^1 w_1^1 + a_1^2 w_1^2 + ... + a_1^m w_1^m\right)p_1 + \left(a_1^1 w_2^1 + a_1^2 w_2^2 + ... + a_2^m w_2^m\right)p_2 + ... +$$
$$\left(a_n^1 w_n^1 + a_n^2 w_n^2 + ... + a_n^m w_n^m\right)p_n\Big]$$

where superscripts and subscripts stand for consumers and goods, respectively.

The Derivation of Excess Demand

As explained in the text, the excess demand of good j is $\varsigma_j(p) = X_j - \sum_i w_j^i$. Therefore, for all j:

(A5) $\varsigma_j(p) = \dot{p}_j = \dfrac{1}{p_j}\left\{\left[\left(a_1^1 w_1^1 + ... + a_1^m w_1^m\right) - \sum_i w_j^i\right]p_j + ... + \left(a_n^1 w_n^1 + ... + a_n^m w_n^m\right)p_n\right\}.$

The mathematical explanation for (A5) is as follows. Self-interest and competition is a scalar potential $\theta(p):V \to \Re$. The scalar potential is twice differentiable and continuous, that is, C^2, on a real vector space $U \in \Re^n$, equipped with an inner product. Then $\partial\theta(p)/\partial p_j = \dot{p}_j = \varsigma_j(p)$. The gradient of $\theta(\cdot)$ is dissipative on some open set $V \subset U$. When $\theta(\cdot)$ is C^2 on V, then the vector field on V is representable by the ordinary differential equation system given in Appendix 2.

On the assumption that each p_j represents a dimension of the gradient,

$$\nabla : \Re^n \to \Re^n,$$

where $\nabla(\theta(\cdot)) = \dot{p} = -\left(\dfrac{\partial \theta(\cdot)}{\partial p_1}, \dfrac{\partial \theta(\cdot)}{\partial p_2}, ..., \dfrac{\partial \theta(\cdot)}{\partial p_n} \right)$; then clearly

$\dfrac{\partial \theta(\cdot)}{\partial p_1} = \varsigma_j(\cdot) = \dfrac{\partial \theta(\cdot)}{\partial t} = \dot{p}_j, \forall_j$, is the jth component of $\nabla(\cdot)$.

$\theta(p)$ can be found by integrating component by component:

$$\theta(p) = \int \frac{\partial \theta(\cdot)}{\partial p_1} + h_1(\cdot)$$

$$\vdots$$

$$\theta(p) = \int \frac{\partial \theta(\cdot)}{\partial p_n} + h_n(\cdot),$$

where the h's are harmonizing functions chosen so that $\theta(\cdot)$ is common to every component. In the Walrasian system, $h_1 = h_2 = ... = h_n = 0$. Then under the assumption that consumers are identical in terms of equilibrium budget shares distribution:

(A6) $$\theta(p) = \sum_{j \in n} \left[(a_k - 1) p_k X_k + a_k \left(\sum_{j \neq k} p_j X_j \right) \ell_n p_k + 0 \right].$$

If consumers are not identical,

(A7) $$\tilde{\theta}(p) = \sum_{j \in n} \left\{ \left(\sum_i a_k^i w_k^i - \sum_i w_k^i \right) p_k + \sum_{j \neq k} p_j \left(\sum_j a_j^i w_j^i \right) \ell_n p_k + 0 \right\}, k \in n;$$

Therefore,

$$\frac{\partial \tilde{\theta}(\cdot)}{\partial p_j} = \varsigma_j(\cdot), \forall_j; \qquad 0 \le a_j^i \le 1, \ \sum_{j=1}^n a_j^i = 1.$$

In order to simplify and still have room to generalize to higher order, we let $m = 3$, $n = 3$. Then from (A7), we have:

(A8)

$$
\begin{bmatrix} \dot{p}_1 \\ \dot{p}_2 \\ \dot{p}_3 \end{bmatrix} = - \begin{bmatrix} 1/p_1 & \cdot & \cdot \\ \cdot & 1/p_2 & \cdot \\ \cdot & \cdot & 1/p_3 \end{bmatrix} \begin{bmatrix} \left(a_1^1 w_1^1 + \ldots + a_1^3 w_1^3\right)\left(a_1^1 w_2^1 + \ldots + a_1^3 w_2^3\right)\left(a_1^1 w_3^1 + \ldots + a_1^3 w_3^3\right) \\ \left(a_2^1 w_1^1 + \ldots + a_2^3 w_1^3\right)\left(a_2^1 w_2^1 + \ldots + a_2^3 w_2^3\right)\left(a_2^1 w_3^1 + \ldots + a_2^3 w_3^3\right) \\ \left(a_3^1 w_1^1 + \ldots + a_3^3 w_1^3\right)\left(a_3^1 w_2^1 + \ldots + a_3^3 w_2^3\right)\left(a_3^1 w_3^1 + \ldots + a_3^3 w_3^3\right) \end{bmatrix}
$$

↑

column

vector $-$ $\begin{bmatrix} \sum\limits_i w_1^i & \cdot & \cdot \\ \cdot & \sum\limits_i w_2^i & \cdot \\ \cdot & \cdot & \sum\limits_i w_3^i \end{bmatrix} \begin{bmatrix} p_1 \\ p_2 \\ p_3 \end{bmatrix} \leftarrow$

of price

change

          column   ↑

          vector   gradient

          of state   matrix

          variables

↑

gradient

matrix

We must remember though that it takes two goods to form a price. Then (A8) has a solution in n-1 dimensions.

Solutions of Various Scenarios

Scenario 1A

In gradient dynamics, convergence to an equilibrium is fast. Hence, transcient solutions are unimportant. It is legitimate, therefore, to observe the system at an equilibrium point. If $a_j^1 = a_j^2 = a_j^3$, for all j, (A8) reduces to:

(A9)
$$
\begin{aligned}
\dot{p}_1 &= \frac{.5}{p_1}\left[\frac{(5-10)}{5}100p_1 + 40p_2 + 40p_3\right] \\
\dot{p}_2 &= \frac{.3}{p_2}\left[100p_1 + \frac{(3-10)}{3}90p_2 + 80p_3\right] \Rightarrow p^* = (2,\ 4/3,\ 1)' \\
\dot{p}_3 &= \frac{.2}{p_3}\left[100p_1 + 90p_2 + \frac{(2-10)}{2}80p_3\right]
\end{aligned}
$$

In order to show that (A9) is a pure gradient when consumers are identical in terms of budget shares distribution, we calculate the Jacobian matrix (A9), evaluated at p^*:

(A9')
$$
J = \begin{bmatrix} -25 & 22.5 & 20 \\ 22.5 & -47.25 & 18 \\ 20 & 18 & -64 \end{bmatrix}_{p^*}
$$

As it can be seen, *J* is symmetric, the system is a pure gradient.

Scenario 1B

In Scenario 1B, consumers are not identical. Values given in the text are substituted in (A8), or we use:

(A10)
$$\begin{bmatrix} p_1^* \\ p_2^* \end{bmatrix} = -\begin{bmatrix} \left(\sum_i a_1^i w_1^i - \sum_i w_1^i\right) & \sum_i a_1^i w_2^i \\ \sum_i a_2^i w_1^i & \left(\sum_i a_2^i w_2^i - \sum_i w_2^i\right) \end{bmatrix}^{-1} \begin{bmatrix} \sum_i a_1^i w_3^i \\ \sum_i a_2^i w_3^i \end{bmatrix}$$

to find $p^* = (1.39, 1.38, 1.00)'$. The Jacobian for the system of Scenario 1B is:

(A10')
$$J = \begin{bmatrix} -42.15 & 25.36 & 23.93 \\ 27.48 & -41.95 & 19.52 \\ 21.00 & 22.50 & -60.50 \end{bmatrix}_{p^*}$$

The Price Elasticity of the Market Demand (D)

(A11)
$$e_{11} = \frac{\partial D_1}{\partial p_1} \times \frac{p_1}{D_1} = -\left\{ \frac{p_2\left(a_1^1 w_2^1 + a_1^2 w_2^2 + a_1^3 w_2^3\right) + p_3\left(a_1^1 w_3^1 + a_1^2 w_3^2 + a_1^3 w_3^3\right)}{p_1\left(a_1^1 w_1^1 + a_1^2 w_1^2 + a_1^3 w_1^3\right) + p_2\left(a_1^1 w_2^1 + a_1^2 w_2^2 + a_1^3 w_2^3\right) + p_3\left(a_1^1 w_3^1 + a_1^2 w_3^2 + a_1^3 w_3^3\right)} \right\} > -1$$

(A12)
$$e_{12} - \frac{\partial D_1}{\partial p_2} \times \frac{p_2}{D_1} = \frac{p_2\left(a_1^1 w_2^1 + a_1^2 w_2^2 + a_1^3 w_2^3\right)}{D_1} > 0$$

II

THE NEW ORTHODOXY

4

THE EMERGING ECONOMIC ORTHODOXY

INTRODUCTION

Part I dealt with theoretical issues in general, and with the scientific status of economics and the determination of the equilibrium price vector in particular. But the determination of the price vector is a technical undertaking. Along the way, I have hinted here and there that the ultimate goal of the theory of economics is the maximization of society's welfare, which is nothing but the modern term for what Adam Smith refers to as the common good. The main task of this chapter is to further elaborate on what society's welfare is supposed to be. In the process, we should be able to circumscribe the domain of economic policy. The idea here is quite simple. If there were an economic definition of welfare, the process of maximization, or economic policy proper, would center solely on technical requirements. Unfortunately, there is no such definition. We must then resort to a mixture of technical and ethical characteristics in order to sensibly talk about society's welfare. Economic policy will, therefore, have to be articulated around two sets of conditions, technical and ethical.

I have also said that the technical goal of economic theory was the demonstration that the equilibrium price vector is well determined. This meant that if the remaining theoretical difficulties, such as the data problem, externalities, public goods, and increasing returns to scale (EPI), the flawed concept of the representative agent, among others, could be resolved, economists would finally earn the same respect due to normal scientists. For, in addition to being able to retrodict, they would be in a position to predict the frequency distribution (or at least the expected values) of the main aggregates such as consumption and employment levels, total output, inflation, growth rates, and so on. Of course, we have seen in Chapter 1 that the social sciences differ from the normal ones. However, if we could at least unambiguously satisfy the technical requirements, we would be taken more seriously by the general public. We still would not have a scientific definition of welfare, but the ability to forecast these aggregates would then put us on the solid ground required to devise credible macroeconomic policy measures pursuant to society's ethical goal. The fact that we cannot, as yet, predict these aggregates complicates the technical task of economists. This also enlarges the gray area of policy domain, which is fueling disputes among various groups jockeying for economic advantage. I will have more to say about these matters later in the chapter. My priority now is to determine what is meant by society's welfare. After that, I should be in a better position to see what the conditions for its furtherance should be.

Unresolved difficulties notwithstanding, the theory nevertheless prescribes that on the technical level our policies must allow, as much as possible, for freedom of choice and competition. For the sake of discussion, I will denote all policy measures promoting the freedom of choice and competition, the necessary conditions. Once this is done, I should be able to show that to promote welfare, however defined, the necessary conditions are not enough. A careful reading of Smith shows that even he did not know how to define society's welfare. Remember that in Chapter 1, I remarked that Smith was appalled by de Mandeville's assertion to the effect that human vices are behind social achievements. Desperate to debunk the implied immorality of the *Fable of the Bees,* Smith cooked up the metaphor of the invisible hand, and next relied on human morality to reach the common good. We should realize that the invisible hand concept is not an objective or falsifiable one. By appealing to human morality, Smith threw the whole construct into the subjectivity arena. We have not been able to do better since. It is, therefore, up to each society to define its ethical directions. These directions may then be spelled out as a different set of conditions about which I shall have more to say in a moment and again in Chapter 6. In the meantime, I will call all policies promoting society's ethical values, sufficient conditions. Eventually, I will define the ultimate goal of economics as the attempt to satisfy these two sets of conditions.

These sufficient conditions constitute a social contract; they are also known as "measures of the welfare state." This last expression was coined in 1941 by Archbishop Temple.[1] Later on, in the *Archives européennes de sociologie,* Briggs (1961) defined a welfare state as a structure in which organized power is deliberately used, through politics and administration, in an effort to modify the play of market forces in at least three directions. In the first direction, individuals and families should be guaranteed a minimum income irrespective of the market value of their properties. In the second, the state should reduce their insecurity by helping them to meet certain social contingencies such as sickness, old age insurance and unemployment. And in the third, the state should offer to them the best standards in terms of a certain agreed upon range of social services regardless of their status or social class. Security and service thresholds were later set by the International Labor Organization (ILO) in areas such as social insurance, social assistance and unemployment, family allowance, housing and educational standards, industrial accident insurance, pensions, public health insurance, among others. From the 1880s to 1945, many states had already adopted some subset of these measures. In the West, it is believed that Germany was the first country to do so, followed by France, Italy, Sweden, the United States, Canada, and the United Kingdom. Many other countries in the South and in Eastern Europe followed suit. However, according to the present overall ranking, Japan, the United States and the United Kingdom are still behind countries such as Sweden, the Netherlands, Denmark, and Norway. By 1970, except for the United Kingdom, the costs of these measures appeared to have exceeded 50% of total public expenditures. By 1981, these costs amounted to about one third of GDP in these countries. It is easy to understand, therefore, that although these measures were thought to be responsible for the transformation of the capitalist economy, the growth of their costs rang an alarm bell in some quarters, and gave rise to the so-called incompatibility thesis.[2] According to this thesis, the welfare measures have led to government failure and overload, which translates into high inflation, erosion of individual responsibility, and independence. This thesis must certainly have played a role in the thinking of Reagan's and Thatcher's administrations in devising their monetarist and supply-side economic policies of the early 1980s. This same thinking was later embraced by the new orthodoxy (to be described shortly) as the justification for the elusive search for individual responsibility.

What should be stressed in this regard is that the growth in the costs of these welfare measures stems mainly from the excessive division of labor demanded by our approach to economic growth. The same division of labor seems to have undermined the security functions previously performed by the extended family system. If, as we will see shortly, the new orthodoxy puts emphasis on individual responsibility, these welfare measures must then be dismantled. It is indeed this drive toward dismantlement that I call the policy of deconstruction within the logic of the new orthodoxy.

The truth is these measures co-existed harmoniously with the capitalist system. In a comprehensive survey of their impacts, carried out by George and Wilding (1984), it was found that the negative consequences outlined in the incompatibility thesis were greatly exaggerated. Although some negative consequences were identified, George and Wilding concluded that they are outweighed by the positive effects of these measures which, in addition, represent a positive source of political stability. I am not saying that public assistance programs should not be made more efficient. However, there seems to be a bent toward exaggerating fraud, dependency, and cost increases on the part of the proponents of the thesis. To shed light on this murky debate, the first step is to dissociate increases in the cost of the social security program from those of income support measures, as I will show in Chapter 6; the two programs should not be casually lumped together, for one is an insurance program, the other is a public assistance program. Next, while focusing on public assistance measures, instead of dwelling on exaggerated fraud and dependency, the proponents should ask themselves why is the number of poor and dependent people increasing so fast in the globalization era? If there is so much fraud and cost increases, who are the culprits? If the beneficiaries are in fact the defrauders, then they should not be sliding so fast into poverty. I can not imagine people deliberately choosing to lose their financial autonomy and becoming dependent on public handouts; this can not be good for their mental health. Maybe the proponents of the thesis should ask whether or not benefits are falling short of people's needs, and how can they become less dependent? More than 50 years ago, the Beveridge Report pointed out the way. Work, it said, is the best route out of poverty and dependency for those who are able to work. Hence, we should focus more on ways of helping people to regain their financial autonomy, and assist those that can not work. Is this not the proper ethical position for rich societies in particular?

The need for both sets of conditions is indeed obvious from what has been said thus far. We saw previously that markets are mere gradients moving toward their minima, and these minima are in turn completely determined by the prevailing technical set-up and the social arrangements. Society naturally has the obligation to judge and decide which one of these minima is desirable in the end. In other words, the crux of Adam Smith's contribution is to tell us how to get on a particular trajectory leading to a particular minimum. It is up to us to choose among all possible minima. Hence, both the necessary and sufficient conditions must circumscribe public economic policy.

These two sets of conditions, I believe, should be the foundation of economic policy. However, before dwelling too much on policy matters, let us first place the notion of efficiency, which is so prevalent in present-day economic discourse, in its proper context.

EFFICIENCY REVISITED

Within the present framework, the notion of efficiency refers only to the necessary conditions. It is indeed a widely used notion, but economic efficiency should neither be confused with mechanical efficiency nor be turned into a political stance. To prevent that from happening, we must always be mindful of its proper context. Although we have dealt so far with pure exchange, we have nevertheless gained sufficient understanding to realize that the equilibrium price vector relates to efficiency in so far as its realization encompasses the two notions of freedom of choice and competition. Put differently, freedom of choice and competition underlie the structure of market gradients. That is, the agents are free to choose their budget share distributions and are sufficiently numerous to ensure competition in the sense that no single agent is able to dominate any other. When production enters the picture, efficiency quite naturally comes to include the presence of a large number of producers that compete with one another, and thereby reduce the costs of production and distribution of Arrow-Debreu commodities. As I have made clear in Chapter 3, this expands supply and allows the flow of a greater volume of commodities than otherwise.

Beyond this presumed outcome (even when there is production), that depends closely on these factors, the concept of efficiency becomes vacuous. Consequently, it can not be offered as dogma, a panacea, or a god-ordained concept, as all of which are beyond debate. I have said rather forcefully, and Professor Robert E. Lane has emphasized in his book *The Market Experience* (1991), that economic agents are not endowed with perfect foresight. They are said to be capable of analyzing and making inferences. Lane calls this cognitive complexity, to be distinguished from the ability to make inferences from what the theory calls facts or objective rationality. But objective reality does not make economic agents rational in the broad sense of the term. They receive market signals, process market information, and make inferences within a given nonlinear mental state, described in Figure 2.2. As no one is better placed to decide for all, we have come to agree that agents must decide for themselves. However, their decisions can in no way be proclaimed best even for themselves, in particular when we know full well that they are not infinitely clever and capable of foreseeing all the ramifications of their choices. Indeed, their choices, as reflected by their budget share distributions, are quite subjective.

The ability to choose notwithstanding, we have already seen how the distribution of initial endowments impinges on market outcomes. But, the theory takes those distributions as givens. It does not question the fairness of either the existing distributions or how they have come to exist. Furthermore, in real markets, there are both small and big firms, and the theory cannot accommodate externalities, the production of public goods and the concept of increasing returns to scale and scope, to use the term of Professor Chandler. The presence of any of these limitations deprives us of our ability to define, let alone to choose among efficient alternative outcomes. Take the case of increasing returns to scale. When they are present, we can no longer claim that as output expand, production costs must necessarily rise. Obviously, resource limitations as well as the scale structure of natural objects tell us that cost reductions should have a limit, but we cannot locate it a priori. Therefore, the concept of *Pareto optimality,* which tells us that a change is optimal if at least one benefits and no one is worse off, becomes empty of meaning in the presence of these factors, and the theory cannot even define optimality on the technical level.

In all, we do possess some theoretical clues, but we are also well aware of the theoretical limitations and contingencies, which we try to address through policy measures. Since markets are incapable of conscious directions, such policies can only arise from a broad social consensus for balancing the concepts of freedom of choice and competition and desired social outcomes. In other words, policies are needed to balance the possible and the desirable. It is not sufficient then to rely on the nebulous concept of efficiency or, even worse, to argue that a democratically elected government need not seek a broad consensus during its mandate. A government is endowed with no more foresight than any citizen. Once a policy is implemented, as outcomes obtain over time, society has no more choices to exercise, except a policy shift which is always costly in terms of social resources. For these reasons, among others, a modicum of prudence must underlie the formulation of public policy. That is, public policy must arise out of social consensus.

Since the 1980s, however, we have seen two governments in the West taking the lead in embarking, with some assurance and without debate, on a radical set of economic policies. Progressively, and in particular since the fall of the Berlin wall in 1989, similar policies are steadfastly being implemented over the North and/or preached with much zeal (but still without debate) over the rest of the world (or the South). The problem here is that the architects of these policies did not follow the normal route to policy formulation and implementation. For the sake of consistency and intellectual honesty, they should have first exposed the theoretical basis of these measures as well as their variants, and then allow for societal debates and choices. We have seen neither. The task of this chapter, therefore, is to partially fill that void. I begin by briefly outlining these measures and probing their theoretical foundations.

THE NEW ORTHODOXY: GLOBALIZATION, DOWNSIZING, AND RESTRUCTURING (GD&R)

As I have said, the 1980–1982 recession was caused by an excessive monetarist reaction to the oil shocks-inflation of the late 1970s. That recession was somewhat unusual in many respects. To begin with, it was truly nasty. It carried consequences that will be felt for years to come. It convincingly showed that old ad hoc theories such as monetarism, supply side, among others, had no answers to falling output and the productivity growth slowdown. I also suspect that that recession has been the needed incentive for the development of a more dismal substitute, known under the acronym GD&R, for globalization, downsizing, and restructuring. During the early 1980s, as the then President of the United States, Ronald Reagan and the British Prime Minister, Margaret Thatcher, had prepared the ground, GD&R found its first fervent adherents in these two countries. From there, it rapidly spread to Chile and New Zealand. In less than a decade, it had conquered the world.

We know that both Reagan and Thatcher were under the spell of two market fundamentalists, but whether GD&R was authored by them or by some invisible college remains a mystery. All that is known about it is that it is a paradigm, articulated around the three programs just mentioned. This is precisely what creates the mystery surrounding GD&R. Normally, most people would be leery about an authorless paradigm. But strangely enough, it was not the case for this one. As if by magic, it was embraced by the financial establishment, headed by the International Monetary Fund and the World Bank. Soon enough, it had captivated executives of central and private banks, brokerage firms, and other international economic organizations such as the OECD; then, CEOs of multinational firms, think-tank economists, and national media fell under the charm of GD&R. By 1987, after field tests in Pinochet's Chile and New Zealand, it was extended to Latin America and Africa as a panacea for debt problems. By 1990, GD&R had arrived in full force in Asia and in the former planned economies of Eastern Europe. Thus, in less than a decade GD&R had been turned into a virtual household acronym, believed to encapsulate the solution to all economic ills, such as high debt levels, the productivity growth slowdown, unemployment, and inflation. In short, GD&R has come to stand for the signposts on the road to economic recovery, although its authors as well as its theoretical foundation remain unknown. More astoundingly, it now underpins all public and private economic policies, though without debate and hence with little understanding on the part of the general public, who nevertheless is bearing its brunt.

As it turns out, beyond its economic impacts, GD&R also has profound implications for representative democracy as well. This will become increasingly clear as we move along. For now, however, I think that it is high time that we take a belated look at what it has come to mean on the economic scene in the 1990s. The International Monetary Fund (IMF) says that:

Globalization refers to the growing economic interdependence of countries worldwide through the increasing volume and variety of cross-border transactions in goods and services and of international capital flows, and also through the more rapid and widespread diffusion of technology.... International commerce and competition, and hence globalization, are, like technological progress, fundamental sources not only of economic growth but also of structural change in economies. (*WEO*, May 1997, 45)

At the United Nations Conference on Trade and Development (UNCTAD), held in Geneva in 1996, the Secretary General of that organization essentially summarized the objective of the phenomenon of globalization as follows:

Given the increasing globalization of the economy and the increasing trade liberalization, firms of all countries will be more and more constrained to adapt their structures of production and trade so as to keep up with the evolution of competitive capacities.[4]

Previously, the Organization for Economic Cooperation and Development (OECD) had described globalization as that structure that gives all countries the possibility of participating in world development, and all consumers the possibility of benefiting from increasing vigorous competition between producers.

At the United Nations Social Summit, held in Copenhagen in March 1995, the U.S. Vice President, Al Gore said:

In our view, only the market system unlocks a higher fraction of the human potential than any other form of economic organization, and has demonstrated potential to create broadly distributed new wealth.[5]

These statements, which are in a sense not new, nevertheless summarize current thinking on GD&R. Notice the key words: Competitive capacities, benefits for consumers, markets and wealth distribution, and growth. They are all concepts of the scientific theory, but taken out of their proper context, they may not at all be meaningful. The truth is that here they summarize something much more important – a paradigm shift, or a new orthodoxy. The aim of globalization is to reform the international economy, in particular the international capital market, and that of downsizing and restructuring is to reform national economies. In this section, I examine their prescriptions and next attempt to uncover their theoretical underpinnings. Their economic and social impacts are left for the next chapter.

Globalization

Globalization appears to rest on the proposition that trade liberalization and the deregulation of capital flows will, on the one hand, allow countries to specialize in activities in which they hold a relative comparative advantage, that is, to specialize in what they do best. On the other, institutional investors (consisting of insurance groups, pension funds, mutual funds, and investment trusts) should change their behavior in the international capital market. In other words, they should be free to seize on investment prospects on the world level and be allowed to diversify their portfolios between national and foreign assets, such as bonds and equities, so as to reduce the volatility of their returns.

These investors used to be regulated by national authorities for prudential reasons and, more importantly, to protect individuals holding claims on them in exchange for certain tax concessions. However, in order to be able to respond rapidly to market developments and speculative opportunities, investors want all such regulations removed. This way they will be allowed to shorten their time horizon and focus more on short-term profits. Also, developments in financial information and communications technology make such changes easier now than they would have been a few years ago. The emergence of the derivative products markets and advances in communications technology, together with the market power of these investors, have opened a whole set of customized products for borrowers, lenders and speculators at the world scale, allowing these investors to by-pass domestic securities houses. In the process, they by-pass national authorities as well.[6] A good example of this is the last attempt of the German government to introduce a withholding tax on interest incomes. It has led to a massive shift of German funds abroad, and to a quick u-turn by the government. Before, domestic investors were dissuaded from venturing into foreign markets with which they were not familiar. Now, as they can operate on the world scale, residents can shift their holdings abroad in response to the least tax-related move by a national government. Hence, one can easily understand why these so-called institutional investors do not want any regulations on domestic capital markets.

Thus, officially at least, by the concept of globalization, the international division of labor and free capital movements should normally lead to increased direct foreign investment, to the diffusion of efficiency and to higher global income. However, there is a proviso. Countries that stand to benefit most are those with the least state interventions and the most free trade regimes.

By 1995, globalization had come to tacitly include the promise of absolute freedom to relocate production and services in any free zone around the world, considerable direct foreign investment, huge capital flows, and tidal world trade volumes. Officially such beliefs are predicated on some selective passages in Adam Smith (1776), to which I will return. Unofficially though, they seem to be based on an anti-Keynesian stance that began to surface in the early 1970s.

It is worth recalling that in the simple exchange economy described in Chapter 3, the equilibrium price vector was reached fairly quickly because the items exchanged were produced and consumed on the same trading day. In real markets, however, it takes time to produce. Producers and consumers must contract in advance at presumed equilibrium prices. Will these prices prevail at the time of delivery? As the information sets of trading partners are always asymmetrical, one party may either be duped or both may be mistaken; hence, agreements may no longer reflect true wants at the time they are executed. If they are not, contracted prices and quantities have to adjust. As producers and consumers have no way of knowing at any given moment whether observed prices are transient or final, by how much should contracted prices be adjusted? Given these contingencies, is it wise to contract now or wait? Although there are no easy answers to these questions, one can see nevertheless why they must be part of the general concern underpinning the decisions of would-be traders.

According to Keynes, these problems characterize real markets more often than not. Consequently, as transactions must be financed, while agents cannot forecast equilibrium prices, the financial system must bear the brunt of the mistakes made in the real sector of the economy. This led Keynes to argue in his book *A Treatise on Money* that governments must have a hand on interest rates, while in *The General Theory of Employment Interest and Money* he assigns to them the role of directing the flow of investment. This implies that government spending is but a means of stimulating the demand for savings in a recession, precisely when the financial system is unable to convince the private sector to act. Thus, Keynesianism is about reorganizing and regulating the financial system so that it can in turn stabilize and foster growth in an open economy.

Some years ago, after studying the reverberations of mistakes committed in the real sector in some details, Professor Robert Clower concluded that these errors do indeed pile up in the financial side in the absence of appropriate regulations. Will Hutton, writing in *The Manchester Guardian* (September 6, 1992), is of the same opinion. He argues that Keynes advocated regulations precisely to prevent credit booms and debt overhang that are sure to follow from mistakes. Therefore, in order for globalization to make financial deregulation one of its cornerstones, it must argue the opposite, that is, controls prevent borrowers and lenders from arriving at optimal bargains, deliberately neglecting to add, of course, that this would be only if agents had perfect foresight.

I will have a chance to look at the preliminary impacts of globalization on the world economy in the next chapter. Suffice it at this point to recall that in Chapter 2, I stressed the fact that the scientific theory does not cover the financial market. Hence, the logical and very important question to ask at this point is: How do we know whether or not the above official statements are meaningful in the sense of Chapter 1? I tackle this difficult issue in the forth section below. Let us now see what is meant by downsizing and restructuring.

Downsizing and Restructuring (D&R)

As the second cornerstone of the new orthodoxy, D&R aim at the removal of governments from domestic economies. To see this, let us return to the statement of Vice President Gore. It is reasonable, I believe, to infer that two strong beliefs underlie it. Only economic organizations can unlock human potential, and that markets distribute wealth in a manner conducive to human fulfillment; but economic organizations, including markets, have existed since time immemorial. If they were the only outlet for human fulfillment, we would all be fulfilled by now. While it is true from experience that markets seem to be better at wealth creation than alternative economic organizations that have been tried, I know, however, of no instances where markets distribute new wealth broadly and equitably. I must, per force, conclude that the vice president had a different structure in mind, perhaps a wide-ranging global market, totally free of regulations. In that connection, I have remarked above that markets are incapable of conscious directions. In many regards, totally free markets can unleash many a social ill. Moreover, I have shown in Chapter 3 that without a minimum set of rules, competition itself may not survive, as markets tend to distribute according to market power that is unfair by definition. Under these circumstances, what is the basis for such a blanket statement on the part of the vice president?

What is also a bit strange about any one of these official statements is that they could have been uttered by officials from a number of places. That is, the IMF, the World Bank, other national central banks, IBM, General Motors Corp., the stock brokerage firms of Wall Street, academic economists, and so on. Stranger still, nowhere else does one find such unanimity among leaders. The statements, summarizing the new orthodoxy, have been preached orally and in annual reports as well in the national press since the early 1980s. They underpin every government decision in both North and South. I have rarely seen such a consensus on economic policy in official circles. What accounts for it?

Spelling out GD&R

More to the point, the above statements also summarize a gamut of specific prescriptions, which may be divided into three main categories:

International Integration Measures. These are the standard ones found in every textbook in economics. That is, the adoption of competitive exchange rate regimes, and the opening of national economies to international trade. They, therefore, conform with the scientific theory.

Austerity Measures. These require reductions in: (1) all government transfers; (2) educational and social protection expenditures;(3) rights, remuneration and the number of public employees; and (4) public deficits, national debt, and infla-tion. Strictly speaking, they do not conform.

Market Freedom and Privatization Measures. These consist of: (1) the removal of all market regulations, in particular those affecting the labor and capital markets and capital mobility; (2) the reduction of taxes on business incomes, capital gains, and high individual incomes; (3) the privatization of public enterprises; and (4) the privatization of public services, including prisons, post offices, hospitals, among others.

In other words, balance the budget and pay the foreign debt, do not get in the way of capital movements, target inflation, free the labor market, and, privatize as much as possible. These are the signposts on the road to full employment and economic growth. What has been the response so far?

In the United States, for example, the more brutal phase of the macroeconomic discipline found expression in the 1995 Republican budget proposal. That budget proposal, coined "The Contract with America" by the Speaker of the House, proposed a $17 billion cut in human services. Some of its main features were cuts of $7.103 billion in housing developments for the poor and Aids victims; $2.23 billion in job creation projects for inner-city youth, training, adult education and vocational training; $2.8 billion in clean water projects and community development; $760 million in school construction and improvement plans, food programs, and library construction; some $664 million in anti-drug programs, and so on. There was also a proposed cut of $200 billion over five years in welfare, Medicare, and civil service pensions. Finally, there was a commitment or perhaps a law to balance the budget over seven years. Money saved from these cuts should be ear-marked to compensate for a tax cut on capital gain, giving 75% of the benefits to those earning more than $100,000 a year.

In the European Union, the Brussels Commission cites the requirements of the Maastricht Treaty and the deadline of January 1, 1999 as additional reasons to accelerate the application of the new phase. The treaty requires that public deficits shall not exceed 3% of gross domestic products (GDP), compared with the actual 1997 average of 4.4%, that inflation and interest rates be targeted, and public debt be reduced. To give the treaty more impetus, a group of experts on competitiveness was set up to study its impact on employment. The group was composed of a former prime minister and a number of ministers, CEOs of multinational firms, and a few union leaders. One of its most insistent recommendations is a new social contract in which the costs of employment are to be reduced (including the minimum wage rate), and social legislations are to be subject to cost-benefit analyses. It was left to individual governments to see where and how to apply the new policy.

Thus, in Germany the first phase has been in place since 1993. But the new phase requires additional cuts in social programs to families, the sick and the elderly, in subsidies, employment assistance, pension funds, among others, totaling DM50 billion for 1997. Concomitantly, taxes on business and on capital gain are to be reduced, but the value added tax (VAT) is to go up from the present 15% to 17%. The government intends to accelerate the deregulation and privatization programs. On May 13, 1996, the Belgian Government received special powers from the parliament to impose the second phase without delay or debate. In France, despite a sizable opposition, the conservative government has reaffirmed its intention to accelerate, among other things, the privatization programs consisting of selling out public enterprises and services. In addition to tax reduction on high incomes, the French privatization program seems to include a weird element not found in similar ones elsewhere, except perhaps in England or Mexico. That is, the government is actually using public funds to buy out the liabilities of nationalized enterprises prior to selling them. Both de Brie (1996) and Halimi (1996) report that such financial gifts amounted to $20 billion by 1994. The story is similar even in socially conscious Sweden. That is, massive benefit reductions in social, health, and employment insurance, accompanied by curtailments in retirement benefits and housing subsidies. After some 16 years of slashing and burning, there is not much left in England to cut or to privatize, except rail services and the nuclear industry. Accordingly, the World Economic Forum (1996) gave that country the highest marks for satisfying the dictates of the new orthodoxy; that is, England scored higher than Germany, France, and Sweden.

In Latin America and the Caribbean, although there are few social contracts to dismantle, countries in that region do not escape the rigor of the new discipline. Many countries in the region have been subjected to the new orthodoxy since their debt crises in 1982. Following the wave of trade liberalization in Chile in the late 1970s and in Mexico in the 1980s, almost every other country followed suit. They had already deregulated interest rates, credit, and banks operations. In the early 1990s, they were instructed to tighten discipline and accelerate reforms so as to attain higher rates of economic growth.

In Africa, the new orthodoxy was first applied in selected countries in 1987. By 1994, all had received the same instructions, that is, to reduce inflation, subsidies on basic foods, and public deficits; adopt flexible exchange rates, privatize public enterprises; and give priority to the export sector. The reluctant countries are told that in order to improve social indicators, they must start by reducing social expenditures. As in the case of the Asian tigers, reduced expenditure levels in conformity with the dictates of the new orthodoxy were to lead to high economic growth rates, and to an eventual reduction in poverty.

In countries in transition, the average real GDP growth rate over the period 1951–1973 was comparable to or slightly better than that of industrial countries, except Japan. But over the 1974–1982 period, it fell below. The immediate reaction of these countries was to borrow abroad. It seems that these loans went to finance unproductive investment. By the end of 1988, the total convertible debt of seven Eastern European countries rose to about $100 billion, with Poland and Hungary carrying some 60% of the total. This then put them in a situation similar to the most heavily indebted developing economies, explaining why their average growth rate remained below that of industrial countries during the 1980s.

As a result of this poor showing, these countries were strongly advised to implement the new orthodoxy during the 1988–1989 period. In order to promote efficiency, they were advised to get rid of state monopolies and to let unprofitable enterprises go bankrupt. Next, they were to apply the standard package, that is, to bring the structure of production and prices in line with what prevails in world markets; to adopt freer trade and competitive exchange rates; to end price controls and subsidies; and to institute legal measures to strengthen the private sector, followed by the widespread privatization of state enterprises. In Hungary, mandatory plan directives were already abolished as early as 1968. In Poland, the large agricultural sector had remained in private hands since the inception of central planning. During the 1988–1990 period, both countries were encouraged to accelerate structural reforms. The minute the new orthodoxy is applied to other countries, including Russia, they were told, international trade and foreign investment will expand; this will spur economic activities in the whole region as well as in the rest of the world. In addition to the standard prescriptions, these countries received two additional pieces of advice. First, the rapid implementation of market oriented reforms is preferable to a gradual approach. Second, the credibility of economic reforms, and therefore the probability of them succeeding, is likely to be greater if the reform package is comprehensive. Besides Pinochet's Chile, there were no true and tried rules or theoretical laws covering either the speed of implementation or the sequencing of reform programs. Why should market oriented reforms, which are after all social experiments, be carried out as fast as possible, mostly when their outcome cannot be predicted? Could it be the fact that the advisors knew very well that public support for reforms would vanish once the public started feeling their brunt? At this point this is a conjecture, which will be examined below.

The new orthodoxy for the resumption of economic growth may be summarized by the following series of tacit propositions addressed to governments and business enterprises:

Globalization: Propositions to Governments

*a Liberate the international financial market.
*b Remove all controls and barriers on the international goods and services market.

Globalization: Propositions to Multinational Firms and Large Institutional Investors and Speculators

a Lower the costs of production and distribution by any means.
b Minimize tax outlays.
c Be mobile; if a host government does not fully adhere to the new orthodoxy, move.
*d Diversify your portfolios and shorten your time horizon.
e Respond quickly to new market developments.

Downsizing and Restructuring: Propositions to Governments

*a Liberate the domestic labor market and use the interest rate to control inflation.
 b Reduce your debt (domestic and sovereign).
*c Disinvest in the domestic economy.
*d Remove all regulations, eliminate all transfers, except perhaps to certain big enterprises.

Downsizing and Restructuring: Propositions to Firms

 a Depress the wage rate, downsize and replace with part-timers so as to increase short-term profits.
*b Become big by mergers and fusions so as to be able to compete internationally.
?c Be attentive to shareholders interests at the expenses of employees.

As the reader might have already noticed, globalization, downsizing, and restructuring are not unrelated. In some quarters, such as the Brooking Institution in Washington, they are seen as a necessary adjustment program. Some scholars such as Ruigrok and van Tulder see them in terms of one global restructuring, involving six actors playing a game in the international arena. On the contrary, I hope to show that they are the three pillars of a vast program of rapid capital accumulation for the few with market power, but with little consideration for society's well-being. Consequently, we are not yet at the point where this can be publicly admitted, which is why these directives are implicit. They are not confined to any single document to my knowledge. It is not even known how they are transmitted to their intended audience, but as directives go, they are rather blunt. Consequently, one would not expect to see them paraded out in manifesto style. Nonetheless, they are in essence the holy writ of the new orthodoxy.

Before going any further, let us note a few things. First, there is no emphasis on long-term investment, innovations, research, and development, nor is there any focus on health, education, coordination failures, fairness in income distribution, infrastructure, spillovers, environmental protection, and certainly no intention of returning to small price-taking firms. Implicit in the new orthodoxy is that all of these missing elements (except the last) should become individual responsibilities. Second, there is no firm evidence as to whether exports lead to growth or the other way around, as shown by the East Asian experience. There is no warning of the danger of opening one's borders to international trade before local industries are able to compete. Nothing is said about the fall in prices when many countries with the same comparative advantages expand production for exports at the same time, as evidence by the catastrophic decline in real commodity prices since 1980. Indeed, between 1980 and 1991, the cumulative terms-of-trade losses of developing countries as a whole amounted to $290 billion. Third, many countries are still not aware of the so-called tequila effect. This term was coined in Mexico when billions of dollars left that country in

December 1994, precipitating an international crisis. Are these countries cognizant of the fact that massive capital inflows in the absence of controls lead to currency overvaluation, exchange rate fluctuations, among other things? Moreover, as argued by the United Nations Development Programme (UNDP) (1997), when national governments compete to attract capital by offering to relax labor and health standards, they are really engaged in a race to the bottom that lowers world standards. Finally, is the creation of mammoth corporations the most efficient way to promote employment and growth? The new orthodoxy seems to affirm this with conviction. Yet, after more than a decade of mergers, there is now a new ad hoc theory advising firms to demerge so as to increase their value. This is no fluke. A well-argued 1996 book by David Sadtler and Andrew Cambell advises multibusiness firms to break up and make an additional $100 billion a year, for they are worth more dead than alive. In order to shed some light on these claims and counterclaims, I now turn to the scientific theory.

THE THEORETICAL FOUNDATION OF GD&R

In Chapter 3, I showed step by step how the economy arrives at the equilibrium price vector. Along the way, we have uncovered some of the basic rules of behavior for the provision of human needs, ranging from basic amenities to the accumulation of wealth. In the process, we have come to realize that human development and fulfillment cannot be pursued without first solving the economizing problem. Subsequently, we extended the goal of economics to the maximization of society's welfare. If, as it is reasonable to suppose, that human development is purposeful, economics falls squarely within the category of social sciences. As such, it ipso facto acquires a social dimension, which incidentally vindicates the vision of both the physiocrats and Adam Smith. However, desirable it may be, we have also said that ultimately the scientific theory can not define welfare proper, so, in order to promote it, we must first define it ethically. Hence, each society must come up with an additional set of conditions that I call sufficient. We then promote society's well-being by trying to satisfy two sets of conditions, that is, those relative to the efficiency of the equilibrium price vector in transmitting information about human desires and resources scarcity, and those relative to the moral requirements of economic decisions impacting on the structure of the market gradient.

As it turns out, these two sets of conditions constitute the very essence of Smith's (1776) contribution. It might be worth recalling once more that Smith's contribution revolves around three main points. The first is the assertion that the principal human motive is self-interest. The second alleges that self-interest together with competition will automatically be transformed by the invisible hand into the common good (welfare). Given the first two, the third is mere advice to policy makers, it simply reminds them that the ideal policy for the promotion of social welfare is a policy which scrupulously respects moral agents' freedom of action. Some zealots are quick to argue that this third point denies any role for the state. However, they fail to see the third point as only a reminder. The first two pertain to what I have earlier referred to as the necessary conditions of welfare maximization. The third becomes superfluous from the perspective of Smith, once we realize that he was operating on the firm belief that economic agents are moral beings, that is, their behavior would always reflect a choice of right over wrong. Therefore, for Smith, the best government economic policy is the policy that interferes the least with human freedom. Put differently, if the material welfare of society is a desirable goal, then freedom of choice and competition are necessary for its obtainment. One of the illustrious successor of Smith, Ricardo (1772–1823) essentially approached international trade in a similar manner. If society's common good is a desirable goal, then freer international trade and the pursuit of relative comparative advantage would bring it about. Hence the efficient allocation of resources is only necessary to the promotion of welfare. Another blatantly selective reading of Adam Smith is now being offered in support of privatization. It is predicated on a passage from Smith (1776, 771) where he says: "No two characters seem more inconsistent than those of trader and sovereign." What he had in mind was the waste of crown land in Europe and the observation that in general people are less frugal with the money of others than with their own. In Book V, Smith recommends the control of interest rates and the banking trade. He also advocates the use of taxation, not as a mean of raising revenue but for social reform and for public works. In Book I, he has a long passage on business people meddling in public policy matters. In this regard, Smith warns against the activities of the landed, moneyed, manufacturing, and mercantile groups, constituting the present-day lobbies. He seems to believe that their interests are always at odds with that of the general public.[7]

Although these remarks are still quite pertinent today, no one would disagree that the economies of today are much more complex than the one Smith had in mind. Besides, as regards the ethical behavior of people, Smith may have been a bit naive. However, it still makes sense to argue that if economics is to be a social science, a set of sufficient conditions must be devised and added to the necessary ones, in order to approach a semblance of what Smith had in mind for the common good. I believe this is exactly what the social contract was all about – an attempt to define and to promote social welfare.

For the purpose of policy formulation, modern economists have rightfully reorganized the prescriptions of Smith around three broad propositions, known as the three theorems of welfare economics. Let us consider them in turn.

Theorem 1: If all consumers and firms are price takers (i.e., they are selfish and numerous), the resulting price vector is Pareto efficient.

In order to take a closer look at what this implies, let us begin by first letting EPI stand for the triplet: externalities, public goods and increasing returns to scale, I have already said that they cause problems for the theory. Next, we recall that *Pareto efficiency* simply refers to a situation in which no agent can be made better off without hurting at least one other. On the other hand, if any price vector is a function of the economy's data (i.e., budget shares and initial wealth distributions), then any price vector is Pareto efficient. The theorem asserts that if the number of consumers (m) and the number of firms (K) are large, then the equilibrium price vector represents a dominant allocation, in the sense that it reveals all the information to be had (without noise) relative to the desires of consumers and to the scarcity of resources. If consumers' choices can not be challenged while firms are both small and big, then Pareto efficiency is a weak normative concept to be accepted on faith because the theorem cannot be proven. We should note that even in the absence of EPI, the price vector remains a consequence of the economy's data. If these distributions had been different, a different allocation would have resulted. Hence, agents actually do not have a choice among alternative outcomes. For lack of anything better, the theory must accept that any equilibrium price vector is Pareto efficient, even one in which one agent ends up with almost everything there is, while the others get almost nothing. In addition, the theory does not allow for the questioning of the initial endowment distribution, say, even one that came about by force or theft. Thus, in terms of the ethical dimension of human well-being, the Pareto efficiency concept is vacuous. In the second place, in real dynamic economies convergence is never obtained, as the data of the economy are always changing. Hence, even if alternative outcomes could be calculated, they could not be compared due to the metaphysical concept of utility; remember, utility levels can not be evaluated. Finally, in many real markets, m and especially K are not infinite, while EPI abounds. In the end analysis, we have a situation where the theorem itself cannot be proven, and three major pitfalls (EPI) may cause it to fail. But the theory does recognize EPI as obstacles. This then leads to:

Theorem 2: Given EPI, Theorem 1 can still be satisfied, provided that non-distorting lump-sum taxes and transfers are imposed on the agents.

Before moving into taxation and transfers, the appropriate question is: Can EPI be eliminated? Economists have in the past considered some alternatives. Back in the 1960s, it was thought that the concept of Coasian entitlement, where the state would extend property rights to the commons, would have been a remedy to externalities. The idea here is that the new owners would voluntarily or through the courts insure that externalities are internalized. There was also what was known as the Samuelson scheme or even an appeal to psychology to help extract true consumer preferences for public goods provision. I will not comment very much on these schemes, except to remark that they have fallen out of favor and were never intended to tackle one of the major obstacles, increasing returns, to which I now turn.

The problem of taxation and transfers happens to be linked to that of increasing returns to scale. First, firms that enjoy increasing returns in the production of private goods do have potential market power. If such firms were to follow the requirements of theorem 1 to set their prices equal to the production costs of their last unit produced, they would register a deficit. Then the state would have to either extend lump-sum taxes to the rest of the economy or take over all activities known to generate increasing returns such as transportation, telecommunications, public utilities, among others (Quinzii 1988). From there an additional difficulty would emerge, because in addition to the production of public goods, the theory would also be inviting the state to be involved in the production of private goods. Finally, the problem of distribution looms large on these difficulties. As the state becomes involved in taxation and distribution, it has the obligation to first evaluate and next determine the best distribution of benefits for welfare maximization. Note that to evaluate, it can neither add up utility levels nor net output. Because, utility is metaphysical, while for the correct assessment of net output, one needs the price vector, which in turn depends on the initial distribution of wealth. While pondering difficult questions, such as: What is an ethical distribution? Is there a scientific definition of welfare? Arrow (1963) was prompted to develop:

Theorem 3: There is no Arrow social welfare function that satisfies the minimum set of conditions of universality, Pareto consistency, independence, and nondicta-torship.

At this point in the discussion, it will not help our purpose to dwell on the latter conditions. Suffice it to say that a large majority of economists agree with Arrow that these conditions constitute the minimum set necessary to prevent the social welfare function from being outright arbitrary. Since 1963, the year when the theorem was formulated, no way has been found to construct such a function. It is almost a tragedy to conclude that there is no scientific approach to the problem of distribution.

Thus, according to theorem 3, there is no scientific definition of welfare; hence, it is vacuous to claim to maximize a nonobservable function. In other words, theorem 3 fails to hold because the theory is unable to scientifically distribute. Both theorems 1 and 2 fail to hold, because of EPI, while the influence of advertising (including untruthful advertising), and the wave of mergers and acquisitions are pushing firms away from the theoretical ideal. Therefore, the meaningfulness of most of the above statements of the new orthodoxy can not be verified. Instead, what can reasonably be inferred from it is that in each society, agents should be numerous, small, and free to choose. Agents and their government should try to internalize unavoidable externalities. Governments should somehow control the production of goods that are either public or coming from industries enjoying increasing returns to scale. Finally, society as a whole should determine the sufficient conditions in accordance with its ethical values. The application of all of these conditions will give rise to a different output-mix in each society. Fair trade among nations should then follow. Accordingly, the above propositions of GD&R, marked by an asterisk, are not meaningful in light of the scientific theory, while the last one is questionable.

Furthermore, most of the directives of GD&R run contrary to the advice of the sociologist and economic historian Karl Polanyi (1957). In his book, *The Great Transformation*, Polanyi convincingly argues against a global market. According to him, a market is an institution that is itself embedded in still larger social and political institutions. The latter institutions *regulate, stabilize* and *legitimize* market outcomes. Without these three functions, even a domestic market is not sustainable, while a free global market (without global institutions) cannot exist for any length of time whithout annihilating the human and natural substance of society. In fact, at one point, he says: "It [the free global market] would have physically destroyed man and transformed his surroundings into a wilderness." (1957, 3) [my addendum]. The essence of Polanyi's enduring insight is implicit in the last two chapters. Indeed, nations had paid heed to Polanyi's advice, since they all had regulating institutions, control instruments, and social insurance schemes that help to bring market outcomes in line with their societies's values. We have to wait until the next chapter to assess the impacts of these directives on countries that have jumped into the global market. For the time being, suffice it to say that most of these directives are not meaningful in terms of the theory.

Returning now to the three theorems, we can see that by themselves they lead to a negative result. In fact, the question as to whether the theory could explain society's welfare or not once placed the followers of Smith in opposition to the partisans of central planning. Today, we are well beyond this unresolved debate. What is reasonable to say, in light of the above conclusion, is that markets seem better able to deliver the goods, thus partially vindicating Vice President Gore. However, left to themselves, they not only produce both goods and bads, but they also distribute them unfairly. Society has, therefore, the obligation to provide a sufficient dose of ethics to counteract negative results. This is exactly what the ordinary person in the street means by the expression "capitalism with a human face."

SEARCHING FOR THE REAL MOTIVATION OF GD&R

Having shown, I believe, that the new orthodoxy has no solid theoretical justification, except perhaps for a selective reading of Adam Smith, it is reasonable now to ask: What is driving it? Could it be the productivity growth slowdown? Is it one of the multiple post-Smith theories that have sprung up since the end of the last century, like the marginal productivity theory? Is it the scare that the growth of the public debt engenders, or is the new orthodoxy driven by ideology? This section examines each possibility in turn. It is important to know what is driving it because its impacts on the well-being of people all over the world are substantial. Indeed, it would be another tragedy to embark on a program of such massive changes, motivated by reasons unknown to those bearing the brunt of those changes.

The Productivity Growth Slowdown

The year 1973 was the harbinger of a curious phenomenon. Everywhere in the world, the growth of the productivity of the factors of production was falling. To make sense of this phenomenon, I must begin by defining a few terms. *Labor productivity*, for example, is the ratio of output over the total hours worked by labor. *Capital productivity* is measured analogously, but both are crude measures. On the other hand, we have what is called the *total factor productivity*, which is a comprehensive measure of factor productivities, but it is even more complicated to measure; we can only approximate it because it does not account for what happens to intermediate inputs. Furthermore, in international comparisons, the measure fails to account for differences in production functions and the ability of the exchange rate to proxy differences in purchasing power. Even so, we define it as the residual in output growth, after deducting the growth attributable to increased uses of labor and capital, weighted by the shares of these factors in output.

According to IMF's figures (*WEO* May 1990, 66), labor, capital, and total factor productivity growth rates, as weighted averages in 16 industrialized countries over the period 1951–1984, were as follows:

	1951–1973	1974–1984
Labor productivity (in % change)	4.8	2.7
Total factor productivity (in %)	3.4	1.3
Capital stock (in %)	4.7	3.2

In Africa, the situation was not rosy over the same periods. From 1970 to 1973, total factor productivity grew at about 3.2%; between 1974 and 1982, it fell to -0.8%. In Latin America, the corresponding weighted averages for Chile, Argentina, Brazil, and Mexico were:

	1951–1973	1974–1984
Labor productivity (in %)	3.2	0.2
Total factor productivity (in %)	1.8	-1.3
Capital stock (in %)	4.7	5.0

A similar situation was observed in the then USSR and in the other centrally planned economies of Eastern Europe. Even in China and Korea where the capital stock grew at impressive rates, total factor productivity growth fell by 65% and 100%, respectively. The phenomenon was indeed worldwide and therefore its explanation is unlikely to lie in the particular situation of a single country.

Nevertheless, the news of the productivity slowdown sent economists scrambling for an explanation. Many culprits were identified, varying from a consumption tax, a fall in aggregate demand, and to the skill level of the labor force. More specifically, Mancur Olson (1988) laid the blame on powerful interest groups in stable economies. Dale Jorgenson (1988), who carried out detailed calculations on the sectoral impacts of the oil shocks of the 1970s, concluded that they were responsible. Evidently, oil shocks are not going to be beneficial to productivity growth. The real question is were they the only culprit? Some economists remain doubtful for two main reasons. First, oil or energy in general is considered an intermediate input; hence, according to them, energy consumption cannot account for the productivity growth slowdown. Second, they claim that labor productivity growth had been falling before the first oil shock. In the United States, for example, labor productivity grew at an average of 2.5% from 1955 to 1968. Over the 1968–1973 period, that is, before the first oil shock of 1973–1974, it fell to 1.5% and to 0.4% per year between 1973 and 1980; in terms of multifactor productivity, the situation was similar in the nonfarm sector. These prompted yet another explanation for the slowdown. The high growth rate of the Golden Period (1945–1973), it is argued, represented a catch-up from the technical advances from World War II; hence, diminishing returns were the culprit. In our view, this is not likely to be a valid explanation. We have had other wars since, some fairly big. We have had many technical advances since, but factor productivity growth continued to fall. Moreover, figures on productivity growth supplied by analysts and institutions are usually at great variance. The above figures for 1968–1973 may well be conservative. In addition, there is no valid reason to consider energy as an intermediate input. If it is, then so are capital and skilled labor. If, on the other hand, energy is treated as a primary input, then the oil shocks are a serious culprit. The technology that was in use during the late 1970s was energy intensive. It seems logical to argue that when the price of oil rose, its consumption fell and output followed.

In the G7 countries, capital productivity growth became negative in the 1970s as shown in Table 4.1. Even after the rise of the new orthodoxy, labor productivity growth remained below its 1972–1981 average. In all industrialized countries, the growth rate remained below its 1972–1981 average during 1982–1984, and it became negative in 1983 and 1988, lending strong support to the energy connection.

However, economists, operating on the received view that energy is but an intermediate input, failed to connect. The scale and extent of the slowdown led to more speculations as to why. They, among others, were, cyclical shocks, inflation, government regulations, unionization, decreases in entrepreneurial ability, and so on. The truth is that nobody seemed to know why. I then conclude that the productivity slowdown cannot be the driving force behind the new orthodoxy, for how can Western governments embark on such a massive change in response to a phenomenon whose cause is still unknown? Or else, if oil consumption is the culprit behind the productivity growth slowdown, why is a new orthodoxy needed?

Table 4.1
The Productivity Slowdown in the G7 Countries

		Labor (%)	Capital (%)	Total (%)
United States	1960–1973	3.1	-0.1	1.9
	1973–1979	1.1	-0.2	0.6
Germany	1960–1973	5.8	-1.5	3.2
	1973–1979	4.3	-1.9	2.1
France	1960–1973	5.9	0.7	3.9
	1973–1979	4.2	-1.1	2.1
Canada	1960–1973	4.2	1.1	2.9
	1973–1979	1.0	-1.6	-0.1
Japan	1960–1973	9.9	0.1	6.6
	1973–1979	3.8	-2.2	1.8
Italy	1960–1973	7.8	1.3	5.8
	1973–1979	1.6	-0.8	0.8
United Kingdom	1960–1973	3.8	-0.7	2.2
	1973–1979	1.9	-2.6	0.3

Source: Kendrick (1982).

Inflation Targeting and the Wage Level

In macroeconomics, aggregate magnitudes are obtained by summing up individual measurements since the Keynesian revolution. Behavior is inferred from there, notwithstanding the danger of drawing different inferences from the same statistics. As these magnitudes fluctuate, Keynes, lacking a sound theory, relied on his observations to forge an explanation of economic fluctuations. Accordingly, optimistic expectations, business profits, business and government expenditures, as well as credit creation are all positively correlated with growth. In a situation where they are all rising, aggregate demand and full employment rise until aggregate demand exceeds output potential, resulting in inflation. As inflation is considered undesirable, independent central banks move to tighten money and credit. Governments too, fearful of inflation, reduce expenditures, and pessimistic expectations set in. High interest rates reduce business investment, and aggregate demand falls until the economy moves into recession. Keynes also pointed out that the desire to save is different from the desire to invest, and that both arise from different groups. Consequently, the rate of interest may fail to bring savings and investment into equality. A pessimistic attitude from bankers and businessmen cause them to hold liquid assets rather than lend and invest. This may then prevent additional falls in interest rates from increasing investment, and economic activities may spiral downward until the level of savings equal the flow of desired investment. If, in the meantime, government spending can not be cut further, public deficits and the national debt will rise.

As it can be seen, Keynes acknowledged the role of, and even encouraged, government interventions in the economy. Government spending (meaning borrowing) on welfare measures can supplement private sector spending, while leakages such as taxes can curb inflationary pressures. Such fiscal policies are to be coordinated with monetary policies controlling the flow of credit. Both sets of policies jointly bring about economic stability. Obviously problems may arise when politicians end up with a license to borrow and spend, but I postpone further discussions on this until I look at the problem of debt.

During the 1970s, most observers were struck by an unexpected set of events. The rate of economic growth, factor productivity growth, capacity utilization in manufacturing were falling, while unemployment, wage, and inflation rates were rising. These were clear indications that the world economy was in a slump. In the Keynesian construct, this was not supposed to happen. The Western authorities took fright and began to heed the attack that had been launched on Keynesianism by the new classicals earlier. They then dusted off the old marginal productivity theory, which is based on the belief that the real wage rate is determined by a worker's contribution to profits. While there may be a correlation, in England and the United States, the "theory" (*sic*) was turned on its head. It became a credo that held that wage flexibility is the route to recovery.

This old marginal productivity theory was linked to inflation in the 1950s. At that time, the conventional wisdom stated that there exists an equilibrium nominal price for each level of money supply. The equilibrium price level in period (t+1) will be just high enough to reduce the real value of period's t's cash balances to the quantity demanded and output level. If economic agents expect higher prices and higher nominal wages in period (t+1), sales may be depressed, and perhaps employment may move away from its equilibrium level. This sort of deduction is straight from Keynesianism, but with a new twist. Back in 1936, Keynes had observed that the money wage rate set by employers is in general rigid, and would not fall sufficiently to become consistent with the prevailing equilibrium; therefore, wage inflexibility is destabilizing. In the early 1950s, an economist by the name of William Fellner had added a twist to this argument. He claimed that successive doses of equal inflation would lose their effectiveness, so that the same effect on unemployment would require ever increasing doses of inflation. Put differently, below normal unemployment, inflation is fueled by liberal monetary and fiscal policies until hyperinflation.

The link between wage and inflation rates definitively entered the collective consciousness with a celebrated paper published by A.W. Phillips (1958). In that paper, Phillips made two central claims: (1) the rate of change of the nominal wage level is a decreasing function of the employment rate; and (2) the rate of unemployment required to maintain the rate of inflation to what we were accustomed to (i.e., 2.3%) was positive. This thesis was embraced without reservation by two influential economists in the United States, Professors Paul Samuelson and Robert Solow. Shortly thereafter, it became a standard ad hoc macroeconomic theory. Subsequently, Robert Lipsey postulated that the rate of inflation is a function of the unemployment level and its rate of change.

Still, the theory was not upheld by observations. The so-called Phillips curve, linking wage and employment levels, was shifting to the right. In the 1970s, to rescue the credo, the New Classical Economists put out an explanation that went like this: "The news of an initial fall in wages is enough for workers to expect that the general wage level will fall to the job-preserving level, so that the level of unemployment will return to its equilibrium level. Otherwise, workers would be charged with repeatedly misforcasting the equilibrium wage level, contrarily to 'rational expectations.'" This explanation, though bordering on weirdness, spurred Professor Milton Friedman to put out a modified version of the ad hoc theory: The rate of change in the wage level is a function of the level of unemployment and the expected rate of inflation.

These developments aptly illustrate the gist of axiomatic theorizing. Starting with the old marginal productivity theory, it makes sense to argue that a firm cannot pay a real wage that is above a worker's contribution without incurring a loss. But the theory does not say in which direction causality runs. Why could it not be the other way around? Investment and innovations raise productivity, aggregate demand, and capacity utilization, which in turn raise the demand for labor and real wage. As a matter of fact, throughout the 1980s, the rates of inflation and unemployment in industrial countries moved in opposite directions, but the rates of growth of real GDP, hourly earnings, unit labor costs, and productivity consistently fell as well. Meanwhile, gross private investment, as a percentage of GDP, remained steady around 20% of a falling GDP (except in England where it was significantly lower), compared with 28% for South East Asia, during the period (*WEO* 1989, 80–83; 1990, 31). In other words, in industrial countries, real total domestic demand growth fell to 0.6 in 1981 and to -0.2 in 1982. While in Japan and in the Asian tigers, the reverse trend was observed. More specifically, in Japan, gross private investment, as a percentage of GDP, went up from the average of 21.4% in 1977–1986 to 33.3% in 1990. In the newly industrialized countries (NICs), gross capital formation was remarkably steady at 27 to 28%; the growth of output per capita grew at least at twice the rates registered in industrialized countries (*WEO* 1990, 127–29).

The above developments have also prompted some researchers to probe deeper into the reasons for these observed differences. In *The Manchester Guardian* on August 6, 1995, Will Hutton reported on a study carried out by Professor Dani Rodrick on the cases of South Korea and Taiwan. Rodrick concludes that in these countries, investment used to be held back by coordination failures until creative government interventions unlocked such market failures and triggered the investment boom of the 1980s. In the Keynesian approach, a coordination failure is the failure to adjust to a superior equilibrium due to price and/or wage inertia. In modern parlance, coordination failures are characterized by the presence of spillovers and strategic complementarities. What is important to note here is simply that the resolution of coordination failures requires either cooperative actions, which are in general unstable because of the incentive to cheat, or third-party intervention (meaning the government). Strategic complementarities, on the other hand, arise when a change carried out by one firm affects the strategy of other firms. This type of coordination failures, which is closer to Keynes' thinking, means that a firm has no incentive to solve a problem that benefits all its competitors as well. Rodrick also determines that exports could not have been the motor of economic growth because they represented such a small proportion of GDP, nor was growth driven by competitive exchange rates. In both countries, the real exchange rate had been remarkably steady during the previous 30 years. Therefore, it was the high levels of investment that drove export growth. In summary, in the 1950s, both economies were trapped in low level equilibria due to coordination failures. It was an array of government interventions that broke the logjam.

Obviously, the examples of Japan and the four Asian NICs are not sufficient to draw macroeconomic inferences. However, such examples are more in line with Keynesianism than with the wage flexibility-inflation targeting theory. That theory has not, to date, received any empirical support. Even in Pinochet's Chile, depressed wages, union bashing, and large-scale privatization did not bring about growth during the 1973–1983 period. In fact, the inappropriate monetary policy imported from Chicago and its concomitant high domestic rates of interest, as well as the reform of the investment code in mining attracted some foreign capital. That inflow of short-term capital caused the peso to appreciate and the national debt to increase. At about the same time, the terms of trade deteriorated, unemployment rose and domestic demand fell. GDP fell by 14% and unemployment rose to 33% of the active labor force. Fortunately, Pinochet's government did address the problem of coordination failures in the mineral, agricultural, and service sectors in the meantime. After the devaluation of the overvalued peso, gross fixed capital formation, as a percentage of GDP, went from 12% in 1983 to 23.3% in 1990. The unemployment rate fell from 12% in 1987 to 4% in 1993. The wage rate went up by 20% from 1989 to 1995. Domestic demand rose, the growth rate increased, and then foreign capital arrived. In the meantime, funds amassed from privatization allowed the public sector to put up roughly $9 billion to rescue some 14 banks and 8 other financial institutions from bankruptcy. These institutions are now in better financial health, although six of them still owe about $4.5 billion to the central bank. The latter had in the meantime taken measures to sterilize and control the inflow of foreign capital, in particular to bar speculative foreign capital since the early 1990s. The recently formed *Administradoras de Fondos de Pensiones* and a healthier banking sector (thanks to government interventions) now make Chile less and less dependent on foreign capital.

Therefore, wage flexibility-inflation targeting, after having failed to bring about the promised economic growth even after ten years, seems nevertheless to be driving the restructuring phase of the new orthodoxy. For further confirmation, let us turn to the apparent problem of the growth of the public debt.

The Management of the Public Debt: A Conjecture

Since World War II, authorities in industrial market economies have managed their economies with a set of policies that rests on two fundamental premises, that is, there exist economic cycles (bounded and irregular fluctuations), and that the general price level can actually be stabilized. These two premises were then translated into what we have identified above as fiscal and monetary policies.

On the assumption that cycles exist (i.e., the economy is a nonlinear system), then in the short term at least, economic policy should aim at overcoming recessions and fighting inflation. Managing the economy then reduces to using variations in public expenditures, taxes, and the money supply as instruments for controlling domestic demand and output. Actually, few still believe in the potency of these instruments, but to maintain credibility, governments continue pretending otherwise.

Of course, the institutional investors, or the new masters of the universe, see things quite differently. For them, if there is any role left for governments, it boils down to either one of two possibilities. They can either attempt to reduce the amplitude of fluctuations around potential output, while recognizing at the same time that maneuverability is limited (see Seater 1993). Or, governments can devise discretionary, temporary, and timely expansionary policies to stimulate their economies out of recessions (Roubini and Sachs 1989). Put differently, governments should simply study, understand, and then address temporary economic shocks, while leaving permanent shocks for structural adjustments. Note however, that the proponents of this viewpoint leave it to governments to distinguish between temporary and permanent shocks. The understanding is that through such behavior, governments may fortuitously stabilize the price level.

In fact, for all intents and purposes, these governments have lost their ability to control their economies. This is primarily due to the need to borrow as well as the growth of public debt since the mid-1970s. Consider the case of the G7 group, for example. In the United States, the ratio (n) of the public debt (D) and nominal GDP fell to 0.45 (or 45%) during the 1960–1981 period; but from 1981 to 1993, it rose to 66%. In Germany, n was more or less stable around 20% up to 1975; from there onward, it began rising to reach 44.1% in 1993. In France, the situation was more or less identical to that of Germany. In Italy, n started at around 25% in 1963, but rose steadily since to reach 119.3% in 1993. In Japan, it rose steadily from 0% in 1963 to about 75.1% in 1993. In Canada, n fell from 1960 to 1975; it rose afterward to 92.5% in 1993. The case of the United Kingdom is somewhat different; n fell steadily during the 1966–1990 period due to inflation (*vide infra*), but rose to 40.4% in 1993. In all industrial countries, n stood at 70% in 1994 to compare with 41% in 1980 (United Nations 1995, 69).

Two important clarifications regarding these ratios are in order at this point. First, the situation is less alarming than it appears. The above ratios do not account for governments' fixed assets as shown in Table 4.2. When these are accounted for, the ratios (except for Italy) fall significantly.

Second, there is no theoretically or empirically defined level of debt a government can carry. Common sense, however, would indicate that there is a ratio beyond which the debt may become unsustainable, but we do not know what it is. This is a judgment call.

For a better understanding of what is involved in the debt problem, let us define the public debt. Obviously, it is the outstanding cumulative amount owed

Table 4.2

The Debt to GDP Ratio in the G7 Countries: 1980–1998 (in %)

		1980–1990	1991	1992	1993	1994	1995	1996	1997[1]	1998[1]
United	gross	49.4	62.1	64.6	66.1	66.0	66.2	67.0	66.5	65.8
States	net[2]	35.4	46.7	50.0	52.1	52.9	53.9	53.8	53.3	52.8
Japan	gross	66.5	66.7	70.0	75.1	82.4	90.1	94.9	98.8	101.2
	net[2]	20.9	4.8	4.2	5.2	8.0	11.8	16.0	18.5	20.6
Germany	gross	40.1	41.1	44.1	48.2	50.4	58.1	60.3	61.5	61.6
	net[2]	21.0	21.4	27.7	35.4	40.7	49.1	51.5	53.0	53.5
France	gross	29.6	35.8	39.7	45.7	48.6	52.9	56.3	57.8	58.9
	net[2]	22.0	27.1	30.2	34.4	40.2	43.5	46.9	48.4	49.5
Italy	gross	79.0	101.4	108.5	119.3	125.5	124.9	123.0	121.5	119.3
	net[2]	73.4	96.3	103.0	111.8	117.3	116.8	116.4	115.0	113.0
England	gross	48.0	33.6	34.8	40.4	46.0	47.3	49.3	49.4	49.6
	net[2]	40.3	26.7	28.1	32.5	37.7	40.9	43.9	45.7	43.1
Canada	gross	60.2	79.4	86.9	92.5	94.6	98.3	99.9	96.5	91.7
	net[2]	30.1	49.7	56.9	61.9	64.7	67.5	68.7	66.3	62.9

[1]IMF's projections; [2]Net debt ratio is the gross minus financial assets held by the social security system.

Source: Compiled using data from *WEO* (May 1997, 22).

by a government. More formally, the public debt is a legal obligation of the government to make interest and amortization payments to holders of designated claims in accordance with a defined and agreed on temporal schedule. In practice, this may comprise the financial obligations of public organizations such as pension funds and social security administrations. But regardless, these obligatory claims are for the most part in the form of bonds.

As the scientific theory is silent on such matters, we only have a few heuristics to go by. During the classical era, economists used to go by a normative principle. That principle suggested that resorting to debt was justified either by nonrecurrent expenditures or the financing of long-term capital projects. However, in the latter case, the principle required a concomitant scheme for debt retirement over the income-yielding period of the investment. Beyond this normative principle, the classicals had nothing else of substance to offer. David Ricardo tried to come to their rescue in 1817. In that connection, he felt that government borrowing and taxation should be viewed as logically equivalent; this is what is now known as the Ricardian equivalence principle. However, common sense indicates, and indeed Ricardo himself never believed for a moment that such an equivalence could exist. Clearly now, given the present high tax context, no one could claim with a straight face that Ricardian equivalence can address the problem of the public debt. Mr. Keynes too had a few ideas on government borrowing, as we have seen above. Over the years however, his ideas were driven to a stance that views public borrowing as a means of cost free financing of demand-enhancing deficits during periods of recession. There are of course two problems associated with such a stance. First, it wrongly assumes that the public debt carries no future burden. Such an assumption is tantamount to wanting it both ways, either it carries a future burden, or it must be financed by noninterest bearing money creation, which may result in inflation. Next, in a democratic society in which politicians vie for votes and power, it was almost inevitable that borrowing and spending would become a vote-gathering mechanism. As the saying goes, the rest is history.

This brief review pinpoints a curious dilemma. On the one hand and despite all the commotion, there is no real guidance as to the appropriate level of debt for an economy. On the other, the reality is that some level of debt is necessary. For example, government bonds are ideal saving and investment instruments for risk averse agents. They are also excellent instruments for controlling the money supply via open market operations. Additionally, governments collect taxes intermittently while they spend continuously, and they must finance infrastructures' projects. To do all of these, they must sell bonds.

Ironically, the level of government debt never used to be a worry for anyone, because it was mainly denominated in domestic currencies. Consequently, there was never any danger of bankruptcy, given the power that governments used to have to tax and draw emergency loans from central banks. Of course, when governments and monetary authorities are not separated, emergency loans from central banks may lead to some concerns. If new money is created following the purchase of new governments' bonds, it may give rise to inflation, unless it is neutralized by an equivalent contraction of credit. But when monetary authorities are independent from governments, there is little danger of that happening. At any rate, all of this has changed with the advent of globalization. Banks and other financial institutions were in the past compelled by regulations to either hold a specified volume of government bonds or have their liquidity ratio fixed in terms of bonds. In many instances and thanks to deregulation and the internationalization of the bond market, these institutions no longer have such an obligation. Hence, governments have lost their ability to tap national saving sources. As a certain amount of debt is necessary, governments must now turn to international sources. By the same token, central banks can at most set short term interest rates to which economic activities appear to be less and less sensitive, whereas, the new masters set long term interest rates. A few examples might make this clearer. In Italy, the central bank was holding some 40% of government bonds back in 1973; in 1989, it held only 13%. On the other hand, in Germany, the percentage of government bonds sold on the international market went from 9% in 1980 to 26% in 1992. In France, it went from 1% in 1986 to 43% in 1992. In Canada, the United Kingdom, Sweden, among others, the story is similar (*WEO* 1995, 69). To further stress the point, I show in Table 4.3 the evolution of crossborder transactions since 1980.

These figures have increased since. In view of this trend, my main point should now be clear. Governments must borrow on the international market,

Table 4.3
Cross-Border Transactions in Bonds and Equities[1]: 1980–1996 (in % of GDP)

	1980	1985	1990	1995	1996[2]
United States	9.0	35.1	89.0	135.3	151.5
Germany	7.7	63.0	120.0	65.1	82.8
France	8.4	21.4	53.6	179.6	229.2
Italy	1.1	4.0	26.6	252.8	435.4
United Kingdom	—	367.5	690.1	—	—
Canada	9.6	26.7	64.4	194.5	234.8

[1]Gross purchases and sales of securities between residents and non-residents; [2]From January to September.

Source: Bank of International Settlements and *WEO* (May 1997, 60).

where the new masters, guided by systemic risk ratings of Moody's and Standard and Poor's, set the level of long term interest rates as well as the rules of behavior in matters of borrowing and debt management. A closer look at these rules will tell us a lot about present-day governments' behavior.

The rules that governments must now abide by are summarized in a simple empirical relationship (see United Nations 1995, 71):

$$(\text{the rate of change of } n) = (\text{the primary deficit ratio}) + (\text{debt service ratio}) - (\text{the economy's growth rate} \times n)$$
$$\dot{n} \quad = \quad (d) \quad + \quad (in) \quad - \quad (gn),$$

where n is the ratio D/GNP; $\dot{n}$ is the rate of change of n; d is the so-called *primary deficit ratio* or the public deficit minus interest payments on D divided by GNP; i and g are, respectively, the average rate of interest on D and the growth rate of nominal GDP. I hasten to add that the new masters let it be known additionally that they want a stable or preferably a falling n; they do not like inflation, and they do not want to be taxed by national authorities.

As it can be seen from the above relationship, every term is a ratio with GNP as the denominator. Moreover, the relationship supposes a negative correlation between g and a positive one with i. Accordingly, the greater the difference $(i - g)$, the faster the growth rate of n in relation to an economy's capacity to support the debt, and vice versa. Hence, in inflationary periods, g is expected to be greater than i. Therefore, n should fall. In fact, according to the UN's Department of Economic and Social Information and Political Analysis, it is thanks to inflation that the United Kingdom managed to reduce its n throughout the 1980s. In contrast, countries such as the Netherlands and Belgium, that tried to maintain the parity of their currencies with the deutsche mark by fighting inflation, saw their n rise to unprecedented levels. If the new masters want a falling n, they should welcome a little inflation. Alas no! Fearful that inflation will chip away at the value of bonds denominated in national currencies, or that local currencies may not appreciate fast enough, they raise interest rates at the first sight of inflation or expected inflation. This is a bit ironic. The new masters require that governments fight inflation (which increases g). But this raises the debt, which causes a concomitant rise in i, unless i is variable or there is indexation. Or else, they want governments to stabilize D over the whole cycle, whose length cannot even be forecasted. Incidentally, among the large number of criteria used by Moody's and Standard and Poor's to determine a country's credit rating, only six play a major role. They are: per capita income, GDP growth, inflation, external debt, the level of economic development, and default history. Except for default history, none is a reliable measure.

Another way of putting it is that when bonds are denominated in national currencies, selling them abroad brings an inflow of capital. Such inflows may cause national currencies to appreciate, while inflation tends to depreciate them. An appreciation benefits old bond holders, a depreciation followed by a risk premium on interest rates benefits new bond holders. Of course, governments are free to denominate their bonds in any hard currency. However, their nationals as well as the new masters are also free to go after the highest yield. The fear of inflation is still there due to the imagined negative correlation between inflation and economic growth. In short, the new masters assess and rate the economy's capacity to earn that hard currency, and the government thereby relinquishes control in their favor. There seems to be no way of breaking the vicious cycle. If the debt ratio is high, a risk premium is put on i, which increases the deficit and consequently the debt. But an increase in the debt leads the new masters to revise the risk premium upward, leading to further deterioration in n.

The only alternative left for governments then is to reduce d. How? Obviously, the easiest way would be to raise taxes. But on whom? The new masters themselves do not want to be taxed nor do they want taxes on the capital gain of their clients. The poor cannot pay. The middle-class has effectively reached it capacity to pay and that class has voting power. At any rate, the average ratio of tax revenue to GDP in industrial countries has already increased from 28% in 1960 to 44% in 1994. In other words, 44% of GDP went to taxes during 1994. The new masters think that this is enough. Of course, not a word is said about the inequity of the tax burden or that another 6% of GDP could be collected on multinational enterprises in order to balance government budgets. In the end analysis, the alternative resorts to cuts in social expenditures or to raids on the pension funds of workers. That is exactly what we are now seeing. Or put differently, this is deconstruction in action, which incidentally violates the sufficient conditions for the promotion of welfare.

All of these conjectures are buried in a technical jargon known in some quarters as *fiscal consolidation,* to which I return in the next chapter. For now, the problem is that national governments in industrial countries have lost their ability to control their economies. Because of the dictates of globalization, they can no longer draw on national saving sources to the extent they used to in the past to finance a necessary level of debt. They must, therefore, revert to international sources. In addition, as what goes on in these countries determines what happens in the rest of the world, it is no exaggeration to say that the new masters call the tune and governments around the world dance to it. Globalization is the battle cry of the new masters.

This fear of inflation and debt is now enshrined in government policy everywhere. The excessive deficit procedure (EDP), for example, is a dominant principle in the Maastricht treaty, governing admission to the European Monetary Union (EMU). Accordingly, during the transition to economic and monetary union, a candidate is required to avoid excessive deficits, defined as a public deficit in excess of 3% and a debt level of 60% of GDP. The justification for this rule is that member states must be restrained from overborrowing to avoid destabilizing the common currency. Because excessive deficits eventually lead to a debt crisis, and the European Central Bank will have to bail out the debt-ridden members, either by keeping interest rates below equilibrium levels or by monetizing the debts. Either way, poor fiscal policies could create inflationary pressures that the bank might find difficult to ignore.

The levels at which the current deficit and the debt are set are totally arbitrary and might not even be effective. As argued by von Hagen and Eichengreen (1996), if the restriction on borrowing were essential for the stability of the common currency, it would have been an essential feature in all monetary unions and in all federated states using a common currency. It is not. Indeed, the only time restriction on a member state's borrowing is justified, as they see it, is when the member does not have its own power to tax. As this is not the case in the European Union (EU), the authors think that EDP is redundant at best, and may even aggravate the very problem that it is designed to solve. Thus, there is a risk that the 3-60 criteria may turn out to be totally arbitrary. Yet the cost of compliance, as I show in the next chapter, is significant.

As we have seen at the outset of this chapter, the IMF says that globalization is about growth, and that growth entails not only the growth of overall production but also a continuous reproportioning of the sectors of the economic system as well as the structure of employment, along with changes in income distribution. Strangely enough, ten years after the inception of the new orthodoxy, the IMF felt that it should leave itself an exit door by adding:

While society as a whole benefits from the process..., the gain are unlikely to be evenly distributed. Some groups may initially gain a great deal, while others may benefit only gradually or suffer setbacks. (*WEO* May 1997, 45)

When it comes to the big question as to whether globalization is adversely affecting large segments of society? The IMF's answer is:

The increasing integration of both developing and transition countries into the global economy has *sparked concerns* that competition from low-wage economies will displace workers from high-wage manufacturing jobs to lower-wage service employment, and in doing so depress living standards in the advanced economies....Yet other *perceived* undesirable consequences of globalization, especially financial globalization, are that it *may* erode the capacity of national authorities to manage economic activity and constrain governments' choices of tax rates and tax systems. (*WEO* May 1997, 45) [my italics]

In the next chapter, I bring forth the available data to see if these perceived concerns are indeed hurting people. In the meantime, I claim that on the surface, the wage-inflation theory and the management of the public debt are the real drivers of the new orthodoxy. Then the obvious question is: How can discredited ad hoc theories and a shaky heuristic be driving present-day behavior? In order to make sense out of this incongruity, I turn toward ideology.

IDEOLOGY

Ideology is a term that is associated with A-L. C. Destutt de Tracy, then a Director at the prestigious Institut de France. Incidentally, he was also an economist who wrote many tracts on economic questions, a *Traité d'économie politique* (1822), and may even be the father of the revealed preference theory, associated with the name of Paul Samuelson. When the debate over the measurement of utility was raging between Bordas and Dupuit in the 1840s, it was discovered that both William Jevons and Jules Dupuit had benefited largely from Destutt de Tracy's approach to indirect utility measurement. More to the point, Destutt de Tracy was also a Newtonian. The Newtonians of his time harbored an uncritical faith in reason and in the scientific method. It was within such a mindset that Destutt de Tracy coined the term ideology for a construct that he associated with a science, whose objective was the study of ideas, their laws, and their origin. His goal, besides furthering the faith, was a frontal attack on metaphysics. Yet, as Katouzian (1980) observed, this misconception of science itself became over the years a full-fledged metaphysical concept. Hegel and Marx both had a hand in this irony. Remember, for Hegel, there was only one truth, it was only our ideological understanding of it that varies from one period to another. Marx added a stint. Ideas alone, he argued, do not determine the course of history. The natural environment, technology, and institutions all influence the individual and the social experience, as well as their changes. Therefore, man's knowledge of truth is consistent with his personal and class interests. Having being brought up in a particular environment, socioeconomic class and moral values, it is natural that he should view the world against such a background. Since Marx then, ideology has come to mean a set of ideas and beliefs reflective of an epoch, a society, or a social class.

Perhaps unwillingly, Marx linked ideology with deception, for if it is a conscious construct within which a particular class or society defends its interests, it is biased or may even be deceptive. Since the turn of the century, the term ideology has then taken on a pejorative meaning. However, ideology may also be confused, even by those employing it, with moral judgment. Hence, it is wise not to dismiss too quickly others' judgments as ideological and therefore not worthy of critical examination. We would be falling head first in the *argumentum ad hominem* trap. The reason I made such a long detour via the various theories was to distinguish between, to use Kartouzian's terms, *limited consciousness*, whereby ideology is confused with moral judgment, and *false consciousness,* where ideology is used deceptively to defend one's class interests. The new orthodoxy, whether originated in academia or on the right of the political spectrum, had to be critically examined to see whether or not it is grounded in economic theory and if it is capable of solving the problems of contemporary capitalism. So far, it is looking more and more like a case of false consciousness.

As we have seen above, the phenomenon of globalization is not to be confused with the period of trade liberalization that preceded World War I. From the 1860s to 1913, trade liberalization was confined to the Western world, operating under the gold standard. The speed and means of communications were not conducive to the development of a global market. There were fewer financial instruments, international trade was regulated, and, national governments were sovereign in the economic arena. The Western economies grew at phenomenal rates. Why then would not globalization simply try to replicate this success? Why is it so keen in wrestling economic sovereignty away from national governments, as it intends to do in the coming Multilateral Agreement on Investment?[8] The goal of this treaty, termed the "constitution of globalization," is to push the deregulatory agenda of the World Trade Organization to an extreme. Some of the clauses of the treaty are so extreme and shameless that the first version was negotiated practically underground. For example, under a chapter entitled "Investor Rights," multinational corporations would have the right to invest in any sector in any country around the world, and the government of the host countries would be charged with the obligation to guarantee the "effective enjoyment" of the investment. To ensure this, investors would be entitled to compensations for any actions a government may subsequently take that may be deemed harmful to investors' profit potential. There is another provision under which a host government may not take any action that restricts an investor's conduct, and that provision as well as the others would be enforced through closed international trade courts, which will determine whether or not actions or even domestic laws must be scrapped for failure to comply with the chapter on "General Treatment." In short, foreign investors would have the power to attack any domestic law or policy (health protection measures, environmental norms, actions preventing civil disturbances, policies promoting regional development, land redistribution laws, laws to protect the natural resource base, and so on) that they alone may deem harmful to their profits. And to top it all, signatory parties can give notice of withdrawal only afters 5 years, and after that the parties are still bound to the treaty's provisions for another 15 years. In brief, foreign investors would have all the rights, and host governments would have all the obligations; this is the mechanism by which multinational corporations plan to disempower governments around the world. If democracies are so unconcerned to the point of letting such a treaty come into force, then the notion of parliamentary democracy itself will be reduced to the simple but meaningless right to vote.

Yet the new orthodoxy is publicly presented as a trinity consisting of: (1) unregulated capital markets; (2) unregulated labor markets and unconstrained multinational firms; and (3) free (unregulated) trade. According to its proponents, no alternative exists. As I was unable to theoretically justify it, I have tried to uncover its true goal. Thus far, it appears that there is indeed a logic behind it all. The evidence that I present in the next chapter seems to show that it is designed to accumulate capital in the hands of a few, but this remains unavowed. Instead, it is hidden behind a panoply of jargons centered around buzzwords such as efficiency, governments' ineptitude, and the like. In private, however, the authors and the beneficiaries of the new orthodoxy, whoever they are, must be singing:

Now where's the action?   Fighting deficit
Fighting inflation   Is none deceit.
And deconstruction   Nor reducing debt.
Are swell for nations.   Both are profit net.
And in addition,

5

THE IMPACTS OF THE NEW ORTHODOXY

INTRODUCTION

The previous chapter examined the prevailing economic orthodoxy in force since the mid 1980s. It demonstrated that, besides its spur for market development, the basic tenets of the new discipline are not totally grounded in the scientific theory of economics; it then looked elsewhere for a possible justification. After a brief examination of the productivity growth slowdown and the wage-inflation theory, among others, it reached the conclusion that the new orthodoxy is driven by the discredited wage-inflation theory, the exaggerated public debt problem, and ideology. Even so, this new orthodoxy nevertheless carries two types of consequence. The first concerns the future of the democratic process, in the sense that the new masters hide their true intention behind economic efficiency while wrestling away the control of national economies from democratically elected governments.[1] However, I will leave this aspect of the danger to the political process. The second type of consequence concerns the economic impacts of the new orthodoxy on the world. This chapter focuses on these economic ramifications in light of the data spanning the last decade.

Obviously, European data cover a relatively short period. They might not either be sufficiently broad or the time span might not be sufficiently long to reveal the full impact of the new orthodoxy. Except for England, most European countries began to apply the second phase of the new discipline in the early 1990s. However, certain European trends, arising out of the application of the first phase, are clearly visible, whereas for Latin America, Africa, the United States and England (the first two of the G7 countries to have adopted the new orthodoxy) almost a decade of data exists. This period is sufficiently long, I believe, to give a good indication as to whether or not the new orthodoxy is capable of putting the world economy on the road to recovery.

The data are drawn from a number of sources. For social statistics, I draw on Halimi (1996); data on corporate capitalization are from the United States Department of Commerce's *Statistical Abstract of the United States, 1995 (Stat. Abs).* But the bulk is from two main sources: The IMF's *World Economic Outlook (WEO)* for the months of May and October 1990, May 1997, and the United Nations' Department of Social and Economic Affairs *Etude sur l'économie mondiale (Etude)* for the years 1979–1980, 1980–1981, 1981–1982, 1993, 1994, 1995 and 1996. In the first four sections of this chapter, I provide, from the data available, a cursory appraisal of the situation. In the last section, I perform some formal statistical tests.

THE WAGE-INFLATION THEORY BEFORE AND AFTER

I have argued that the wage-inflation theory and the management of the public debt provide the seeming logic of globalization and restructuring. However, that logic might not be that clear to everyone. For a greater understanding, therefore, I take another look at the wage-inflation theory before and after the inception of the new orthodoxy, except that this time around, I examine a slightly modified thesis that happens to be more in line with current thinking that begins by implicitly assuming that inflation is bad for economic growth. Additionally, it posits that a positive level of unemployment, beyond frictional unemployment, is the price to pay for slowing down the growth of wage rates. Increases in wages are assumed to fuel inflation, which in turn depresses the growth rate of GDP. Consequently, if a period of high inflation happens to coincide with a productivity growth slowdown, high wages, and high unit labor costs, it is natural for a believer in the wage-inflation theory to embrace the restructuring phase of the new orthodoxy without a second thought. After all, if wages could deliberately be depressed, inflation would be tamed even at the risk of a higher level of unemployment. Productivity growth would somehow resume, and GDP growth would follow. And, in theory at least, economic growth is capable of eventually solving the unemployment problem. All labor has to do is to stay calm, swallow the brunt of the adjustment, and wait for better days. This has been the leitmotif in the discourse of the political leaders who venture an explanation of the so-called new thinking. Frequently though, their reasoning appears confused and contradictory. However, we must be cognizant of the fact that they are repeating, with little or no understanding, a lesson learned from bankers and academic economists. Even so, the interesting question is: Are these relationships meaningful, in the sense of Chapter 1? To check, I turn to the data forthwith.

I start with Table A5.1 in the Appendix, which shows movements in factor productivity growth. It is clear from the table that, on the average, the growth of labor productivity between 1973 and 1979 fell significantly below its 1960–1973 level in all industrial market economies, including G7 countries. The same trend was observed with regard to capital and total factor productivity growth, but the data for later periods in all industrial countries are not available. Over the

1982–1991 period, labor productivity growth improved somewhat, in particular in the United States and the United Kingdom. However, I must emphasize here that Kendrick's figures appear way higher than those supplied by the United Nations (see *Etude* 1995, 323). Just as there is no consensus on why the slowdown occurred, we do not know why labor productivity rose during 1982–1991, if in fact it did. Some observers suspect that the improvement is due to the slight rise in oil consumption, but I will return to that later. Nevertheless, I can understand why many adherents of the wage-inflation theory would quickly find some ground for rejoicing over this mixed result. As far as I am concerned though, this is not the whole story.

In order to thoroughly examine the validity of the theory, we need a few technical definitions. The *wage rate* is currently defined as the total compensation per employed person, whereas *unit labor costs* are the total compensation of employees per unit of output. *Nominal GNP,* on the other hand, is the total physical output produced in any period of time t, conventionally a year, valued at the price level of the period t (p^*). It is not difficult to see that this measure does not give a true picture of the variation in physical output from $(t-1)$ to t, since the price level may have changed. Because of this, we make use of the *real GNP* concept, which isolates the change in physical output in the whole economy between different periods of time, by valuing the physical output at the previous period price level (i.e., at the same price level or at constant prices). Thus, valuing the physical output in time t at the price level of period $t-1$, we get the real performance of the economy over the period $[t-(t-1)]$. Using these concepts, I can now define two different measures of inflation (deflation), which is a rise (fall) in the general price level. The first and most familiar measure of inflation is a rise in the consumer price index (CPI); it measures the price changes of a basket of goods consumed by an urban wage earner, but the basket of goods in question is supposed to remain the same from year to year. This is not realistic, so a better measure of inflation is the rise in the *GNP deflator* (or the implicit price deflator) between two periods. The GNP deflator is the ratio of nominal GNP to real GNP over a given period taking therefore into account what is actually produced in the whole economy from one year to the next.

In Table A5.2, I show variations in the CPI index for developed market economies and for the G7 group. Considering this imperfect but popular measure, the control of inflation in these countries during the 1980s was a success. Based on figures supplied by the IMF (*WEO* May 1990, 132–133), Figure 5.1 shows variations in the wage rate, unit labor costs, and in the GNP deflator in the G7 group. In order to aggregate over various countries, moving average weights of the 12 previous quarters of the U.S. dollar values of their respective GNP/GDPs were used. As it can be seen, the growth rates of all three variables reflect two clear shocks, one in 1973–1974, the other in 1979–1980; moreover, all three variables moved together.

In Table A5.3, we see that the unemployment rate shot upward, reaching unprecedented level in 1984, except in Japan. Over the 1985–1990 period, the

Figure 5.1
Indices of Percent Change from a Year Earlier in the Wage, Unit Labor Costs,
and the GNP/GDP Deflator in G7 Countries: 1973=100

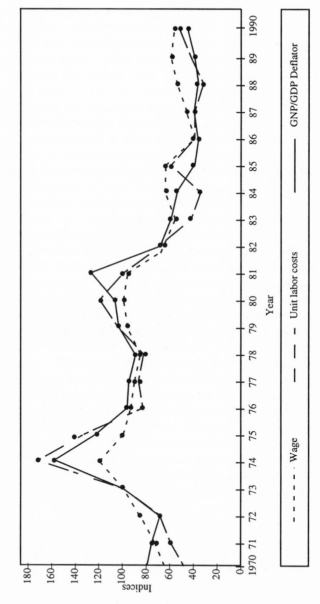

unemployment situation improved in some countries, remained about the same in Japan, and worsened in France and Italy. Thus, as the growth rates of wages and inflation moved downward, the unemployment rate moved upward, lending some support to the theory. In other words, the expected happened. It remains now to see whether or not the taming of wages and inflation paid off in terms of output growth.

The way the theory is supposed to work is as follows: A rise in productivity growth lowers the costs of production, shifts supply to the right, lowers the price level, and increases the total output demanded and GNP growth. To check the meaningfulness of this proposition, we move to Figure 5.2, constructed with data from *WEO* (October 1990, 6; May 1990, 65, 128; May 1997, 133–141) and *Etude* (1993, 22). Data from GNP growth clearly show that the proposition is not upheld. The rate of growth of real GDP remained lower than the 1961–1973 average throughout the whole decade of orthodoxy in industrialized market economies (G7 group included). As regards other parts of the world, it is either too soon to draw a similar conclusion as in the case of the transitional economies, or the growth observed is not due to the new discipline. For example, the success of the newly industrialized economies (NICs) of Asia, recalling Rodrick's study, was due to creative government investment and the taming of coordination failures rather than the new orthodoxy. In fact, in a more recent study of growth in China, Hu and Khan (1997) confirm Rodrick's findings. The two authors conclude that education, reforms that create incentives, and capital investment combined to raise Chinese labor productivity to unprecedented levels after 1984. More specifically, from 1979 to 1994, labor productivity increased at an average annual rate of 3.9%; this means that after correcting for the poor performance prior to 1984, the post 1984 average had to be even higher.

As I have said, one could very well argue that the situation in the G7 group is not conclusive, since three out of the four European countries included in that group were late in applying the second phase of the new orthodoxy. To this, I would reply: What about the United States and the United Kingdom, Latin America and Africa? Table A5.4 shows these specific situations. According to the table, considering also that the Unites States and the United Kingdom were among the first in the G7 countries to apply the new orthodoxy, the data on economic growth do not support the link between lower inflation and economic growth.

Before turning to other aspects of the new orthodoxy, I wish to look at the link between inflation and growth in a more explicit manner. This link used to fuel a passionate debate between the proponents of a negative relationship, and opponents claiming that a moderately high rate of inflation is a necessary by-product of economic development. According to the proponents, a high rate of inflation is a symptom of fundamental macroeconomic imbalances (e.g., Blejer 1983). In addition, a high rate of inflation affects the financial sector in various

Figure 5.2
Real GDP Growth Rates of Industrial Countries

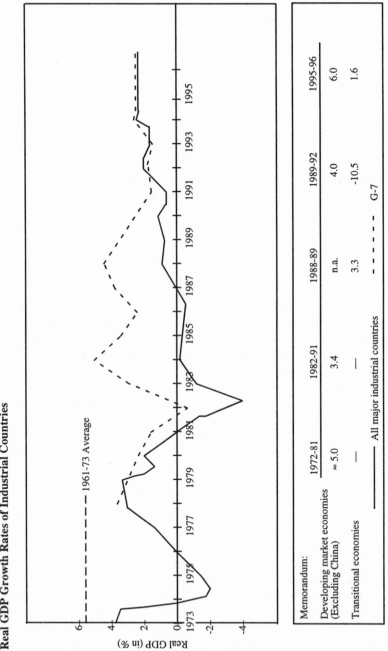

Memorandum:	1972-81	1982-91	1988-89	1989-92	1995-96
Developing market economies (Excluding China)	≈ 5.0	3.4	n.a.	4.0	6.0
Transitional economies	—	—	3.3	-10.5	1.6

— — — G-7

——— All major industrial countries

ways. Among others, it shortens the planning horizon and, of course, negatively affects the real rate of interest. For these reasons, they argue, high inflation may be expected to be associated with poor economic performance.

In a search to confirm this assumed negative correlation, a study was carried out by the IMF on a sample of 88 developing countries (Table 5.1). The countries were divided into three groups according to their inflation rates over the period 1983–1989 (*WEO*, May 1990, 57). Countries with annual average rates of consumer price inflation below 6% were characterized as "low inflation"; those with annual average rates above 6% and below 15% were characterized as "moderate inflation," and those with rates over 15% as "high inflation." The thresholds were chosen so as to put roughly an equal number of countries in each group. Weighted averages were obtained using GDP weights. The results were as follows.

Statistical significance tests were also carried out for differences between groups and for each variable, using unweighted averages. Values for high inflation were found to be significantly different at the 90% level from those of an unspecified lower group. However, considering the quality of economic data, it may be inferred that high inflation may indeed be harmful to growth. But no such claim can be made for inflation rates up to 10%. It is fair to say, however, that there might be some substance to the negative link argument at rates approaching 20% and higher due to the kind of uncertainty that arises at such rates.

I do not have the benefit of a similar study for industrialized market economies. I note, however, that for these countries as a whole and, for three of them in particular, the situation was more or less similar.

Intercountry differences are for memorandum because the sample is too small to draw inferences. For all industrial countries, there is a significant drop in both inflation and real growth rates between the three periods. Combining this result with that of the more extended study above, it is safe to conclude that the data do not justify the obsessive fear of the negative impact of inflation below 10%; if anything, it seems that the rates of inflation and growth move in the same direction.[2]

There is more to this inflation story. To understand what is driving it, we must begin by asking why a segment of society is so scared of inflation? In fact, the scare is fueled by tales of the German and Hungarian hyperinflations of the past and by an onslaught of negative publicity that began in the early 1970s with a timely series of books (Back 1972; Friedman 1973; Jones 1973). These books have managed to equate inflation with hyperinflation. The truth is that inflation is a balancing force that does not need government intervention, except to stop it from spiraling upward. Let us take retirees on fixed incomes. Inflation erodes the purchasing power of their earnings only to the extent that their state pensions are not fully indexed for inflation. Savers lose only if the rate of interest on savings is lower than the inflation rate, and when governments tax nominal interest incomes, but it does not have to be this way. During inflation,

Table 5.1
The Link Between Inflation and Economic Growth

	Low inflation	Moderate inflation	High inflation
Number of countries	28	31	29
Inflation rate			
unweighted average	3.2	9.6	84.8
weighted average	2.8	9.2	183.1
Gross fixed capital investment (as a percentage of GDP)			
unweighted average	22.8	22.2	17.2
weighted average	27.5	24.7	18.2
Growth rate of exports			
unweighted average	5.2	5.6	3.4
weighted average	10.9	9.2	6.1
Growth rate of real per capita GDP			
unweighted average	1.4	1.0	-0.3
weighted average	4.3	4.0	0.1

Source: Compiled using data from *WEO* (May 1997, 57).

Country	1971–1980		1982–1989		1990–1997	
	Average rate of		Average rate of		Average rate of	
	inflation	growth	inflation	growth	inflation	growth
Canada	8.0	4.6	5.2	3.3	1.7	1.5
France	9.6	3.6	5.8	2.1	2.1	1.4
Italy	14.0	3.1	8.9	2.4	5.0	1.1
All industrial countries	9.5	3.1	4.3	3.0	2.9	2.2

governments pay out more for services but also receive much more since they tax nominal incomes in addition to what they expropriate from savers by taxing nominal interest incomes. They also pay more on new borrowings but they pay out less on outstanding debt. Labor gets more from firms by adjusting wages to inflation but pays more to the same firms for goods and services. It is the same for raw material suppliers. To put it all into perspective, let us suppose that there is a sudden rise in the costs of raw materials, labor and capital. This will cut business profits. In the absence of world competition, firms will compensate by raising prices of goods and services. The resulting inflation will cut the real costs of these inputs. On the other hand, if these costs were to fall, business profits would rise and new investment would push up the costs of labor, raw materials, land, and capital. What about borrowers and lenders? As long as the nominal rate of growth (inflation plus real) of GDP is equal to the nominal rate of interest, the division of the national income remains unchanged. In short, borrowers gain when the real rate of interest is negative, while lenders gain when it is positive. Over the last two decades, for how many years was the real rate negative? During the 1970s![3] Thus, when upon the advice of bankers, governments intervene to fight inflation, instead of stopping it from accelerating upward, they upset the natural equilibrating force and hurt one group. Guess which one?[4] Anyway, let us leave the relationship between inflation and growth there for the time being. I will return to the supposed negative link between inflation and economic performance in the section on statistical analyses.

THE SITUATION OF THE LATE 1970s: A CONJECTURE

The examination of the data in the preceding section, albeit cursory, turns up no evidence that the new orthodoxy was a spur for economic growth. Yet we must admit that the world economy experienced difficulties in the late 1970s. In the early 1980s, it was plunged into a nasty recession; this much is not in dispute. However, having found no valid explanation for the recession in the wage-inflation theory, I now offer my own conjecture.

Following the massive balance of payments deficits in the Unites States and the end of the Bretton Woods Agreement in the early 1970s, the world economy experienced two oil shocks. The first was in 1973–1974, the other in 1979–1980. On a basis of 1975 = 100, the indices (nominal and real) of the price of oil were as follows:

	1973	1974	1978	1979
Nominal Price Index				
OPEP reference price	22	100	118	205[1]
world average fob price	22	100	117	215[1]
Real Price Index				
OPEP reference price	29	102	96	138[1]
world average fob price	40	112	95	145[1]

[1] IV-Quarter 1979.

The price of oil continued to rise until 1981; it remained high until its brutal fall in 1986. These two massive shocks in the price of one of the principal energy inputs of the world economy are reflected quite clearly in the movements of the GNP/GDP deflator in Figure 5.1. In developed market economies, the CPI passed from the 1969–1972 average of 5.1% to 11% between 1973 and 1975. In developing market economies, it went from 8.9% to 19.0% over the same period. Because of the oil shocks, industries in industrial countries adapted, oil consumption rose very little from 1973 to 1979, but fell significantly during the 1980s. Table A5.4 and Figure 5.3 depict the situation before and after the oil shocks. In fact, comparing Figures 5.2, 5.3, and Table A5.4, one can almost see the positive correlation between oil consumption and economic growth found by Beaudreau (1995).

Figure 5.3
OPEP Nominal Reference Price Index: 1973–1993

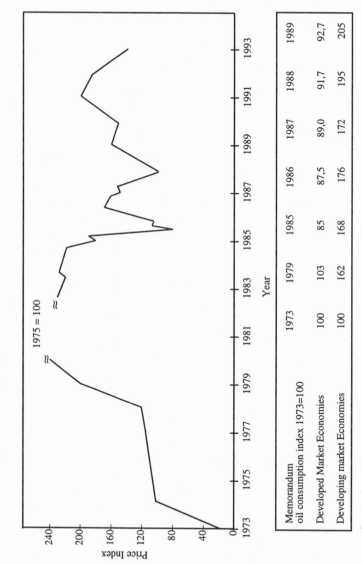

Memorandum oil consumption index 1973=100	1973	1979	1985	1986	1987	1988	1989
Developed Market Economies	100	103	85	87,5	89,0	91,7	92,7
Developing market Economies	100	162	168	176	172	195	205

Source: Compiled using data from *WEO* (May 1990, 95).

As industries passed along the oil price increases to consumers, the reaction of governments in the G7 group, except Canada, was to institute a restrictive monetary policy; Canada came on board in the third quarter of 1979. Incidentally, the contraction in the money supply, shown in Table A5.5, was more severe in the United States and the United Kingdom, precisely the two countries where the rates of growth of GDP were the lowest during 1979–1982.

Concomitant to the contraction of the money supply, nominal and real interest rates, shown in Table A5.6, rose sharply between 1978 and 1981. Gross fixed investment, as a percentage of GNP, fell. Except in Japan, the rate of change of this variable became negative in every country in the G7 group. As G7 governments moved to a contraction mode, their economies received a chill. Real domestic demand fell (Table A5.7). The story was similar in all industrial countries (Figure 5.4), where domestic demand and capacity utilization fell. The public deficit (as a percentage of GDP) rose by 26% in the G7 group by 1981, while in of all industrial countries it rose by 54%. Thus, all industrialized economies plunged into recession.

The recession was in fact a worldwide phenomenon. At the same time, in developing oil exporting economies, the real growth rate of GDP fell from an average of 5.5% during 1971–1979 to 1.4% in 1980 and to -0.5% in 1981. In developing oil importing countries, the rates for the same periods were 5.6%, 4.1%, and 1.4%, respectively. The price of primary products (except oil) fell by 15.6% by 1981; manufactured products prices fell by 5.0% (*Etude* 1981–1982, 69). The balance of payments (in current prices) of developing oil exporting countries improved, but that of oil importing economies went from a deficit of $23.9 billion to $69 billion in 1980. In Eastern Europe, a similar situation was observed (*Etude* 1979–1980, 43).

In summary, the oil shocks seemed to have been the main cause of the inflationary surge of the late 1970s. The monetarist reaction of G7 governments was to contract the money supply and raise real interest rates. Pessimistic expectations set in; business depressed investment and domestic demand fell. Labor reacted to inflation by demanding higher wages, and unit labor costs rose in response to higher wages and falling output. But even after the wage rate growth had fallen by almost 50% by 1982, output continued to fall. Since the wage rate stayed low but economic growth remained sluggish in the G7 and in all industrial countries, I conclude that my conjecture is more plausible than the assertions of the wage-inflation theory.

THE PRELIMINARY IMPACTS

The growth of the public debt and a mistaken view of the relationship between wage and inflation seem to explain, at least in part, the zeal behind the new orthodoxy. Whether justified or not, its application nevertheless has enormous consequences. In order to appreciate its impacts on the world

Figure 5.4
Indices of Domestic Investment as a Percent of GDP and
Capacity Utilization: Industrial Countries

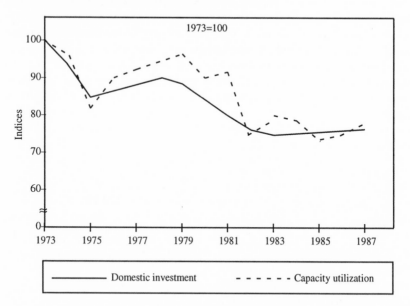

economy, I turn toward the determination, albeit preliminary, of who loses and gains from its application. I begin with a preliminary assessment of the impact of globalization, to be followed by a similar one for downsizing and restructuring.

Globalization

The projected benefits of globalization were essentially massive financial transfers, increased and diversified international trade, the reduction of sovereign debt, improvements in balance of payments, among others. These developments were supposed to be followed by explosive economic growth. These predictions will now be examined to see to what extent they have been either fulfilled or are likely to be realized. But beforehand, let me remind the reader once more that the data span a relatively short period; hence the qualification preliminary, although, I believe nevertheless that in the cases of the United States, United Kingdom, Latin America, and Africa, the data set seems sufficiently long to at least determine the general trend.

Resources Transferred

Tables A5.8 and A5.9 in the Appendix to this chapter show the net resource transfer to poorer regions during the 1980s, both as a percentage of GDP and in absolute amounts.

The tables are quite revealing in the sense that, on the one hand, the most indebted countries (Argentina, Bolivia, Brazil, Columbia, Chile, Ecuador, Ivory Coast, Mexico, Morocco, Nigeria, Peru, the Philippines, Uruguay, Venezuela, and the former Yugoslavia) were net exporters of capital during the 1980s. On the other, the bulk of the outflow of capital went to Western Asia, whose success in terms of growth, I have already said, was not initiated by foreign capital inflow. Nonetheless, by 1996 Asia was receiving some 49% of the total net private capital flow to developing contries. Indeed, this figure seems to indicate that foreign capital generally follows growth rather than the other way around.

Trade

During the 1982–1992 period, the value of exports of developed market economies as a whole increased from $1.6 trillion to $2.6 trillion, i.e., a 124% increase. At the same time, their imports increased by 120.3%, leaving them with an improvement in their current account balance. The situation in countries in transition remained virtually unchanged up to 1991; if anything, their exports increased from $74.4 billion in 1982 to $75.3 billion in 1991, while their imports went from $65.1 to $74.5 billion during the same period. On the other hand, the developing market economies registered an increase of 81.8% (i.e., from $506.9 billion to $921.5 billion) in their exports. At the same time, their imports rose by 95.1%, leaving them with a deficit in the current account balance over the period (*Etude* 1993, 403–07).

The trends in trade volume and value are not surprising. However, to pinpoint the impact of globalization more accurately, I truncate the period into two subperiods: 1988–1992 and 1984–1988, avoiding the disturbances of the 1982 recession. On this basis, Latin America's exports increased by about 6% per year between 1988 and 1992, but the rate was about zero during 1984–1988. Under the same conditions, Africa's exports went up by 9.7% during 1988–1992 to compare with -4.3% during the 1984–1988 period. The situation in Western Asia was similar to that of Africa, whereas in Eastern and Southern Asia, exports increased at a rate of 15.3% per year the 1988–1992 period, compared with a rate of 18.7% per year over 1984–1988. Hence, globalization did not affect the latter region's trade, but it can be said that elsewhere its impact on trade was positive. From 1990 to 1997, the trade volume in goods and services of advanced economies increased at about 6.2% per year, compared with 5.0% per year between 1979 and 1988. During the same period, that of developing economies increased at 8.7% per year, compared with 2.1% per year during the 1979–1988 period. However, over the same period the terms of trade of nonfuel goods and primary products producers was negative, except for 1994 and 1995. The ten-year average (1990–1999) annual percentage change in the terms of trade of all developing countries is projected by the IMF to be around –0.6.

Trade Diversification

As to whether or not globalization encourages trade diversification, the answer is negative. Table A5.10 shows that the old pattern of the 1960s had not changed by much by the 1990s. More specifically, from 1980 to 1991, trade among developed market economies increased by some 10%; between developed and countries in transition it increased by 12.6%, but it decreased by 2% between developed and developing countries. Countries in transition did not manage to increase their trade with any other group, but substantially decreased it between themselves. Developing market economies reduced their trade with rich countries by almost 10% and increased it between themselves by over 4%. The story of Table A5.10 seems to be that the three blocks trade mainly among themselves. However, if anything, the impact of globalization on trade diversification seemed to have been an increase in trade among the rich countries and among rich and countries in transition. From 1990 to 1997, countries in transition increased their trade flows with advanced economies, and reduced them with all other groups.

Current Account Balance, Foreign Debt, and Currency Speculation

The impact of globalization on developing economies, in terms of the current account balance and debt, seems to fall short of the predictions. I show these in Tables A5.11 and A5.12. The current account balance was negative throughout the whole period. According to the IMF (*WEO* May 1997, 169), in 1994, the current account balance of all developing countries was $-24.0 billion. In 1997, it fell to $-112.5. The sovereign debt (Table A5.12) of these countries increased by 82% during the period under consideration, despite the much talked about power of globalization to reduce it (see the discussion on the relationship between inflation and the growth of the public debt in Chapter 4). So far the elimination of capital and exchange controls, together with reductions in trade barriers, have increased trade volumes, but not necessarily the concomitant benefits of trade. Instead, multinational corporations and investment houses have increased their power over national governments, even over governments in industrial countries, as exemplified by the wave of speculation against the Swedish krona and the French franc in 1995. This danger and the volatility of the foreign exchange market have compelled national governments to settle for the lowest common denominator, be it in wages, health, or education. I am not the first to voice such an opinion, however. Professor Paul Krugman, in a speech at the London School of Economics in June 1995, went as far as coining the term globaloney to describe globalization. Another observer, Professor Ajit Singh of Cambridge University, finds no evidence that globalization has been good for the West as a whole. To the extent that it is symbiotically linked to deflationary macroeconomic policies, he argues, it is positively harmful.

Over the 1980 decade, Tables A5.11 and A5.12 show two revealing facts: Increasing imbalance in current accounts and increasing short and long term foreign debts. The combination of bank lending and portfolio investment in bonds and equities have been sufficiently large to finance the current account deficits. I see two likely consequences of these developments: Potential upheavals in this global market and the eventual need for new regulations. A huge and unregulated international capital market is bound to be very volatile. A sudden change in any country, due to market rumors (true or false) or to reactions to a policy change, may greatly disturb its economy. Incidentally, this danger is well illustrated by events following the stock market crash of October 1987 and by those observed in Mexico in December 1994 and in Asia in 1997. Since portfolios are now internationalized, asset holders may decide at any time to change their composition for whatever reason. What I mean is that should they suddenly decide to reduce their dollar or any currency holdings, the surge may give rise to a sudden and sharp deterioration in the position of these currencies.

The process through which a country may end up by losing its foreign exchange reserves or even go into debt is depicted in Figures 5.5 (a) and (b). In Figure 5.5 (a), I show the initial demand curve DD for foreign exchanges in country A, for example, whose currency is the peso. The supply curve of foreign exchanges is given by SS. If the foreign exchange market was in equilibrium, the quantity E_e would have changed hands at the equilibrium rate e^* pesos/ dollar. But here, I suppose that the government, or the central bank of country A, maintains an official exchange rate e_o, which is below the equilibrium rate. This causes the peso to be overvalued and, consequently, there exists an excess demand equal to the difference between E_d and E_s. This means that importers or speculators in country A demand E_d units of foreign exchanges, but exporters are only willing to supply E_s units at the official rate. Also, at e_o imports are deemed too cheap and exports too expensive. This situation may produce other symptoms as well, such as shortages of dollar reserves, deficit in the current account, price distortions, and it might be fueling a black market in dollars. In order to keep the rate e_o, the government would have to make the amount of the excess demand available each period; otherwise, there would be a constant pressure to devalue the peso. As no government likes to devalue, it might take a speculative attack to force its hands.

A speculative attack here may mean that those holding peso assets decide to convert them into dollars just before the imminent devaluation. Once they join up with the importers, the demand curve DD shifts to D_f D_f, and the excess demand at e_o increases. If now the government is unable to supply the excess demand at e_o, the peso will have to be devalued to e_f. As was the case in Mexico in December 1994, under pressure, the government wanted to established a 30% floating band, centered around e^*. But speculators had an other idea. They forced a devaluation of more than 100%. The country could not produce the extra foreign exchange demanded. In order to avoid all the consequences of that, an emergency loan package had to be arranged for Mexico. The economy received a devastating shock, and its foreign debt went up over-night. Here, however, one can say that the speculators precipitated an overdue correction. According to the neoclassical economics rationale, whether exporters are selling the sweet water supply of

Figure 5.5
Operations of the Foreign Exchange Market

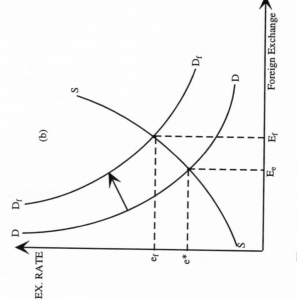

(a)

At the official rate e_0, the peso is overvalued exemplified by the excess demand ($E_d - E_s$). To maintain e_0, the central bank must supply ($E_d - E_s$). Otherwise speculators shift demand & devalue the peso. The exchange rate rises to e_f.

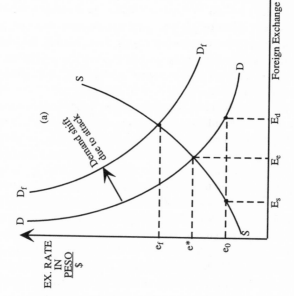

(b)

The market is in equilibrium (E_e, e^*). A speculative attack devalues the currency. To maintain the exchange rate, the Central Bank loses reserves or country must borrow a broad.

country A in order to import champagne, the laws of supply and demand must be obeyed. To avoid such hasty and disruptive actions, the exchange rate should be set by the market.

However, a country may find itself in deep trouble even when these laws are obeyed. Consider Figure 5.5 (b). The market is in equilibrium at E_e and e^*. But a speculative attack occurs, for whatever reason, even a false rumor. The currency must be devalued just the same. Whether the government feels that the attack is justified or not, it must come up with the excess foreign exchange demanded by the market. For example, as of July 1997, the Thai Central Bank reported that it had some $32 billion in reserves. One month later, the IMF and the Pacific Rim countries had to supply Thailand with a $16 billion loan to defend its currency, the baht. Despite that, the baht was devalued by more than 20% against the dollar by September, and the foreign debt to GDP ratio of Thailand rose to about 125%. Prior to that, Thailand was viewed as a growth model. But its uncontrolled finance companies exaggerated in borrowing abroad (from Western bankers with excess cash) to finance the construction of skyscrapers. Clearly, it is dangerous to borrow in a foreign currency, convert the loan into a local currency, and invest it in some questionable investment scheme. Speculators can just compare the amount a country has to pay on its foreign debt at a particular date and the amount of its reserves. Insufficient reserves are enough to trigger an attack. If an uncontrolled financial sector exaggerates, its trouble quickly becomes the country's trouble; the speculators know fully well that the government will surely intervene to bail out an overexposed financial sector.

When the speculators had finished with Thailand, they turned against the Indonesian rupiah. As in the case of Thailand, Indonesia had a surplus of $970 million and some $21 billion in foreign reserves as of May 1997. Did those figures depict the true situation? If yes, then the currency was not overvalued. However, by August of that year, the central bank was buying its own rupiah at the tune of $200 million a week in an attempt to neutralize the attack of speculators who had believed a rumor that a free float was imminent. The government was compelled to institute, and then scrapped, a 12% intervention band. Nonetheless, the rupiah still plunged against the dollar, costing some $55 billion in foreign debt, including a loan package of $37 billion from the IMF. When observers ask why, since the economy's fundamentals were deemed right? A jittery market, was the reply. This kind of answer reflects either ignorance or phony economic magnitudes.

Many other countries in the region underwent a similar experience lately, despite having fought similar rearguard actions against speculators. In August 1997, the Malaysian ringgit and the Singapore dollar had significantly fell against the dollar. By mid-October, the cumulative average rise in exchange rates exceeded 30% in Indonesia and Thailand, and 20% in Malaysia and the Philippines, and 6% in Taiwan. Until October 1997, South Korea, for example, was considered by bankers, the IMF, and the self-styled Western analysts, prosperous enough to be included among industrial countries. By December 1997, that country was on the verge of defaulting on its financial obligations, and required a $57 billion emergency loan from the IMF. Then, the same Western experts who, three months earlier, were lauding the Korean capitalist miracle, became busy predicting its death knell. The same people, who could not even see the crisis coming a few months earlier, suddenly had an explanation for it. It is not caused by globalization, they had the temerity to say, but by bad management. Thus, when a sizable portion of asset value evaporates (*The Guardian Weekly*, January 25, 1998, estimates the Asian asset value lost at $1 trillion so far), when the sovereign debt increases overnight (after many years of painstaking effort to reduce it), when the rosy growth rates must be revised downward, it is due to mismanagement and not to an uncontrolled market. Therefore, the Asian crisis, which is still at its beginning, is being blamed on Asian corruption and mismanagement. There must be some truth in these tales, but surely they do not explain the whole drama. The unregulated international financial system itself must have helped triggering the financial debacle. How else can the closure of 56 finance companies in Thailand, 16 banks in the Philippines, and 14 merchant banks in Korea be explained?

To shed more light on this burgeoning crisis, let us consider again the case of South Korea. The Korean people have been working hard, creating wealth since the mid-1960s. Up to October 1997, the Korean economy was the eleventh biggest in the world. Bankers and speculators were stumbling on each other to loan money to Koreans. From 1995 to 1996, Korean entities issued some $16 billion worth of bonds on the international market, that is, 38% of the total money raised by the tigers, according to the IMF (*International Capital Markets 1997*, 77). However, as in the case of Mexico in 1994, a significant share of the total foreign debt of Korea, as well as that of the other tigers, is short-term and dollar-denominated. And as it was to be expected, when money is flowing, people become greedy. Corrupt politicians and the herd investment mentality encouraged the money centers, credit rating agencies on Wall Street and elsewhere to overlook all signals of danger. But when the massive dollar-denominated payments came due at the end of 1997, and that international banks and investors decided not to continue extending credit, it became clear to everyone that debtors and the government did not and never had enough dollars to pay off. All of a sudden, we begin to hear from, for example, Credit Lyonnais Securities that only 13% of the Korean nonfinancial firms were solvent (*The Guardian Weekly*, January 11, 1998), and that the conglomerates or chaebols are collapsing under the weight of their debt. Share prices plummeted. The exchange rate of the won rose 50% against the U.S. dollar, and urgent calls went out to the IMF.

The IMF went in with a $57 billion loan package, destined to pay off the foreign banks and the institutional investors and, in exchange, Korea was forced to deregulate and to liberalize, that is, the standard deflationary package. Put differently, the IMF simply rescued the institutional investors from the consequences of their unwise decisions, without however asking them to change their behavior. What does all of this imply for Korea? Korean shareholders, depositors, and workers will in the end be the net losers as the country moves to implement the austerity package required by the IMF. Now, since foreigners can now acquire up to 55% of any Korean business, while the won has lost about 50% of its value against the U.S. dollar, Korean firms are up for grab by foreigners at bargain prices. Thus, a significant share of the wealth created by Koreans over the last 30 years will fall on the laps of Western capitalists.

We must now extend this analysis to the other tigers in order to proffer the potentiality of the unfolding crisis. Among other things, the tigers will, in the short term, face higher unemployment. Thailand, Malaysia, and South Korea may begin expelling their foreign workers; some 2 million might be affected. Next, these countries may well begin a round of competitive devaluation in the pursuit of the illusory export-led growth. Then, China, Japan, and the West would have to act in order to protect their market share. If, in addition, Japan decides to call off its loans from the West ($269 billion in U.S. treasury bonds and $258 billion in UK bonds), then the Asian storm will become truly global.

There are a few lessons to be learned from this unfolding crisis. First, attempts to create wealth from short-term foreign loans are always risky. Second, countries can not easily export their way out of trouble on the back of depreciating currencies. Last but not least, in an uncontrolled international financial market, footloose capital moving around the globe, from currency to currency, in search of higher and higher profits, does not bring about economic stability. It is ironic though that it now takes a George Soros, the speculator par excellence, to recognize that we now need greater regulation of the international financial market.[5]

To highlight the problem connected with currency speculations and the need for some minimum regulation, let me make a little digression into the derivative market. Derivatives are financial instruments whose values are derived from the value of some real assets, such as currencies, commodities, stocks, and bonds. One of their basic functions is to transfer and to spread risks, as well as the hedging of opportunities to individuals and institutions. The two most common forms of derivatives are *futures* and *options* contracts. A futures contract is a forward contract involving the obligation to purchase or to sell an Arrow-Debreu commodity or a financial instrument at a specified price, at some specified time in the future. A typical forward contract is one in which a party (a farmer) commits to sell, for example, 100,000 bushels of wheat, 3 months hence, at $2 a bushel to a buyer (a baker). The baker is sure to have the wheat when needed and knows now what it will cost him. The farmer can now buy equipment, supplies, and labor services to produce, and can even compute now his future profits, no matter what happens to the price of wheat. Both decrease their risks with this futures contract. A stock option, on the other hand, gives someone the right to sell or buy a specified stock or stocks at a specified price, on or before a set date in the future. For example, for an option premium of $15 a share, a buyer commits to take 100 shares of a stock at $100 a share within a specified time. Such call options exist on all major stocks, bonds, foreign currencies, and so on.

There is much talk about the easy money to be made on derivatives, but little is said about the risks involved. In the above wheat example, if in 3 months, the price of wheat rises to $3 a bushel, the farmer will lose an opportunity to make an additional $100,000; if the price falls to $1 a bushel, the baker will lose $100,000. In the case of the call option, the buyer might have bet that the price of the stock will rise to $150 a share. If he or she is right, he will earn $5,000 or 50% return, neglecting commissions, on his investment of $10,000. However, if the share price falls below $100, he can refuse to exercise the option and lose the investment of $1,500; if he exercises it, we can say that he will make 233% on the sum he risked. In the case of foreign currencies, someone may buy a position of $100,000 in a currency for future delivery, by putting a margin of $1,500. Now suppose at delivery time the currency is depreciated by 3%, something that may happen at any minute. Then, he or she will be liable for a loss of $3,000, that is, twice his or her initial investment. These examples are given only to show how easy it is for traders controlling billions of pension funds of other people, to make big gain or to suffer huge losses. Even the financier George Soros, the man reputed to have the Midas touch did manage to lose more than $500 million in 1994 on a single currency.

Since the collapse of the Bretton Woods System of fixed-exchange rates, the above type of speculation on foreign currencies has dramatically increased the volatility of exchange rates. The need for regulation is well illustrated by what can and has already happened in the futures markets. There, a big buyer can buy and hoard a huge volume of a commodity on the spot market (thus restricting supply) and, at the same time, accumulate significant positions on the futures market of the same commodity (thus increasing demand). This way, he can force the price upward and make a killing. This kind of fraud, called cornering or manipulating the market, vividly illustrates a simple fact: the development of new markets always needs a concomitant set of regulations to prevent frauds.

The danger represented by an uncontrolled currency market may be resumed as follows. The enormous volume of transactions involved in the international currency market can easily overwhelm the capacity of any government or institution to react to a market disturbance. As the World Bank has observed, at times of system overload, credit risks can significantly increase as the completion of transactions becomes doubtful. The reason for this is that clearing systems typically deal with the failures of participants. Their bad debt is normally covered by a guarantor, which may be a clearing house or a government, since all transactions involving failed participants have to be unwound. Alternatively, the unwinding of all transactions with failed participants may leave an unexpected pattern of uncovered exposures, leading to more and greater failures. Who is then supposed to be the last resort lender in such cases? The very size and scope of the present international financial system raise serious doubts as to which national or international authorities are responsible, or capable of injecting sufficient liquidities in it in the event of a serious crisis.

If anything, the overall situation is getting worse as time passes. In 1989, the total volume of international transactions was estimated at $718 billion per day. In 1995, the Bank of International Settlements estimated it at $1.571 trillion per day; 84% of which involves foreign exchanges and 16% involves bonds. These transactions are going on day and night in London (39%), New York (16%), Tokyo (10.2%), Singapore (6.6%), Hong Kong (5.7%), Switzerland (5.3%), and in other places (17.2%) as distant as France and South Africa. Rates between major currencies may change up to 20 times per minute, and a given participant may carry up to 4,000 operations in a 24-hour period. In the midst of all of this, it is not uncommon for the amount involved in one transaction to exceed the capital of a participant. Furthermore, considering that transactions are executed during the working hours of the place where they originate, say, point A, to be settled in point B at some other time, such transactions are subject to both liquidity and Herstatt risks. The latter risk arises when a participant runs the risk of failing before making a settlement; the cases of the Bank of Credit and Commerce and Baring, for example, illustrate the nature of the Herstatt risk. We must, therefore, be mindful of the fact that in the case of a crisis, insufficient, or delayed actions in one country could spread the crisis to other countries at electronic speed. Because of this, together with the increasing volatility of the international capital market, policy makers must now spend more of their time thinking of issues of stability and systemic risk. If financial crises are to be prevented, regulatory measures must be put in place. That is, measures to ensure an adequate capital base for financial institutions; to ensure that clearing houses and settlement systems function safely; to place limits on market volatility, and to coordinate procedures for crisis management. As a matter of fact, the Agreement on Bank Capital Adequacy reached in the forum of Basle Committee on Bank Supervisors in July 1988 is step in the right direction. The recommendations of the International Organization of Securities Commission (IOSCO), which met in Venice in September 1989, are another. As time passes, or as more crises develop, we may finally understand why real markets cannot function well without regulation.

The so-called Asian crisis can teach two main lessons to those who want to learn. The first is about the gist of Keynes's contribution. He is associated only with deficit spending, while the main Keynesian insights are about the potential failure of markets to clear, and the imbalance between the real economy and the whims of unregulated financial markets. The second lesson is that for freer trade in goods and services to coexist with real growth and maximum employment levels, controls on capital movements and bounded exchange rate fluctuations are preconditions. This is what the Bretton Woods System was all about. Unfortunately, that system was enchored on the U.S. dollar rather than on world credit; curiously, currency fluctuations have been more violent, and growth has been sluggish since 1973, precisely the year when the United States killed the system.

What About Fiscal Consolidation?

As indicated earlier, in 1994, the ratio of tax revenue to GDP in industrial countries amounted to 44%. During the same year, however, the ratio of government expenditures to GDP was 50%. According to traditional Keynesianism, attempts to reduce government deficit may cause recessions. In other words, if a government suddenly applies the brakes, even in pursuit of a well-intentioned effort to balance its budget, it will throw people out of work and cut off the flow of funds to its economy. Globalization claims that this is false. When government budgets are in balance, the business community is impressed by the apparent determination of governments to stop wasting tax money. Businessmen and investors will spend more on renovating plants, updating equipment, and investing for future growth. Does this hypothesis hold water? In 1996, McDermott and Wescott decided to put it to the test. They defined a successful fiscal consolidation as a continuous fall in $\dot{n}$ (the rate of change of the debt to GDP ratio) or at least a 3% fall in n three years after fiscal consolidation began, but without causing a recession. They then examined the results of 74 episodes of fiscal consolidation in industrial countries over the 1970–1995 period in order to see if the concept has any substance. According to the results, 64% of the episodes failed; 16% were inconclusive; and 18% were successful.[6] Among the 18% success rate, however, the experience of New Zealand figured rather prominently. The reader may get a real feel for what success means here simply by ascertaining what New Zealanders now think of fiscal consolidation, or by checking the preliminary results below.

It is early to draw definitive conclusions on globalization, however, if history is a guide, since the mid-19th century, the game has been the same: Trade barriers go up when one is threatened by international competition. In the meantime, one grows faster behind the barriers. Once one becomes the dominant player, one asks that trade barriers and regulations be removed. Of course, this is not a plea for protectionism. I simply note that during the Golden Age of 1945–1973, ordered trade (i.e., within the framework of rules) was only one of the three pillars of economic growth. The others were Keynesianism and post-war reconstruction. There is no doubt that internationalism and ordered and fair trade are to be preferred to nationalism and protectionism, but history suggests that it is growth and rising incomes that lead to increased trade rather than the reverse.

Downsizing and Restructuring (D&R)

In the United States, the impacts of restructuring translate into increases in low paying jobs and falling hourly wages, erosion of civil liberties and increased social insecurity. During the 1980s, the number of low paid workers rose to the point that one third of the labor force is now included in the poor category due to their low salaries. About one-fifth of American children now live below the poverty line, 10% of them in complete deprivation. Meanwhile, corporations that fail to deliver to shareholders have found refuge in downsizing and restructuring. When in March 1996, *The New York Times* reported that since the early 1970s some 40 million jobs have been lost through D&R, President Clinton instructed the chairman of the President's Council of Economic Advisers to undertake a formal study of the impact of D&R. Strangely enough, the study reached the conclusion that D&R may have been positive for the economy. This conclusion seems to be based on the finding that people who lost their jobs in the 1980s have been more quickly absorbed into the workforce rather than those who lost their jobs in the 1970s. The study additionally claims that 68% of all the new jobs created over the last two years have been in industries that pay above average wages, forgetting that the average itself is way below what it used to be. On the other hand, the consulting firm, Mercer Management, has studied the effects of D&R on 131 firms over the 1985–1990 period.[7] It found that only 27% are doing better now than before downsizing and restructuring.

The New York Times of October 1995 estimated that the gross value of mergers and acquisitions has multiplied by more than ten during the 1980s. This jump was facilitated by the lack of controls and by the willingness of banks to make short-term loans available for the purpose. It follows that during the period, a large share of the return on productive capital went to debt service, while the pressure to raise short-term profits was translated into massive lay-offs. During the fourth quarter of 1995, some 18% of the 108,000 layoffs of that year were triggered by merger and acquisition activities. Thus, instead of financing productive investment and innovations, increased profits (due to layoffs) fueled stock speculations and debt service. After all of this, there is now a new trend to demerge so as to further increase profits.

Meanwhile, income distribution has worsened. In the 1970s, the top 5% of family incomes was ten times those of the lowest 5%. In 1993, the ratio stood at 15 to 1. According to *U.S. News and World Report* (January 22, 1996), between 1983 and 1989, the richest 1% got 81.6% of the increase in the national wealth, while the bottom 80% had to make do with 1.2%. A similar incongruity was observed in compensation packages for CEOs of big corporations, leading the D&R revolution. They had not forgotten themselves. Going back to 1975, the ratio of the average CEOs salary to that of the average worker was 41 to 1 (i.e., $326,000/$8,000); in 1980, it was estimated at 42 to 1; in 1992, it was 148 to 1, and it jumped to 185 to 1 ($3,700,000/ $20,000) in 1994. Official 1990 figures taken from the *The Guardian Weekly* of May 1992 indicate that 33.6 million Americans were living below the poverty line of $7,650 per year for a household of four. But 1% of the richest households owned 40% of America's total wealth.

Despite the obvious deterioration in the social situation in the United States and in other OECD countries, the OECD (i.e., the organization) relentlessly scorns its members for not implementing the new orthodoxy fast enough. Recently, Switzerland came under severe criticisms for not privatizing its regional banks. Two of Canada's provinces, Ontario and Quebec, received blame for not deconstructing fast enough. France is tagged a bad student for not reducing the number of public employees, social expenditures, and the minimum wage fast enough. The organization went as far as arguing that governments should not focus on income distribution at any given moment. Because, during a given year, according to the OECD, many wage earners earn little, but in subsequent years, a large proportion of them passes to higher income levels. To add insult to injury, the organization cites England for being its best student. There, we are told, union monopolies are broken; firms' profits are up; real wage growth rates are below productivity growth; and firms are freer to hire and fire. This is the right way to go to stimulate job creation (see Halimi 1996). Meanwhile, as the European Union is pushing to meet the criteria of the Maastricht Treaty, the number of unemployed has risen to about 20 million and the number of poor people jumped to 55 million.

This might just be a coincidence, but The World Economic Forum (1996), under the chairmanship of the Prince of D&R, Jeffrey Sachs, listed England first on its list of winners for international competitiveness. Why? England satisfies the criteria of the new orthodoxy better than any other country in Europe. At the same time, however, the 2,000 CEOs polled by Mr. Sachs place England 35 on 49 in terms of educational service delivery; 48 on 49 for saving and investment; 5 on 49 for its attitude on the precepts of the new orthodoxy; 4 on 49 in terms of labor market flexibility and 2 on 49 in terms of the costs of overseas communications.[8] On the other hand, a recent study by the Confederation of British Industry (CBI) shows that Britain's most vulnerable workers have suffered pay cuts over the last two years; in particular, the number of people earning less than $3.70 per hour whose ranks swelled by 20% during 1994–1995. Furthermore, the level of schooling of 16 to 19-year-olds is below the European average; income disparities which widened during 1995–1996 are increasing faster than in most OECD countries. *The Guardian Weekly* of January 25, 1998 reports that one in five persons lives on less than half the average income, compared with one in ten in 1979. What is going on here? Is the OECD operating on a different set of beliefs than the CBI? I also note in passing that, over the last 10 years, OECD's operating budget of F1.7 billion has doubled, while none of its economic forecasts have proven right. Why shouldn't an organization such as this one be among the first to be privatized?

In Latin America, the situation is mixed, with growth in some countries (Argentina, Chile, Honduras) and stagnation or deterioration elsewhere. When we add the Caribbean area, we see that the growth rates of production in 1991 and 1992 were 3% and 2.2%, respectively. Income per head remained virtually unchanged. The collapse of December 1994 robbed Mexico of its title of next best student of restructuring (a title given by the OECD), and revealed the fragility of uncontrolled foreign exchange markets. All over Latin America and the Caribbean, the reform package took its toll on society. Unemployment rose, wages fell, social expenditures fell, and about 40% of the population of the region plunged into extreme poverty. I cannot claim that this is solely due to restructuring, only that so far restructuring in the region is a flop.

In Africa the terms of trade improved during two years (1984 and 1987) and worsened during the remaining years of the decade spanning 1982–1992. As I have already shown (Table A5.11), Africa's current account balance remained in the red throughout the whole period. Short and long-term debts increased by 55% and 115%, respectively during the 1982–1992 period. Its economic growth picture was comparable to that of Latin America, but its real per capita growth rate, except for the year 1985, was negative, whereas its average rate for the 1972–1981 period was 0.3%.

In the economies in transition the overall economic picture is almost tragic. Output per head has fallen by about one third in the states of the former USSR, and by about one quarter in the rest of Eastern Europe since the imposition of the new orthodoxy. More specifically, in Poland, gross capital formation in 1992 was about 80% of its 1988 value; the unemployment rate stood at 14%; and the inflation rate was at 43%. In Hungary, gross capital formation in 1992 was about 75% of what it was in 1989; unemployment and inflation rates were at 12.3% and 23%, respectively. In the Czech Republic, for the same variables the figures were 70%, 5.1%, and 10.8%, respectively. Table A5.13 depicts the growth picture in that region up to 1993.

In the G7 group, the flagship of the new orthodoxy, the growth rate of the money supply fell from 5% in 1989 to zero in 1992. The rate of unemployment rose from 6.5% in 1989 to 8.3% in 1993. Short and long-term interest rates remained at about 8% in 1993, that is, slightly higher than in 1986. Finally, the public deficit, as a percentage of GDP, went from 1.6% in 1989 to about 4.0% in 1993. In the midst of all of this, I note a singular contradiction, depicted in Tables A5.14 and A5.15. From 1980 to 1993, in peacetime, military expenditures, except in the United Kingdom, rose sharply. More astoundingly, Table A5.15 shows that from 1985 to 1993, firms in the G7 countries dramatically increased their net worth. Market capitalization, that is, the total amount of various securities (bonds, debentures, and stocks) issued by corporations in these lean years tells very clearly who the beneficiaries of the new orthodoxy really are.

In the European Union the exigencies of GD&R are encapsulated in the Maastricht criteria of 3/60. In order to meet these criteria, members of the European Union had to strain their economies during the last decade. As the deadline for admission into the EMU approaches, candidates were high-strung as it would have been absurd not to qualify for admission, mostly after having delt such a terrible blow to their economies. As of March 1998, 4 out of 15 met both criteria, but 11 members were declared admissible, while 4 have opted to stay out of the first wave. However, among the 11, only 3 (France, Luxemburg, and Finland) meet the 3/60 rule, while others such as Germany and Italy had to use clever if not dubious accounting manipulations to reach the deficit criterion. As pointed out in the previous chapter, the 3/60 rule appears quite arbitrary, and its impact on economic growth is not yet visible. If we consider two 10-year period averages, 1979–1988 and 1989–1998, that is, before and after the inception of the orthodoxy, the overall result is difficult to judge. In terms of the annual percentage changes over the two periods, unit labor costs in the EU fell from 5.6 to 3.7, the GDP deflator and consumer prices went from 7.8 to 3.5 and from 7.5 to 3.6, respectively (*WEO*, October 1997, 159–160). However, during the same two periods, the annual percentage change of real domestic demand and gross fixed capital formation also fell from 2.3 to 1.8 and from 2.2 to 1.8, respectively. In terms of real GDP growth rates, among the 4 out of 15 that have met both Maastricht criteria, 3 of them had lower rates than Greece that had a deficit of 4% and a debt ratio of 108.7%. In fact, the average real growth rate for all 15 members fell from 2.3% during 1979–1988 to 2.1% during 1989–1998 (*WEO*, October 1997, 148). Meanwhile, the number of unemployed persons soars to 19 million officially. In the next chapter, I show that this 19 million figure is grossly underestimated.

In summary, therefore, I have shown that the new orthodoxy is articulated around three well orchestrated subprograms. Globalization, which promised explosive trade and economic growth rates, but which ended up by creating a monstrous financial international market, responsible to no one and to no institution, not even to all the central banks of the G7 group put together. And downsizing and the restructuring of national economies to the advantage of large corporations, at the expense of labor and the needy. However, in the orchestrated and rehearsed official discourse, the story is quite different. The aim of globalization-downsizing-restructuring is, it is argued, to propel the world economy into a new golden era of economic growth. Table A5.16 reflects the overall impacts of the new orthodoxy in terms of growth. There was some growth in developing market economies, but according to Beaudreau (1995), this is due to firms from rich countries moving out to low wage areas. There was also growth in Asia, but the likely explanation for that is well exposed in Rodrick's study. Thus far, this is what I have observed, but then again perhaps it is too early to tell.

THE EXPERIENCES OF CHILE AND NEW ZEALAND

Previously, I said that Chile and New Zealand were the first countries to have carried out field tests on the new orthodoxy. Is there any lesson to be learned from the experience of these two countries? Prior to reforms, both countries were experiencing an economic downturn. Both had an overregulated economy, inefficient agriculture, and a chronic balance of payments deficits. Following the 1982 recession, Pinochet's government introduced the new orthodoxy *manu forti,* supported by the extreme right of the political spectrum, (the opinion of the center and unions were simply not solicited). As I have already said, reforms began in agriculture and in the public sector. From the mid-1980s to 1994, Chile experienced impressive nominal economic growth rates, benefiting a minority of its citizens. I will have more to say about reforms in Chile in the next chapter. For now, suffice it to say that, economic growth has benefited a few; that is, the rich have become richer. But, as it is always observed, the rate of pollution increased two or three times faster than the growth rate of the economy. In terms of the welfare of the population, the costs of old-age protection felt entirely on workers, while only 78% of the workforce is thus far covered; projections indicate that many will end up with acquired benefits less than the guaranteed minimum. If the average citizen is not worse off today, it is because the two governments that followed Pinochet's regime have made a conscious effort to smooth out the rough edges of the new orthodoxy.

In New Zealand, the reforms initiated in 1984 were applied in stages. During the 1984–1987 period, the financial market was deregulated and agricultural transfers were eliminated. The 1987–1990 period was devoted to the privatization of public enterprises. In 1990, the former Minister of Finance, Ruth Richardson, presented what was called then the mother of all budgets. It called for reductions between 5% to 27%, depending on specific programs, in social transfers, such as family assistance, unemployment insurance, old-age pensions, health, and education, among others. In 1991, all social legislations protecting workers were abolished; in other words, the labor market was deregulated, and the union movement was decimated. What are the results thus far?

The answers one gets vary by sector. For the OECD, the World Bank, the IMF, the Heritage Foundation, and the right, everything is fine and on course. For those who are at the receiving end, that is, those at the lower end of the distribution of income, the Garden of Eden that New Zealand was in the 1960s, because of its pioneering social legislations, has been replaced by Dante's Inferno, to use the expression of Serge Halimi. What is the story in terms of numbers? As shown below, it is rather mixed.

	1983	1986	1991	1995	1996
Current account balance (% of GDP)	-4.2	-6.2	-2.1	-4.2	-5.5
Public deficit (% of GDP)	-6.8	-3.5	-2.4	3.0	3.0
Consumers' price index (in %)	3.8	17.0	1.8	3.5	2.1
Unemployment (in %)	5.7	4.0	10.9	6.3	6.2
Net public debt (% of GDP)	32.0	46.0	52.0	35.0	—
Real GDP growth (in %)	6.8	1.8	-1.8	3.4	2.7

As it can be seen, there have been improvements in current account balance, inflation, and public deficit, and deterioration elsewhere. What is of interest is the real growth rate of the economy. In 1983, just before reform began, the real growth rate stood at about 6.8%. However, it fell from there until 1991; from 1993, 1994, and 1995, growth rates were 4.6%, 6.3%, and 3.4%, respectively. For 1996, it was 2.7 %, and optimistic projections for the long term put it at no more than 3%. Hence, in terms of growth, New Zealand has performed less well than the average country in the region. There have been no visible improvements in the balance of payments, labor productivity growth is stagnant, poverty has increased, and the average citizen is now more insecure. Meanwhile, between 1984 and 1994, the growth rate per head fell by 10%. It is hard, therefore, to find a lesson to be learned from this experience.

STATISTICAL ANALYSES

In the previous sections, the reader was presented with an overview in tabular form. I have also commented a number of formal studies, namely, IMF's study on inflation, McDermott and Wescott's on debt reduction, and Mercer Management's study on restructuring. Everything leans in the same direction, it seems. That is, after reviewing the material, one does not become more confident in the ability of the new orthodoxy to deliver on its promises, but there remains rooms for disagreement. Fortunately though, the new orthodoxy also generates a few testable propositions that can be put to a formal test. I will now put three of them to the *between* and *within* column variance analysis test.[9]

Transition to Market Economy Versus Economic Performance

The new orthodoxy is categorical on the following pronouncement: The experiment with central planning (not dictatorship) is a failure on economic ground. Countries that were under such a regime must reverse their inward-looking legacy in order to catch up with the world economy, whose performance has been clearly demonstrated (*WEO* May 1997, 93–98). The countries in question took the challenge, and they are now up to seven years into the great transformation. What has been achieved?

The European Bank for Reconstruction and Development (EBRD) has recently used nine indicators to rate the progress of countries in transition toward restructuring, downsizing, and liberalization. These are all countries that had previously signed the obligations of Article VIII of the IMF's Articles of agreement. Those that were declared more advanced toward reform are the same that received a greater volume of direct foreign investment and a grade equal to or greater than 3.00. The less advanced ones received less direct foreign investment and a grade lower than 3.00. According to the logic of the new orthodoxy, therefore, we should then expect the more advanced ones to do better than the rest in terms of real economic growth.

I will now submit this to the variance test. Normally, I would have computed the average growth over the six-year period under consideration. However, many of these countries were at war at one time or another during the period, in particular those with lower grade. Since the evaluation was made in 1996, I decide to test the proposition for 1996. The Null Hypothesis reads as follows:

The Null Hypothesis: The variance estimate between group means (S_b) and the variance estimate within groups (S_w) were from the same population of countries in transition with respect to the variance of the population.

I then take random samples from both groups that are next analyzed in Table 5.2.

Table 5.2
Testing the Transition to Market Against Economic Performance

	Group I (grade p greater than 3.00)				Group II (grade p less than 3.00)		
Country	p ..	Growth of real GDP (in %) x	x^2	Country	p ..	Growth of real GDP (in %) x	x^2
Czech Rep.	3.4	4.2 0	17.64	Lithuania	2.9	3.50	12.25
Hungary	3.4	1.00	1.00	Russia	2.9	-2.80	7.84
Estonia	3.3	3.10	9.61	Albania	2.7	8.20	67.24
Poland	3.3	5.50	30.25	Kyrgyz Rep.	2.7	5.60	31.36
Slovak Rep.	3.2	7.00	49.00	Moldova	2.7	-8.00	54.00
Croatia	3.1	5.00	25.00	Kazakstan	2.6	1.00	1.00
Slovania	3.1	3.50	12.25	Macedonia	2.6	1.10	1.21
Latvia	3.1	2.50	6.25	Romania	2.6	4.10	16.81
	n = 8	---------	----------	Armenia	2.4	6.60	43.56
		31.80	151.00	Georgia	2.4	10.50	110.25
				Ukraine	2.4	-10.00	100.00
				Uzbekistan	2.4	1.60	2.56
				Azerbaijan	1.8	1.30	1.69
$S_b^2 = 23,64$				Belarus	1.8	2.00	4.00
$S_w^2 = 446.21$				Mongolia	—	3.00	9.00
Fcal = (23.64/1)446.21/21) = 1.11					n = 15	---------	----------
Fo.o5 = 4.32						27.70	472.77

Source: Compiled using growth data from *WEO* (May 1997, 106, 141, used by permission of the International Monetary Fund).

From the result and with the criterion Fo.o5, the Null Hypothesis can not be rejected. This means that no significant differences between them were found, because either the EBRD ranking does not really discriminate between the two samples or there is no significant difference to be found.[10]

Deficit-Debt Reduction Versus Economic Performance

The statement coming out of the new orthodoxy relative to deficit and debt reduction is unambiguous. Countries must reduce their operating deficit, or better, reduce the growth rate of their gross public debt to GDP ratio ($\dot{n}$) so as to increase economic performance. For this test I consider only countries for which I have better data, that is, those of the European Union, the United States, Japan, and Canada. As we all know, they have tried their best to deconstruct in an attempt to reduce this famous ratio over the last three or more years. Some have succeeded, others have failed. I then select two random samples from the two groups. Group I consisted of countries that have managed to reduce the growth rate of the ratio during three consecutive years (1995–1997). Group II comprised those whose gross debt to GDP has increased over the same period, as they were unable to reduce their operating deficit.

If, as claimed by the new orthodoxy, reduction in the ratio is a worthwhile exercise, then we would expect to find a real difference between the two groups in terms of economic performance. The Null Hypothesis in this case is:

Null Hypothesis: The variance estimate between sample means and the variance estimate within groups were from the same population with respect to the variance of the population.

Again, based on the result shown in Table 5.3, I have accepted the Null Hypothesis at the 5% level. I must therefore conclude that there is not a significant difference between the two groups.

Inflation Targeting Versus Economic Performance

As I have remarked in the last two chapters, there is a real frenzy in the boardrooms of central banks over the level of inflation. Accordingly, inflation rates over 2% send a shriving chill down the spine of the big players. This is the sign for not-so-big players, such as ministers of finance, bonds sellers, and so on, to begin the refrain: "Inflation is deadly to economic performance."

I then draw three random samples from 103 countries according to their average inflation rates over the 1990–1996 period. Group I consisted of 31 countries whose average inflation rates were less than 5%. Group II was made of 35 countries with average inflation rates between 5% and 12%. For theremaining 37 countries, their average rates were above 12%. I then performed two tests. In the first, all three groups were tested together against their average real growth rate of GDP over the seven-year period. In the second, I tested the low and moderate inflation groups against the same variable. In both tests, the acceptance criterion was the 1% level of significance.

This time around, the Null Hypothesis reads as follows:

Null Hypothesis (Ho1): The variance estimate between low, moderate and high inflation group means and the variance estimate within the three groups were from the same population with respect to the variance of the population.

As can be seen in Table 5.4, in the first test, the Null Hypothesis is rejected at the 1% level. On this basis, I conclude that there is a real difference among the three groups.

The purpose of the second test was to verify whether or not there is a significant difference between low and moderate groups. Hence the second Ho was:

Table 5.3
Testing the Level of Sovereign Debt Against Economic Performance

	Group I Countries with 3 consecutive years of debt reduction (1995–97)[1]			Group II Countries with 3 consecutive years of debt augmentation (1995–97)[1]	
	Growth rate of real GDP in 1997 (in %)			Growth rate of real GDP in 1997 (in %)	
Country	x	x^2	Country	x	x^2
Italy	1.00	1.00	Germany	2.30	5.29
The Netherlands	3.00	9.00	France	2.40	5.76
Belgium	2.30	5.29	UK	3.30	10.89
Sweden[2]	2.00	4.00	Spain	2.80	7.84
Denmark	2.70	7.29	Finland[3]	4.40	19.36
Greece	3.00	9.00	Luxembourg[3]	3.70	13.69
Portugal	3.30	10.89	United States	2.60	6.76
Ireland	6.30	39.69	Japan	3.00	9.00
Austria[2]	1.70	2.89	n = 8	---------	---------
Canada	3.50	12.25		24.50	78.59
n = 10	--------	---------			
	28.80	100.90			

$S_b^2 = 0.15$
$S_w^2 = 21.51$
Fcal = (0.15 / 1)/(21.51/ 16) = 0.11
F$_{0.05}$ = 4.49

[1]Based on information available up to March 1997; [2]Countries whose debt ratio increased slightly in 1996, but was lower in 1997 than 1995; [3]Countries whose debt ratio decreased slightly in 1996, but was higher in 1997 than 1995.

Source: Compiled using growth and debt data from from *WEO* (May 1997, 27, 132, used by permission of the International Monetary Fund).

Ho2: The variance estimate between low and moderate inflation group means and the variance estimate within the two groups were from the same population with respect to the variance of the population.

Again, as shown in the table above, Ho2 is also rejected at the 1% level. In other words, in terms of economic performance, there was a significant difference between the two groups but, surprisingly, this does not confirm the conventional wisdom. Let me first remark that the purpose of the test was not to explain the source of economic growth. However, the data seem to rather confirm my hunch (Chapter 5, second section) to the effect that moderate inflation rates are not harmful to economic growth. While it is true that the low inflation group distribution has a lower mean and a lower variance. Indeed, the measure of relative dispersion (standard deviation/mean) shows that the moderate inflation group distribution is about 6% less uniform than the other. If a policy choice is needed, it would boil down to choosing between more uniformly lower growth rates and more dispersed but higher rates. At any rate, the argument that lower inflation rates are compatible with better economic performance is not upheld by the data. We would have to look elsewhere for the justification of the inflation frenzy.

Table 5.4
Testing the Level of Inflation Against Economic Performance

Group I Average 1990–1996 inflation rate of less than 5% Average real GDP growth 1990-96 (in %)			Group II Average 1990–1996 inflation rate between 5% and 12% Average real GDP growth 1990-96 (in %)			Group III Average 1990–1996 inflation rate above 12% Average real GDP growth 1990-96 (in %)		
Country	x	x^2	Country	x	x^2	Country	x	x^2
United States	1.88	3.53	Thailand	8.61	74.13	Argentina	4.87	23.72
Japan	2.27	5.15	Ivory Coast[1]	2.30	5.29	Brazil	1.92	3.69
Malaysia	8.77	76.91	Jordan	6.38	40.70	Chile	6.82	46.51
Canada	2.83	8.00	Kuwait	7.91	61.00	Libya	2.30	5.29
Antigua &			Fiji	3.27	10.69	Guyana	5.87	34.46
Barbuda	2.58	6.66	Nepal	4.86	23.62	Guatemala	3.92	15.36
Barbados	-0.10	0.01	China	10.51	110.46	Albania	-1.30	1.69
The Bahamas	0.34	0.11	Papua New			Hungary	-1.95	3.80
Germany	2.57	6.60	Guinea	5.32	28.30	Vietnam	7.91	62.57
Seychelles	3.14	9.86	Maldives	8.08	65.29	Mexico	2.61	6.81
Malta	5.20	27.04	Spain	1.80	3.24	Romania	-0.27	0.07
Grenada	2.41	5.76	Indonesia	8.00	64.00	Myanmar	5.53	30.58
St Vincent	3.59	12.89	India	5.42	29.38	Honduras	3.36	11.29
Oman	5.90	34.81	Pakistan	4.84	23.42	Poland	0.82	0.67
Belgium	3.41	11.63	Botswana	4.82	23.23	Iran	5.48	30.03
Ireland	5.86	34.34	Trinidad &			Haiti	3.37	11.36
Finland[1]	0.25	0.06	Tobago	1.47	2.16	El Salvador	5.37	28.84
Denmark	1.97	3.88	The Gambia	2.08	4.33	Estonia[1]	5.28	27.88
Austria	2.20	4.84	Namibia	3.58	12.82	Venezuela	3.13	9.79
Sweden	0.82	0.67	Syria	6.37	40.57	Kenya	2.51	6.30
United Kingdom	1.20	1.44	Philippines	2.78	7.73	Zimbabwe	2.15	4.62
Norway	3.45	11.90	South Korea	7.73	59.75	Jamaica[1]	1.45	2.10
Netherlands	2.48	6.15	West. Samoa	0.15	0.02	Nigeria	3.44	11.83
Switzerland	0.26	0.07	Hong Kong	5.07	25.70	Sao Tome &		
St Lucia	3.07	9.42	Mali	2.60	6.76	Principe	1.07	1.14
New Zealand	2.28	5.20	Mauritania	2.93	8.58	Uruguay	3.45	11.90
Singapore	8.40	70.56	South Africa	1.00	1.00	Egypt[1]	2.08	4.32
Panama	5.48	30.03	Tunisia	4.87	23.71	Peru[1]	3.87	14.98
Nether. Antilles[1]	1.21	1.46	Portugal	1.84	3.38	Uganda	7.41	54.91
Taiwan	6.31	39.82	Bolivia	4.13	17.06	Paraguay	2.91	8.47
Australia	2.62	6.86	Mauritius	4.93	24.30	Turkey	4.56	20.79
	------	------	Morocco	3.28	10.76	Czech Republic	-2.01	4.04
n = 31	93.99	347.48	Italy	1.21	1.46	Costa Rica	3.56	12.67
			Buthan	5.31	28.20	Columbia	4.27	18.23
			Solomon Islands	5.20	27.04	Dominican		
			Sri Lanka	5.21	27.14	Republic	3.23	10.43
			Swaziland	4.49	20.16	Ecuador	3.14	9.86
				------	------	Ghana	4.41	19.45
			n = 35	158.25	915.38	Tanzania	4.48	20.07
							------	------
						n = 37	104.00	590.52

Ho1

$S_b^2 = 60.70$

$S_w^2 = 560.56$

Fcal = (60.70/2)/(560.56/100) = 5.41
Fo.o5 = 3.09
Fo.o1 = 4.82

Ho2

$S_b^2 = 36.47$; Fcal = (36.46/1)/(262.37/64) = 8.90

$S_w^2 = 262.37$; Fo.o1 = 7.04

[1]Five year average.

Source: Compiled using data from *WEO* (May 1997, 132–149) used by permission of the International Monetary Fund.

APPENDIX 5

Table A5.1
Factor Productivity Growth Outlook in Industrial Market Economies (in %)

	Country G7 (Average Values)[1]	Labor	Productivity Capital	Factor
United States	1960–1973	3.1	-0.1	1.9
	1973–1979	1.1	-0.2	0.6
	1972–1981	2.1	n.a.	—
	1982–1991	3.4	-0.5	0.2
Germany	1960–1973	5.8	-1.5	3.2
	1973–1979	4.3	-1.9	2.1
	1982–1991	3.0	-1.1	1.4
France	1960–1973	5.9	0.7	3.9
	1973–1979	4.2	-1.1	2.1
	1982–1991	3.6	1.9	1.3
Canada	1960–1973	4.2	1.1	2.9
	1973–1979	1.0	-1.6	—
	1982–1991	2.5	-2.0	-0.2
Japan	1960–1973	9.9	0.1	6.6
	1973–1979	3.8	-2.2	1.8
	1982–1991	3.4	-1.7	1.2
Italy	1960–1973	7.8	1.3	5.8
	1973–1979	1.6	-0.8	0.8
	1982–1991	3.9	-0.2	1.2
United Kingdom	1960–1973	3.8	-0.7	2.2
	1973–1979	1.9	-2.6	0.3
	1982–1991	4.4	-0.9	-0.2
Industrial countries[2]	1960–1973	5.2	—	—
	1973–1978	2.8	—	—
	1974–1984[3]	2.7	—	1.3
	1980–1985	2.6	—	—

Sources: Compiled using data from *Etude sur l'économie mondiale* (1994, 2); and *WEO* (May 1997, 131–141) used by permission of the International Monetary Fund.

Table A5.2
Consumer Price Index in Industrialized Market Economies: 1972–1996 (variation in %)

Countries average	1972–1981	1982	1983	1984	1985	1986	1987	1988	1989	1990	1991	1996
G7 Group	9.1	7.0	4.4	4.5	3.8	2.0	2.8	3.1	4.2	4.1	3.6	2.0
All Indust. countries	9.2	7.5	5.0	4.8	4.1	2.4	3.0	3.3	4.4	4.2	3.6	1.9

Source: Compiled using data from *WEO* (May 1990, 132).

Table A5.3
Levels of Unemployment in Selected Developed Market Economies:
1967–1996 (period average)

Countries[1]	1967–1974	1975–1979	1980–1983	1984	1985–1990[2]	1996[2]
Australia	2.1	5.5	7.2	8.9	—	4.7
Austria	1.5	1.9	3.0	3.8	—	8.6
Belgium	2.6	7.0	11.5	14.0	—	12.6
Denmark	1.3	6.5	9.9	n.a.	—	8.8
Finland	2.5	5.1	5.4	6.1	—	16.3
Ireland	5.6	7.0	9.7	n.a.	—	12.4
Netherlands	2.2	5.8	9.9	14.0	—	7.6
Spain	2.7	5.8	14.6	n.a.	—	22.1
G7 Group[1]						
United States	4.6	6.9	8.4	7.4	6.3	5.4
Germany	1.1	3.5	5.4	8.6	7.7	10.3
France	2.5	4.9	7.5	8.6	10.1	12.4
Italy	5.6	6.8	8.6	10.2	11.3	12.1
Canada	5.2	7.5	9.4	11.2	9.0	9.7
Japan	1.3	2.0	2.3	2.7	2.6	3.3
United Kingdom	3.4	5.8	10.9	13.2	9.3	7.5

Sources: Compiled using data from [1]Bean and Layard (1986, S1); and [2]*WEO* (October 1989, 77; May 1997, 135, used by permission of the International Monetary Fund).

Table A5.4
Real GDP Growth Rates in Countries Under the New Orthodoxy for
More than 5 Years: 1976–1995 (variation in %)

Countries	Average 1976–1979	Average 1981–1988	1989	1990	1991	1992	1995
United States	4.7[1]	2.8	2.5	0.8	-1.2	2.1	2.3
United Kingdom	2.4[1]	2.8	2.3	1.1	-2.3	-0.5	1.9
New Zealand	—	—	0.8	-0.2	-1.8	0.9	3.4
Latin America and Caribbean	n.a.	1.4	1.1	0.1	2.0	2.2	1.3
Africa	3.8	1.8	3.0	2.0	1.3	0.7	2.9

Sources: Compiled using data from [1]*Etude sur l'économie mondiale* (1980–1981, 30); and [2]*WEO* (May 1990, 124; May 1997, 133, used by permission of the International Monetary Fund).

Table A5.5
Real Rates of Change in the Money Supply in G7 Countries: 1979–1980

Country	1979				1980			
	I	II	III	IV	I	II	III	IV
United States	-1.6	-3.4	-3.4	-5.0	-4.6	-5.2	-3.9	—
Germany	7.4	6.6	3.4	1.4	1.0	-0.6	-3.6	—
France	3.3	2.7	1.7	2.2	-1.2	-2.6	-5.6	—
Italy	5.9	4.6	3.5	1.4	-3.2	-4.4	-7.0	—
Canada	7.6	10.1	9.7	7.4	8.0	5.2	0.6	—
Japan	9.9	7.9	7.7	3.3	1.4	-0.6	-2.5	—
United Kingdom	0.8	0.7	-3.6	-4.1	4.7	-5.4	0.1	—

Source: *Etude sur l'économie mondiale* (1980–1981, 50). The United Nations is the author of the original material.

Table A5.6
Loan Rates, Nominal and Real, in G7 Countries: 1978–1981 (in %)

Country	December 1978		December 1979		December 1980		December 1981	
	nominal	real	nominal	real	nominal	real	nominal	real
United States	11.75	2.8	15.25	1.8	21.50	8.1	15.75	6.3
Germany	5.50	3.0	9.75	4.1	11.50	5.8	13.00	6.3
France	9.80	0.1	12.50	0.7	12.25	-1.3	14.00	n.a.
Italy	15.00	3.1	19.50	0.5	20.50	-0.7	22.50	5.2
Canada	11.50	3.0	15.00	4.1	13.25	6.3	13.00	4.0
Japan	4.50	0.9	6.51	0.7	8.16	0.7	7.00	2.6
United Kingdom	13.50	4.7	18.00	0.7	13.00	-0.1	14.50	2.2

Source: *Etude sur l'économie mondiale* (1981–1982, 34). The United Nations is the author of the original material.

Table A5.7
Real Total Domestic Demand Growth in G7 Countries: 1971–1983 (annual changes in %)

Country	Average 1971–1980	1981	1982	1983
United States	2.5	2.2	-1.9	5.1
Germany	2.7	-2.7	-2.0	2.3
France	3.5	-0.1	3.5	-0.7
Italy	2.9	-1.2	0.3	-0.6
Canada	4.9	4.7	-6.6	4.1
Japan	4.2	2.1	2.8	1.8
United Kingdom	1.7	-1.5	2.2	4.8

Source: Compiled using data from *WEO* (October 1989, 74).

Table A5.8
Net Transfer of Financial Resources to Developing Economies: 1980–1991 (as a percentage of GDP)

Group of countries	1980	1985	1990	1991
Africa	2.4	2.4	3.8	2.7
of which: 15 most indebted countries	1.1	-4.9	-2.8	-0.8
Latin America	1.4	-4.8	-2.6	-0.5
of which:				
Mexico	2.3	-5.1	0.5	3.2
Argentina	2.2	-6.6	-7.4	-2.3
South East Asia	2.3	-0.1	0.7	0.6
of which:				
China	0.0	4.1	-3.5	-3.2
Korea	7.4	-1.3	0.6	2.6
Thailand	6.3	2.8	8.0	7.2
Developing nonoil-exporting countries	4.0	0.8	0.0	0.1

Source: Adapted from *Etude sur l'économie mondiale* (1993, 389). The United Nations is the author of the original material.

Table A5.9
Net Transfer of Resources to Developing Economies: 1982–1992 (in billions of dollars)

Regions	1982	1983	1984	1985	1986	1987	1988	1989	1990	1991	1992
Africa	16.2	9.7	3.8	-2.6	7.6	2.1	7.0	4.8	-5.8	0.9	-1.6
Latin America and the Caribbean	3.4	-25.7	-34.9	-30.2	-11.4	-17.4	-21.6	-28.9	-26.0	-7.2	6.9
Western Asia	2.3	27.1	12.9	20.2	36.7	21.8	25.0	15.0	3.8	41.6	27.2
Other Asian	8.6	5.7	-4.6	4.1	-12.3	-30.8	-18.4	-10.4	-5.1	7.3	12.4
Mediterranean	3.8	1.4	-0.1	-1.6	-2.0	-3.3	-7.0	-4.9	8.3	4.7	7.0
All countries	34.3	18.3	-22.9	-10.1	18.7	-27.9	-15.0	-24.5	-24.7	47.3	51.9
Memorandum 15 most indebted	9.4	-23.9	-40.6	-40.5	-22.0	-28.4	-30.9	-37.8	-32.0	-12.8	2.5

Source: Adapted from *Etude sur l'économie mondiale* (1993, 167). The United Nations is the author of the original material.

Table A5.10
World Trade Pattern: 1980–1991 (in %)

	Developed market economies				Countries in transition				Developing market economies			
	1960	1985	1990	1991	1960	1985	1990	1991	1960	1985	1990	1991
Developed market economies	66.7	73.1	78.0	77.3	29.3	22.3	34.9	42.8	62.7	59.2	61.8	60.8
Countries in transition	3.3	3.2	2.7	3.1	54.7	60.4	45.5	41.9	6.5	7.8	5.1	4.9
Developing market economies	30.0	23.7	19.3	19.6	16.0	17.3	19.6	15.3	30.8	33.0	33.1	34.3

Source: Adapted from *Etude sur l'économie mondiale* (1993, 394). The United Nations is the author of the original material.

Table A5.11
Current Account Balance[1] of Developed and Developing Market Economies: 1982–1992 (in billions of dollars)

Countries	1982	1983	1984	1985	1986	1987	1988	1989	1990	1991	1992
128 Developing market economies of which:	-75.6	-54.0	-21.4	-32.7	-54.0	-13.7	-27.3	-20.5	-15.7	-83.3	-87.4
Latin America	-42.1	-8.8	-2.3	-4.9	-20.4	-13.3	-11.8	-7.9	-7.1	20.7	-33.7
Africa	-24.8	-18.0	-12.0	-6.2	-15.6	-12.9	-18.5	-16.9	-7.3	-12.3	-10.3
Western Asia	12.2	-8.8	1.7	-5.9	-19.4	-7.8	-9.7	1.4	7.4	-31.4	-16.9
South Eastern Asia	-19.2	-16.2	-6.7	-15.0	2.0	20.1	8.8	0.2	-2.8	-15.3	-21.4
Memorandum 100 oil importers	-57.1	-38.1	-25.5	-31.4	-21.1	-9.5	-6.3	-15.7	-29.8	-42.9	-50.0
Developed Market economies of which:	-8.9	-1.4	-29.2	-28.7	6.6	-17.9	-12.2	-31.4	-45.1	12.3	20.2
Germany	11.1	10.8	15.9	23.3	47.7	56.9	62.3	69.8	62.1	10.0	-1.2
Japan	8.1	22.2	36.4	50.5	87.5	89.7	82.6	60.3	40.4	84.7	121.0

[1]Commercial balance plus services and private transfers; (+) stand for a surplus, (-) for a deficit.

Source: Adapted from *Etude sur l'économie mondiale* (1993, 403–409). The United Nations is the author of the original material.

Table A5.12
Foreign Debt of 122 Developing Economies:
1982–1992 (in billions of dollars)

Countries	1982	1983	1984	1985	1986	1987	1988	1989	1990	1991	1992
All countries of which:	781	856	880	967	1066	1210	1201	1213	1288	1344	1419
long term	619	719	751	838	944	1068	1052	1050	1098	1142	1200
short term	162	137	129	128	122	142	149	163	190	202	219
Latin America of which:	354	385	397	412	434	474	456	451	463	470	478
long term	263	323	346	366	397	428	405	389	392	400	402
short term	91	62	51	46	37	46	51	62	71	70	76
Asia of which:	236	263	268	302	341	391	394	402	445	489	539
long term	190	215	220	253	291	332	333	340	371	403	448
short term	46	48	48	49	49	59	61	62	74	86	91
15 most indebted of which:	385	416	431	449	474	520	501	494	510	516	526
long term	280	341	366	392	432	475	450	434	441	447	454
short term	105	75	65	57	42	45	51	60	69	69	71

Source: Adapted from *Etude sur l'économie mondiale* (1993, 424–426). The United Nations is the author of the original material.

Table A5.13
GDP Growth Rates of Countries in Transition: 1983–1996

	1983	1985	1987	1989	1990	1991	1992	1993	1994	1996
Eastern Europe of which:	4.2	2.6	2.3	0.0	-11.8	-10.8	-8.8	-4.0	-1.8	1.6
Bulgaria	3.4	2.7	6.1	-9.1	-4.7	-16.7	-13.0	-8.0	—	-9.0
Hungary	0.7	-0.3	3.8	3.8	-4.0	-11.9	-5.0	-0.6	—	1.0
Poland	5.6	3.6	2.0	0.2	-12.0	-7.6	0.0	2.0	—	5.5
Rumania	6.1	-0.1	0.8	-5.6	-7.4	-13.7	-15.0	-6.0	3.9	4.1
G D Republic	4.0	5.5	3.3	2.4	-25.0	—	—	—	—	—
Czechoslovakia	2.4	2.2	0.8	1.3	-4.7	-15.9	-7.2	-2.0	—	—
States of the former USSR	4.3	1.7	2.8	3.0	-4.0	-8.0	-20.0	-13.5	-13.4	1.6
All Countries in transition	4.2	2.0	2.6	2.1	-6.3	-9.0	-16.8	-10.0	—	—

Sources: *Etude sur l'économie mondiale* (1993, 381). The United Nations is the author of the original material; *WEO* (May 1997, 141), used by permission of the International Monetary Fund.

Table A5.14
Military Expenditures in G7 Countries: 1980–1993
(in billions of dollars)

Country	1980	1993	% variation
United States	212.10	297.60	40.30
Germany	33.00	36.70	20.30
France	31.20	42.60	36.50
Italy	14.90	20.57	38.00
Canada	7.62	10.30	35.10
Japan	18.10	41.73	130.00
United Kingdom	32.53	34.02	4.50

Source: *Statistical Abstract of the United States* (1995, 880).

Table A5.15
Market Capitalization of Firms in G7 Countries: 1985–1993
(in billions of dollars)

Country	1985	1990	1992	1993	% variation since 1985
United States	2324.60	3089.60	4757.90	5223.80	124.70
Germany	183.80	355.07	348.13	463.50	152.10
France	79.00	314.40	350.90	456.00	477.20
Italy	58.50	118.80	129.20	136.15	132.70
Canada	147.00	241.92	243.01	326.50	122.10
Japan	978.67	2917.70	2399.00	2999.75	206.50
United Kingdom	328.00	848.90	927.13	1151.46	251.00

Source: *Statistical Abstract of the United States* (1995, 872).

Table A5.16
World Real Rates of GDP Growth: 1981–1997 (in %)

Countries by category	1981–1988	1989	1990	1991	1992	1993	1994	1995	1996	1997
Developed Market Economies	2.8	3.3	2.4	0.7	1.6	1.0	2.0	2.0	2.5	2.9
of which:										
United States	2.8	2.5	0.8	-1.2	2.6	3.0	3.0	2.0	2.4	3.0
European Union	2.1	3.4	2.8	0.7	1.1	-0.4	1.5	2.5	1.6	2.4
Japan	4.0	4.7	4.8	4.3	1.1	0.1	1.0	1.4	3.6	2.2
Economies in transition	3.1	2.1	-6.2	-8.8	-15.2	-8.6	-6.0	1.6	-0.8	0.1
Developing Market Economies	3.1	3.5	3.0	3.4	4.9	5.2	5.0	5.0	—	—
of which:										—
Latin America & Caribbean	1.4	1.1	-0.1	2.8	2.1	3.3	3.0	1.3	3.2	
Africa	1.8	2.8	2.2	1.6	0.8	1.6	2.2	2.9	5.0	4.7
Western Asia	-1.7	3.2	1.9	-0.2	5.7	3.5	3.2	n.a.	—	—
South-Eastern Asia	5.9	6.1	6.4	5.3	5.2	5.4	6.0	n.a.	—	—
China	9.9	4.3	3.9	8.0	13.2	13.4	10.0	10.5	9.7	—
Mediterranean	2.5	0.4	1.1	-5.6	-1.9	-0.3	4.0	n.a.	—	—
World	2.9	3.2	1.6	0.3	0.8	1.1	2.5	3.7	4.0	4.4
GDP per capita	2.8	1.5	0.0	-0.2	-0.9	-0.6	0.6	1.0	—	—
World trade	—	8.0	5.6	4.6	5.5	2.7	6.0	6.0	9.2	5.6

Sources: Compiled using data from *Etude sur l'économie mondiale* (1994, 2); and *WEO* (May 1997, 131–141). Used by permission of the International Monetary Fund.

III

POVERTY, GROWTH, AND DISTRIBUTION

6

UNEMPLOYMENT AND SOCIAL SECURITY IN THE AGE OF DECONSTRUCTION

INTRODUCTION

As we have seen in the previous chapter, the benefits of the new orthodoxy are yet to be seen, but its negative consequences are all around us. In this chapter, I probe the two impacts that are closely linked to poverty, that is, unemployment and the menace that the orthodoxy poses to social security. The idleness or the unemployment of a portion of the active labor force of an economy represents a significant cost. Besides, unemployment is also associated with a host of other psychological and social problems, including negative repercussions on future employment prospects. On the other hand, the impacts of social security programs, whose financing depends on employment, are eminently positive. Wherever such programs exist, they have been found to be expensive, but they also boost people's well-being in a number of ways. For example, they provide workers with some means of consumption after their retirement; economists term this smoothing out the life consumption schedule of workers. They represent an important means of capital accumulation. They alleviate the adverse selection problem (i.e., the likelihood of being cheated when buying unknown products) in private insurance markets, while allowing for some form of intergenerational exchange and risk sharing arrangements. They legitimize the market distribution of risks and rewards, and they prolong the life expectancy.

This chapter examines employment and social security systems, and attempts to link their impacts to economic well-being. More specifically, I hope to show that both unemployment and certain trends in employment breed nefarious effects, while the impacts of social security systems are beneficial in terms of well-being. However, the presence of one and the absence of the other are closely linked through poverty, for high unemployment is detrimental to the viability of social security systems, and both seem to receive minimal attention relative to inflation in the new orthodoxy. According to Professor John Kenneth Galbraith, it is because inflation affects everyone, while unemployment touches only a small percentage of the active labor force. But regardless of the reason, it is important to stress that through its obsessive fear of inflation, the new orthodoxy does exacerbate the problems of unemployment and threatens the beneficial effects of social security systems. I begin with a cursory review of unemployment in both the North and South in the age of deconstruction.

Most aggregate economic magnitudes are not accurately measured; unemployment rates, published at regular intervals by public institutions, are no exception. Even when the methods of gathering the figures are clear, consistent, and immutable, it does not mean the figures will reveal the true picture. In most cases, they can only convey improvements or deterioration in this particularly disturbing statistic. I will address the problems inherent to the measurement of unemployment shortly. But beforehand, I wish to focus on unemployment as a social problem rather than the way it is perceived within the new orthodoxy.

Unemployment first surfaced as a traumatic experience during the great depression of the 1930s. It is reasonable to suppose that although the political leaders, who devised the welfare programs of the late 1940s, had themselves no firsthand experience with unemployment, they nevertheless must have had an intuitive feel for its impacts. They must have, no doubt, observed for the first time the surprising fact that the market mechanism was capable of both creating and destroying wealth. Having seen this and, principally seen how easily the old ways of thinking could easily unleash untold sorrow to humankind, they and the rest of the Western World were ready to enter a new era, one of high economic growth, fueled in part by the optimism of the immediate aftermath of World War II. All of this meant rising employment of labor. The United Nations Charter, in its Article 55, paragraph a, saw fit to explicitly promote full employment as a key element in the creation of the conditions of stability and well-being of nations. Many Northern states that were members of the UN gave full employment priority in their macroeconomic policy packages. Many even took the lead in enacting specific measures such as the U.S. Employment Act of 1946. The socially planned economies of Eastern Europe saw full employment as a social manifesto. Even the countries of the South, which were in no position to attain full employment, adopted it nevertheless as a worthy objective. What has happened since the mid-1970s? Why is the concept of full employment now banished from the economic landscape?

I have already explored the relationship between unemployment, the oil shock-inflation of the late 1970s, and falling domestic demand. This is how it all began. I believe that the subsequent sketchy attention given to unemployment and to its unprecedented rise in the 1980s are due mainly to a shift in thinking. In setting the new orthodoxy, policies are influenced mainly by narrow interest lobbies, bankers, institutional investors, and CEOs of multinational firms. In the mind of these actors, the concern for the full employment of labor appears minimal, and it shows. However, in the eyes of a part of the public and, principally, for the victims, unemployment carries unacceptable costs. Political leaders are therefore caught in the middle. Unable to adequately address the problem, they all too often fall back on stratagems and lip service, aimed at their national audiences, and vague promises made at international conferences. In the meantime, the problem is being exacerbated by greed and new technologies. The question now is, will governments continue responding in the same way to the future public outcry, that is, with more double speak and more international conferences such as the one sponsored by the UN in Copenhagen in March 1995? It is highly likely.

Clearly then there is a need, I believe, to refocus on unemployment for what it actually is. But first, let us begin by briefly defining the required concepts.

ON DEFINITIONS AND MEASUREMENTS OF ECONOMIC MAGNITUDES

Normally, countries supply the level of unemployment in their economies, as a percentage of their active labor force, every year, or at shorter intervals. Let us then begin with the definition of the *active labor force*. The reader will probably be surprised to learn that it is not the sum of employment and unemployment levels. Within the panoply of concepts relative to labor markets, the active labor force is not even uniquely defined. It may refer to all those who fall within the legally defined age brackets to work, that is, 16 to 65 year-olds who are willing to work. Sometimes, it is distinguished from the population falling within the age brackets. When this is the case, it then includes those that are no longer within the age brackets to work but who continue to work. By the same token, it excludes those that are not actively looking for work, such as people engaged in domestic services, military personnel, and students. On the other hand, it includes those that are in the informal sector, those engaged in voluntary services, and so on. Hence, it is not the sum of officially defined employment and unemployment. The arbitrariness is not limited to the arithmetic. It exists in ways that are not immediately apparent. For example, the age brackets are defined by demographic and legal considerations proper to each country. The logic as to what is to be included or excluded is arbitrary. For example, the logic as to why military personnel are excluded, while private security guards and the police are not, when all these groups are protecting assets, is far from being clear. The reader should then brace him or herself for more of such idiosyncrasies as we move along.

Any inaccuracy in the measurement of the active labor force is per force carried over to the panoply of types of unemployment rates regularly found in official statistics. There are quite a few. To begin with, we have the notion of *frictional unemployment,* which refers to those that are in transition from one job to another, due to continual changes in a relatively free economy; it used to be estimated at 2 to 3% of the total rate, but these days it is put at 1% or less. Next, there is what is known as *structural unemployment* that results from fundamental changes in the economy, where workers are said to lack the flexibility necessary to adapt to other jobs, for example, when coal mines are mechanized. There is also what is called *seasonal unemployment*, which is due to the seasonal nature of some types of work (this type is sometime included in frictional unemployment). We also refer to the notion of *hidden unemployment*, which arises from the fact that the economy is not operating at its potential. This type would include those workers that are not included in the active labor force, but who would seek out work if the economy were operating at higher levels. There is no problem or disagreement about the nature of some categories such as seasonal unemployment. However, there is intense disagreement about other categories such as cyclical, natural, technological, and voluntary unemployment, and about their importance and sometimes their very existence. A good example of this is structural unemployment; economists agree about its existence but not about its extent and cause.

All of these categories are expressed as a percentage of the active labor force. Since so many are completely without purpose for us here, I will only make passing reference to them. What is important is the official unemployment rate, which refers to those workers who are without work, who are actively searching for work, and who are unable to find any, expressed as a percentage of the active labor force. The concept of full employment, on the other hand, refers to a condition where the demand for all factors of production (labor, capital, among others) is equal to their supply. Under this condition, their market prices become elements of the equilibrium price vector discussed in Chapters 2 and 3. In the labor market, therefore, there is full employment when the number of job openings is equal to the number of workers willing to accept these openings. We have little use for the concept of full employment; our main thrust will be on the consequences of unemployment. As far as the rate of unemployment is concerned, it should be clear that it is a contextual figure that may give a rough idea of the magnitude of the problem. Hence, its value is limited to an indication of the direction of change.

How is the official unemployment rate measured? There are three principal ways of measuring it, family surveys, unemployment registers, and record of unemployment insurance claims. For the sake of comparison, the International Labor Organization (ILO) recommends the standard definition just given. But the ILO explicitly asks its member states to omit part-timers and discouraged unemployed workers, as well as those included in training programs. However, even there there is room for differences since some countries consider people involved in training programs employed while others do not.

The survey method consists of asking a controlled sample of idle individuals to fill out a questionnaire to determine the nature of their idleness and the effort they have deployed to find work. Although there are some differences with regard to the questions, the survey method nevertheless makes intercountry comparisons more meaningful. The main reason why it is not widely adopted is that it is costly.

Mainly for cost reasons, most countries find it easier and cheaper to pick out the number of unemployed persons from unemployment registers. The problem with this method is that an unemployed individual would only register if there is some hope of getting a job from the process. To prevent the data from becoming obsolete, the unemployed must reregister at regular intervals. Therefore, discouraged workers drop out progressively, when, by word of mouth, would be applicants quickly know whether or not it is worth reregistering or registering in the first place. Hence, in countries where the employment service has a poor track record in finding employment, the data collected on unemployment are practically worthless.

The third method simply counts those that are drawing unemployment benefits. This method does not favor intercountry comparisons since the number of unemployed drawing insurance benefits depends on a given country's regulations. People who collect benefits are unemployed according to the ILO's definition, but not all unemployed persons are collecting benefits. In fact, in some instances, people who are theoretically unemployed are reported to be holding bogus jobs long enough to qualify for benefits.

To make matters worse, ILO's definition counts individuals who have worked for at least one hour during a given period (usually one week) as employed. Here then we may have cases where clearly unemployed persons are not counted. For all of these reasons, therefore, it is no exaggeration to say that the number of officially unemployed people around the world is grossly understated.

THE UNEMPLOYMENT BURDEN IN THE NORTH

Since the mid-1970s, industrial countries in the North are faced with a situation that one expert describes as: "A remorseless rise in unemployment." Obviously, the level of unemployment differs markedly from country to country. For example, the situation in Japan and in some of the Scandinavian countries can hardly be compared with what exists in the rest of the OECD countries. Even in those cases, however, today's levels of unemployment are much higher compared with past performance. If we add the situations of Southern countries and those countries in transition, it can be said that the trend toward higher unemployment levels in the new orthodoxy is universal.

Almost everyone, whether employed or unemployed, realizes that unemployment carries a significant economic cost. That cost cannot easily be broken down into its constituent parts, nor will I attempt to do so here. I am more interested in addressing the least talked about components, that is, the social cost that those with first-hand experience with unemployment characterize as a real psychological burden. Those that are unable to find work to support themselves and their families often end up losing their self-respect, and this has untold repercussions on their mental health and on everybody around them. Unemployment also seems to fuel social violence, school drop-outs, urban decay, poverty, and even the mortality rate. As can be observed in the United States and the European Union, unemployment feeds ethnic intolerance, xenophobia, and even fascism. More important for our purpose, idleness deskills the work force, which in turn exacerbates the problem. Assuming that these issues are likely, the problem cannot be left solely in the hands of labor economists who, despite the classic Lane's (1991) study, continue to regard the supply of labor as a unique choice between work and leisure.

Obviously, the determinants of the supply and the demand of labor are numerous and may be common to both. But whatever they are, costs figure prominently in them, that is, real wages, the costs of hiring and firing, social and nonpecuniary costs of employment, etc. To these we must add the increasing role of a new element, the progressive divergence between competence and needs. This new element arises from technical shocks, where the prevailing technology requires higher and higher skill levels. Economists refer to this phenomenon as the skill mismatch constraint.

Those involved with the problem of employment or unemployment are now taking the mismatch factor much more seriously. However, to arrive at a solution by dint of effort, they must first cleanse their mind of all preconceived notions. One such notion is that the rise in unemployment is primarily a consequence of the rapid labor force growth with the supply of jobs lagging behind the demand; this way they confuse the skill mismatch factor with excess supply. Obviously, the number of job applicants has increased, but is there an excess supply? True, there has been a rise in women's participation, and we must be mindful of the baby boom phenomenon and its echo, but these appear to have been more than muted out by the men leaving the work force, for they do not show up in the labor force growth as shown in Table A6.1 in the Appendix to this chapter. Prior to the mid-1970s, we were accustomed to unemployment rates in the 2 to 3% range. Now, in the mid-1990s, we are dealing with figures between 8 and 12% in the richer countries. In absolute terms, this represents a staggering figure in 1996–1997, meaning that in the European Union, the OECD and the world, the numbers of unemployed people are estimated at 18 million[1], 35 million, and 150 million, respectively. Since, as I have argued, the figures are conservative estimates, this alarming phenomenon cannot be explained by labor force growth.

Women's participation figures prominently in the total participation rate, principally that of married women. Table A6.2 shows that from 1973 to 1992, the population of inactive women fell in selected Northern countries, while the employed number has risen. At the same time, however (except in Japan), the reverse trends are observed for men.

Rather than blaming women's participation, labor force growth, and rising real wage, decision makers must realize that it is globalization, through its emphasis on bigness, that is exacerbating the unemployment problem, and restructuring that has changed the nature of employment toward more independent, part-time, and temporary work. In changing the demand for labor, the new orthodoxy finds it convenient to raise further the skill level required. The share of skilled labor in total employment in industrialized countries has gone up by some 10% in the last 20 years, but the big upswing began in the 1980s. Meanwhile, the level of unemployment of unskilled workers during the 1980s was between two or three times that of skilled workers. Other factors, such as the introduction of labor saving technologies, falling domestic aggregate demand, tight monetary policies, the rise of imports and offshore production, among other things, have also aggravated the problem. However, in keeping with my promise not to bother the reader with long tables, figures on unemployment and inactivity rates in selected countries are shown in Table A6.3 in the appendix.

Another misleading concept, which should be evacuated from the mind of decision makers, is the so-called non-accelerating inflationary rate of unemployment (NAIRU). The NAIRU is a magic unemployment rate below which an economy is not supposed to go in order to avoid episodes of accelerating inflation. The NAIRU is one of those concepts that is increasingly used to foster false consciousness. In my view, at least, it only justifies the indifference of decision makers vis-à-vis the unemployment problem. In order to see why, let us begin with the mindset that has produced the concept.

For greater clarity, I return to the so-called Theory of Aggregate Supply, the earlier version of the ad hoc wage-inflation theory, which unfortunately rests on a number of unverified assumptions. Namely, overemployment drives nominal wages upward. Nominal wages drive production costs upward, which in turn are passed on to consumers in the form of higher prices, hence inflation. Conversely, unemployment leads to falling nominal wages and production costs and, therefore, to deflation. This dynamic adjustment of inflation and wages comes to an end only when the economy reaches its full potential with full employment. Hence, the rate of unemployment corresponding to full employment is called the natural rate of unemployment. As I have said, none of these assumptions can actually be empirically confirmed, but the theory lives on and is even expanding.

During the 1970s, new features were introduced. In order to see how they all fit together, let us denote the actual rates of inflation and unemployment as f and u, respectively. Next, I let f^* and u^* stand for the expected rate of inflation and the natural rate of unemployment. Then, on the assumption that at any time, actual, expected, and natural rates may diverge, they may nevertheless be related through the simple formula:

(the actual rate of inflation) = (the expected rate of inflation) − (the difference in actual and expected

rates of unemployment)

$$(f) \qquad = \qquad (bf^*) \qquad a(u - u^*),$$

where b and a are coefficients. According to this view, the excess of unemployment, $(u - u^*)$ causes wages to fall, while rates of unemployment below the natural rate cause wages to rise. From our previous discussion of this matter, we know that the direction of causality has not been established. The above assumed one is nevertheless so firmly anchored in the minds of the protagonists that they proceed to link inflation and unemployment in the above formula. You may also note in passing that in the underlying assumptions, labor is treated as any Arrow-Debreu commodity, subject to the laws of supply and demand.

The above formula is termed the *expectations-augmented Phillips curve*, the same discredited Phillips curve encountered in Chapter 4. To make the formula operational, it is next supposed that if $u = u^*$, both labor and firms expect the same rate of inflation, and nominal wages would increase at this expected rate. Because labor, the commodity, will attempt to protect its real price, all firms will oblige and the actual rate of inflation will be equal to the expected rate. The other thing to notice is that labor cost, a fraction of the total production costs, is passed on to prices in a one-to-one relationship. Any young student that comes across this formula will retain its main message, that is, inflation is caused by wage increases. Two other obvious truths should normally flow out of the formula. The first is that, if $(u - u^*) < 0$, then $f > f^*$, that is, if actual unemployment happens to be below the natural rate, actual inflation will exceed expected inflation. It follows, therefore, that if $(u - u^*) > 0$, we should observed deflation. However, even after some 16 years of falling wages, no deflation has been observed. To rescue the theory, its protagonists argue that the natural rate has gone up.

The next sets of implications that follow straight from the formula are the following. In the short run, the expected inflation rate, which can only be based on past values, is assumed constant. The Phillips curve is then negatively sloped or there is a tradeoff between inflation and unemployment. This means that in the short run, the unemployment rate can be reduced only at the cost of higher inflation. If now the curve is observed shifting all over the place, it is in response to variations in expected rates of inflation. Again, there is no way of verifying such an assertion, because every shift can be explained by a different level of inflation previously guessed by labor. In fact, the coefficient, b, can take any value less than one that happens to correspond to the location of the curve in inflation-unemployment space. For example, if $u = u^*$, and we have a tradeoff, then $b < 1$; we are then in the short run. In the long run, on the other hand, the actual inflation rate is equal to the expected rate. The coefficients a and b are both equal to one, and the curve must be vertical. Within this logic, if you were to ask: What rate of inflation would prevail when $u = u^*$? The answer would be simple. Inflation is what was expected, that is, $f = f^*$. Then, according to Professors Friedman and Phelps, when $f = f^*$, meaning in the long run, macropolicies become impotent against unemployment. Once this viewpoint is established, it is a simple intellectual leap to arrive at the conclusion that if u were to fall below u^*, we would have accelerated inflation.

The reader will notice that in this paradigm, short and long runs are distinguished by the value of the b coefficient. However, the Phillips curve was initially presented by Phillips as a long run empirical regularity, based on data spanning almost 100 years. And this is where the tradeoff between unemployment and wage inflation was first detected. Further, back in the 1960s, the same curve was accepted as a good description of the facts. In the 1970s, when it became apparent that the rate of unemployment was increasing over time, the notion of expected inflation was brought in; in the 1980s, the $b = 1$ argument was added. Despite these adjustments, however, there is neither a consensus on a vertical Phillips curve nor a plausible explanation as to why we have not had deflation in the presence of unprecedentedly high unemployment. These troublesome questions are countered with the argument to the effect that money wage behavior is asymmetrical. This means that wages rise in the presence of excess demand for labor or with expected inflation, but they do not fall in the presence of high unemployment or expected deflation. Hence, to make the theory work symmetrically, the new orthodoxy recommends that we arbitrarily depress wages.

The modern concept of the NAIRU must be seen against this background. In the economic literature, it is formally defined either as "a rate of unemployment below which an economy cannot go without accelerating inflation, or as the unemployment rate compatible with a rate of inflation that does not deviate from the expected rate of inflation."[2] The reader will no doubt realize that that rate is the NAIRU or the natural rate of unemployment. What is natural about it? Obviously, since labor (the commodity) cannot be easily exported when it is in excess supply, we have become accustomed to unemployment in any given period. But moving from there to the belief in the existence of a natural constraint called the natural rate is both ludicrous and misleading. Moreover, if in fact labor is an ordinary ADC, why should there be a natural rate? Why have we not a natural rate of oil output, or capital usage, or banana production?

More astoundingly, estimating the NAIRU has become a real research industry (see e.g., Coe and Gagliardi 1985; Calmfor 1993; Layard et al. 1993). Some estimates of the NAIRU carried out in industrial countries with coordinated salary negotiations are offered as support for the idea that unemployment is sensitive to wage; others do not and instead show that the functioning of the labor market remains as complex as ever. Stranger still, estimates of the NAIRU seem to vary from one subperiod to another within the same country. For example, for the United States, Adams and Coe (1990) estimate that in the 1960s, the NAIRU was around 3.5; in 1980, it rose to 7.25 and fell to 5.75 in 1988. In 1996, Akerlof et al.(1996) put it between 4.5 and 5.3. In Germany, it went from 1.6% to 8.0% over a ten year period. In France, it went from 3.3 % to 9.0% in five years. In the United Kingdom, it was estimated at 2.6% in 1967–1970; at 7.2% during 1971–1975; and from 1981–1983 it fell to 5.9%. Beside shifting values, 1980s estimates in capitalist countries, as similar in terms of institutions as Germany and Austria, are very different, that is, 8.0% for Germany and 2.4% for Austria. How can such discrepancies be explained? In order to stress the absurdity of the concept, Professor Solow (1986) asks: Are we to understand that we would have accelerated deflation in Germany and in Austria should their unemployment rates go above 8.0% and 2.4%, respectively? This is a straightforward question, but I am not sure that Professor Solow will ever get a straight answer.

The reader may have noticed also that both of the above definitions of the NAIRU are associated with the discredited Phillips curve. The first is compatible with a long run Phillips curve with a negative slope but with a vertical segment at the left at a positive unemployment rate. That rate is precisely the NAIRU, as

I have already explained. The second definition assumes a completely vertical long run Phillips curve, where the long run is now a state in which actual and expected inflation rates are equal. Those who estimate the NAIRU from the first definition often cite factors such as changes in the composition of the labor force, skill requirements, unemployment insurance benefits, obstacles to labor mobility, and so on, to explain these shifting long run values. With the second definition, the method of solution consists in setting the coefficient of expected inflation at unity and equating current and expected inflation rates. As it can be seen, the above factors do not appear in the latter solution concept, yet they are offered just the same as explanations for variance and shifts in the estimates. Solow summarizes the difficulty with the NAIRU concept as follows: "One can always define the unemployment rate to be below the natural rate whenever inflation is accelerating. But then it is vacuous to say that inflation is accelerating because unemployment is below the natural rate."[3]

It should also be pointed out that the importance given to the NAIRU and the frantic effort to estimate it are motivated by the desire of central banks to control inflation. As I have emphasized in Chapter 5, if rates on loans are fixed for a time, an inflationary surge that pushes the inflation rate above the nominal rate of interest would produce negative real rates and losses for bankers. Thus, hedging the fear of inflation reduces to the ability to forecast it. Milton Friedman (1968) first used the term natural rate of unemployment while attacking the monetary policy rule that prevailed at that time. At the end of the 1960s, there was a strong belief that there was a stable negative relationship between unemployment and inflation. Friedman's intention, therefore, was to remind the monetary authorities that only one of the two values could be preselected. Instead, and perhaps inadvertently, he unleashed the frantic effort to estimate the natural rate of unemployment in a futile attempt to provide central banks with an empirical regularity to back up monetary policy.

Following Friedman's address to the American Economic Association, his followers began developing a standard characterization of the joint behavior of wage and price inflation and the unemployment rate. To bring this to fruition, they started out with the demand for labor that posits that the rate of change in the price level is positively related to the rate of change of wage. They also produced a supply equation in which the rate of change of wage is positively related to the expected rate of inflation and negatively correlated with the unemployment rate. Substituting one equation into the other yields the following relationship:

$$f(t) = a + f^*(t-1) - b\,u(t) + \text{error term}$$

This is essentially the same as the previous equation, except that the latter is thought to be derived from demand and supply, incorporating rates of change rather than absolute levels. As we have seen, the demand and supply of labor are not so simple to formulate. In his book, *The Tyranny of the Market: A Critique of Theoretical Foundations* (1995), Douglas Vickers argues that: "The marginal

Product of labor cannot be specified.... Then the demand curve for labor that purports to derive from the marginal product conception is vacuous." If he is right, then the empirical link between inflation and unemployment is both weak and imprecise in both demand and supply. This frantic search for a theory underpinning Phillips' finding has led to the practice of first regressing changes in inflation on changes in unemployment. Next, coefficients are manipulated so as to produce estimates of the natural rate. However, as I have already indicated, the belief is that if in the long run, actual (f) and expected (f^*) inflation rates are equal, then the Phillips curve is vertical and the natural rate $u^* = a/b$. It follows that if u is less than u^*, f is greater than f^* and we should have a magic acceleration in inflation. On the other hand, if $u = u^*$, we should have stability in inflation and unemployment.

The reader may have already noticed that the long run is simply defined by setting $f = f^*$ and the rest follows. As the economist James K. Galbraith has remarked, all subsequent works focused on finetuning the above procedure to obtain smaller standard error of the constant term of a regression of one endogenous variable on another. The curious thing is that the data do not support this ad hoc theory. We nevertheless end up with a characteristic behavior that boils down to this: If inflation occurs, then the actual unemployment rate must be below the NAIRU. If inflation is stable and the actual rate of unemployment is higher than the previously estimated NAIRU, then the previous estimate must have been too low. This behavioral response is what Galbraith calls "a 30 year predictive failure."[4]

The point I wish to stress with regard to the NAIRU concept is that it may well be taken as a license for inaction. Suppose for a moment that a natural rate of unemployment really exists, then instead of saying that the current level of unemployment is far above the natural rate, policy makers may simply assume that the current rate is high because the natural rate, taken as a technical constraint, has shifted upward. Such an assumption would have numerous implications for policy, for what can be done against a high and shifting natural rate?

Finally, it may be asked: Could the unemployment insurance programs and/or labor market regulations hold the key to the puzzle of high unemployment? I attempt to sketch an answer by comparing the situations in the United States, the European Union, and in Japan. *Etude* 1994 summarizes them as follows. The U.S. situation is characterized by: (1) a 26-week long unemployment insurance program, but the rules for collecting are very strict; (2) a federal minimum wage that is low relative to the average salary in the economy; (3) a 16% unionized rate, and little or no coordinated salary negotiation, and; (4) an unregulated labor market, except in matters of outright discrimination. Consequently, the labor turnover rate is about twice as high as that prevailing in the Japanese economy (see Blanchflower and Freeman 1994), and the unemployment rate in 1993 was 6.7% and falling.

In the European Union, the situation is characterized in a similar way, that is: (1) a relatively generous unemployment insurance program in which affiliates receive between 60% to 70% of the average salary during 12 to 30 months; (2) a minimum salary determined either by the government, as in France and Spain, or by collective agreements as in Germany and Italy; (3) an elaborate work legislation whose aim is more than the equality of opportunities; it regulates work hours, recruiting, and firing procedures, as well as the social costs of employment. The average unemployment rate in 1993 was about 10% and rising.

In Japan, on the other hand, we have: (1) an unemployment insurance program that pays benefits up to 30 weeks; (2) a well-coordinated system of salary determination; (3) a regulated labor market where employment is regulated by type of industry (big firms usually offer employment for life but small ones may not); and (4) a well-coordinated retraining program with a proven record for improving the skill level of workers. To wit, the proportion of young workers within the ages of 25 to 34 with a first university diploma, is about twice that of those within the ages of 45 to 54. However, the proportion of young workers with less than a secondary education went down significantly over the last 20 years. The unemployment rate in 1993 was estimated at 2.5%.

What lessons can these three cases teach us? It is difficult to say. Unregulated labor markets and stingy insurance benefit programs do not necessarily produce low unemployment rates, although there is a temptation to draw just such a conclusion from the European experience. However, we should not be too quick to draw such an inference. It is contradicted by Japan and by other countries (such as Holland) as well. In countries such as Austria and Norway, for instance, women's participation is high; labor markets are regulated; unionized rates are relatively high; and unemployment insurance programs are generous. Yet, unemployment rates are relatively low, and we do not observe the social degradation that characterizes the United States and United Kingdom economies. Nonetheless, there must be a lesson in all of this. Let us continue probing the problem of unemployment in order to see if a clear lesson will finally emerge.

THE IMPACTS OF TECHNOLOGY ON UNEMPLOYMENT IN THE NORTH

The distinction between frictional and structural unemployment, for example, has always been an ambiguous one. Nevertheless, economists seem to agree that frictional unemployment is by any definition a transitory type based on the labor turnover rate, and that can be addressed by policy on labor mobility. Structural unemployment, on the other hand, appears to be a more intractable and persistent phenomenon, in particular when it is caused by a mismatch in the labor market. The degree of the mismatch itself may be so great and so deeply rooted in the educational system of a country that it needs be addressed outside the labor market.

Back in 1821, the economist David Ricardo provoked an uproar with his remark to the effect that the employment of machinery was not detrimental to the interests of the laboring class. Obviously, there are instances where the introduction of new technologies may even boost employment, although with an adjustment lag. However, even Ricardo had to backtrack from the above remark as the evidence on unemployment caused by rapid technical changes began to pile up. Today, the fact that the rapid process of innovation does lead to structural unemployment is so well established that the debate would be incomplete without at least a mention of the role of modern technology. In this regard, it should also be emphasized that the application of new technologies to the productive process is a major cause of wealth creation. However, it carries a huge cost in terms of unemployment that should not be slipped under the rug either; in particular when it is well-known that more often than not the design, introduction, and propagation of new technologies are carried out with one eye on profits and the other on wage growth, which boils down to the same thing.

The Northern market economies account for some 95% of the total expenditures on research and development. In these economies, new technologies are being incorporated in fixed capital assets at a very rapid pace (*Etude* 1995, 315), that is, the rapid development of computer technology, the incorporation of smart chips to machinery, among other things, are done with the goal of replacing labor in almost every sector of these economies. At times, one gets the impression that, outside Japan, the ultimate objective seems to be the transformation of the work place into a non-human environment (see McKinsey Global Institute 1994a; OECD 1992). As shown in Figure 6.1, new jobs are mainly in high technology areas which make use of scientists, engineers, and high-level cadres. From 1970 to 1992, the index of employment in high technology jobs in industrial countries rose by more than 10%; that of medium technology level remained more or less unchanged. But, the fall in employment requiring low skill levels and in manufacturing in general was drastic. Suppose that the United States's case, aptly described by Rebecca Blank (1996), represents a trend in the new orthodoxy, then the fall in low skill level jobs becomes a matter of great concern, for it may be irreversible. Blank has found that in the United States it is becoming harder and harder for low skill workers and poor families to escape poverty. For these workers, declining wages mean that work by itself has become a less effective way of escaping poverty.

Among men with less than a high school diploma who worked full-time all year, real wages declined by 22% from 1979 to 1993. Consequently, they faced far worse work opportunities than their fathers did.

Among women, with less than a high school diploma, who worked full-time all year, real wages declined by only 6% over the same period. However, these women started out with more deplorable conditions and continued to earn about 71% of the average salary of low skilled men, therefore, they faced more or less the same work opportunities as their mothers. If this trend is going to be preserved and reinforced in the North, then the unemployment problem is going to be intractable.

Figure 6.1
Employment Index by Technology Level in 17 Industrial Countries: 1970–1992

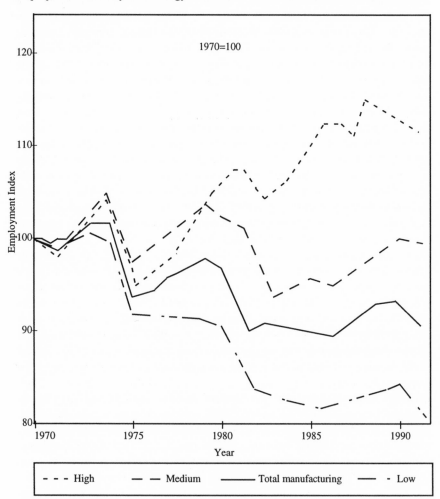

Source: *Etude sur l'économie mondiale* (1995, 315). The United Nations is the author of the original material.

UNEMPLOYMENT AND NEW FORMS OF EMPLOYMENT IN THE SOUTH

Compared with the North, countries in the South present a wider variety in terms of economic development and institutional setting. For the present purpose, suffice it to say that these countries have huge rural and informal sectors to which the above concepts and measurements of unemployment are not really applicable. When they are applied, the imprecision inherent to the measurement of various forms of unemployment is not only magnified, but the whole exercise reflects, albeit roughly, the situation in the urban areas.

In the North, sketchy evidence suggests that if the official definition of unemployment were to include discouraged workers and all those not counted for one reason or another the figures of open unemployment would significantly increase. Consider two examples. Back in 1992, the official unemployment rate in the United Kingdom was around 10%. Five years later, it is claimed that some 2 million workers are officially unemployed, representing about 6.9% of the active labor force. What is not said, however, is that in the meantime one million workers were not counted because they were considered not actively looking for work. Another 200,000 had been excluded from the roll on the ground that they were not immediately available for work. If these people were not excluded, the official unemployment rate would have been 11% rather than 6.9%.[5] In the United States of 1997, some 8 million individuals were officially unemployed, representing 5.6% of the active labor force. This is hailed as an exemplar of economic dynamism under the new orthodoxy. At the same time there were some 5 million discouraged and 4.5 million involuntary part-time workers. Then the actual rate of unemployment was between 9.1% and 12%. What are we then to make of these official figures?

In order to have more realistic unemployment rates in the South, bigger correction factors would be required. For example, Tokman and Garcia (1981) estimated open unemployment in Latin America to be around 20% of the active population. Squire (1979) obtained 26% for Asia and 40% for Africa. When these figures are expressed in proportions of the active urban labor force, they climb to 25%, 50% and 61%, respectively. Adjusting these already rough estimates either upward or downward still leaves them unacceptable. Now imagine the havoc being created by restructuring and downsizing in such settings. The case of Bolivia (*Etude* 1994), seems to be a good illustration. Back in 1985, when the new orthodoxy was first applied, Bolivia was suffering from hyperinflation in its modern sector. Its official unemployment rate was reported at 6%. Immediately thereafter, some 20,000 miners were dismissed from the publicly owned mines. Real wages were reduced by about 25%, while other restrictive measures were applied without mercy. Three years later, the official unemployment rate had already doubled. The case of Bolivia may or may not be typical, but it can serve as a reference case to gauge similar situations in the absence of specific studies. Of course, such situations would have to be studied in the light of the impacts of external shocks, debt service, wars, natural disasters, demographic growth, and economic embargoes.

Weird Trends

In the South, greed, vices, and the exigencies of the new orthodoxy combine to exacerbate an already precarious situation. This is exemplified by the appearance of some weird trends in employment. Two of the most revulsive ones, that is, child labor and slave factory work, are already prominent in the dark alleys of Asia, Latin America, and Africa. In order to place them in focus, I now turn to the last ILO report on child labor and to one story from China.

The ILO estimates the number of child workers in the South at 250 million. I cannot vouch for this figure. However, the scale of this new problem appears so great, by any comparison, that the ILO recommends urgent actions be taken to forestall the exploitation of children in dangerous industrial employment, and in the sex trade involving some one million children. The Report details the long hours and diseases that child workers are exposed to in mining, agriculture, ceramics and glass factories, deep-sea fishing, and construction. There are two aspects of the problem that many may find shocking, some of the worst conditions are found in factories producing goods for export under contracts to Western-owned multinational firms, and children as young as three-years-old are reported to be working in fireworks and match factories across the Indian subcontinent.

In 1995, the ILO survey was restricted to children aged 10 to 14. The number of child workers was estimated at 73 million. In 1996, the survey was extended to children within the ages of 5 to 14. The number climbed to 250 million, with 153 million in Asia, 80 million in Africa, and about 18 million in Latin America. Some 120 million of the total were working full time. As I have already indicated, the 250 million figure seems dubious. However, since it does not include children under 5, nor those engaged in domestic services (due to the hidden nature of the latter), nor the situation of Eastern Europe, the world total may very well be staggering. Some experts in the matter, such as Assela Bequele of the United Nations, attribute this sad state of affairs to the IMF's structural adjustment programs, the rapid transition to a market economy in Asia, and the collapse of state structures in some parts of Africa.

The second weird trend observed in employment practices in the South, more prominent in Asia than anywhere else, must squarely be laid at the doorstep of globalization. It is illustrated by a Chinese case. Imagine platoons of workers, marching in step and shouting in unison: Be loyal! Love my work! Thanks to the boss! This is more or less the way Anita Chan, writing in *The Guardian Weekly* of November 17, 1996, describes the new factory reality in some parts of China, the country which recently tops the economic growth list. I might also add that the spur of offshore production of goods for exports, such as Nike and Reebok shoes, is straight from the loins of globalization. This is also a growing trend in numerous factories in China, supervised by Taiwanese and South Korean bosses, which is now spreading to Vietnam and Cambodia.

As noted by Chan, popular wisdom has it that the success of Chinese and Korean overseas businesses is due to the Confucian culture in which mutual trust, flexibility, and interpersonal relationships dominate. No, says Chan. The so-called Asian economic miracle consists of giant factories, staffed with the rural poor, and managed by ruthless military discipline so as to gain the maximum cost advantages required by globalization. She finds a hankering for military standards of discipline and unquestioned loyalty under the supervision of retired army officers. For example, security guards must snap to attention and salute factory managers at each encounter[6]; employees must run a mile per day and do as many pushups as they can in one minute. This discipline, by itself, could at first sight appear salubrious, until it is put in its proper context. The context consists of 12-hour day and night shifts, compulsory overtime, dormitory life, corporal punishments, a penalty of one half a day's wage for lateness, and a subsistence nominal wage of $0.25 per hour.

Why are these developments now taking place in China? Because nominal wages in Taiwan, Hong Kong, and Korea have risen. Within the logic of globalization, as wages begin to rise in China, the bosses begin to move their factories to Vietnam and Cambodia rather than paying higher wages. In this sense, Paul Krugman is quite right in saying that the present phenomenal growth rates of Asia are bound to be ephemeral.

Of course, think-tank theorists, financed by multinationals, will certainly argue that such situations, encountered in Latin America as well, are better than no work at all. After all, no one obliges the rural poor to accept such working conditions, one of them has already argued. Professor Robert Solow has a counter argument for this kind of reasoning. He had the concept of *voluntary unemployment* in mind when he said: "[B]y this standard (reasoning), all the American soldiers who were killed in Vietnam could be counted as suicides since they could have deserted, emigrated to Canada or shot themselves in the foot, but did not" (1986, S33). Just the same, in order to see how voluntary such employment opportunities are, one has just to consider the turnover rates of these factories. They are so high that factory bosses feel compelled to require two weeks to a month wage plus ID cards as a deposit on hiring to make sure that workers do not leave before the expiration date of their contract. Is this the road to economic growth and democracy?

WHAT IS THE LESSON?

The implicit consensus within the new orthodoxy is that countries with high unemployment should follow the United States and United Kingdom's examples. Because unemployment is seen as a lesser world problem than the consequences of high social costs of employment. Is collective social insurance really an impediment to full employment? The Japanese economy would seem to attest to the contrary. That economy is now in a slump due to the misbehavior of its unregulated banks, yet its official unemployment rate is the lowest among the economies of the G7 group, perhaps the lowest in the world. Because its operation rests on a wholly different conception of the labor market, the obligations of employers to employees produce a structure of social insurance in which the labor market is organized to reduce individual workers' risks. Within such a structure, the obligations of cadres are to their employees first, their customers second, and their shareholders last. This means that workers know that the large firms at least will make them redundant only as a last resort. This also means that in guaranteeing work throughout good times and absorbing lower profits during bad times, the large firms carry a cost that the new orthodoxy advises against. In the West, however, large firms are instead in thrall to their shareholders. Hence, they are unable to see that providing the certainty of employment relieves the pressure on social security systems.

Social costs, in terms of taxes and national insurance contributions, can be lower and secure a wider notion of economic efficiency through high employment rates. In addition, by taking responsibility for their employees, large Japanese firms expect and indeed obtain a reciprocal commitment that brings higher compensatory productivity. Moreover, the guarantee of employment benefits these firms in at least two indirect ways, that is, it keeps the consumer market relatively buoyant and it reduces social tension. More specifically, the large firms have built around them an array of subcontractors, called small firms, on whom they displace a part of the risk of economic fluctuations. This way, their own work force remains stable, while that of the small firms does not. Meanwhile, the small firms design a wage structure that is geared to economic fluctuations. The result is that productivity is extremely high in the big firms involved in the export sectors and low elsewhere. But big and small firms interlock to produce an overall economic and social structure characterized by high average productivity and low average social costs. Of course, I have just described the pre-1995 Japan. By 1995, and after resisting American pressure to move toward the wild form of laissez-faire specific to the United States, Japan had finally yielded to globalization. The resulting havoc, created by unregulated bank activities (over $1 trillion of bad debts), has destroyed consumer confidence and encouraged capital flight (estimated at over $1 billion per day). The collapse in Japan's finance sector has also caused employment in the construction and public works sectors to fall by some 11% as of July 1998, while enemployment is fast rising in all sectors.

In the other G7 countries, the efficiency gain from labor market flexibility, expounded by the new orthodoxy, consists mainly in laying workers off and replacing them with machines in the name of a concept termed substitution by the theory. While it is technically correct to argue that the economic value of work must equal wage, it is nonetheless disastrous socially when no one assumes the responsibility for providing work. In a setting in which no other pattern of behavior is permitted due to the deep-seated belief that the unemployed are deep down undeserving, firms' costs are lowered, but that of society increases. Then the new orthodoxy tells us that because social costs are rising, individual workers must provide for their old age, sickness, or even their own employment. No doubt many will, but a bigger share will not be able to. It then follows that, within such a setting, all notions of welfare maximization must be dropped. But the Japanese experience suggests otherwise. Therefore, countries in the North and in the South with high unemployment, and which care about the welfare of their population, would do well to look toward the pre-1995 Japan for a way out.

SOCIAL SECURITY AND ECONOMIC WELL-BEING

The purpose of social security (SS) systems is to first and foremost finance the period of retirement of workers. In most countries where such programs exist, benefits paid to the elderly are typically in the forms of annuities that continue until the death of the recipient. Depending on statutes, social security systems may provide benefits to the disabled, surviving spouses, and children at levels that depend on the recipients' needs and on previous contributions made by them while working. Beyond these forms of income support, social security systems provide insurance. Here I refer to social security systems which include income supports and disability and survivors' benefits; the latter represents the primary source of disability and life insurance to the public.

There are a number of valid economic reasons for social security systems. First, although costly for present and future generations, these benefits nonetheless transfer resources to a needy generation of elderly, and thereby smooth out their consumption schedule. Second, when benefits paid out to the elderly are positively related to earnings of the younger generation, there is some intergenerational risk-sharing, which counteract the adverse selection problem of private insurance markets. Finally, although these benefits may adversely affect the saving rate, they improve social welfare as evidenced by increased life expectancy. However, within the new orthodoxy, a huge problem looms large over the future of such systems.

Social security systems are funded through taxes levied on workers' salaries, and often equally on employers as well. In either case, such programs may either be *fully funded* or *underfunded.* When these systems are fully funded, they allocate each dollar contributed to a dollar's worth of old age annuity and insurance benefits. Most countries have set up underfunded, or pay-as-you-go, systems; this type allows for the possibility of intra and intergenerational distributions. This makes it unnecessary to have a huge trust fund, as in the case of fully funded systems, because, rather than paying from past contributions, underfunded systems use current tax contributions to pay for current benefits. Theoretically, a pay-as-you-go system may benefit the start-up group of elders and penalize the initial young and future generations. For the latter groups, the present expected value of their contributions may be less than the present expected value of their benefits. The reason for this is that a mature underfunded system can only pay, on average, a return on contributions equal to the rate of population growth (k) plus the productivity growth rate (g) and a negligible second order term. If this return is less than the economy's steady rate of interest (r), workers receive a smaller return than if they had saved and invested in the economy themselves. As shown by Paul Samuelson (1958): If $r > k + g + kg$, they will be worse off; if $r < k + g + kg$, they will be better off, and; if $r = k + g + kg$, expected present values balance out and no further increases in contributions are necessary. However, the reader will no doubt realize that these conclusions can only serve as a bench mark; they arose from crude calculations done in an oversimplified partial equilibrium two-period model. In real underfunded social security systems, any increase in the number of recipients, or any decline in the earnings of contributors, requires either a reduction in benefit levels or an increase in payroll taxes. Such adjustments to changing demographics and overall economic conditions can be significant in terms of costs.

It is not uncommon in countries with enlightened governments and enough wealth for SS systems to offer extensive coverage, such as medical care, unemployment insurance, disability insurance, work accident insurance, maternity insurance, family assistance, rent subsidies, among other things, which constitute what I have previously termed the sufficient conditions for the promotion of welfare. When coverage is so extensive, it is safe to say that social security programs benefit adults of 65 and over (the elderly), as well as children under 15 years old (the future workers). All of these forms of protection were deemed necessary for welfare 45 years ago when there was greater social cohesion and economic growth. Since then, these programs have been at one time or another subjected to elaborate studies by economists that have looked at the welfare lost due to the taxes levied to finance them, their impacts on national saving, their impacts on employment, and so on. The major criticism levied against such underfunded programs is that taking money from the young savers and giving it to old spenders reduces national saving and addles the next generation with debt. This is however, hypothetical, for this argument pre-supposes that the young generation is not now benefiting from social security systems. At any rate, there is no real consensus as to the net effects of these programs except in one area life expectancy which is one objective index of their beneficial effects. Assuming that coverage is more extensive in richer countries than in poor ones, Table A6.4 examines the situation in ten countries in the North and in seven in the South. The intuition that extensive coverage is beneficial in terms of life expectancy is borne out by the comparison.

Returning now to the problem of financing these systems, one should note that the proportion of 15-year-olds, who will be the future contributors, is falling almost everywhere. At the same time, the proportion of 65-year-olds and over, the recipients of benefits, is rising almost everywhere in the world. Hence, to maintain a given level of well-being in underfunded systems, the amounts of resources devoted to these programs must increase. In the North, in addition to a rising proportion of the elderly, a lower proportion of the active labor force is working and contributing to these systems. Meanwhile, in the South, social security coverage has increased, but a far lower percentage of those in need are actually covered. How then can an adequate level of well-being be maintained in the North and extended to all deserving souls in the South in the age of deconstruction? This, in a nutshell, is the present problem of social security systems.

According to the United Nations, in 1990, some 160 countries had some form of social security in place, compared with only 80 countries at the end of the 1950s (see also Otting 1993). The significant progress made since is now being threatened by demographic shifts as shown in Table A6.5, and by the dictates of the new orthodoxy. The United States is one of those countries with extensive coverage which is now grappling with the financing problem. Let us use this case to size up the problem.

Financing Social Security Programs in the United States

The U.S. program began with the Social Security Act of 1935. Today, it is mainly seen as a public underfunded program, financed by payroll taxes. As workers pay in, they accumulate credits toward benefits at retirement. At any point in time, tax inflows and benefit outflows can be projected, based on various economic and demographic assumptions, so as to determine the actuarial viability of the program. In order to keep the benefit outflows stable in an underfunded system, where each generation of elderly is supported by the next generation, one relies on a combined employer-employee tax rate on taxable wages.

Projections show potential problems, and steps are being taken to revise the requirements, whose details are outlined in Gramlich (1996). Here, I comment on the factors used to determine the actuarial viability of the program.

As I have said, a social security program may comprise various forms of assistance, the U.S. program is one of those. It is a package that includes Medicare Hospitalization Insurance (HI) and Old Age, Survivor, and Disability Insurance (OASDI). The reform proposal aims at combining the trust funds of these programs, because the benefits paid out are financed by the same workers' contributions. In 1995, it was estimated that the OASDI trust fund will dip below what is called its safety level in 2030; the safety level is defined as a year's worth of benefits. The HI trust fund, on the other hand, was projected to become unsafe in 2002, but one of the avowed objectives of the U.S. system is to make these funds actuarially safe for one generation, that is, for 75 years. An advisory council, formed in 1994, was then asked to determine, among other things, the combined employer-employee tax rate (t) that would preserve the actuarial safety just defined. The formula proposed by the council is as follows: Let the ratio, a, denote the average level of social security benefits, divided by the average taxable wages, and call it the aggregate replacement ratio; this ratio is, therefore, the rate at which wages are replaced by social security benefits at retirement. Next, define the ratio, b, as the number of social security recipients, divided by the total number of workers, and call it the dependency ratio. It follows that the combined employer-employee tax rate necessary to pay for benefits is: $t \equiv ab$.

In the case of the United States, and most likely in that of the European Union as well, the demographics show that people are living longer and they are not having enough children to stabilize the population share of young people (see Table A6.5). As a result, the dependency ratio (b) is steadily rising. At present, it is about 0.29, but it is projected to rise to 0.50 by 2030, the year in which the last members of the baby boom generation will reach retirement. And by the end of the 75 year forecast, it is expected to rise to 0.56.[7] Assume now thať the replacement rate (*a*) remains constant, then t must rise in order to pay for an agreed benefit level.

As of 1995, *t* was set at 12.4%; that is enough until 2030. Beyond that, it must rise to 17% until 2070, and to 19% and rise steadily afterwards. It is important to bear in mind that these projections are based on a constant ratio *a.* This may not be so in the age of deconstruction. The actual trends are falling wages and employment due to the application of the new orthodoxy, and rising number of recipients due to the demographics. Hence, in order to preserve a given level of benefits, *t* might have to rise much faster than the above projections show.

Many other counties, such as Argentina, Peru, Colombia, Sweden, Australia, New Zealand, Canada, among others, have revised or are in the process of revising their schemes. The questions of interest for them are: Where should accumulated funds be invested? Should countries move to private social security schemes for greater efficiency? In that connection, there has been much talk about the success of the Chilean system, which I will now examine it, albeit briefly, in order to see whether or not it could be a model for other countries to follow.

The Chilean Social Security Program

Chile was certainly among the first of the countries in the South to have instituted a social security scheme in 1924. Its coverage was relatively wide, ranging over the informal and formal sectors. By the 1970s, however, it began to show signs of great strain. It was run by more than one bureaucracy and the structure of benefit paid-out was set by industry and occupation. In short, it had become complex and inefficient. Consequently, in 1981, it was reformed and privatized.

At the heart of the reform is a mandatory savings plan, which is linked to a market for indexed annuities for the conversion of accumulated funds into retirement benefits. Affiliates of the previous public program were offered two options, that is, either stay with the public program or join one of the private regimes. Those who chose to go private received a premium that depended on their accumulated contributions as bonds (*bonos de reconocimiento*). However, new entrants in the labor market are given no choice but to adhere to the private regimes at a cost set at 10% of their monthly earnings. Those who want additional benefits such as disability and survivor's insurance must pay an additional 3.5% of their earnings. We can already see that compared with the U.S. public system, the Chilean private scheme costs slightly more on average for similar benefits; that is, 12.4% versus 13.5%, respectively.

In the Chilean scheme, the amount of benefits paid out depends on accumulated funds, which in turn depend on the rate of return of invested funds. A worker can draw his share of capital at retirement in the form of phased withdrawals, or he or she can buy an indexed annuity. The state guarantees a minimum pension (at 65 for men and 60 for women) to those not having sufficient contributions to provide them with between 22% to 25% of their average previous earnings.

The resources contributed to this funded system are managed by 21 highly regulated *Administradoras de Fondos de Pensiones* (AFP). Affiliates are free to choose between them, depending on competence and performance, measured in terms of rates of return. According to Gillon and Bonilla (1992), the private regimes have thus far done much better in terms of capital accumulation, compared with the old regime, and invested funds have earned relatively higher rates of return. These two factors have contributed to the popularity of the Chilean scheme, and seem to support the view that privatization is the route to higher efficiency. In this regard, two observations are in order.

In terms of capital accumulation, it is true that the records of the privatized regimes are impressive. As of June 1992, total accumulations came to about 35% of GDP, and reached 43% of GDP in 1993, compared with only 1% of GDP by 1981. Equity holding by the AFPs represented more than 11% of the total value of the Santiago Stock Exchange by 1994; they also hold some 55% of government bonds, 59% of corporate bonds, and 62% of mortgage bonds. In terms of rates of return, the average rate was 14.5% per year from July 1981 to July 1992. On this score, however, it seems that these high rates are due more to the performance of the Chilean economy as a whole over the same period than to the ingenuity of private administrators. Even so, the system has thus far played a significant role in the process of capital accumulation.

The second observation relates to costs. We have already seen that the U.S. system, with a tax rate of 12.4%, will remain viable until 2030. In the Chilean system, the tax rate for similar benefits is 13.5%. Valdes-Prieto (1994) estimates the administrative cost of the Chilean system at about 2.94% of taxable earnings. This is translated into about $89.1 per affiliate per year, compared with $18.7 per affiliate per year in the public U.S. system. This high administrative cost is perhaps due to a huge sale force and to wasteful advertising of the AFPs in their competitive drive for new clients, thus, it costs affiliates over 16% of their earnings. It might be worth drawing attention at this point to another strange feature of the Chilean system. Employers have no obligation to contribute to the plan; this clearly has a bearing on affiliate costs. In addition, the initial cost of transferring from the public to private regimes, estimated at about 4% of GDP, was borne entirely by the public purse. Finally, when administrative costs of similar schemes are compared across countries, the Chilean scheme fares well compared to Jamaica (10%) and Zambia (50%), but less well in relation to Malaysia (2.5%), Norway (2.1%), and Singapore (0.53%).

The Chilean plan should be considered for its capital accumulation power and for demonstrating that any given part of a social security scheme can be privatized. However, countries that are considering reproducing it should be aware of its transition and administrative costs, and of its unexplained feature whereby employers have no obligation. Also to be considered are certain drawbacks inherent to privatization. One of them relates to the intergenerational risk-sharing element already mentioned. This element will most likely be absent from privatized systems because the private sector cannot sign contracts with unborn future generations. Another is the ever present danger of exacerbating the adverse selection problem, which refers to the vulnerability of buyers of new products whose quality-price characteristic cannot be observed. On the other hand, a privatized system is likely to give households a grater choice in the management of their retirement funds. However, if they happen to be less well informed about risks and return, and/or are unable to make wise investment decisions, the additional choice could turn out to be detrimental to their well-being in a less secured private system.

We have seen since Chapter 4 that markets by themselves are not sufficient to promote people's welfare. The evidence from the very first countries to have embraced the new orthodoxy clearly shows this much. If maximum welfare is really the ultimate goal of society, as claimed by economic science, then high employment levels and various income support and insurance schemes cannot but play a significant role in its obtainment. We have also seen why, in this respect, falling wages and employment as well as the downsizing demanded by the new orthodoxy are worrisome. As revealed by Blank's (1996) study, supported by data from Canada, there is an almost perfect positive correlation between unemployment and child poverty. This situation is exacerbated by cuts in various income support programs. True, paying for them is quite demanding. However, postponing the sacrifice now will only make it more costly later. Child poverty produces dysfunctional societies and dysfunctional adult workers. Embracing the attitude and the philosophy expounded by the new orthodoxy can only mean turning one's back on the goal of welfare promotion.

The other point that should be stressed is that the above formula relating wage growth and inflation, which is now guiding attitudes toward unemployment is based on unverifiable assumptions. None of the variables (inflation, actual, and natural rates of unemployment) can be accurately measured. The direction of causality is not firmly established. There is thus considerable room for maneuvering in a situation such as this and, obviously, different interest groups interpret it so as to further their interests. But, my point is: After seeing that the formula cannot explain the stylized facts, why not turn it around for once? Instead of adding concepts, like epicycles to the Ptolemaic construct, why not change the interpretation? Maybe, investment in education and training, leading to productivity increases, to high wages and low unemployment, and finally, to little or moderate inflation, would better fit the stylized facts. It seems to me that by trying, only "false consciousness" would be put at risk.

APPENDIX 6

Table A6.1
Labor Force Growth in Developed Market Economies: 1961–1993 (in %)

Period	OECD Countries	European Union	United States	Japan
1961–1973	1.1	0.3	2.0	1.3
1974–1990	1.2	0.5	1.9	1.0
1991–1993	-0.1	-1.1	0.3	1.3

Source: Compiled from *Etude sur l'économie mondiale* (1994, 327). The United Nations is the author of the original material.

Table A6.2
**Employment, Unemployment, and Inactivity in Selected Countries: 1973–1992
(proportions of the 25 to 54-year-old men and women in the total population)**

			1973	1979	1990	1992
United States		a)	91.6	90.6	88.5	86.2
	men	b)	2.3	3.1	4.1	6.0
		c)	6.1	6.3	7.4	7.8
		a)	49.7	59.0	70.6	70.2
	women	b)	2.3	3.2	3.3	4.4
		c)	50.3	37.8	26.1	25.4
Japan		a)	96.7	95.5	96.1	96.2
	men	b)	1.0	1.6	1.4	1.4
		c)	2.3	2.8	2.5	2.4
		a)	53.8	55.1	62.9	64.1
	women	b)	0.5	1.1	1.3	1.3
		c)	45.7	43.8	35.8	34.6
United Kingdom		a)	93.5	91.8	86.3	81.3
	men	b)	2.1	3.8	6.3	11.5
		c)	4.4	4.4	6.3	7.2
		a)	58.3	62.0	71.0	70.2
	women	b)	0.3	1.3	2.0	3.2
		c)	41.7	36.7	27.0	26.6
France		a)	94.5	93.3	89.6	88.5
	men	b)	2.3	3.1	5.6	6.5
		c)	3.2	3.7	4.6	5.0
		a)	52.8	59.5	65.1	66.4
	women	b)	1.3	3.5	7.8	8.5
		c)	45.9	37.0	27.1	25.1
Sweden		a)	92.7	94.0	93.8	87.9
	men	b)	1.6	1.3	1.3	5.4
		c)	5.7	4.7	4.9	7.2
		a)	66.8	79.5	89.2	85.2
	women	b)	2.1	1.6	1.2	3.5
		c)	31.1	18.9	9.6	11.3

a) employed b) unemployed c) inactive

Source: Compiled from *Etude sur l'économie mondiale* (1994, 330–31). The United Nations is the author of the original material.

Table A6.3
The Anatomy of Unemployment in Selected Developed Market Economies (in %)

Country	Unemployment Rate			The Inactivity Rate of	
	1990	1993	Long term as % of total in 1990	25 to 54 year-olds since 1990	25 to 54 year-olds 1974-1992
Canada	8.1	11.3	5.7	18.1	10.2
United States	5.4	6.7	5.6	13.8	5.4
Australia	6.9	11.1	21.6	15.9	11.8
Japan	2.1	2.5	19.1	3.8	0.5
Germany	4.8	5.9	46.3	18.7	13.9
France	8.9	11.7	38.3	11.5	7.3
Spain	15.9	23.1	54.0	18.7	13.9
Italy	10.3	10.3	71.2	14.2	6.6
Netherlands	7.5	8.5	48.4	10.5	3.2
Austria	3.2	4.4	—	—	—
England	6.8	10.4	36.0	18.7	12.2
Finland	3.4	17.9	6.9	20.8	11.0
Norway	5.2	6.1	19.2	13.7	5.0
Sweden	1.5	9.4	4.8	12.2	6.8
Ireland	13.4	16.7	67.2	19.6	7.5

Source: Adapted from *Etude sur l'économie mondiale* (1994, 335). The United Nations is the author of the original material.

Table A6.4
Life Expectancy of 60-Year-Old Men and Women in Selected Countries: 1950 and 1990 (in approximate number of years beyond 60)

Country	men		women	
	1950	1990	1950	1990
Developed				
United States	15.5	18.6	18.5	22.5
Germany	16.5	17.2	17.2	21.8
France	15.0	19.0	18.1	24.2
Italy	16.0	18.0	17.5	22.6
Canada	16.5	18.5	18.6	23.1
Japan	14.2	20.0	16.5	24.1
Sweden	17.0	19.0	18.0	23.2
Switzerland	16.0	19.0	17.7	23.7
Norway	18.4	18.1	19.0	22.7
Spain	15.0	18.8	13.0	19.2
Developing				
Mauritius	11.0	14.2	14.6	18.1
Guatemala	14.7	16.5	14.5	17.5
India	11.2	14.6	13.0	16.6
Colombia	12.0	17.2	13.0	17.5
Philippines	16.0	15.5	18.2	17.2
Ecuador	14.2	17.6	16.3	19.2
Costa Rica	14.9	18.8	15.8	21.9

Source: Adapted from *Etude sur l'économie mondiale* (1995, Figures xv.1 and xv.2, 380–81). The United Nations is the author of the original material.

Table A6.5
Proportions of Dependents in the Total World Population: 1970–2025

	1970	1990	2025
Developed Regions of which	36.2	33.5	36.8
less than 15	26.6	21.3	17.8
65 and over	9.6	12.2	19.0
Developing Regions of which	45.8	40.1	33.8
less than 15	41.8	35.6	25.8
65 and over	3.7	4.5	8.0
Africa	47.9	48.0	38.9
less than 15	44.8	45.0	34.8
65 and over	3.1	3.0	4.1
Latin America	46.4	40.7	34.3
less than 15	42.5	35.9	25.7
65 and over	3.9	4.8	8.6
Asia	44.3	37.9	32.2
less than 15	40.3	32.9	22.6
65 and over	4.0	5.0	9.6
World of which	42.9	38.5	34.2
less than 15	37.5	32.3	24.5
65 and over	5.4	6.2	9.7

Source: *Etude sur l'économie mondiale* (1995, 383). The United Nations is the author of the original material.

7

GROWING ECONOMIES IN A FINITE ECOSYSTEM

INTRODUCTION

From one year to the next, the absolute size of an economy, measured by the quantity of goods and services it produces, may decrease, increase, or remain the same. We normally refer to these situations as *negative* economic growth, *positive* economic growth, or the *steady-state* economy, respectively. This chapter deals with the last two. However, there are a few important concepts to clear up before we begin. In the past, positive economic growth and economic development were used synonymously. Even today, the two may be easily be confused unless they are explicitly distinguished. Therefore, for present purposes, I define economic development as a process by which an economy provides its agents with the means to realize their potentiality, by gradually bringing them to a fuller, greater, or better state. Whereas, (positive) economic growth will refer to a natural increase in size by additions or through a more efficient organization of economic activities. However, what we call efficiency is taste and technology dependent, as we have already seen, and as such, it is governed by these two factors. An increase in size due to additions simply implies additions of material, through assimilation and accretion. In such a set up, the concept of availability is of central importance. As it may be known, there is a considerable amount of energy stored in the raw materials found in nature. When we use these raw materials, we consume the availability of the stored energy in doing useful work, but not the stored energy itself. In thermodynamics, the concept of availability is associated with entropy, a measure of disorder that is also inversely related to the concept of availability of useful energy; that is, when entropy is low, availability is high. We may then say that the entropy of the stored energy is low and, as we decrease its availability entropy increases. We may express the second law of thermodynamics as the principle by which all physical processes end up by increasing the entropy (disorder) of the universe. According to Georgescu-Roegen (1971), the whole economic process may be described as a process that feeds on low-entropy materials found in nature. In this inquiry, I am more concerned with the type of growth that results from the increased transformation of low-entropy inputs into high-entropy artifacts and services.[1] In the end analysis, my aim is to provide an answer to the basic question: Can this process go on for ever, as the economic establishment has led us to believe?

Curiously enough, during the Middle Ages, a period that spans some one thousand years, economic growth, as defined here, was absent from the economic and social calculus. It is much later, in the time of Adam Smith (1776), that economists have begun to concern themselves with growth proper, that is, the minute they began pondering the question as to whether the invisible hand could generate the desired pace of economic expansion. Nonetheless, from Adam Smith to the end of World War II, the focus first was on the long run growth of England. Later, attention shifted to the rest of Western Europe and North America. However, very little was known about the process itself. Growth theorizing proper was merely confined to a series of reflections of a few individuals who were primarily interested in the development of trade. In the mid-1930s, a Harvard Professor, Joseph Schumpeter, attempted to put the process of growth/economic development on a more analytical footing. The effort of Schumpeter then paved the way for the subsequent analyses done along the lines of Domar (1947) and Harrod (1948). These theories somehow marked a real turning point in the sense that they inadvertently fostered the idea that the growth process had no end. From there on, modern industrial societies began regarding economic growth as synonymous with progress. Little by little, growth became a panacea for all problems. Now it is seen as a signal indicating the path that these societies must follow in order to create a material and technological paradise on earth.

At times, one gets the impression that growth means whatever suits one's purpose. According to Douthwaite, the economic establishment first identifies growth with Pigou's (1932) "economic welfare" and later with "society's welfare." Both bilateral and multilateral aid agencies have taken up the habit of equating growth with rising living standard and, therefore, with the eradication of poverty. From its inception in 1945 through the 1960s, the World Bank, for example, focussed exclusively on big projects, convinced that it was fighting poverty through economic growth. The results have been some growth but also the so-called debt crises, social and environmental degradation, and increased relative poverty. The fiction that relative poverty can only be fought with growth is so pervasive that it is risky to even question it. In the North, almost everyone is brought up to think that the future will always be materially richer than the present and the past. This pattern of thought is shared by millions in the South who, despite recent evidence, still believe that things can get better only through economic growth. The belief is so solidly embedded in the social consciousness that anyone who dares question its basic premises runs the risk of being branded a pariah (Douthwaite 1993, 5–7 passim).

The problem I want to draw attention to is that our notion of growth may be a good or a bad thing, depending on how it is defined or measured. In the North, the benefits of economic growth seem to receive all the attention, while its drawbacks are carefully kept out of view, hence growth is always cast in a good light. In the South, however, this is harder to do. Drawbacks such as pollution and the depletion of natural resources, being simply too obvious, have overshadowed the benefits of growth. This negative result then gave rise to a second wave of growth analyses, spearheaded by the work of Robert Solow (1956), also known as the traditional neoclassical theory of economic growth. Solow's model was, of course, never free of weaknesses. Its omissions and deficiencies led to a third wave of theorizing, now known as the theory of endogenous growth, developed along the path pioneered by Romer (1986) and Lucas (1988). Due to the lack of space, I restrict myself to these theories because they seem to be the most representative of the lot, but there are countless models of growth in the economic literature. In fact, the field seems to jump from one growth model to another in an attempt to understand the process and, more importantly, to avoid difficult questions such as: Where is economic growth taking us? How long can it go on? What are its true benefits and costs?

A few thoughtful economists have had the courage to question our growthmania. Professor John Kenneth Galbraith, for example, in his book *Economics, Peace and Laughter* (1971), remarks that since no one in the advanced countries has ever asked what society was trying to achieve, people were unaware that there was any need for choice about how resources were used. Professor Kenneth Boulding (1964) raised a similar concern with his now famous remark: "Anyone who believes exponential growth can go on forever in a finite world is either a madman or an economist." More recently, Richard Douthwaite, in a well-documented and well-argued book, *The Growth Illusion* (1993), draws attention to the high costs of growth. While it is true that economic growth has improved the lives of many in both North and South, it has also accomplished something else, something that we have shied way from. The unpleasant task of bringing it to the fore falls on some courageous analysts like Edward Goldsmith who, referring to the impacts of growth in the Third World in the preface of the *The Growth Illusion*, puts it this way: "Economic development [growth], by destroying people's families and communities, annihilating their natural environment and forcing them off their land and into the slums, is in fact the greatest source of their present insecurity." Why can not troublesome questions about growth be asked? As I have just alluded to, I believe that it is because, in the North, statistics are collected on the short term and on the observable benefits of growth, while negative impacts are relegated to the wilderness. Under these circumstances, very few have found it necessary to bother to ask whether or not the assumed benefits of growth exceed its costs. Such neglect is of course further justified by the huge gap between the time benefits are perceived and the time costs are felt. And when the costs finally arrive, they are perceived as new problems whose solutions reside in more growth.

Here I shall try to balance various views on growth, starting with the initial effort outlined in the works of Domar and Harrod. I hasten to add, however, that Harrod's paper, after attracting much attention, was subsequently found to be incomplete. Domar's paper then took the lead in providing directions for new research for a time. Whatever deficiencies that remained in it were supposed to be addressed in Solow's model, which I take as the real point of departure of growthmania. Against the background provided by Solow, I take a quick look at the third wave, touched off by Romer and Lucas, before moving on to a more realistic approach to economic growth in a finite world.

ECONOMIC GROWTH AS SEEN BY ECONOMISTS

Economists have somehow found it easier to look at economic growth in mathematical terms. In an attempt to shed light on the process and to extend the scope of the scientific theory, they have naturally constructed various ad hoc growth models. As is usually the case, dominant ones are succinct representations of dominant viewpoints. Hence, through these models one can form a fairly good idea of the evolution of economists' understanding of the process of growth. In order to do that though, I must first define a few variables and review a couple of assumptions. Let O stand for output, K for the stock of physical capital, Y for the level of income, and I for investment or realized saving (because the two are supposed to be equal in equilibrium). We next make two basic assumptions. First, the rate of economic growth (g) is the product of the investment-output ratio (I/O) and the output-capital ratio (O/K). Second, investment is taken to be proportional to the capital stock (or, equivalently, proportional to the level of income), and output is proportional to the capital stock. We may then write: $I \cong sY$ and $O \cong bK$, where b is a proportionality constant and s is the constant marginal propensity to save (*i.e.*, the variation in income divided by the variation in saving). This implies that investment, being also proportional to the stock of capital, determines the rate of growth of both output and capital for a given level of capacity utilization. Once these relations are accepted, it then follows that the saving-income ratio is identical to the investment-output ratio.

Output is assumed to be produced with capital and labor. If the labor force (L) grows at the rate (e) and labor productivity is $\lambda = O/L$, then output must grow at the rate ($e + \lambda$) in order to keep all the labor force employed. In other words,

$$g = (I/O)(O/K) = (sY/Y)(bK/K) = sb = e + \lambda$$

From this equilibrium set up, it can be seen that if (sb) is greater than ($e + \lambda$), the economy has run out of workers. If, on the other hand, (sb) is less than ($e + \lambda$), unemployment has increased beyond bounds. Hence, equilibrium means the above equality. For a time, this was the received view despite the obvious fact that growth is primarily associated with disequilibrium.

Solow was among the first to realize that this reasoning was too simplistic. In every economy, people are obsessed with growth, Solow then asks: If growth was dependent on four little parameters, taken two at the time, why could economies not just pick their desired rate of growth? From the perspective of the productivity growth slowdown, discussed in Chapter 4, another appropriate question that could have been asked is: If the rate of growth is completely determined by (sb), for example, why could not the problem be easily understood and fixed? According to Solow, the reason is that not all the above parameters are independent or exogenous to the economy. It was the attempt to resolve incongruities such as these that led to the neoclassical model, in which Solow tried to make at least b or λ endogenous. However, to do this, the model had to put emphasis on the economy-wide production function. That function happens to incorporate (in addition to the two factors, L and K) a constant, reflecting the prevailing technology as well as its exogenous rate of change. The function also admits the concept of diminishing returns to capital, meaning that successive and identical increments of capital produce lower and lower increments in output. The inclusion of diminishing returns to capital causes the long run rate of growth to be independent of s but completely dependent on ($e + \lambda$). If so, then the rate of technological progress remains exogenous.

This result triggered a new wave of dissatisfaction. Why should the rate of technological progress be exogenous? This would be tantamount to saying that the main factor behind growth is left unexplained. Most economic agents are intuitively aware of the role increasing returns to scale in production and in distribution; most are aware of the concept of externalities; and most are aware of the impacts of research and development. It would indeed be strange if any or all of these had nothing to do with growth. The fact that they are sidestepped by the neoclassical model was a matter of concern.

It is precisely these concerns that the endogenous growth theory sought to address. This theory naturally dispenses with diminishing returns to capital, and accepts increasing returns instead. It also recognizes that the underlying form of markets is monopolistic (consisting of large sellers) rather than perfect competition. But sadly enough, it retains the fictions of the representative agent and optimizing behavior over an infinite horizon. We may note that with increasing returns to scale and monopolistic competition, the model departs from the scientific theory, while the representative agent concept is an unnecessary appendage, adding nothing of value. This is not to say that there was no progress in the search for a greater understanding, however. Many other theoreticians have had time to augment the content of the model, even though it fell outside the theory's domain. Changes in research and development, the effects of environmental and safety regulations, investment in physical and human capital, among others, have since been incorporated (see Madison 1987). Obviously, these additions constitute a worthy effort. However, in the end the value of the model boils down to either its ability to provide us with plausible explanations of puzzles such as the productivity growth slowdown, or empirical studies to confirm at least one of its principal statements. One such statement concerns the differences in growth rates in the OECD countries with the same capital structure (Denison 1985). In this regard though, the result of the empirical study carried out by Christensen, Cummings, and Jorgenson (1980) is negative. Because the study was designed to test the convergence in the growth rates of these countries, the result is negative because it found convergence. This then implies diminishing returns to capital, which are not supposed to be there according to the endogenous growth model itself.

In fairness, let me add that the result of the Christensen-Cummings-Jorgenson study is not too convincing. Cross-country regressions of growth rates on a variety of determinants are very sensitive to the choice of countries, to the period, and so on. No convergence has been observed outside the OECD. In fact, Lant Pritchett (1997, 10), using data from the Penn World Tables, found that the ratio of GDP per capita of richest to poorest contries increased from 8.7 in 1870 to 38.5 in 1960, and to 45.2 in 1990; this divergence can not be explained by differences in population growth alone, and there are many other such examples. The notion of convergence itself may either be flawed or poorly measured. Its absence does not necessarily uphold the endogenous growth theory nor does it invalidate the neoclassical model, because increasing returns to scale may exist only on a portion of the domain of the production function. In addition, the growth process may be more complicated than it has been heretofore assumed, or it may be heavily dependent on noneconomic factors, such as attitude, political stability, and other variables.

In summary, we may say that economists' views on growth have evolved from the incomplete model of Harrod, and from Domar's model, which focusses on equilibrium, to a neoclassical model that leaves the main impetus for the growth process unexplained. Then they moved to an endogenous model which does not seem to have any empirical content. All of these models have much to say about expanding possibility frontiers, exogenous realization of states, rational expectations, and so on, but most of them leave out the demand side of the market as well as the impact of growth on the environment and on resource depletion. However, in the midst of all these incongruities, economists' points of view on growth still dominate the landscape. In fact, the most striking feature of these incongruities, that is, the viability of the process of economic growth itself, is not even discussed.

GUIDING THE INVISIBLE HAND

Every time someone attempts to talk about the actual costs and benefits of economic growth, he or she is accused of being against cars, refrigerators, central heating, and summer holidays. Arguing against positive growth is to argue against progress, it seems. Since it has always been difficult to have an earnest debate, most economic agents have never come to grips with the limitations of economic theory in this regard. Therefore, it has never been realized how limited our measures of progress actually are. The misunderstanding about the limits of the theory, coupled with the false consciousness of the leaders of our economic institutions, has led us to believe that our measures of economic growth are in fact signs of progress. By words and actions, we continue to propagate this misunderstanding despite evidence to the contrary. Why? Douthwaite gives a partial answer. He states that: "The groups that make investment generating growth are getting good returns. They then, having access to the media, glorify growth, and carefully avoid mentioning that their good returns might be at the expense of everybody else" (1993, 3). To this we must add that the damaging impacts of growth, in particular those related to planet earth, have yet to be fully felt. The new orthodoxy stands to make matters worse. For, according to this new thinking, all economic decisions should be left to the market. It is for consumers, it is believed, to decide, through the distribution of their budgets, what should be produced. And that markets guarantee both efficiency and individual freedom *lato sensu*. The danger of this kind of thinking, as I have already stressed, is that markets are incapable of conscious directions. There are, for example, many socioeconomic outcomes that can be brought about only by collective actions and not by markets. Are we to understand that they should be dispensed with?

As things stand today, there is an urgent need to find a way to avoid future conflicts between social goals and market outcomes. According to Douthwaite, a shift in thinking must come first. He reminds us that: "It is the job of political parties to lay before the electorate alternative views on the direction society and, consequently, the economy should take. Once we have chosen between their proposals... the resulting government should legislate accordingly, leaving the market to work out the fine details, not the overall direction" (1993, 4).

Douthwaite is clearly combining what I have labeled sufficient and necessary conditions. In this regard, I have said that society should choose between various potential minima of the market gradient by preselecting the economic structure. What the new orthodoxy recommends instead is for governments to shirk the responsibilities conferred on them by representative democracy by surrendering to market lobbies. Indeed, at times, present day governments act more as the representative of the lobbies than as people's representative. If this uncharted course is followed, Douthwaite believes that our future will be one that none of us has sanctioned and very few desire. In the remaining sections, I attempt to make a case against the myth of positive economic growth by arguing for economic development instead.

GNP per Capita Versus Economic Welfare

Over the years, we have managed to equate standard of living with economic welfare, which in turn are equated with GNP per capita. This is the way things have evolved, although by the turn of the century economists had accepted the obvious fact that the consumption of goods and services was but one of the factors determining living standard or economic welfare. However, as most of these factors have proved difficult to quantify, economists first turned to Pigou's definition of welfare,[2] but with a twist. For Pigou, economic welfare increases with production and consumption (therefore with national income), provided that the share of national income accruing to the poor is not decreased. Clearly, for him, economic welfare, though proportional to national income, was only a part of citizens' total welfare, taken in the sense of Jeremy Bentham and perhaps in the spirit of Wilfredo Pareto. As Douthwaite put it, unable to define total welfare, economists simply claimed that it the same thing as national income. This may or may not be true, depending on our definition of national income. Even so, little by little, we began to forget Pigou's definition and began to equate total welfare with anything that appears convenient; that is, to standard of living, the quality of life, and so on. As a result, people began to take it for granted that a rise in production and consumption means a rise in total welfare or in the quality of life.[3] Once this equation is firmly entrenched in the social consciousness, it is but a short step to arrive at the belief that economic growth is necessarily a good thing for everyone. This is precisely where the problem lies. Economic growth, as measured by increases in GNP/GDP, may not be a good thing for everyone.

It is not difficult to find vivid examples to the contrary. Think of instruments of torture, such as electric batons and belts, electric pistols, anti-personal mines, and so on. Such production increases GDP, and it is a good thing for their producers, but everyday hundreds of people around the world are tortured with these instruments, killed (10,000 a year) or maimed (15,000 a year) by these mines. How then can it be claimed that growth in GDP is good for all? I further stress the point with an historical example. Improvements in tools and in transportation in the seventeenth century increased the accessibility of natural resources to the Europeans. The increase in their natural resource base fueled their economic growth, but also created a labor shortage to exploit it. From this narrow perspective, growth appeared a good thing for Europeans, but not for the inhabitants of the Americas and Africa because the labor shortage gave rise to colonization, genocide, and the slave trade. Again, it is hard to support the claim that growth is good for everyone. Moreover, in a modern economy, consumers' tastes are, to a large extent, created by advertising. Thus, a large part of total expenditures goes to satisfy the wants that it generates. From another perspective, increases in GNP pollute the environment and create much involuntary consumption (such as highway congestion, accidents insurance, police services, delays, road maintenance, indoor air filters, taxes, and so on). To what extent these items increase the living standard or the quality of life is a mystery. Yet, they all go on to swell the GNP measure.

Economic growth means increases in GDP which, it is recalled, is a measure of the market value of recorded and traded goods and services during a year. Granted, the way GDP is now measured leaves much to be desired, but it can be objectively measured. Whereas notions such as quality of life, or total welfare, among others, are subjective concepts. They cannot so conveniently be equated with economic growth, measured by GNP per capita.

Some time ago, Nordhaus and Tobin (1972) decided to tackle these difficult issues head on. They tried to come up with a sensible measure of economic well-being for the United States, that could serve as a proxy for people's welfare, they termed it a measure of economic welfare (MEW). They next computed the net national product (NNP) by deducting depreciation from GDP before correcting for inflation. Then they compared the two measures and concluded that from 1929 to 1965 NNP per capita grew at 1.7% per year while MEW per capita grew at 1.1% per year.[4] However, Daly and Cobb (1989) were not satisfied with the Nordhaus-Tobin approach. They decided to compare the MEW measure with GNP itself and for shorter period lengths. As a result, between 1935 to 1945, per capita GNP rose by about 90%, but per capita MEW went up by only by 13%. From 1947 to 1965, the two growth figures were 48% and 7.5%, respectively. They next constructed a new index of MEW that accounted for the depletion of the natural resource base (NRB), pollution, and human capital depletion (as measured by the capital value of health and education). The result was that from 1950 to 1986, per capita GNP increased by 105%, but per capita MEW rose by only 40%. In fact, the per capita MEW in the United States reached a peak in 1969; it remained more or less constant for the next 11 years, and then began to fall. However, from 1969 to 1986, while per capita MEW was constant or falling, inflation-adjusted GNP per capita went up by about 36%, showing that this measure of economic welfare is not even proportional to the national income as Pigou had supposed. The divergence appears to be even more pronounced since globalization. Those that are interested in knowing more about the divergence between economic welfare and GDP growth are referred to Douthwaite (1993, 13–17 passim).

There is no question, and this must be emphasized, that economic growth brings benefits. However, there are also valid reasons to be concerned about the way benefits are being measured, about the proportion of those benefits that goes to satisfy wants created by growth itself, and about the inequity in income distribution that the growth of markets brings about. But that is not all. By far, the most worrisome aspect of economic growth is its cost in terms of the demand it makes on our finite stock of natural resources, and in terms of environmental damage. To be aware of the damage, we must remember that positive economic growth first and foremost involves production. The act of production necessarily involves the depletion of the natural resource base (NRB) of the planet, followed by a gradual degradation of the environment. The portion of the NRB lost each year as waste products is not known for sure. By all estimates it is significant, and its impact on the environment is nonnegligible. If it is properly accounted for, the GDP figures would be much less without, however, making it proportional to MEW. To account for the depletion of the NRB, we must focus on the act of production itself, beginning with an attempt to get a rough estimate of the value of the NRB.

Estimating the Present Value of the Natural Resource Base

The total wealth of a nation comprises its physical and human capital stocks and its NRB. The NRB in turn consists of the water supply, agricultural land, forests, minerals and fossil fuels deposits, among other things. We use them to produce the stocks of human capital and artifacts that deplete with use and over time. In other words, a part of the NRB must then be devoted to the replenishment of the stock of capital, while the rest is used to produce additional artifacts and services. As I have said, no one knows the exact size of the NRB. We only have rough estimates. What is known for sure, even if we divide the NRB into renewable and nonrenewable resources, is that the stock is finite. If we continue exploiting our renewable resources at rates that exceed their natural rates of growth, then these renewables will soon become, for all practical purposes, non renewables. At present rates of exploitation, many observers feel that we run a serious risk of running out of nonrenewable resources in the not too distant future. The next section concerns the question of how to manage these resources until we know more. But first, let us try to get an idea of their present value and their distribution.

The World Bank, in its *Monitoring Environmental Progress* (1995, 1996), tries to estimate the NRB in present dollar value per person and by region. The estimate obviously depends on the assumptions made with regard to the social rate of discount and the useful life of proven and supposed reserves. I will not go into details since no matter how they are looked at the figures will remain rough estimates. As shown in Table A7.1 in the appendix, agricultural land represents more than 50% of the total wealth of all regions, except for the Middle East and North Africa. As it can be seen, regions that appear poorer in terms of GNP per capita are the richest in terms of agricultural land. Can they afford to let overgrazing and bad agricultural practices destroy land fertility? Obviously not. A similar remark applies to the Middle East and North Africa where 88% and 61%, respectively, of the NRB are in nonrenewable resources. How can these vital resources be protected when we know that the growth process in essence consists of transforming the finite low entropy NRB into high entropy artifacts, services, and waste? Until we have a better idea, the appropriate question must be: How should they be managed so as to maintain their productivity and prevent irreversible environmental degradation? This is the question that I attempt to address.

ECONOMIC GROWTH AND THE ECOSYSTEM

In the previous section, I said that the NRB is made of two types of resources: renewable and nonrenewable. Actually, there is a third type that may be designated global resources. This type comprises: water resource (marshes, lakes, rivers, the oceans, and so on), the atmosphere, and biodiversity. These resources are usually designated as global, in the sense that they belong to all living creatures. They presently concern us because their life supporting capacity is also both limited and threatened by economic growth. To make this point clear, let me begin with a brief review of the potential danger of perturbing their functions within the scheme of things.

Sweet Water and Oceans

Sweet water is indispensable to health, life and, of course, to economic growth and development. However, the total of sweet water available on the planet is inequitably distributed; in addition, it is being wasted and increasingly polluted. At this point in time, industry takes about 69% of the total, agriculture uses about 23%, and 8% goes to serve household needs. Clearly, industry and agriculture represent the two main sources of pollution. In industry, the chief polluter is the petrochemical sector. But in comparison, agriculture pollutes even more. Although it takes only 23% of the total water available, it is responsible for 80% of the damage already done. The chief pollutants are nitrates, phosphorus, and pesticides. Gershon and Le Moigne, writing in *Finance & Development* (June 1994), estimate that each year sweet water pollution incapacitates some one billion people around the world, and kills three million. Besides pollution, there is another danger that looms large over the horizon, pure shortages. The absolute quantity of sweet water available per person is steady falling. According to midterm demographic projections made by the UN, some 34 countries around the world are on the verge of a water shortage, defined as less than 1,000 cubic meters per person. Their situations will become critical by the year 2025.

At the UN Conference on the Environment and Development, held in Rio de Janeiro in 1992, member states explicitly recognized the danger represented by the pollution and the waste of water resources. They then approved a new policy, stressing, among other things, the need to base allocation decisions on a combination of prices, regulations, and demand management. The integrated management of water resources is not going to be an easy task. Already, it is estimated that it will take between $600 to $700 billion over the next ten years to implement a sound water management program, just in the South. These countries are being advised to base their plans on the 1992 French legislation, considered a model in this regard. Where would the money needed for their implementation come from? From economic growth perhaps? Most likely not, since industrial and agricultural pollution seems to increase 2 to 3 times faster than the average growth rates of the Southern countries.

The oceans of the world provide a livelihood for millions through fisheries. They serve the needs of transportation, circulate and supply water for the growth of vegetation, reduce the carbon dioxide concentration in the atmosphere and thereby cool the planet. However, the demands of economic growth are pushing them to the limit of their capacity to support life and biodiversity on earth. They are now serving as a final depository of toxic trace pollutants released by industry and agriculture. Scientists have identified the four most damaging types of pollutants in the oceans, two of which have been found to be particularly dangerous. They are heavy metals (beryllium, cadmium, and mercury) and organic chemicals, in particular polychlorinated biphenyls (BCPs). These pollutants are extremely harmful to life itself, yet they have already gone from the seabed to our food chain.

The Atmosphere

Any talk about atmospheric pollution brings us right back to the act of production. To be sure, we can always substitute a new resource for the dwindling supply of another, or improve the service yield of scarce ones while keeping the pollution associated with bioeconomic activity to a minimum. However, our preoccupation with economic growth causes us to overestimate our capacity to do so. Our arrogance has even led us to think of our atmosphere as a sink with the infinite capacity to absorb pollution. This overestimation of our ability and capacity leads, in turn, to greater and more optimistic projections of sustainable growth in the economy. Such optimistic projections of growth appear ubiquitous. They fuel the belief that we can always come up with substitutes, or at least the general belief that the terrestrial dowry of natural resources and environmental sinks are sufficient to provide sustenance for even larger populations and larger economies. Behind these beliefs lies another more fanciful one, that is, even if there were limits, technological advances will occur at rates that exceed the rates at which resources and environmental sinks become exhausted. However, everyone familiar with the problem sees these beliefs as seriously misleading.

Let me emphasize once more that I am not denying the benefits to be had from economic growth. Take the Asian tigers, for example. Even if their high growth figures are somewhat misleading, the majority of their prople live better today than they did 30 years ago. In questioning our approach to growth, I do not wish to disparage such benefits, much less the efforts of those that made it all possible. My point is that we seem to be afraid of facing the problems associated with the growth process, although these problems stand to bring the process itself to an end. We must, therefore, muster enough courage to look at the process in a more realistic fashion. This, however, requires a more technical discussion along the lines already developed in the classic work of Georgescu-Roegen (1971) and in Dominique (1994); that discussion is confined to Appendix 7B.

Should Global Resources Be Managed?

In order to answer this question, we must first attempt to understand how things fit together in the geosystem. According to the Gaia hypothesis (see Margulis and Lovelock 1974), the complex geosystem, involving the atmosphere and the biosphere, constitutes a feedback or cybernetic system which is not only self-regulated, but which also seeks an optimal physical and chemical environment for the biota. I cannot do justice to the more elaborate argument subsequently put forth by Lovelock, but I will try to convey the idea with this example. The presence of carbon dioxide in the atmosphere lies behind the growth of green vegetation, including trees, through the so-called fertilized effect. Trees retain soil moisture and preserve land fertility. The oceans, trees, the rock weathering process, and microorganisms act as a pump removing CO_2 from the atmosphere and thereby maintaining a comfortable temperature in the geosystem. Dimetyl-sulfide (resulting from the death of unicellular algae in the oceans) allows clouds to form which, in turn, produce wind and ocean currents. Ocean currents bring nutrients to algae and fauna, while wind currents and the heat flow from the equator to the poles bring water from ocean clouds to land and trees. Although the decay of green vegetation produces carbon dioxide, at the same time green vegetation gowth buries carbon and produces life supporting oxygen. This is just an illustration of the complex interaction of everything in the geosystem. Put more succinctly, various biological processes, including those that I have just described, control not only atmospheric composition, but the acidity of water, atmospheric aerosols, electron concentration, and the circulation of elements such as sulfur and phosphorus. This complex interrelationship keeps conditions in the geosystem within limits tolerable to life. As can be seen, this Gaia hypothesis is a provocative way of looking at the overall process of life on earth, and to which all sorts of investigations in different fields can be referred. What is then its main message for the proponents of growth? Do not disturb the global balance.

The other thing to keep in mind is that the above complex interrelationship is fragile. Awareness of this fragility began only some 20 years ago, yet we have already arrived at some sort of acceptance of the idea that the geosystem should be managed, that is, social costs should be internalized. User fees and taxes on certain types of pollution should be levied and marketable permits for other types of pollution should be issued. These actions may help, but I do not think that they are enough or appropriate for the preservation of the balance of forces shaping the geosystem. According to data gathered from shorelines records, from the limits of glaciers, pollen deposits, ice cores, fossils of foraminifera, and oxygen isotope ratio measured in the carbonate of fossil seashells, there have been widespread glaciations and hot periods over the last 1.5 million years. But the mean temperature of the geosystem fluctuated within a band of less than 8 degrees centigrade (Schackleton and Opdyke 1976). This means that the geosystem possesses its own fragile but equilibrating mechanism. My experience makes me fear man's management. The best strategy, in my view, is to adopt a code of behavior requiring economic agents simply not to interfere in this natural process.

There are other reasons why human beings should not be allowed to disturb the global balance. Issuing marketable CO_2 permits will allow rich firms and nations to continue on increasing the CO_2 concentration. First, a 2 or 3 degree rise in the actual mean temperature of 15.3 degrees celsius will significantly affect the organization of economic activity. Higher mean temperature will favor the growth of some crops over others at various locations. Calculations show that an increase in carbon dioxide concentration will increase the so-called El Nino effect; hence precipitation patterns will be altered and major droughts are to be expected in some regions. Marginal farmland will no doubt require additional capital expenditures either for irrigation or flood control. Rising temperature and humidity will alter the levels of water tables as well as the intensity of precipitation. Regions of increasing rainfall might experience flooding and soil erosion, while coastal management will certainly be affected by the rising sealevel. Changes in water distributions and run-offs might affect hydroelectric generation as well as the demand for electricity for new cooling needs. Certain industries such as fisheries, tourism, transportation, and aquatic sports are likely to undergo major shifts. Warming trends will certainly carry risks to human health from the transmission of malaria and waterborne infectious diseases. There might also be significant population movements with all their ugly consequences. In other words, we stand to experience significant changes in relative prices due to changes in market structure. Scientists on the Intergovernmental Panel on Climate Change (IPCC) are now more united than ever before; they have emphasized that a 60% reduction in current carbon dioxide emissions is urgently needed to prevent dangerous climatic changes. The main culprits in this process are: the United States, with less than 5% of the total world population, but the country that accounts for about 25% of the emissions; Europe, with 9% of the total population produces some 19%; China accounts for 13.5%; and countries of the former Soviet Union produce about 10.2%. Politicians in these countries claim that they accept the warnings about global warming. They further accept that from 1960 to 1998 the total cumulative carbon emissions in the atmosphere has increased by more than 200 billion tons. At the same time, the world mean temperature is increasing at about 0.1 degree centigrade a decade. Yet, industry lobbies in the Unites States mainly continue to block attempts to set target reductions, while the reactions of political leaders remain woefully inadequate.

Second, at present, global resources, the atmosphere in particular, are viewed as unpriced goods. Therefore, they do not figure in the economizing calculus. Efforts to price them may not decrease uses significantly enough to prevent saturation. In addition, the benefits of past growth are inequitably distributed, as everyone knows. No doubt, future ones will also be inequitably distributed. The scientific theory does not treat inequitable distribution as a market failure, but it is likely to be a source of social conflict in the future. The efforts to price global resources may reinforce income maldistribution and irreversibly perturb the complex and interrelated function of these resources.

Third, there is, on the one hand, simply too much uncertainty as regards the future consequences of tampering with the global resources to allow for their adequate reflection in present choices. On the other, no moral or economic justification can be found whereby one species has the right to bring about changes whose costs will be borne by all other species rather than just the agents of changes. Finally, as results are uncertain they may be nondesirable and/or nonmarginal. Hence, we come to the point where the best strategy is obviously to avoid tampering with these resources.

SUSTAINABLE GROWTH IN THE MEANTIME

Until we come to grips with the true costs of economic growth, and agree to promote economic development instead, our approach to production should embody the principle of sustainability. However, before discussing how, let me clarify an important point. Sustainability means different things to different groups. I start by defining it for the present purpose before proposing ways of applying it to the exploitation of renewable and nonrenewable resources.

There are various definitions of sustainability. For the so-called deep ecologist, sustainability seems to refer to the maintenance of all resources unaltered for future generations of all species (O'Riodan 1988). The environmentalist, on the other hand, views sustainability in terms of the capacity of the NRB to maintain or even increase human welfare; this view is forcefully argued in the Brundtland Report (Brundtland 1987). Whereas, the environmental economist is more prone to a view of productivity (i.e., the exhaustion of some resources is inevitable). Hence, the idea of restoration is incompatible with the goal of economic growth. He then suggests that the NRB be first subdivided into particular classes and that the contribution of each class to economic growth be assessed. When there exist competing uses for a given class, its use should then be determined by its social value (Mikesell 1992). Here, I adopt the view that the sustainable management of the NRB implies preserving its productivity on an intergenerational basis.

Sustainability in Renewable Resources

Within the category of renewable resources, I include all primary products of terrestrial photosynthesis and other resources whose depletion and degradation are reversible. Among these, we can safely include elements such as soil fertility, water quality, and animal populations. When it comes to the exploitation of renewable resources, the conventional model posits a level of exploitation Q', determined by equating the marginal natural growth rate (g') and the market rate of interest (r), as shown Figure 7.1. However, amenities may be derived from a resource in its status *quo ante*, and damage to the environment may result from its exploitation. For me at least, the sustainable exploitation of a renewable resource involves a serious effort to assess its market value as well as whatever other intrinsic value it may have by the judicious use of contingent valuation techniques. Such intrinsic value is usually the sum of option, existence, and/or bequest values, assessable by the principle of willingness to pay. On the other hand, there might also be hidden costs of exploitation such as environmental negative outcomes, including human illness and death. To simplify, we could put together the costs of preserving intrinsic value and repairing environmental damage and call them *defensive expenditures* (E). Such expenditures could then be introduced in the calculus. As shown in the figure, as r is greater than zero, the owner of the resource will exploit it at the level $Q' < Q^*$. However, if he has

Figure 7.1
Optimal Level of Exploitation of a Renewable Resource

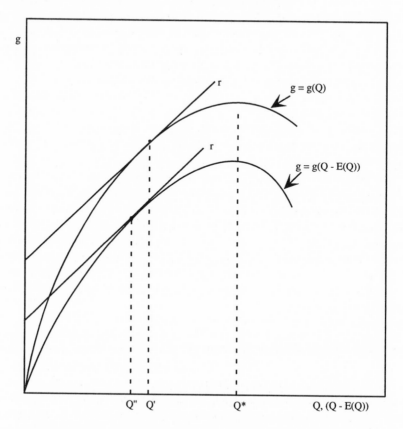

to account for defensive expenditures, the level of exploitation will be less. For, he now has: $g'(\cdot)=(\partial g(\cdot)/\partial Q)-\partial g/\partial E(\partial E/\partial Q)=r$, where I assume the the variation of E with respect to Q is positive. The optimal level of exploitation then falls to Q''. At the same time, the optimal gestation period, that is, the period that gives the maximum net present value, is thereby lengthened. Of course, all those nonowners enjoying benefits from the resource *quo ante* status may now have to compensate the owner according to their willingness to pay. In the end, the nonmarketable amenities may be preserved and the environment is protected. This, I believe, is a more sensible way of being mindful of intergenerational rights in the case of renewable resources.

Sustainability in Nonrenewable Resources

Nonrenewable resources are here defined as those resources whose stocks cannot be replaced once depleted. This category consists of plant and animal species, but principally fossil fuels and minerals. The exploitation of fossil fuels and minerals is now governed by the so-called Hotteling rule. According to this rule, the owners of these resources are encouraged to extract them over a number of years when the expected rate of increase in their present-value prices are equal to or greater than the rate of interest (r), and to deplete them as fast as possible otherwise. Clearly, this rule clashes with the notion of sustainability; it also goes against the notion of resource accounting, enunciated long ago by John Hicks. According to Hicks: "[True] income is the maximum value that an individual can consume during a time period and still be as well off at the end of the period as he was at the beginning" (1946, 172). This Hicksian principle clearly places exhaustible resources on the same footing as machinery and equipment, by treating the reduction in their value or quantity as capital consumption.

Applying this principle to the present situation means that a certain amount is to be subtracted from the yearly net revenue from extraction and invested. This implies that consumption over a given period must be limited to that amount that will leave the owner of the resource as well off at the end of the period as he was at the beginning. In the cases of fuels and minerals, this means maintaining their productivity over time. To do this, a share of net revenue must be invested in other capital assets such that the total present value of the stock is preserved.

The principle of resource accounting may be applied to the management of nonrenewable resources in two ways. It can be integrated into costs-benefits analyses by simply deducting an amount $(S(t))$ from the yearly income flow. $S(t)$ should next be invested at, for example, a rate r each year such that it becomes equal, over the extraction period, to the net present-value of the resource. This way, the net present-value is simply converted into an equivalent capital asset.

The second way is to combine the investment strategy with a quota scheme à la Daly (1974b). The Daly quota scheme is shown in Figure 7.2, where the curve DD represents the market demand for the resource and SS is the supply curve which includes the costs of exploitation and restoration for environmental damage, if any. Without the quota, a quantity Q would be produced and sold at a price given by the point E (for equilibrium). Once a quota of Q^* is imposed, the price per unit rises to the level OP_d. Out of this price, the resource owner receives the amount OP_s and the government keeps the amount P_dP_s. Thus, out of the total willingness to pay OP_dHQ^*, the area under the supply curve $(OSGQ^*)$ represents costs, and the amount SP_dHG is the rent drawn from the exploitation of the resource. How does this this rent come about? It should be stressed that the owner recovers the costs of production and restoration for each unit sold at OP_s, but this amount is still higher than the cost of all inframarginal units from 0 to Q^*. Hence, if he receives a price of OP_d, the area SGP_s is a differential rent and the area GHP_dP_s is a pure scarcity rent. A rent is by definition an unearned income. Without the quota, the price would be at the level of E, and the owner would appropriate all the unearned differential rent, which encourages depletion. However, with the quota the owner still retains the reduced differential rent. But the unearned scarcity rent is appropriated by the

Figure 7.2
Daly's Depletion Quota Scheme

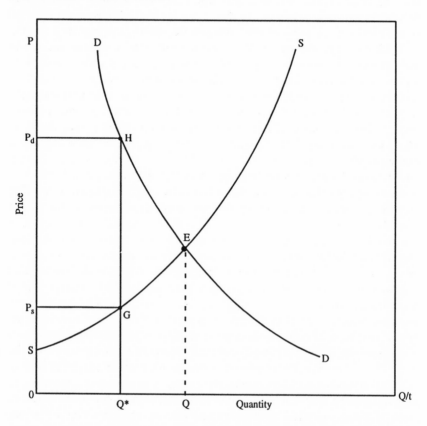

government issuing the quota. As in the above case, the scarcity rent can be invested at a rate *r*. In fact, the quota level can be adjusted to give the amount which, when invested at the rate *r* each year will grow over the duration of the exploitation so as to become equal to the net present-value of the stock of the resource.

THE ALTERNATIVE TO ECONOMIC GROWTH

For ordinary people, economic growth means a better life, whereas for the architects of the capitalist system, economic growth means market opportunities and increased profits. Increased profits lead to more investment and increased labor productivity. Investment, in turn, raises the national income and enlarges productive capacity. But, to paraphrase Douthwaite, increases in national income eventually peter out, while capacity has been increased for good. Hence, for a growing and more productive economy, we need more investment and more debt to finance it. Therefore, we need more rapid growth, more opportunities, and more profits to satisfy the growthman and to avoid increased unemployment and idle capacity. Besides, growth means legitimacy for dictators, reelection for democratic governments, and more profits for business. Whereas, zero growth means debt overload, idle capacity, falling profits, and negative growth.

What does this all mean? As it now stands, the capitalist system can survive and flourish only by continuing to grow. However, more growth means more resources, which happen to be finite. This is a real dilemma. In the first place, nothing on earth can grow indefinitely. In the second place, at their present scale, economies are already showing signs of unsustainability. In the previous section, I looked at sustainability as a stopgap measure. As the reader may have noticed, sustainability is not a completely viable answer to the need to grow. It can only postpone the crossover point. Of course, we can continue deluding ourselves into believing that growth can go on forever, on the grounds that it is the only way to alleviate poverty or to increase welfare. However, labeling growth sustainable will only delay the inevitable transition and make it more painful.

This is not to say that we should not reduce the exploitation of labor, alleviate poverty, and improve on the quality of life. The question is how? It is interesting to note that in the time of John Stuart Mill, classical economists used to believe that private property (or wealth) was a legitimate bastion against exploitation. However, Mill (1881), who was known for his great insight, reminded them that: "When some own a great deal of [private property] and others have little, it becomes the very instrument of exploitation rather than a guarantee against it." According to current thinking, the new orthodoxy will take us forward in this regard. However, in his book, *Slow Reckoning* (1997), Tom Athanasiou reminds us of the limitations of the new orthodoxy. According to him, it combines worn-out democracies with rusty institutions, on the one hand, and corporations dictating government agendas, on the other, while the gap between rich and poor is widening by the minute. Put differently, he too realizes that the new orthodoxy is fostering exploitation, among other things.

Alleviating poverty and improving on the quality of life do not mean scrapping the capitalist system. What is needed is an the alternative to what we expect from it. As I see it, the alternative is to first shift our thinking from economic growth to economic development without growth. This would lead straight to the steady-state economy proposed by Daly (1994a). To paraphrase Daly, the steady-state is defined by four characteristics: (1) stabilized populations of humans; (2) equality between investment in the capital stock and its depreciation; (3) equality between the rate of exploitation of renewable resources and their natural rates of growth, and the progressive conversion of the stock of nonrenewable resources into a permanent income stream; and (4) allowing technology, information, wisdom, goodness, and product mix to grow. The second-best way is to seriously address the question of income distribution so as to alleviate poverty and exploitation, and to provide more representative governments with the wherewithal to mitigate negative market outcomes. Under the present circumstances, one of the two ways appears *sine qua non*. As I have already said quite a bit about our approach to economic growth, I now tackle the difficult issue of income distribution.

APPENDIX 7A

Table A7.1
Estimation of the NRB by Region: 1994 (dollar value per person)[1]

	Agricultural Land	Forests & Protected Areas	Minerals & Fossil Fuels	Total
North America	8177.3	3857.2	3394.3	15429.0
Australia, New Zealand & Japan	4691.6	1638.3	1117.0	7447.0
Western Europe	3810.7	1288.9	504.3	5604.0
Middle East	6934.5	630.4	55476.0	63041.0
Eastern Europe & Central Asia	4857.0	1165.7	3691.3	9714.0
Eastern Asia	2846.2	328.4	474.3	3649.0
Southern Asia	3259.8	144.9	217.3	3622.0
North Africa	1037.1	56.0	1709.8	2803.0
South America	4506.3	1993.2	2166.5	8666.0
Central America	2450.1	700.0	31.8	3182.0
Caribbean Area	4188.2	252.3	605.5	5046.0
Eastern & Southern Africa	1944.8	658.2	388.9	2992.0
Western Africa	3531.0	470.8	706.2	4708.0

[1] Rounded off figures.

Sources: Adapted from World Bank. *Monitoring Environmental Progress: Expanding the Measure of Wealth.* Washington DC, 1995, 1996; J. A. Dixon and K. Hamilton. "Élargir la définition de la richesse nationale." *Finance & Développement* 33 (1996, 15–18), reproduced by permission of the International Monetary Fund.

APPENDIX 7B

As I have alluded to above, the process of economic growth begins with the act of production. To put it succinctly, the way economists study production is to first assume that there are three main inputs to the process. They are, labor (L), in which health and education are embodied, capital (K), which incorporates technical progress, and natural resources (N), available either in infinite supply or which have an infinite number of substitutes. Once these inputs are defined, the production process reduces to the simple application of some unknown input-output map (f), such that:

$$f: (L(t), K(t), N(t)) \Rightarrow Y,$$

where t is a real time index, and Y is the final output of the application of the map. It is then easy to see that this conventional representation goes a long way in blurring our understanding of the process of growth. First, Y is the end product only as far as the production process is concerned. We must bear in mind that Y consists of artifacts (A), services (S), waste products (W), and direct heat (H). Apart from services that are consumed, everything else eventually becomes waste products. Second, the other factors (L) and (K) do not undergo any net transformation. A part of N (or the NRB) is used to keep labor alive and to replace the portion of capital worn out in the act of production. Neglecting both, this replacement and the so-called learning effect, both L and K may be viewed as mere catalysts. Third, the very capacity of the environment to absorb waste products is limited. In reality, all the N fed to the process comes out as services, waste products, or heat, which either perturb the functioning of the global resources and reduce the productivity of the NRB, as shown in Figure A7.1.

In this representation, it is easier to see that (f) is in fact converting a given amount of natural resources into an equivalent quantity of consumption objects, waste products, and heat. This is in accordance with the First Law of thermodynamics, which states that the sum total of matter-energy (of the planet in this case) is constant. Accordingly, we may transform energy from one form into another, but in so doing energy must be conserved. The above representation, due to Dominique (1994), adds more realism to the conventional one with a catalytic loop and a negative gain (G) or a negative feedback loop. On the one hand, the negative feedback loop addresses the concern of those who believe that the accumulated waste is beginning to pose a serious threat to both our habitat and the productivity of the NRB. On the other, from the notion of the input-output map, it becomes obvious that the pursuit of growth involves the continuous drawdown of low entropy stores (even with recycling), in conformity with the Second Law of thermodynamics. Then clearly a point will eventually be reached where the NRB becomes either unproductive or completely depleted. There is no way to tell which will come first. Hence, economic growth, thought to be necessary, is also a source of danger. This dilemma has ushered in the concept of sustainable growth. It is clear from the above representation that this concept can only delay the inevitable, for economic growth is not sustainable in the long term. In fact, growth might come to an end well before complete depletion. If our habitat is being damaged and if the damage is reducing the productivity of the NRB, sooner or later it will take more energy to extract a given amount of energy. Production will then cease. In order to see how this gloomy scenario may come about, let us turn to the atmospheric damage that results from the act of production.

Anthropogenic Inputs into the Atmosphere

As we have seen, production in the pursuit of growth puts considerable amounts of waste into the atmosphere. That is, solid and liquid waste, heat, and harmful gases. As determined by the Intergovernmental Panel on Climate Change (IPCC), composed of 170 scientists from 40 different countries, the most urgent problem that all living creatures now face is global warming. The main question is how to halt the concentration of greenhouse and trace gases in the atmosphere?

At this point, human metabolism alone releases some 560 billion watts into the atmosphere, and human populations are still growing. In addition, human

Figure A7.1
The Production Process

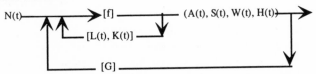

processes are continuously producing unrecoverable heat. Based on very conservative estimates, about half of all the energy input to power plants goes up directly as heat. The total thermal pollution is now estimated at more than 10 trillion watts (Dominique 1994, 268). Furthermore, economic activities produce a significant quantity of gases of all sorts. Among which we have: carbon dioxide (CO_2), nitrogen compounds (N_2O, NH_3, NO, NO_2), sulfur compounds (CSO, CS_2, SO_2, H_2S), chlorocarbons (CH_3CL, CH_2CL_2, $CHCL_3$), chlorofluocarbons (CFC-11, CFC-12) and hydrocarbons (CH_4, C_2H_3, CO). Gases such as CO_2, N_2O, SO_2, CH_4, the CFCs, and H_2O are identified as greenhouse gases, and the others as trace gases. Except for SO_2, these gases increase the temperature of the geosystem (earth surface and the atmosphere) and, therefore, enhance global warming.

To better understand global warming, imagine, for calculation purposes, the earth and its atmosphere as a disc. At the outer fringe of the atmosphere, the disc receives some 1370 watts per square meter from the sun in visible wavelengths, lying between 0.4 and 0.7 microns (a micron is one thousandth of a millimeter). About one half of this solar flux is scattered and absorbed by the atmosphere, while the other half falls on earth's surface. The surface, in turn, absorbs a part and radiates the rest to interplanetary space in infrared wavelengths between 1 micron and 1 millimeter. The quantity of heat absorbed by the surface and the atmosphere is measured in the form of the average temperature of the geosystem. The role of greenhouse gases is to block and absorb the outgoing radiation. For example, CO_2 absorbs and radiates back to the surface mainly in ranges lying between 2.36 and 3.02 microns, between 5 and 8 microns and between 12.5 and 16.7 microns. Nitrous oxide and methane do the same between 50 and 100 microns and above 10 microns, respectively. The trapped radiation forces the world mean temperature upward and causes more water to evaporate. Water vapor in turn absorbs in ranges lying between 2.2–3.27, 4.8–8.5, 12–15, and 50–100 microns. In other words, our atmosphere is completely transparent to the incoming visible light and may become, with greenhouse gases, almost completely opaque to infrared radiation. Bearing in mind that a body radiates according to the Stefan-Boltzmann law, this makes the quantity of heat radiated proportional to the temperature of the body raised to the fourth power. Hence, because of this temperature backlog, the geosystem cannot significantly discharge energy to interplanetary space until the outer fringe is warm enough. But, by that time, the surface temperature may be unbearable. This explains the fear of global warming.

By far the most damaging of the greenhouse gases is carbon dioxide, coming from the decay of vegetation, volcanic eruptions, and principally from the combustion of fossil fuels supporting economic growth. To give the reader a feel for the increases in concentration, consider the measurements of CO_2 concentration in parts per million by volume carried out at the Mauna Loa Observatory. In 1900, the CO_2 concentration was estimated at 293 ppmv. In 1997, it is at 370 ppmv, and is increasing almost exponentially. Calculations from climate models indicate that doubling the concentration from 300 to 600 ppmv could raise the mean temperature of the geosystem by 2.8 degrees celsius. In the meantime, methane concentration has gone from 0.8 to 1.7 ppmv since the beginning of this century. During the same period, nitrous oxide concentration went up from 288 ppbv to 310 ppbv. When we add the effects of the other greenhouse gases, thermal pollution and water vapor, we have feedbacks working in conjunction to raise the temperature faster. In the midst of all of these, what must be forcefully stressed is that life on earth and all the good things that we all take for granted are not going to be the same under a 3 degree rise in the mean temperature. As indicated in the text, the global mean temperature is increasing at the rate of 0.1 degree celsius per decade since the 1940s. In 1997, the experts of IPCC have termed this situation dangerous, because the process of heat flow is not linear, and during the last 20 years or so, the global temperature has gone up 0.3 degree.

8

POVERTY AND INCOME DISTRIBUTION

INTRODUCTION

Chapter 3 presented a simple model of pure exchange. Albeit oversimplified, it nevertheless was capable of showing how an economy responds to changes, or how it produces the equilibrium price vector, once its structure is given. This simple model led to another important result that has always been corroborated by observations, that is, the gain created by exchange is never equitably distributed. It follows, by extension, that when an economy expands, it continues on creating inequality. However, not so surprisingly, from the 1990s experience of the former socialist countries of Eastern Europe, we have observed that when an economy implodes, it still generates inequality. This negative and asymmetrical relationship between market development and distribution has become more and more credible. The proponents of market development may try to let it slip by, but it can not be denied.

Some forty years ago, Professor Simon Kuznets formulated an empirical relationship that was so widely accepted that for a time it enjoyed the status of a theorem. According to Kuznets, the relationship between income per head and the inequality of income distribution forms an inverted U-curve.[1] This means that at low income per head levels, the inequality of income first increases with increases in income per head and then decreases. Put differently, the share of income received by the poorest group decreases with economic growth, and it takes about 60 years before that group regains its initial share. However, to my knowledge, there is no theoretical support for such a thesis. Kuznets' empirical study should not be interpreted as the way it must be, but simply as a reminder of the incompleteness of the scientific theory of economics. This chapter does not attempt to prove or disprove Kuznets' assertion, instead, it sizes up the problem of income distribution, sees how it is affected by economic growth, and how it impinges on poverty. If it can be shown that poor distribution underpins poverty, while economic growth does not improve distribution. We would then have no choice but to find a way (other than growth) of mitigating such negative outcomes.

MEASURING AND TAMING INEQUALITY

In Figure 8.1, I show the prevailing inequality in our world as measured by the Lorenz curve. I will have more to say about this curve later on. For now, suffice it to say that if the cumulative income share is represented on, for example, the vertical axis, while the cumulative share of population is on the horizontal axis, perfect equality is given by the diagonal line of the unit square. In reality, the Lorenz curve is always displaced toward the lower right hand corner, dividing the area of the lower rectangle into two parts, A and B. If each 1% of the population receives exactly 1% of the total income, we would have a uniform distribution and the curve would be a straight line falling on the diagonal. Whereas if one person receives 100% of the total income, the curve would lie on the lower half of the perimeter, passing through the lower right hand corner. Economists measure the extent of inequality with the so-called Gini coefficient (G). As it can be seen, a uniform distribution lying on the diagonal would be represented by a $G = A/(A+B) = 0$; this is the signature of perfect equality. For a curve lying on the right hand corner, $G = 1$, since the area $B = 0$; this case would represent perfect inequality.

As Kuznets' assertion is not proven, economists must continuously fall on the Gini coefficient to assess how actual markets distribute gains. However, this practice has never produced a $G = 0$ nor a $G = 1$. In all cases, the data problem notwithstanding, the Lorenz curve falls below the diagonal, where $0 < G < 1$. Indeed various Gini coefficients calculated by the staff of the World Bank show that lower values are associated with richer economies, but also that these economies are those in which greater attention is paid to people's welfare. Could this be a mere coincidence? Or could this be due to the Kuznets effect? For example, the coefficients for Latin America and Sub-Saharan Africa were both about 0.50 in 1993. In Asia as a whole, the coefficients fell between 0.35 and 0.40. For the European Union, with 12 members in 1993, it was 0.35. For the OECD countries, the average was about 0.30 in 1993. Of course, one could easily infer that the values are lower in richer regions and higher in poorer ones, as postulated by Kuznets. However, this would be misleading somehow for a number of reasons. First, Kuznets' assertion has no theoretical foundation, as I have already remarked; it is an empirical relationship waiting for some sort of theoretical support or, more appropriately, it means that the interpretation of the theory is unsatisfactory. Second, in Latin America and the Caribbean region, GDP went from $175 billion in 1970 to $1250 billion in 1991. Over the same period, that of Sub-Saharan Africa went from $76 billion to $289 billion. There is then no valid reason why both regions would have the same coefficients, unless it can be shown that the two regions are on different branches of the inverted Kuznets U-curve. This does not appear to be the case in light of additional information. For example, prior to the demise of socialism in Eastern Europe, the average G-value for these countries was historically lower than the OECD average. Yet, we now know that they were in fact much poorer in terms of income. Obviously, I do not have many such examples to go by since most rich countries do have welfare measures. The evidence from the former socialist countries is nevertheless compelling. Hence, I am inclined to think that the G coefficient is lower in the presence of the welfare measures, discussed in Chapter 6, that tame naked market forces.

There is another problem associated with Kuznets' thesis. What message does it send to the poor? Why can not economic growth help the poor before 60 years? Who is benefiting in the meantime? In the last decade or so, the direction of direct foreign investment and the origin of world trade have significantly changed. Technological innovations have stimulated economic integration in general by reducing the cost of information. Modern telecommunications enable capital markets to function 24 hours a day. A significant share of these measured benefits went to Asia. For example, investment as a share of GDP rose from an average of 27% to 39% in Eastern Asia and the Pacific Rim. It went from 20% to 23% in Southern Asia. It fell almost everywhere else during the same period. The story is the same with regard to trade. The ratio of Asian exports to GDP increased significantly from 1985 to 1995, but remained stagnant almost everywhere else, if we exclude oil exports from the Middle East. The GDP of Eastern Asia increased at an average rate of 10.3% per year from 1990 to 1995. During the same period, GDP grew at an average of 4.6% in Southern Asia, and by about 2% in other countries. Undoubtedly, Asia as a whole was richer in 1995 than it was 15 years ago. Did the poor benefit, or should they be told to wait another 55 years?

What about the world as a whole? It has been enjoying economic growth for quite some time, in particular since 1945. Yet, some 2.3 billion people around the world live on less than $2 a day, some 1.3 billion of whom must make do with less than $1 a day, and 1 billion are either unemployed or underemployed. At the same time, pollution has increased faster than economic growth, that is, a cost borne by the poor as well as the rich. Should the poor be compensated or should they be told to wait? Is it reasonable at this point to suspect that economic growth alleviates *absolute* poverty, but increases *relative* poverty and pollution? Even so, as I have alluded to in Chapter 7, if pollution is properly accounted for, and if in fact it is reducing the productivity of the natural resource base, then economic growth might even be increasing absolute poverty in the longer term. I am not convinced that a definitive answer can be provided by regression analyses. The scientific theory produces neither good enough data to do that, nor is greater precision really needed, so I will continue on probing, as I have been doing, to see if economic growth is indeed alleviating the inequality that seems to underpin both absolute and relative poverty.

ASSESSING WORLD INEQUALITY

The Origin of World Product

In order to see how world income is distributed, it would be useful to start by estimating the total. However, one of the main problems of estimating the world product is that of proper exchange rates. National income data are labeled in various national currencies. Even when exchange rates are determined by market forces, they do not accurately reflect the actual purchasing power within national borders. They more often than not reflect the relative prices of goods and services traded on international markets. However, these markets are affected by all types of factors, such as foreign direct investment, transfers, remittances from abroad, fluctuations in domestic interest rates, anticipation, and so on. Due to these factors, international comparisons and the conversion of national currencies into one common currency, such as the U.S. dollar, fail to accurately reflect the actual purchasing power in domestic markets. In addition, given the differences in the relative sizes of the modern sectors of each country, specific studies have shown that market exchange rates tend to underestimate the domestic products of less developed market economies relative to those of more developed markets.

In an attempt to make comparisons more meaningful, the United Nations (1991) carried out a survey of 183 countries and regions using four different methods to convert domestic currencies into U.S. dollars. In the first method, the UN used the so-called monetary exchange rate (MER) compiled by the IMF, which is the average annual rate applied to current transactions transmitted to the IMF by the authorities from each country. As these rates are influenced by nonofficial rates as well, a corrected exchange rate (CER) was also used; it is claimed that CER accounts for high inflation and for the gap between domestic prices and official exchange rates. The World Bank for its part regularly supplies a list of exchange rates (WA), which is based on a 3 month moving average of previous values and on the implicit assumption that exchange rates align themselves on variations in domestic prices over a period of three months. The WA rates were also used. Lastly, the UN looked at the concept of purchasing power parity (PPP) to convert domestic currencies into U.S. dollars. However, as it was to be expected, each one of these conversion methods reveals its own strength and weaknesses. Consequently, the UN study produced four different results, but the results of MER and WA were relatively close. My analysis is based on values obtained through MER, but as economists are especially fond of the PPP method, which does not necessarily depend on exchange rates, I explain forthwith why I prefer to discard it for the present purpose.

Purchasing Power Parity (PPP)

The PPP is a specification which supposes that over any time period, the exchange rate between any two countries' currencies is determined by changes in the relative price levels in these two countries. This specification produces two versions of PPP: absolute and relative. The absolute version relies on the so-called Law of one price of competitive markets. From this law, the exchange rate is just the PPP which, in turn, is the ratio of the value of a standard basket of goods valued in the local currency over the value of the same basket valued in the foreign currency. This then boils down to the ratio of the domestic and foreign price indices. Thus, regardless of monetary and real disturbances, a standard basket of goods should have the same worth in any country due to instantaneous and costless market arbitrage. On the other hand, the relative version simply restates the same thing, but it additionally accounts for changes in relative price levels and in actual exchange rates.

Whether expressed in absolute or relative terms, PPP remains as controversial today as when it first appeared in the sixteenth century. Some economists believe that in the absence of monetary disturbances, PPP accurately reflects differences in domestic purchasing power. A few empirical studies appear to support this view but only in periods of high inflation. The problem though is that during high inflation, differing adjustments in wages, prices, and exchange rates are more likely to produce variability in relative prices, hence in PPP. For this reason, time series studies of PPP relationships were carried out. Results show that aggregate price indices, as well as other factors, have exhibited persistent and large deviations over the last 20 years. These other factors are capital flows, productivity growth differentials, the absence of competitive markets, external shocks, and differences in policy mixes. This should not be surprising, because productivity level differences influence real income which, in turn, influences the relative prices of traded and nontraded goods within a country. Hence productivity differences influence price levels across countries and across time.

Because of all these unresolved difficulties, many experts consider PPP a grossly misleading simplification. They offer the large currency fluctuations of the 1970s and the 1980s, as well the ruinous currency experiments carried out in Latin America as examples. They then conclude that the absolute version of PPP is demonstrably wrong, while the relative version is empty of content. I have two other reasons for discarding PPP in favor of MER. The sample of countries used in the PPP approach was smaller. More importantly, the total value of world GDP obtained through PPP was not only unconvincing, but it differs too much from those derived from other methods.

The Analysis

The UN study[2] was carried out for two selected years, 1970 and 1991, over a world divided into nine main regions: North America, Western Europe, countries in transition, Japan and Oceania, Latin America and the Caribbean region, North Africa, Sub-Saharan Africa, Western Asia, and Eastern and Southern Asia. Except for the so-called countries in transition and China, these regions were under market capitalism in 1970. In 1991, it can be said that they were all market economies.

As a result, in 1970, they produced goods and services valued at $3.205 trillion; in 1991, their GDP climbed to $22.9 trillion. If we now use the level of income per head as a benchmark, despite its imperfection, these regions may be divided into rich market economies ($2,000 per head and over) and developing market economies (less than $2,000 per head). Accounting for population levels, it was found that the rich region, with 10.6% of the total world population in 1970, accounted for 67.6% of world GDP. This meant that the poorer regions, with 89.4% of the world population, produced only 32.9% of world GDP. Under the same classification, the richer regions with 15.1% of the total population were responsible for 74.9% of total world product in 1991. The remaining poorer regions, with 84.9% of the total population, produced about 25%. This is the way it was after a 21-year period. The poorer regions lost in population and in economic weight, due, among other things, to the change in the status of Japan. The question now is how was the total world product distributed during this 21-year period?

Distribution

As we have just seen, by 1991 market capitalism, for all practical purposes, had taken over the world as the main form of economic organization. There had also been shifts in income and in the population base of rich and poor regions. During the period under consideration, that is, between 1970–1991, the UN study found that the first but the poorest quartile of the world population lost 1% of its share of world product. The second and third quartiles went down by 1.3% and 4.6%, respectively. However, the fourth and richest quartile gained up to 6.9% (see Figure 8.1 and *Etude* 1994, 508).

The situation is vividly depicted by the Lorenz curves in Figure 8.1. To construct the curves, regions were first classified by GDP per capita in ascending order. The vertical axis depicts the cumulative share of world product, while the horizontal one represents the cumulative share of total population. As I have already explained, the 1991 curve bulges further toward the right hand corner. This means that, under MER, the inequality of world income worsened from 1970 to 1991, according to the United Nations' finding. Figures for 1997 show a further deterioration.

Leaving the Kuznets thesis aside for the moment, by 1995, one would expect this negative outcome would have improved at the regional level due to the progress made in Asia. After all, Asian countries have a historically high level of education. During the period under consideration, and beginning in the 1980s, five of the richest ones had addressed the problems of coordination failure head on. In addition, they had maintained the highest level of domestic investment. In that connection, I should emphasize also that during that period, the economies of Asia and the Pacific Rim received the major share of direct foreign investment. This trend continued uninterrupted during the early part of the 1990s; for comparative purposes, during 1990–1994, the economies of Asia and

Figure 8.1
The Distribution of World GDP Among the World Population by Region:
1970–1997

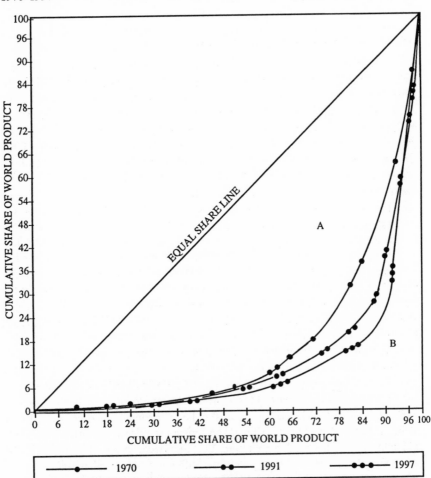

Source: Data for 1970 and 1991 are from *Etudes sur l'économie mondiale* (1994, 502).
The United Nations is the author of the original material.

the Pacific Rim received about 54% of all direct foreign investment, compared with Latin America (29%) and Sub-Saharan Africa (4%). Suppose we now remove Turkey and Cyprus, which were previously included in the Asian bloc, and we add Japan. Then, in 1970, the Asian bloc, with 54% of the population of the world, produced about 14% of world GDP. By 1995, and considering only Asian countries that had registered significant growth rates since 1970, the Asian bloc comprised 55% of the world population and realized about 32% of the world GDP. In the meantime, Western Europe and North America, with 11.7% of the world population, produced 53% of world GDP in 1995, compared with 58.7%

in 1970; for 1997, the situation was more or less similar. Asia made the difference. Our next question is, does growth alleviate poverty as it automatically assumed?

GROWTH AND RELATIVE POVERTY

In order to answer the question as to whether economic growth reduces income inequality, I now consider the three poles of growth as they stood in 1995, that is, the European Union, North and South America, and Asia. Let us start with the European Union, with its 15 member states, it had about 380 million people in 1995 and a GDP of $6.67 trillion in constant 1993 dollars (*Stat. Abs.* 1995, 857). The second bloc, the American one, consists of the United States, Canada, Mexico, Chile, Brazil, and Argentina, with 594.1 million people in 1995, producing a GDP valued at $8.046 trillion. Finally, I consider the Asian and Pacific Basin bloc, comprising countries where economic growth has been nothing short of spectacular, that is Japan, China, Indonesia, Malaysia, the Philippines, Pakistan, Thailand, Myanmar, Nepal, Vietnam, Bangladesh, Sri Lanka, South Korea, Hong Kong, Taiwan, and Singapore. In 1995, that bloc had 3173.5 million inhabitants and a GDP of $8.0 trillion.

I next derive the Lorenz curve for each bloc taken as self-contained units. The result is shown in Figure 8.2. As it can be observed, the Gini coefficient for the European bloc, which has been historically low, remained low in 1995. However, the curves for the American and Asian blocs departed significantly from the European one. Here, the question is why is the intercountry distribution in Asia looks so bad, mostly when it is known that the intracountry income distribution is somewhat better there then in the Americas? To answer this question, consider first the American bloc. The United States is a high income country, and it alone accounted for 44.4% of the total population of the bloc and 78% of its GDP. Whereas in Asia, the high income countries were Japan, Taiwan, Hong Kong, South Korea, and Singapore. These countries represented not quite 7% of the total population. Yet, they were responsible for 63.2% of the GDP of the bloc. This explains the difference, but it is marginal to our purpose. The fact remains that with the same method of calculation and with the same constraints, the Asian bloc, whose growth rates were the envy of the rest of the world, exhibits the highest level of intercountry inequality; indeed, its level of inequality seems to exceed that found previously for all regions. However, the point that I want to stress may be revealed by reversing the question, that is, why is the level of inequality so low in the European Union? Again, the Kuznets thesis offers the easy answer. However, by virtue of our previous discussion on this matter, this answer does not appear satisfactory. Without a more detailed analysis, it seems more reasonable to look toward labor market regulations, unionization, and welfare measures for the answer. In fact, as we will see below, among the countries in the three blocs, inequality appears to be higher wherever these factors are conspicuously absent.

Figure 8.2
Inequality in Three Growing Economic Blocs: 1993

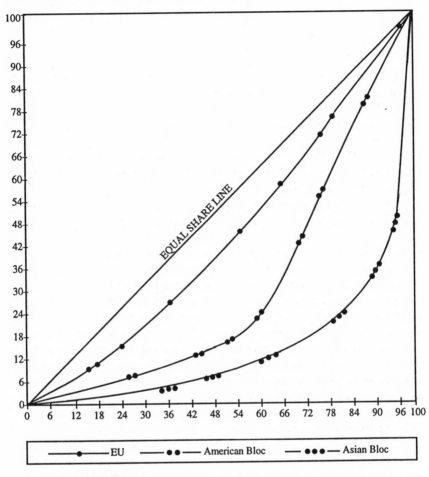

Source: *Stat, Abs*, (1995).

Growth, Pollution and Poverty

As we have seen above, the benefits of economic growth are not equitably shared, and the poor even seem to be penalized. Clearly, one of the ways growth impinges on poverty, in the absence of specific mitigating measures, is through environmental degradation. Consider the sketchy evidence shown in Table 8.1 that I was able to gather to that effect. The positive correlation between growth and the environment is clearly visible. The one between growth and poverty is not so obvious. However, when it comes to poverty, it must be realized that the official definition of this variable varies from one economic space to the next. Let us agree that *absolute* poverty is associated with the basic inputs necessary

Table 8.1
Economic Growth, Pollution, and Poverty

Region[1]	Annual Rate of Growth		CO2 Emission[2]	Yearly Rate of Deforestation	Poverty Index in 1990[3]
	1970– 1992	1982– 1992	1981– 1990		
Eastern Asia[4]	5.2	6.2	990	1.6	13
Southern Asia[5]	2.0	3.0	600	0.7	48
Eastern Europe	1.1	1.2	na	na	8
Middle East & North Africa	0.1	-1.8	360	na	33
Sub-Saharan Africa	0	-1.1	300	0.9	48
Latin America	1.1	-1.6	250	1.0	23
All Developing Countries	1.8	0.8	na	na	30

[1]Rough estimates; [2]Tons of carbon per million dollars GDP; [3]Percent of population living in poverty; [4]South Korea, China, Thailand, Indonesia, Malaysia, Philippines, and Myanmar; [5]Pakistan, India, Nepal, Bangladesh, and Sri Lanka.

Source: Ernest Stern. "L'Asie en développement: Un nouveau pole de croissance." *Finance & Développement* 31, (June 1994, 19), reproduced by permission of the International Monetary Fund.

to support life. Under this definition, I have no doubt that economic growth may alleviate this type, unless the process is deliberately blocked by policy, as it was in South Africa under Apartheid. On the other hand, the best definition of *relative* poverty that I have seen is that given by the European Statistics Agency (Eurostat). According to that definition, the relatively poor are: "Persons, families and group of persons [for whom] resources (material, cultural and social) are so limited as to exclude them from the minimum acceptable way of life in the member states in which they live."[3] Based on this definition, my contention remains that growth automatically increases *relative* poverty unless the process is mitigated by policy. As I have already said, although the cases of the European Union and the countries in transition lend more credence to this view, I present further evidence in this regard.

Obviously, a definitive answer can only come from studies carried out at national levels instead of regional ones. Again, not having detailed data for individual countries, I can only rely on sporadic figures gathered here and there. For example, according to a study carried out by the OECD (1996, 99), from 1973–1993, the adjusted real income of the poorest 10% of the U.S. population fell by 21%, while that of the richest 10% increased by 22%. The way the U.S. situation has evolved since the 1980s is as follows: From 1980 to 1993, four-fifths of income earners lost ground, while the highest quintile improved its position by 11%. Interestingly, the top 5% increased its share by about 20% but, at the same time, poverty increased among both children and adults (Table 8.2). More astoundingly, *U.S. News and World Report* in January of 1996 reported that, between 1983 and 1989, under the Reagan-Bush Administration, 1% of the U.S. population appropriated 61.6% of the increase in the national

Table 8.2
Income Distribution in the United States: 1980–1994 (in %)

	1980	1993	1994[1]
Lowest fifth	5.2	4.2	3.6
Second fifth	11.2	10.1	—
Third fifth	17.5	15.9	—
Fourth fifth	24.5	23.5	—
Highest fifth	41.5	46.2	—
Top 5 %	15.3	19.1	21.1
Children in poverty (%)	17.9	22.0	—
Adults in poverty (%)	13.0	15.1	—

[1]Estimates.

Source: Stat. Abs. (1995, 475).

wealth, while the poorest 80% got 1.2% of the increase. The U.S. situation seems to support my initial contention that growth may alleviate absolute but increases relative poverty.

It is quite clear that based on some historical evidence labor market deregulation and their concomitant de-unionization have had a strong impact on the rise in inequality in the United States. The 1935–1945 period is known to have been one of great improvement in wage equality, exemplified by a significant compression in the wage distribution. That period also coincided with the enactment of a series of measures that promoted equality. For example, following the passage of the National Labor Regulations Act of 1935, the unionization rate rose from 12% to 35% from 1934 to 1946; there is no doubt that unionization brings improvement in the lower end of the wage distribution. On the other hand, the Fair Labor Standards Act of 1938 gave rise to all the minimum wage laws. As a result, the federal minimum wage represented 40% of the average hourly earnings in the manufacturing sector, and 55% of that of nonsupervisory personnel in the service sector by 1946. Finally, through the National War Labor Board (1942–1945), the federal government took an active part in wage settlement in the whole of the private sector. There is now a consensus among experts that these measures were responsible for the improvement observed in the wage distribution.

As I have pointed out in Chapter 4, one of the main demands of the new orthodoxy is the complete deregulation of labor markets; a request to which the federal government was happy to oblige. The first consequence of the unprecedented rise in unemployment, following the deregulation of the financial, communication, energy, and transportation sectors, was a fall in the unionization rate from 24% to 17% from 1980 to 1988. The second was a 30% fall in the real value of the minimum wage between 1980 and 1989. It is, therefore, hard not to conclude that these changes exacerbated the rise in inequality. Compared with countries such as Germany, France and Sweden, among others, the United States went farthest in deregulating its labor market during the 1980s. It is also in the

United States where wage inequality rose the fastest, compared with other OECD countries.

England presents another example worth mentioning, because it comes right after the United States in terms of wage disparity. That country has earned the title of best student from the OECD for its Tory government's zeal to deconstruct. The aim of that government's master plan was to raise economic growth by changing the entire culture of the country, including planned privatization worth $300 billion, the elimination of subsidies to the poor, and the reduction of the tax burden on the rich. According to the proponents of the new orthodoxy, direct foreign investment is now on the rise because the labor market is completely deregulated, and both employment and investment are on the rise. However, *The Guardian Weekly* of April 27, 1997 reported widespread falsification of the job placement figures in order to reach election targets, a situation already discussed in Chapter 6. Between 1980 and 1996, the English economy grew by only 1.9% per year, compared with the OECD's average of 2.1%; here we have a case where the extra growth did not even happen. In terms of a common measure of income, the EU definition of relative poverty is translated into 50% of the net mean income, or £123 per week in England. According to a study of relative poverty in 12 member states carried out by Eurostat in 1993, it was found that:

- 5.5 million British households, or
- 12.8 million individuals, of whom 3.9 million children, or
- 23% of households

fell below the 50% the net income line. These figures have worsened since 1993. Put differently, the Gini coefficient of the U.K.'s economy stood at 0.37 in 1993, that is, 2 percentage point above the EU average. Thus, for over 16 years of Tory's rule (the Tories being one of the staunchest defenders of growth and globalization, and the star pupils of the OECD), the real income of the poorest 10% of society fell by 13%, while that of the richest 10% increased by 65%. It is difficult to tell what happened to absolute poverty because many of the welfare measures had been watered down. There is no doubt, however, that relative poverty increased. For example, figures released by the new Labor government in 1998 show that one in five people live on less than half of the average income, compared with one in ten in 1979, and that the poorest 20% of people get a lower share of social security benefits than they did in 1979. (*The Guardian Weekly*, January 25, 1998).

Japan seems to follow a slightly different approach in the fight against income inequality. In that country, welfare measures are less generous, compared to countries in Europe, but the Japanese society relies more on family support, high employment, taxes, and transfers. For the last 40 years, the Liberal Democratic Party has relied on this three-pronged approach to create a society that tries to put every citizen comfortably in the middle of the income distribution. Although there are still pockets of poverty, this equality objective is slowly being realized. In 1996, the average per capita income was close to $32,000. The per capita income ratio of the richest to the poorest regions was 1.8. Only 2% of Japanese households had incomes of less than $16,000 a year, and only 2% had incomes over $160,000 a year. Though different in its approach, the Japanese case still shows that inequality is to be fought with policy rather than with growth alone.

Data on income distribution and poverty levels in developing countries are even harder to come by. The levels of poverty in Trinidad and Tobago, Chile, and Costa Rica appear to be low by any standard, but there is no indication that the situation is up to standards elsewhere. Deininger and Squire (1997, 36–39) offered a sporadic view in selected countries. According to these authors, on the average, the richest quintile appropriates some 60% of the national income. More specifically, in Senegal, the top quintile gets 59%; in South Africa, the figure is estimated at more than 63%; in Chile, it is around 60.5%. Brazil presents one of the worse cases; the top quintile grabs up to 67% of the national income. The poverty of income distribution in the South can be gauged another way. As is well known, a big chunk of the wealth of these countries is held in the form of land. The Gini coefficients for land in India, Indonesia, and South Korea are respectively 0.63, 0.55, and 0.35. In Thailand, Tunisia, and Peru, the Gini coefficients for income are around 0.40, but for land, they are respectively 0.45, 0.64, and 0.93 (Deininger and Squire 1997). Thus, on the whole, inequality in developing countries appears to be worse than in the United States, the United Kingdom and Australia, which happen to be among the worse among rich countries.

However, when we look at the *within* country distribution on a per capita basis, Asian countries fair better than the Latin American ones, contrary to what is shown in Figure 8.2. In Table 8.3, I used data compiled by the United Nations Development Programme (1997) to compare the share of real per capita GDP of the richest and poorest 20% in some selected countries and regions.

As it can be seen, the situation is far better inside the Asian countries (due to tradition), compared with that inside the Latin American ones. The low values for the former socialist countries also lend support to my contention as regards the equalizing role played by the welfare measures. There is one sad note to this story, however, Michael Walton recently reports in *Finances & Développement* (September 1997) that, as a result of high growth rates of income, inequality is now rising in Asia. China represents a notable example. There, the Gini coefficient for income went from 0.30 in 1985 to 0.39 in 1995; this rise, by the way, is the highest ever observed in the world over the last thirty years.

The global situation of income distribution between the North and the South may be summarized as follows: In 1970, the GDP ratio of rich to poor countries was 2.08; in 1991, it was 2.96. If we now compare the situation of the richest and poorest 20% of countries, we get another graphic picture of inequality. Thus, in 1960, the richest 20% of the countries had incomes 30 times greater than the poorest 20%. In 1990, the richest 20% had 60 times more, despite the progress

Table 8.3
The Share Ratio of Real GDP per Capita of the Richest 20% to that of the Poorest 20% in Selected Countries and Regions over the 1980–1994 Period

Country	Ratio	Country	Ratio
G7 Group		*Latin America*	
Unites States	8.91	Chile	17.42
Germany	5.75	Costa Rica	12.67
France	7.48	Panama	28.90
Italy	6.02	Venezuela	16.21
Canada	7.05	Mexico	13.49
Unites Kingdom	9.63	Colombia	15.50
Japan	4.31	Ecuador	9.74
		Bolivia	8.60
Asia		Honduras	15.10
New Zealand	8.76	Guatemala	30.00
Australia	9.59	Nicaragua	13.13
Hong Kong	8.70		
Singapore	9.58		
Thailand	9.41	*Eastern Europe*	
Malaysia	11.67	Czech Republic	3.56
Sri Lanka	4.41	Slovakia	2.63
Philippines	7.35	Hungary	3.85
Indonesia	4.68	Poland	3.93
China	7.08	Belarus	2.96
Vietnam	5.63	Bulgaria	4.73
Pakistan	4.72	Estonia	7.01
Bangladesh	4.03	Romania	3.78
India	5.01	Latvia	3.82
		Tukmenistan	6.38
Regional Average		Ukraine	3.72
North America	8.72	Moldova Republic	6.01
Western Europe	6.25		
South Asia	4.83		
South East Asia & the Pacific	6.60		
Eastern Europe & the CIS	6.60		
Nordic Europe	5.61		
Latin America & the Caribbean	18.66		

made in Asia. Much much more could be said about such disparities, but that would not serve our purpose at this point. Those that are interested in knowing about the income gap between the rich and the poor in greater detail are encouraged to consult the last two human development reports, compiled by the United Nations Development Programme (UNDP).

Before moving on, let me emphasize that the poverty engendered by poor income distribution in developing countries is not confined to the absence of basic needs; it takes a toll on many other aspects of life. A good case in point is health. According to the World Health Organization (1995), a third of the world's children are undernourished. Some 12.2 million children die each year, in most cases, for lack of treatments costing about $ 0.20. One million die of measles, and half a million die of tetanus each year.

As far as I am concerned, the picture is sufficiently clear. By itself, economic growth does not alleviate relative poverty, whereas, as revealed by a number of specific studies, the welfare measures do. One of the latest reports on European incomes shows that countries with the most generous welfare measures have lower proportions of relatively poor. Put differently, countries that have gone farthest in deconstruction (such as the United Kingdom), or never had much to deconstruct (such as Greece) have a far higher percentage of relative poverty than those with generous welfare measures (such as Denmark). Yet, under the new orthodoxy even Northern politicians not on the right of the political spectrum continue calling for deconstruction, while pretending or openly denying that it increases relative poverty. As the argument goes, welfare measures, as a burden on business and competitiveness, represent an institution subversive to individual self-reliance. According to these politicians, money will be better used elsewhere to lower the social costs of doing business.

I see two dangers in these simplistic arguments. The first is that the proponents of the new orthodoxy dominate the economic landscape and supply the faulty notions and even the vocabulary. They are so successful in this respect that even the well-intended middle class and those that wish to see more solidarity are buying into these defective notions, making analyses and debates more difficult. The second danger is more ubiquitous. These arguments conceal the fact that social costs are different from production costs in the sense that they seem to increase with inaction. If I am right in this, then the social costs in deconstructor states will be huge in the not-too-distant future.

Therefore, if economic growth is increasing relative poverty, while welfare measures are indeed a bulwark against relative poverty, then governments still have an important role to play.

WHAT CAN GOVERNMENTS DO TO ALLEVIATE POVERTY?

As we have seen, a cursory reading of the statistics points toward a clear relationship between income distribution, poverty, and welfare measures. Economic growth seems to do little to alleviate absolute poverty. Instead, it damages the environment and increases relative poverty. The fight against poverty will require an all out effort and many specific measures. No matter what these measures turn out to be, employment and income distribution must lead the list. According to present trends, it seems that in the economy of tomorrow, only two sectors will be able to offer employment, that is, the market and the civic (or voluntary) sectors. But the market that I have in mind is the so-called knowledge market. Clearly that market will not be able to absorb all those in the present blue collar sector for obvious reasons. Consequently, the only immediate alternative that I see is a 30-hour week. Additionally, although the redistribution of income is not the concern of the scientific theory, there seems to be no alternative to an exogenous intervention to redistribute. However, this is a touchy matter. Income redistribution is violently opposed by the rich and the powerful, and it goes against the dictates of globalization. Yet, I see no real alternative if we want more equitable and peaceful societies. In this section, I examine the least conflictive way I know to redistribute income.

Consider the situation in which most governments found themselves in the mid-1990s. In the rich countries, in particular, governments were spending more than they received. Compelled by the logic of globalization, they went as far as they could in cutting spending and transfers; they did so with zeal and yet budgetary deficits persist. If debt and deficits are as bad as we are told, it seems reasonable to assume that the alternative is to increase revenues by raising taxes. I must, therefore, return to a question that I raised before: On whom? We have already seen that almost everywhere the middle class is losing ground. The lower class is rapidly sliding into poverty. To stop and reverse this unhappy outcome, welfare measures must be maintained and even be extended in scope. To pay for them, governments must raise taxes wherever the capacity to pay happens to be, that is, in the biggest and still growing market around, the international financial market. Although this idea may not seem to be in line with current thinking, it nevertheless points directly to what is commonly known as the Tobin tax.

The Tobin Tax

Since 1972, the international community has been engaged in an off-again on-again discussion relative to the feasibility of a Tobin tax. One commentator compares the Tobin tax to the Loch Ness monster, except that, it regularly resurfaces in times of crisis and, unlike the monster, is unpleasant but compelling. Indeed, it has received support from a minority of eminent economists and from a number of political leaders. For example, François Mitterand, the former President of France, raised it during the Copenhagen Summit in 1994. It received support from Dr. Boutros Boutros-Ghali during his tenure as the UN Secretary General. It was warmly endorsed by Jacques Delors, the then President of the European Commission, and even by Barber Conable while presiding over the World Bank.[4] Yet during the Halifax Meeting of the G7 group in 1995, the idea of the Tobin tax never went beyond informal corridor discussions. In subsequent years, it was not discussed at all. Before we attempt to demystify the opposition to the tax, let us see what it is all about.

The initial Tobin tax proposal is the brainchild of Professor James Tobin (1972), the 1981 Nobel Laureate in economics. In proposing the tax, Tobin wanted to discourage speculation on hard currencies and thereby reduce the volatility of exchange rates. The tax would have made it slightly more costly to convert one currency into another. The reason is that theoretically, a tax increases transaction costs. Hence, speculations against currencies would also become less tempting. This in turn would stabilize capital flows and therefore exchange rates.

There are at least three main advantages to such a tax. First, by reducing the portion of the total volatility due to speculation, the tax would allow operators to react only to real changes in national economies. In such a case, governments would no longer be compelled to turn to protective measures. Second, the application of the tax would most likely be coordinated by a single international institution, and this would insure coordination at the international level. Last, the proceeds of the tax would be distributed among governments and would relieve the pressure to dismantle much needed welfare measures.

At first the tax did raise one major concern and a few minor objections. The major concern was how to distinguish between bona fide transactions and speculative moves. To address this concern, Paul Spahn (1996) proposed a dual tax structure, that is, a low rate would apply to ordinary transactions and a surtax would be levied on the profits realized on very short term transactions that one can reasonably associate with speculative attacks on currencies. Within such a structure, exchange rates would freely move within established limits. The surtax would then be applied to the gap between the observed rates and the band limits. This way, exchange rates would be kept within well established limits by means of taxation rather than by actions of central banks.

What are the remaining points of objection to the tax? The first, of course, centers on the question of efficiency. In that connection, its opponents argue that it would impede the operation of the international financial market by creating liquidity shortages without dissuading speculators. In other words, speculators in general aim at making 3% profit on each speculative attack. Therefore, a 1% tax should not discourage them. Another point raised is how broad such a tax should be? Should it be imposed on all transactions, whether from states, financial institutions, or the producers of goods and services? If financial institutions were to be exempted, would that not encourage them to take market shares from others? On the other hand, taxing them too would simply increase transaction costs and reduce market efficiency. Furthermore, even if only foreign exchange cash transactions are taxed, agents could very well avoid the tax by moving toward derivative products, commercial papers, among other things. As is well known, derivatives, short-term operations, financial swaps, and so on, could allow operators to transform long-term positions into short-term; this, it is argued, would have repercussions on the cash market. The third objection is specific to some official quarters where the Tobin tax is simply branded unrealistic. Here I must confess that I am not sure why, except that for the proponents of globalization any tax is unrealistic. Anyway, this last point seems to be the main justification for not putting the tax on the agenda of the annual meetings of the G7 group. Last but not least, the opponents worry about how the proceeds should be shared. Believe it or not, they are concerned about the possibility that the bulk of the money collected would go to countries with well-developed capital markets such as the United States, England, and Japan.

The Question of Efficiency

Among the reasons given for opposing the tax, the efficiency argument seems to be the weakest. From the laws of supply and demand, a tax that is not a lump sum tax or that is not applied on profits is associated with a deadweight loss. To my knowledge, however, attempts to measure the loss have produced insignificant values when the tax is in the order of 10%. In the case of this tax, it initially was a question of a 1% tax on complete transactions (buying and selling). On the one hand, we are told that 1% might not be enough to dissuade speculators. On the other, we are told that a higher percentage stands to put financial intermediation at risk. Let us be serious. The deadweight loss associated with a 1% *specific* or *ad valorem* tax would probably be too small to measure. Anyway, if the imposition of the tax is to be a policy measure, the right approach is to do a cost-benefit analysis on the difference between *ex-ante* and *ex-post* situations. In other words, what is the cost of excessive volatility, and what is the benefit of exchange rate stability? In the dual structure proposed by Spahn, the surtax is supposed to act as a circuit breaker applied to the negative externalities associated with excessive volatility, otherwise it would have no effect. Hence, it is identical to the stabilizing mechanism of the European Monetary System. As far as I can see, the stability sought would reduce the risk of speculative bubbles that distort market signals. By the same token, it would probably improve resource allocation, reduce risk premia, and give back to governments and central banks the autonomy they used to have prior to the advent of globalization.

The Rate

In Chapter 5 we saw that the Bank of International Settlements estimated that the total value of transactions on the international financial markets of foreign exchange and bonds amounted to $1,571 billion per day in 1995. Some 84% of this total represented foreign exchanges alone. Assuming 250 working days per year, a tax of 1% on foreign exchanges would have brought in $3.3 trillion per year. Spahn's dual structure proposes a tax of 2 base points on speculative actions and a 1 base point tax on derivative products. Even if we leave derivatives aside, a 2 base point tax on foreign exchange would raise $660 billion per year. At such a low rate, all arguments about efficiency become vacuous, while all budgetary deficits would be eliminated after a couple of years. If I take the proponents of globalization at their word, countries without well-developed capital markets should eventually benefit from the growth promised in the absence of deficits. Why then is the G7 group not more sympathetic to this solution? Is it because the tax is really unrealistic?

On the Realism of the Tobin Tax

As I have said, I do not quite know why the tax is charged with whimsicality. Even so, in 1995, a group of eminent economists decided to seriously study the feasibility of the tax in light of what was then known about the international financial market. The conclusion was that it was worthy of serious consideration. A year later, a collection of specialized papers appeared (Ul Haq, et al. 1996). On the whole, the experts agreed that the tax deserved to be studied in depth. Strangely enough, the establishment press maintained media silence on Ul Haq's book. Why? I suspect that in some quarters, the tax (including Tobin himself) is considered too Keynesian and therefore too politically incorrect. If I am right, this would be a first in the annals of the Nobel Prize. Tobin, it is recalled, is the 1981 Laureate precisely for his contributions in this area. Should his ideas be proven wrong so soon afterwards, what would that imply for the Nobel Prize in economics?

Curiously enough, those who oppose Tobin's ideas, claiming that they are no longer à la mode, are the same who hold on tightly to defunct ad hoc theories long after they have been discredited by the facts. When the Bretton Woods System collapsed, it is recalled, the quasi-totality of the economics profession rallied behind Milton Friedman's thesis on flexible exchange rates. Accordingly, flexible exchange rates were supposed to do away with speculation and solely reflect the fundamentals. This thesis has been clearly discredited, yet the opponents of the Tobin tax hold on to it. Indeed, to palliate this anomaly, they even give it a twist: "Speculators help the market to operate more efficiently." What are we to understand from this? That speculators of Mexico (1994), Asia (1997) stabilize markets!

In general, the proponents of globalization are fond of the argument to the effect that restrictive measures are always destabilizing. Thoughtless and longer term measures probably are, but thoughtful short-term measures do not have to be. Consider the case of Chile. In the 1980s, Chile instituted a whole series of short-term measures designed to discourage short-term incoming capital associated with speculation.[5] As a result, Chile has since known a much greater monetary stability than other Latin American countries that were experimenting with globalization. In a nutshell, the adherents of globalization have managed to scare the whole world over the deficit-debt problem. If governments, grappling with this problem, cannot go after those with the ability to pay, then the deficit-debt crisis will be with us for many years to come.

SUMMARY AND CONCLUSIONS

INTRODUCTION

This final chapter recapitulates the content of the three constituent parts of this work; better to be charged with repetition than with parsimony, I believe. The first objective of this book was to clear up the scientific status of economics. In light of this clarification, the second objective was to examine the scientific foundation of the prevailing economic orthodoxy. In the process, I discussed what I consider to be the modern criteria of scientificity. After applying these same criteria to economics, I came to the conclusion that economics is indeed a social science, albeit one that is incomplete and full of defunct ad hoc models still vying for acceptance. As we pushed farther toward understanding what distinguishes normal from social sciences, we discovered that the social sciences have additional reasons to preserve their defunct models. The important thing to stress is that the social sciences do have social goals. Economics' goal is the promotion of society's well-being, which is not objectively defined. This explains in part the persistence of the defunct models. However, the theory of economics spells out very clearly the preconditions for the attainment of the ultimate goal. On this ground then it does not support the new orthodoxy. In addition, the new orthodoxy seems to have its own goal which, as far as I was able to discover, is capital accumulation in the hands of the few. In this, it is admirably successful, but such a success cannot be squared with the goal of the scientific theory. To make itself more palatable, its strategy is to wrap itself in a number of buzzwords and concepts originating in the defunct models. This is the tentative conclusion reached thus far. I will now briefly review and amplify the analytical steps that led to this conclusion.

PART I

Chapter 1

This chapter locates economics on the spectrum of scientific activities. Before that could be done, however, the chapter had to clear up some common misconceptions about science in terms of both theory and practice. One such misconception is the commonly held view that the scientific process is both objective and infallible. To dispel that view, the various viewpoints that used to dominate the process in the past were reviewed; it was shown that each one was limited. Over time these viewpoints evolve, but do not vanish. If anything, the practitioners of science make a genuine effort to control for their particular viewpoints but, as we have seen, this is easier to do when their particular interests are not directly involved. In short, it can be said that the underlying priors of modern scientists may not be consciously held axioms, but they are nonetheless structurally implicit presuppositions that may impair the characteristics of objectivity. As far as the characteristic of infallibility is concerned, it is simply not attainable.

In order to arrive at these conclusions, the chapter offers a modern definition of a scientific theory, and explains the role it plays in the development and practice of a science. Therefore, there is no science without a scientific theory because it is the scientific theory that defines the covered domain, the concepts, the facts, and the statements that are pertinent to a particular area of knowledge. The practice of science, however, refers to a modus operandi by which the meaningfulness of statements thrown off by the scientific theory is determined. However, there are two caveats. The scientific theory is a mathematical construct. As such, it offers the advantage of economy of words and explicitness but it is primarily axiomatic. Thus, upstream, axiomatic structures cannot escape the drawbacks of inconsistencies and incompleteness. Downstream, two of the four characteristics of meaningfulness, namely, objectivity and reliability are not guaranteed. Put differently, no known scientific activity has successfully avoided these two caveats, although some fare better than others.

With these clarifications in mind, Chapter 1 tackles an often asked but seldom answered question. What distinguishes *normal* from *social* sciences? The normal sciences use a number of signposts, such as repeated measurements of relatively stable phenomena, and laws of symmetry to decipher the workings of the four basic forces of nature. In the process, these sciences, particularly physics, have formulated a plausible story as to the objective of each of the four forces, cast as a law of nature. In other words, if these laws did not interact with each other, each would steadfastly pursue a particular objective that may be put as follows: If left alone, the strong nuclear force would only produce heavier and heavier elements up to iron. The weak nuclear force would only produce stable nuclei. The electromagnetic force would only give complex but fragile forms, and gravity would fill up the observed universe with black holes. However, since they do interact, the outcome is a multifarious universe whose goal, if any, is both unknown and imperturbable. Nonetheless, the known objective of each of the four forces underlies the apparent reliability and objectivity of normal sciences that happen to fall in ranges where a particular force predominates, and where structural presuppositions are controlled for.

The social sciences, attempt to discover and decipher forces that shape human societies, if any. However, they face an additional difficulty. On the organizational scale of matter and energy, human societies fall on the complex portion of the scale where the electromagnetic force is predominant. A particularity of that force is its dual nature, or its dual polarity. This means (see section 4, Chapter 2) that each living entity is a "point" electromagnetic field endowed with a polarity or appreciatory judgment that in turn is subject to polarity reversals. Appreciatory judgment is what is surmised to be free will. But free will and polarity reversal have an additional consequence for the social sciences, that is, their outcomes are *collective averages* of judgments, and therefore are statistical in character.

With these qualifications in mind, the chapter concluded that: (1) Economics is a social science because it possesses a scientific theory and an experimental design to determine the meaningfulness of its statements, but it is weak on the characteristics of objectivity and reliability; (2) economics is *primus inter pares* among the social sciences, but, as any other social science, its truths are contextual and this makes them vulnerable to ideological spins.

Chapter 2

Chapter 2 retraces the salient turns in the developmental path of economics from political economy to a formalized social science; it also reviews its definitions, hypotheses, concepts, and goal. In the process, it is shown that in order to reach its goal, which is none other than the promotion of society's welfare, it must meet a few preconditions. The first precondition is that the theory of economics must demonstrate that under free choice and competition the equilibrium price vector is well determined. In other words, it must show that there exists an inherent market force which, whatever the initial conditions, is capable of adjusting so as to arrive at a final state of balance; moreover, that state must be unique and stable. These properties legitimize the claim to the effect that the competitive interdependent market system is capable of achieving a desirable (hence, collective) allocation of resources under its own power. In the absence of the triplet limitations that I term EPI in Chapter 4, such a nontrivial result is achieved under Walrasian assumptions, formulated (in Appendix 3) as a dissipative and differentiable scalar potential of unrealized opportunities.

However, a large majority of economists favor the Arrow-Debreu solution concept. The seeming elegance of that solution resides in its axiomatization, which casts aside all concerns for realism and experimentation. Debreu himself once remarked that axiomatization facilitates the detection of logical errors. As the logic is embedded in the axiomatic structure itself, it is no safeguard against whimsicalities which are far removed from the reality that economics purports to explain. Thus, the Arrow-Debreu solution has three types of limitations: The

Gödel type, minor and major. There is no doubt that, except for the Gödel type that is common to all sciences, the remaining limitations, which include the elimination of EPI as preconditions can be adequately addressed over time. If not, then the system can only come close to a 'second-best' allocation. In the meantime, there must first be a shift in thinking. Economics permeates all of social life. If its theory and its practitioners are to be relevant to society, a two-step approach is needed. The remaining limitations must be addressed, perhaps through the Walrasian route, and economists must come to grips with the fact that, according to the second precondition, the ultimate goal of economics is people's fulfillment and not necessarily capital accumulation by the few.

The main conclusions to be drawn from this chapter are: (1) The augmented Walrasian construct outlined here shows that, technically, the final state of the system is dependent on the structure. Society must, therefore, influence the structure so as to reach the desired outcome; and (2) many noneconomists often deride the field for the poverty of its predictions. This seems to be due to a series of misconceptions about the scientific process in general and about the nature of economics in particular. Chapter 2 has an important lesson for them too. Consider a system that confronts millions of agents seeking their own selfish interests without any precommunication. In the absence of EPI, and with free choice and competition, the system is capable of achieving a desirable state of balance in which these millions of diverse and conflicting desires converge. Such a system cannot be trivial. It is up to economists to work hard to foster a greater understanding of this remarkable achievement.

Chapter 3

Chapter 3 sets up a simple exchange model in which a nonzero excess demand system is taken as the nabla of a dissipative scalar potential of unrealized gains. It is shown that this simple set-up is enough to make the determination of the equilibrium price vector concept constructive. In what may be construed as a series of thought experiments, the model demonstrates the meaningfulness of statements such as: (1) When the supply of a good is fixed in quantity, the price of that good moves in the same direction as collective preferences, expressed as budget shares; (2) the notion of an identical or representative agent is meaningless; (3) if there is no change in the demand for money, changes in the general price level are positively correlated with changes in the money supply; (4) if an economy moves from a competitive to a monopolistic regime, the general price level rises; (5) the determination of value in the market is nothing but a reflection of collective choice and available technology; (6) the notion of efficiency is meaningless outside the conditions given in (5) above; and (7) in pure exchange, the equilibrium price vector is well determined within a given structure, but it wobbles through economic space and time according to structural changes in the market gradient. When there is production, prices may fluctuate more. If there is production and conflict among the owners of the factors of production, there will be cycles in addition to irregular fluctuations. In other words, if the objective of capital accumulation and workers' consumption are in conflict, the system may produce a cycle in employment ratio and in the growth rate of income. Perhaps not under globalization but, ideally, high profits lead to high growth rates and increases in wages, which in turn squeeze profit rates. Employment level, growth rate, and output fall, and profits are restored as productivity exceeds the growth of the wage rate. The system is then Liapunov stable with unchanging coefficients, and orbitally unstable otherwise. In the absence of conflict, the production coefficients can probably be incorporated in the gradient matrix given in Appendix 5.

PART II

Part II, consisting of Chapters 4 and 5, is devoted to a study of the economic orthodoxy that came into vogue in the mid-1980s. The task of Chapter 4 is to determine whether or not this new orthodoxy is grounded in the theory outlined in Part I. Chapter 5 simply looks at the impacts of the new orthodoxy on society's well being.

Chapter 4

This chapter begins with an attempt to unravel Adam Smith's concept of the common good. Over the years, economists have, perhaps inadvertently, equated it with welfare maximization and the like, but there is a big caveat. The scientific theory leaves welfare undefined. In this sense, therefore, the proposition that economics maximizes welfare is meaningless. At best, it can define the necessary conditions for welfare improvement or promotion, that is, under the assumptions of freedom of choice and competition, the economic system is capable of calling on available technologies to bring diverse agents' choices into balance, but in the absence of EPI. However, since there is no sure way of getting rid of EPI, while the welfare function itself remains undefined within the theory, we are not in a position to make the claim that economics maximizes welfare. Nonetheless, economics, being a social science, has a consciously and collectively chosen dimension. Sound economic behavior implies first leaving the provision of public goods to the state; attempting to internalize externalities so as to prevent them from distorting market signals too much; and accounting as much as we can for the presence of increasing returns to scale. Second, devising a set of sufficient conditions dealing with the distribution of wealth and income to promote society's well-being. This last set of conditions boils down to choosing the structure of market gradients through economic policy.

These results imply that the process of formulating policy in a democratical-ly organized society rests on societal consensus. Chapter 4 voices some concerns with regard to the implementation of the new orthodoxy labeled GD&R. This major policy shift is being implemented without consultation, without debate, and, it seems, without the understanding of those that are called on to bear its brunt. The new orthodoxy calls for the withdrawal of the state from economic affairs, the dismantlement of all income support measures, and an emphasis on individual responsibility in the economic arena. However, in the theoretically gray areas, and whenever statements are meaningless, the state must intervene. In this sense, at least, the income support measures are in line with the theory's goal, and individual responsibility makes good sense only when the economic playing field is leveled, which is unlikely. Hence, the principal propositions of the new orthodoxy are not meaningful in the context of the theory. This being so, Chapter 4 tries to find their justification elsewhere.

However, after careful examination, the closest we come to a justification is the interplay of the wage-inflation theory and the management of the public debt. This should normally raise many an eyebrow. The wage-inflation theory is a defunct ad hoc theory, while the debt management approach is a shaky heuristic. How could they be the force driving a major policy shift that, in addition, has managed to produce near perfect consensus in the economic establishment? Chapter 4 has no answer. However, after reconsidering the role of false consciousness in human affairs, the inescapable conclusion is that the main objective of the new orthodoxy is really capital accumulation. To make it more palatable, the establishment has wrapped the new orthodoxy in a cloud of buzzwords, such as efficiency and growth, which further shelter it from public debate.

The principal conclusions of the chapter are: (1) market economics can promote society's common good by promoting free choice and competition, by devising measures that help to circumvent EPI, and by respecting society's ethical values; (2) the prevailing economic orthodoxy, known under the acronym GD&R, is not a sound policy by virtue of (1) above; (3) instead, GD&R leans on defunct ad hoc models and on a strong dose of false consciousness to gain acceptance. As far as Chapter 4 can determine, its unavowed goal is not primarily economic growth, but capital accumulation on the world scale.

Chapter 5

GD&R, in vogue since the mid-1980s, has puts forth a number of tacit prescriptions outlined in Chapter 4. In return, it pledges to increase foreign direct investment, increase and diversity international trade flows, reduce sovereign debts and improve balances of payments, and resume world economic growth. Chapter 5 examines these pledges in light of data spanning the decade 1987–1997. The official inception of the new orthodoxy dates back from the mid-1980s, but at the time of this writing, a complete set of data beyond 1996 was not yet available. Up to that date, the results were as follows:

A. The financial resources transferred to Southern countries, as a percentage of GDP, decreased from 1980 to 1991, except for Mexico and Thailand (Table A5.8). More specifically, it decreased from 1.1% to -0.8% for the 15 most indebted countries. Between 1982 and 1992, the net absolute amounts transferred to Africa, Western Asia, and the Mediterranean were positive. They were negative in the cases of

Latin America and the Caribbean, the rest of Asia and, of course, the most indebted countries. By a strange turn of events, the most indebted countries transferred $257 billion to the richer countries over the period (Table A5.9).

B. The value of international trade increased, but still in a context of increased polarization. The current account balance improved for developed market economies and for countries in transition, but it worsened for developing market economies. The current account balance showed persistent surpluses for Germany and Japan between 1982 and 1992. During the same period, it showed persistent deficits for a sample of 128 developing market economies. From 1992 to 1997, the current account deficit of all developing countries increased from $24 billion to $112.5 billion. On the other hand, there was a slight shift in the pattern of world trade from 1980 to 1991. However, the three main blocs continued to trade mainly among themselves (Tables A5.10, A5.11).

C. Between 1982 and 1992, the sovereign debt of a sample of 122 developing market economies increased from $781 billion to $1419 billion, that is, an 86% increase. The short-term debt of the 15 most indebted countries decreased from $105 billion to $71 billion, but their long-term debt went from $280 billion to $454 billion. By 1997, the total external debt of all developing countries had increased to $1853.4 billion. However, from 1992 to 1997, their ratio of external debt to GDP went from 38.2% to 30.2%.

D. During the second half of the period under consideration, the value of exports of Latin America and Africa increased at 6% and 2.4% per year, respectively. Those of Western Asia, on the other hand, went from 18.7% per year in the first half down to 15.3% per year during the second half.

E. In terms of real growth rates, the situation improved in some regions and worsened in others. For example, marked improvements were observed in Southern and Eastern Asia, Latin America, and the Caribbean. However, growth remained sluggish in industrial countries and dramatically deteriorated in countries in transition. On the average, the world real growth rate, during the 1981–1988 period, was 2.9%; by 1993, it fell to 1.1%, and in 1994, it climbed back to 2.5%. In terms of real per capita growth rates, that statistic stood at 2.8% per year during the 1981–1988 period. It fell to -0.6% in 1993 and rose to 0.6% in 1994. According to the medium-term baseline scenario of the IMF (*WEO* 1997), the four-year average (1995–1998) of real GDP growth rates were 2.7% in advanced economies, 6.4% in developing ones, and 1.8% in countries in transition. Interestingly enough, the preglobalization eight-year averages (1979–1986) were 2.6%, 4.1% and 2.8%, respectively.

F. Downsizing and restructuring increased the profits of a minority of firms. According to a study of 131 firms carried out by Mercer Management, Inc., only 27% reported better days after downsizing and restructuring. In the meantime, the ratio of the average CEOs salary to the average worker's salary went from 42 to 1 in 1980, to 185 to 1 in 1994, and to 187 to 1 in 1997.

G. In the first eight years following the general acceptance of GD&R, in the G7 countries where growth was sluggish, the rates of market capitalization of big corporations increased anywhere from 15.6% to 59.6% per year.

H. Finally, in terms of economic growth, variance analyses showed that there is neither a significant difference between more advanced and less advanced countries in transition, nor between countries that have reduced their debt load and those that have increased it during the last three consecutive years. The same type of test showed that, with regard to the relationship between growth and inflation, there is a significant difference among low, moderate, and high inflation countries. It also showed that there is a significant one between low and moderate groups, but countries with moderate inflation rates performed better than countries that had either low and high inflation rates. However, I am the first to admit that the test on countries in transition does not appear satisfactory mainly due to the fact that only the year 1996 was considered. Although, for lack of data, I could not demonstrate it, I nevertheless think that there is a real difference between countries that are en route to capitalism. My hunch is that when the data are in, it will be found that countries with more efficient governments and economic institutions, that are capable of seriously addressing the problems of coordination failures and corruption, perform better than those with weak and corrupt institutions.

Admittedly, if we exclude the cases of Chile and New Zealand, the period examined is relatively short. But the evidence presented for this short period showed that GD&R has not yet delivered on its pledges, and might never do since its main policy recommendations are not upheld by the data.

PART III

Part III, consisting of Chapters 6, 7, and 8, focuses on the social impacts of GD&R. As stressed in Part II, GD&R claims that its official objective is economic growth through market development and individual responsibilities. However, we saw that the average rate of economic growth under GD&R is lower than that recorded for past performances. Instead, in its wake we find unemployment, deconstruction, and increased inequality. Part III attempts to shed more light on this incongruity.

Chapter 6

Chapter 6 looks at the specific threat that GD&R represents for employment and social security systems. Unemployment is, among other things, a grave social ill. Society must be watchful so as not to let governments, jockeying for votes, use this statistic as an expedient. Chapter 6 begins by mounting a defense against such potential manipulation by shedding light on the way unemployment is measured. It shows how poor various measures of unemployment are, and argues that, at best, they can only convey the direction of changes. Next, the chapter looks at the various costs associated with unemployment. On the psychological level, unemployment shatters self-confidence and self-esteem. On the social level, it fuels violence, urban decay, school drop-outs, ethnic intolerance, and racism. On the economic front, it represents lost opportunities and, in addition, deskills the labor force which, in turn, exacerbates the problems of unemployment. More importantly for our purpose, unemployment is a major cause of poverty.

Clearly, if unemployment has many extra-market dimensions, it cannot be left to the whims of profit maximization. Instead, we must address it both within and outside the labor market. However, for that to be possible, we must beforehand clear up a number of misconceptions, provide better estimates of unemployment by category, and reform our general attitude and our institutions.

The income support measures in place since World War II represent another bulwark against poverty. Specific studies of these measures unambiguously confirm this fact. These measures, principally disability and survivors's benefits and social security, benefit mostly the young and the elderly. Both are financed through employment and both are threatened by changes in economic conditions and demographics. Put differently, unemployment has increased under GD&R. The proportion of the population under 15 years old, that is, the future work force, is falling in both developed and developing market economies. The proportion of 65-year-olds and over is on the increase. These three phenomena combine to threaten to the financial viability of income support measures.

Naturally, there is now a drive in most countries toward reform. The inclination, encouraged by GD&R, is to privatize. This chapter argues that moving from publicly financed programs to privately financed ones is no panacea. The switch involves transition costs, higher administrative costs, and higher tax rates for participants. On the one hand, the change from public to private financing may give households a greater choice in the management of their contributions. On the other, it may exacerbate the adverse selection problem, and may prove detrimental to the well-being of those that are less well versed in the appreciation of risks and return.

In terms of principal conclusions, we have the following:

A. Unemployment is a multifaceted problem that is poorly measured. The national figures are grossly underestimated and intercountry comparisons are meaningless. A better method of assessing unemployment is urgently needed. As a suggestion, consider: (1) a definition of the *active* labor force as the bracket of 16 to 65-year-olds; (2) a measure of the *actively employed* as the difference between the employed total and the number of over 65-year-olds still working; (3) a measure of the *inactive* labor force as the difference between (1) and (2); and (4) *unemployment* is then the *inactive* labor force minus students, the sick, and refusals (i.e., those not interested in working).

B. The unprecedented rise in unemployment around the world is not due to increased women's participation, the baby-boom phenomenon (Table A6.1), the generosity of income support measures, or a rise in the NAIRU. The real culprits seem to be skill mismatch and greed.

C. Under the impulsion of GD&R, dangerous trends in employment, such as slave and child labor, are emerging, principally in the South; they must be resisted. In the meantime, attitude and institutions must be reformed along the examples of Japan and, perhaps, Holland.

D. Publicly financed income support measures are a bulwark against poverty, and they have a positive effect on life expectancy (Table A6.4).

E. Demographic trends present a real menace to the financial viability of income support measures, and they are expected to continue unabated until the year 2025 (Table 6.5).

F. In response to the risk of bankruptcy, most countries are leaning toward privatization. The solution is not there. Under pressure from the advocates of GD&R, governments may be tempted to shirk through such a move. Citizens should make sure that the move to privatization is warranted by cost-benefit analyses.

Chapter 7

It is generally argued that economic growth is the only realistic approach to alleviating poverty. GD&R, then, appears attractive precisely for its emphasis on growth. Chapter 7 looks at growth in a finite world, and finds that it has been astutely equated with a number of appealing concepts, such as economic welfare, living standard, quality of life, among others things. This stratagem has been so successful that the majority of people in both North and South now think that with economic growth the future can only be better and richer. Economists, for their part, have made an earnest effort to analyze the process of economic growth. That effort has not produced meaningful results, however. The process is still not well understood. What seems to be certain is that growth is necessary for the survival of the capitalist system. As there seems to be no viable substitute for the market system at present, it must live on. But, it cannot do so in its present form; it is damaging to the ecosystem, while increasing relative poverty. Chapter 7 argues that when both benefits and drawbacks are taken into consideration, we come to an inescapable conclusion; that is, society would be better off by moving away from its fixation on quantitative growth and toward development. In the meantime though, the principle of sustainability should be seen as a stopgap solution.

The main conclusions are the following:

A. Quantitative economic growth is first and foremost a process that involves the continuous drawdown of finite low entropy stores, while producing additional bundles of goods, services, heat, and waste products. Services are consumed immediately. Artifacts are enjoyed for a time before being turned into waste. Waste and heat are reducing the productivity of existing resources, and are damaging the environment. If quantitative growth has the potential to alleviate absolute poverty, it increases relative poverty.

B. The GNP or GDP per capita measure does not reflect the true cost of quantitative growth. Hence, we have no solid ground to claim that it is proportional to economic welfare.

C. Sustainability is a stopgap principle with the potential for mitigating the impacts of quantitative growth on the ecosystem and relative poverty. Until the thinking of society shifts from this form of growth to development, sustainability should embody three subprinciples. Namely: (1) The process of growth should not promote the misleading idea that society can manage the geosystem. In no way should the process of quantitative growth interfere with the global natural balance; (2) the net (after clean up) rate of exploitation of renewable resources should not exceed their natural rates of growth; and (3) nonrenewable resources should be exploited according to the principle of resource accounting. More explicitly, the net-present value of a nonrenewable resource should be converted over time into an equivalent capital asset. This means that the consumption rate of such a resource is bounded from above by the growth rate of capital.

Chapter 8

Chapter 8 closes the discussion of inequality and income distribution. Since Part I, we became aware of the fact that markets not only produce both goods and bads, but that they distribute them unfairly. The chapter provides an overview of inequality around the world. Intercountry inequality is worse in Asia, followed by the Americas. The European Union fare best on this score, while Asian and the former socialist countries fare best on intracountry income distribution. A cursory analysis of the reason for such disparities points to the absence of income support measures, among other things. Briefly, these measures seem to do more to alleviate poverty than economic growth. As GD&R has launched a frontal attract on both employment and income support measures, it is hard not to conclude in the end that it is exacerbating poverty around the world.

This is worth repeating. Off-shore production, due to lower wages and lower social costs, creates a lure of economic growth in the South and contributes to unprecedented unemployment in the North. Unemployment in the North, in turn, threatens the funding of the income support measures. However, these measures together with employment are safeguards against the poverty created mainly by poor wealth and income distribution. It is reasonable, therefore, to argue that GD&R is exacerbating poverty in a double way. First, by emphasizing individual responsibility and downsizing, it encourages unemployment and the elimination of public assistance to the poor. Next, it encourages income and wealth maldistribution that, in turn, increases relative poverty.

The alternative is for governments to create conditions promoting employment while maintaining funding for income support measures in the meantime. The big question is: How can they do so without incurring more debt? Chapter 8 sees no alternative to a Tobin tax on the financial market. In this regard, the conclusions are:

A. The Tobin tax would reduce the exchange rate volatility associated with speculation, foster international coordination in this regard, reduce risk premia, and perhaps improve resource allocation. More importantly, it would provide governments with the badly needed resources to promote society's well-being.

B. The Tobin tax is opposed, because of its associated deadweight loss; such a loss is probably too small to be measured. It is nevertheless hard to see how a 2 base point tax on the profits realized on short-term foreign transactions could be less efficient than a situation subject to volatility, risks, and uncertainty. If the case of Chile is any guide, the Tobin tax stands to stabilize the foreign exchange market, and perhaps stop the drive to deconstruct.

In conclusion, let me remind the reader that the simple exchange economy described in Chapter 3 was only an exercise. When production is added, the Lotka-Volterra process, transposed to the economic scene by Goodwin, better characterizes the real economic situation. However, I hasten to add that it too is an ideal type, which nevertheless provides me with the appropriate backdrop to conclude this essay. In the Lotka-Volterra-Goodwin parable, labor's share of the output plays the role of the predator and the employment ratio is the prey. Normally, if the prey population is deliberately depressed by external forces, that of the predator can only follow suit. Equivalently, if labor's share is falling, capitalist's share (the prey) will grow without bound, unless there exists a natural inhibiting factor to limit it; in such a case, the growth of capitalist's share follows a logistic path. One should not be misled, however. This parable characterizes a wide class of problems, although I will be the first to recognize that human economic interaction is not so simple. Nevertheless, the lesson here is that capital has become completely mobile under globalization, while labor is not. It is as if the prey were free to move to other locations where the dangerous predator can not follow. In each new environment, however, local predators are weak and inept. In other words, the prey appears to be well organized, while predators are disorganized and outmaneuvered.

However, I am the first to acknowledge that the Goodwin parable does not quite describe the situation of the mid-1990s. The present inquiry indeed shows that GD&R is more or less a prey-predator process, but one in which both species compete for a common resource. Mathematical analyses and ecological observations show that such a process produces two stable equilibria (a) and (b) and many unstable equilibria. In (a) there is a positive population for both species, and in (b) one is wiped out. However, if we happen to be in (a), a slight change in any one of the environmental parameters results in a jump to (b), i.e., an ecological catastrophe. For me, the moral is clear, I sincerely hope that this essay will also make it clear to those in charge.

NOTES

INTRODUCTION

1. This new orthodoxy is to be distinguished from past episodes of trade and capital liberalization. This one stands out from the others by its scale and its scope. It is a general rule of behavior, covering not only world trade and capital movement, but public policy, including the dismantlement of all social protection measures, and the dissemination of the American culture. See, for example, Watkins (1995), and the World Commission on Culture and Development (1995).
2. See Hawking (1988).
3. There are may examples, such as Mishan (1969), Galbraith (1971), Henderson (1981), among others.

CHAPTER 1

1. For an interesting account of the origin of analytical economics, see Rima (1967), Ch. 1.
2. Smith (1776, Bk II, 255).
3. For an account of the link between *The Theory of Moral Sentiments* and *The Wealth of Nations*, see Morrow (1928).
4. For Smith's reference to Mandeville's ideas on private vices and public benefits, see Smith (1911, 451).
5. Arrow and Hahn (1971).
6. Quoted in Barrow (1988,10–26 passim), by permission of Oxford University Press.
7. For more precise definitions of the term, see Kuhn (1970).
8. For an extended discussion on what separates these families, see Barrow (1988), Ch. 1.
9. See Tipler et al. (1980, 97), Einstein (1921), among others.
10. Laplace (1974). For this and the discussion of the appendix to this chapter, see Poincaré (1911, 1968), Weinberg (1980).

11.For a proof of Gödel's First Incomplete Theorem see Behnke et al. (1974, vol. I, 72–79).
12.See Casti (1994, 138).
13.No one can claim that she fully understands the quantum theory, but the non-specialist can begin with Bohr (1958), Heisenberg (1959).

CHAPTER 2

1. This connection is consistent with the one made by Ingrao and Israel (1990), Chs. 8 and 9.
2. See the 1954 English translation of Walras by William Jaffe (1981).
3. Jaffe (1981, 313–336).
4. Samuelson (1947), Ch. 9.
5. See Grether and Plott (1979), Slovic and Lichtenstein (1983), among others.
6. Muth (1961, 315–335), Lucas (1976).
7. Quoted in Ingrao and Israel (1990, 287–288), by permission of MIT Press.

CHAPTER 3

1. Brouwer (1910, 176–180), Kakutani (1941); for a simplified presentation, see Varian (1978, 142–144).
2. For the kinds of complication that may arise from fixed-point equilibria, see Baumol and Benhabib (1989, 77–105); Koçak (1986), Ch. 3 and Lesson 11.
3. For an excellent primer on gradient dynamics, see Hirsch and Smale (1974), Ch. 9.

CHAPTER 4

1. It seems that Archbishop Temple first used the term to distinguish the measures of economic well-being in England from similar concepts in use in Nazi Germany. The term welfare was again used in the Beveridge (1942) Report.
2. The incompatibility thesis is thought to have been central to the right wing agenda of the Thatcher and Reagan governments. For an account, see Mishra (1984).
3. See Lane (1991, 43–45).
4. Speech of the Secretary General, delivered at the 9th Session, Geneva, 1996.
5. Speech of Vice President Al Gore at the United Nations Social Summit, held at Copenhagen in March 1995.
6. See, for example, Rodrik (1994).
7. Smith (1776, Bk. I, 10 and Ch. 11, passim). For other views on the invisible hand and on public works, see Book IV, Chs. 2, 4 and 9 and Book V, Part 3.
8. For an assessment of the threat that MAI poses for the sovereignty of Canada, see Clarke (1997), Clarke and Barlow (1997).

CHAPTER 5

1. See to that effect the Multilateral Agreement on Investment (MAI). Although citizens and most legislators have been kept in the dark, the treaty has been under negotiation at the OECD in Paris since 1995. The original version was not signed in April 1998 as planned, thanks to strong opposition in some quarters (France, Canada, New Zealand).

2. The link between inflation and economic growth will be reexamined in the fifth section of this chapter.
3. The sharing of the proceeds of growth between lenders and borrowers is well illustrated in a study carried out in the United Kingdom. From 1957 to 1969, as the long-term real rate of interest was around zero, lenders and borrowers were found to share the proceeds of growth fairly evenly. During the 1970s, the real rate became negative and borrowers gained. However, when Mrs. Thatcher began targeting inflation, the real rate became and remained positive for her entire period in office. Consequently, the richest 2% of the population appropriated as much of the national income as the bottom 50%. (Douthwaite 1993, Ch. 5).
4. For a clear account of the impacts of the inflation-targeting policies in the United Kingdom, see Green and Sutcliffe (1987).
5. Soros seems to favor the creation of an international credit insurance corporation, which would compel borrowers to reveal their true credit position so as to determine the maximum amount of loan to be insured. In this regard, Professor Kunibert Raffer has another idea; he raises the possibility for countries to seek protection from their creditors by using American style bankruptcy codes. For more on these proposals, see *The Guardian Weekly*, January 18, 1998. Another alternative measure is, of course, some variant of the Tobin tax, discussed in Chapter 8.
6. The term consolidation is used in conjunction with restructuring to mean efficiency-enhancing structural changes, such as closures, mergers, and other alliances, and, of course, labor shedding. For more on the claims of globalization as regards consolidation in the European banking system, see IMF (*WEO*, May 1997, 24–25).
7. See *The Wall Street Journal Europe*, Brussels, December 9, 1996.
8. *Le monde diplomatique*, July 1996, quoted by permission.
9. Since samples are disposed column wise, there are J colums with x_{ij} observations in each. There are m_j observations in each column, and $\sum_1^j m_j = N$ total observations. Column means and the grand mean are denoted $\bar{x}_{ij}$ and $\bar{x}$, respectively. The sum of the squared deviations of column means from the grand mean is S_b^2, while the sum of the squated deviations of x_{ij}, from $\bar{x}_{ij}$ is S_w^2. The total estimated deviation is $\sigma^2 (= S_b^2 + S_w^2)$, while σ^2 is the true variance of the population. The objective of the test is to compare S_b^2 with S_w^2 in order to ascertain wheter or not S_b^2 differs more than might be accounted for by chance, with S_w^2 as a reference value of chance variation. The numbers of degrees of freedom associated with S_b^2 and S_w^2 are $df_1 = (J–1)$ and $df_2 = (\sum_1^m x_{ij} - 1)$, respectively. On the ground that variance estimates are independent and drawn from a normally distributed and homogeneous population, S_b^2, S_w^2 and $\hat{\sigma}^2$ are espected to be good estimates of σ^2. Otherwise, hetegeneity is present; in such a case, S_b^2 and $\hat{\sigma}^2$ will be affected, but S_w^2 will not be, since it is a reference measure. The ratio S_b^2 / S_w^2 follows the F-distribution with df_1 and df_2 degrees of freedom. For more details on the 'between' and 'within' column variance test, see Frederick E. Croxton, et al. *Applied Statistics*, (Englewood Cliffs, NJ: Prentice-Hall, 1967), pp. 605–619.
10. Three of my students, using a more complete data set from 1989 to 1996, have found a real difference between a sample of countries more advanced toward transition and another sample of less advanced ones. Any requests for a copy of their term paper should be channeled through the author.

CHAPTER 6

1. *Le monde diplomatique*, July 1996.

2. See Solow (1986, S30).
3. Solow, ibid. S31.
4. See James K. Galbraith (1997, 93–108).
5. See Farnetti (1997, 16), quoted by permission of *Le monde diplomatique*.
6. *The Guardian Weekly*, November 17, 1996, quoted by permission.
7. Gramlich (1996, 57).

CHAPTER 7

1. Georgescu-Roegen (1971), Chs. IX and X.
2. See the 4th edition of Pigou (1932).
3. Douthwaite (1993, 6–8).
4. In developing the MEW index, Nordhaus and Tobin (1972) hoped to prove that the level of GNP was indeed closely related to their definition of economic welfare. They were quite satisfied with the result, that is, until other analysts began reexamining their basic assumptions.

CHAPTER 8

1. The primary reference is Kuznets (1975), but here I am relying more on the analysis of Deininger and Squire (1996, 565–591). See also Deininger and Squire (1997, 36–39).
2. See United Nations (*Etude* 1994, 485–511).
3. See Eurostat (1990).
4. *Le monde diplomatique*, February 1997.
5. For more detail, see *The Guardian Weekly*, January 18, 1998.

BIBLIOGRAPHY

BOOKS AND ARTICLES

Adams, C. and D. Coe. "A System's Approach to Estimating the Natural Rate of Unemployment and Potential Output for the United States." IMF Staff Papers 37 (June 1990): 232–293.

Akerlof, G., W. Dickens and G. Perry. "The Macroeconomics of Low Inflation." *Brookings Papers on Economic Activity* 1 (1996): 1–26.

Arrow, K. J. *Social Choice and Individual Values.* 2nd ed. New York: John Wiley and Sons, 1963.

Arrow, K. J. and G. Debreu. "Existence of an Equilibrium for a Competitive Economy." *Econometrica* 22 (1954): 265–290.

Arrow, K. J. and F. H. Hahn. *General Equilibrium Analysis.* San Francisco: Holden-Day, 1971.

Athanasiou, T. *Show Rechoning: Ecology After the Cold War.* London: Secker & Co., 1997.

Back, G. L. *The New Inflation, Its Causes and Effects.* Englewood Cliffs, NJ: Prentice-Hall, 1972.

Bairoch, P. and R. Kozul-White. "Globalization Myths: Some Historical Reflections on Integration, Industrialization and Growth in the World Economy." UNCTAD Discussion Paper No. 113, March 1996.

Barrow, J. D. *The World Within the World.* Oxford: Clarendon Press, 1988.

Baumol, W. and J. Benhabib. "Chaos, Significance Mechanism and Economic Applications." *Journal of Economic Perspectives* 3 (Winter 1989): 77–105.

Bean, C. R. and P. R. Layard. "The Rise in Unemployment: A Multi-Country Study." *Economica*, Supplement 53 (1986).

Beaudreau, B. "The Impact of Electric Power on Productivity." *Energy Economics* 17 (1995): 231–236.

Behnke, H. et al. eds. *Fundamentals of Mathematics.* Vol. 1, translated by S. H. Gould. Cambridge, MA: The MIT Press, 1974.

Beltrami, E. *Mathematics for Dynamic Modeling.* New York: Academic Press, 1987.

Beveridge, W. H. *Social Insurance and Allied Services.* London: Cmmd 6404, HMSO, 1942.

Blanchflower, D. G. and R. Freedman. "Did the Thatcher Reforms Change British Labor Market Performance?" In *The UK Labour Market: Comparative Aspects and Institutional Developments*, edited by Ray Barrel, 51–92, London: Cambridge University Press, 1994.

Blank, R. M. "Labor Markets and Public Assistance Programs." *NBER Reporter* (Fall 1996): 11–13.

Blejer, M. I. "On the Anatomy of Inflation." *Journal of Money, Credit and Banking* 15 (November 1983): 469–482.

Bohr, N. *Atomic Physics and Human Knowledge*. New York: Wiley & Sons, 1958.

Boulding, K. E. *The Meaning of the Twentieth Century*. New York: Harper and Row, 1964.

Briggs, A. "The Welfare State in Historical Perspectives." *Archives européennes de sociologie* 2 (1961): 221–259.

Brouwer, L. E. "Uber einendeutige stetige transformationen von flächen in sich." *Mathematische Annalen* 67 (1910): 176–180.

Brundtland, H. G. *Our Common Future: Report of the World Commission on Environment and Development*. London: Oxford University Press, 1987.

Calmsfors, L. "Centralization of Wage Bargaining and Macroeconomic Performance." Working Paper No. 131, OECD, Paris, 1993.

Casti, J. L. *Complexification*. New York: Harper Perennial, 1994.

Christensen, L., D. Cummings and D. Jorgenson. "Economic Growth, 1947–82: An International Comparison." In *New Developments in Productivity Measurement*, edited by J. Kendrick and B. Vaccara, 595–691. Chicago: University of Chicago Press, 1980.

Clarke, T. *Silent Coup*. Toronto: James Lorimer & Co., 1997.

Clarke, T. and M. Barlow. *MAI: The Multilateral Agreement on Investment and the Threat to Canadian Sovereignty*. Toronto: Stoddart, 1997.

Coe, D. T. and F. Gagliardi. "Nominal Wage Determination in Ten OECD Countries." Working Paper No. 19, OECD, Paris, 1985.

Colander, D. *Beyond Microfoundations: Post Walrasian Macroeconomics*. New York: Cambridge University Press, 1996.

Conference des Nations Unies sur le Commerce et le Développement. *Manuel de la statistique du commerce international*. Genève: UNCTAD, 1979.

Cournot, A. *Recherches sur les principes mathématiques de la théorie de la richesse*. Paris: M. Rivière, 1838.

Daly, H. E. "The Economics of the Steady State." *Papers and Proceedings of the American Economic Association*. May 1994a: 15–21.

Daly, H. E. "The Steady-State Economy: Toward a Political Economy of Biophysical Equilibrium and Moral Growth." In *Valuing the Earth*, edited by H. E. Daly and K. Townsend, Cambridge, MA: The MIT Press, 1994b.

Daly, H. E. "Sustainable Growth: An Impossibility Theorem." In *Valuing the Earth*, edited by H. E. Daly and K. Townsend, Cambridge, MA: The MIT Press, 1994c.

Daly, H. E. and J. Cobb. *For the Common Good*. London: Green Print, 1989.

Debreu, G. "Economies With a Finite Set of Equilibria." *Econometrica* 38 (1970): 287–292.

Debreu, G. *Theory of Value: An Axiomatic Analysis of Economic Equilibrium*. New York: John Wiley and Sons, 1959.

De Brie, C. "Les Européens dans la nasse de l'austérité." *Le monde diplomatique* (July 1996): 1, 9.

Deininger, K. and L. Squire. *A New Data Set Measuring Inequality*. Economic Studies of the World Bank 10 (September 1996): 565–591.

Deininger, K. and L. Squire. "Nouveau regard sur le rapport entre croissance et inégalité des revenus." *Finances & Développement* 34 (1997): 36–39.

Denison, E. "Explanations of Declining Productivity Growth." *Survey of Current Business Part II* (August 1979): Table 1.

Denison, E. *Trends in American Economic Growth 1929–1982.* Washington DC: The Brookings Institution, 1985.

Destutt de Tracy, A.L.C. *Traité d'économique politique.* Paris: Hachette, 1822.

Dixon, J. A. and K. Hamilton. "Élargir la définition de la richesse nationale." *Finances & Développement* 33 (1996): 15–18.

Domar, E. "Expansion and Employment." *American Economic Review* 37 (1947): 243–355.

Dominique, C-R. "Belief and Deterministic Randomness in a One-Sector Discrete Time Optimal Growth Model: The Case of Hong Kong." *Journal of International Economic Integration* 5 (August 1990): 21–27.

Dominique, C.-R. "An Empirical Assessment of Endogenous and Exogenous Fluctuations in a Goodwin Growth Model with Belgian Data." *Asian Journal of Economics and Social Studies* 10 (April 1991): 107–122.

Dominique, C.-R. "Feedbacks and Discontinuities in the Productivity of the Natural Resource Base: With Emphasis on the Earth Atmosphere." *Asian Journal of Economics and Social Studies* 13 (1994): 257–276.

Dominique, C.-R. "Market Choice Formation and Reversals Studied as Fields' Interactions: With Special Emphasis on the Role of Information." Working Paper No. 92–73, Laval University, 1992.

Dominique, C.-R., F. des Rosiers and L. Kiss. "Nonlinearity and Limits to Forecasting in the Canadian Residential Housing Market." Working Paper No. 9605, Department of Economics, Laval University, 1996.

Douthwaite, R. *The Growth Illusion.* Tulsa: Council Oak Books, 1993.

Eichengreen, B. *Globalizing Capital: History of the International Monetary System.* Princeton, NJ: Princeton University Press, 1996.

Einstein, A. *La théorie de la relativité restreinte et générale.* Paris: Gauthier-Villars, 1921.

Eurostat. *Basic Statistics of the Community.* Luxembourg: Eurostat, 1990.

Farnetti, R. "Excellents indices économiques pour un pays en voie de dislocation." *Le monde diplomatique* (February, 1997): 16.

Field, J. and R. Pressel. *Our Economy.* New York: University Press of America, 1993.

Friedman, I. *Inflation: A Worldwide Disaste.* London: Hamish Hamilton, 1973.

Friedman, M. "The Role of Monetary Policy." *American Economic Review* 58 (1968): 1–17.

Galbraith, J. K. *Economics, Peace and Laughter.* London: Deutch, 1971.

Galbraith, James. "Time to Ditch the NAIRU." *Journal of Economics Perspectives* 11 (Winter 1997): 93–108.

Gautier, J-F. *L'univers existe-t-il?* Le Mejan, France: Acte Sud, 1994.

George, V. and P. Wilding. *The Impact of Social Policy.* London: Routledge and Kegan Paul, 1984.

Georgescu-Roegen, N. *The Entropy Law and the Economic Process.* Cambridge, MA: Harvard University Press, 1971.

Gershon, F. and G. Le Moigne. "Une gestion équilibrée des ressources en eau." *Finances & Développement* 31 (June 1994): 24–27.

Gillon, C. and A. Bonilla. "La privatizacion de un regimen nacional de pensiones: el caso de Chile." *Revista Internacional del Trabajo* 111 (1992): 193–221.

Goodwin, R. M. "A Growth Cycle." In *Socialism, Capitalism and Economic Growth,* edited by C. Feinstein, 54–58, Cambridge, MA: Cambridge University Press, 1967.

Gramlich, E. M. "Different Approaches for Dealing with Social Security." *Journal of Economic Perspectives* 10 (Summer 1996): 55–66.

Green, F. and B. Sutcliffe. *The Profit System: The Economics of Capitalism*. London: Penguin, 1987.

Grether, D. and C. Plott. "Economic Theory of Choice and the Preference Reversal Phemenon." *American Economic Review* 69 (1979): 623–638.

Halimi, S. "Economistes en guerre contre les salaires." *Le monde diplomatique* (July 1996): 10.

Harrod, R. F. *Toward a Dynamic Economics*. London: Macmillan, 1948.

Hawking, S. *A Brief History of Time*. New York: Bantham Books, 1988.

Heisenberg, W. *Physics and Philosophy*. New York: Harper & Row, 1959.

Henderson, H. *Politics of the Solar Age: Alternatives to Economics*. New York: Doubleday, 1981.

Hicks, J. R. *Value and Capital*. 2nd ed. Oxford: Oxford University Press, 1946.

Higgins, M. and J. William. "Asian Demography and Foreign Capital Dependence." Working Paper No. 5560, National Bureau of Economic Research, 1996.

Hirsch, M. W. and S. Smale. *Differential Equations, Dynamic Systems and Linear Algebra*. New York: Academic Press, 1974.

Hu, Z. and M. S. Khan. *Why Is China Growing So Fast?* Washington, DC: IMF Economic Issues, 1997.

Ingrao, B. and G. Israel. *The Invisible Hand*. Cambridge, MA: The MIT Press, 1990.

International Labor Organization. *1992 Yearbook of Labor Statistics*, 51st ed. Geneva: ILO, 1993.

International Monetary Fund. *World Economic Outlook*. Washington, DC: IMF WEFS, April 1989.

International Monetary Fund. *World Economic Outlook*. Washington, DC: IMF WEFS, May and October 1990.

International Monetary Fund. *World Economic Outlook*. Washington, DC: IMF WEFS, May 1995.

International Monetary Fund. *World Economic Outlook*. Washington, DC: IMF WEFS, May 1997.

International Monetary Fund. *International Capital Markets: Developments, Prospects and Key Policy Issues*. Washington, DC: IMF WEFS, November 1997.

Isnard, A. N. *Traité des richesses*, 2 vols. Lausanne, 1781.

Jaffe, W. "Another Look at Léon Walras' Theory of Tâtonnement." *History of Political Economy* 13 (1981): 313–336.

Jones, A. *The New Inflation*. London: Penguin, 1973.

Jorgenson, D. W. "Productivity and Postwar US Economic Growth." *Journal of Economic Perspectives* 2 (Fall 1988): 23–41.

Kakutani, S. "A Generalization of Brouwer's Theorem." *Duke Mathematical Journal* 8 (1941): 457–458.

Katouzian, O. *Ideology and Method in Economics*. New York: New York University Press, 1980.

Kendrick, J. W. "International Comparisons of Recent Productivity Trends." In *Contemporary Economic Problems: Demand, Productivity and Population*, edited by William Fellner, Washington, DC: American Enterprise Institute, 1982.

Keynes, J. M. *The General Theory of Employment, Interest and Money*. New York: Harcourt, Brace & Co., 1936.

Keynes, J. M. *A Treatise on Money*. London: Macmillan, 1930.

Kirman, A. P. "Whom or What Does the Representative Individual Represent?" *Journal of Economic Perspectives* 6 (1992): 117–136.

Klein, P. A. *The Role of Economic Theory*. Boston: Kluwer Academic Press, 1994.

Koçak, H. *Differential and Difference Equations Through Computer Experiments*. New York: Springer-Verlag, 1886.

Kuhn, T. S. *The Structure of Scientific Revolutions*. Chicago: Chicago University Press, 1970.

Kuznets, S. *Economic Growth and Structure*. London: Heinemann, 1975.

Lane, R. E. *The Market Experience*. New York: Cambridge University Press, 1991.

Laplace, P-S. *Exposition du système du monde*. Paris: Fayard, 1974.

Layard, R., S. Nickel and R. Jackman. *Unemployment: Macroeconomic Performance and the Labor Market*. London: Oxford University Press, 1991.

Link, A. N. *Technological Change and Productivity Growth*. New York: Harwood Academic Press, 1987.

Lucas, R. E. "Econometric Policy Evaluation: A Critique." In *The Phillips Curve and the Labor Market*, edited by K. Brunner and A. Meltzer, Amsterdam: North-Holland, 1976.

Lucas, R. E. "On the Mechanics of Economic Development." *Journal of Monetary Economics* 22 (1988): 3–42.

Madison, A. "Growth and Slowdown in Advanced Capitalist Economies: Techniques of Quantitative Assessments." *Journal of Economic Literature* 25 (1987): 649–698.

Mandeville (de), B. *The Grumbling Hives: Or Knaves Turn'd Honest* (1705), republished under the title: *The Fable of the Bees or Private Vices, Publik Benefits* Vol. 1. Oxford: Clarendon Press, 1714, 1732, 1924.

Margulis, L. and J. Lovelock. "Biological Modulation of the Earth Atmosphere." *Icarus* 21 (1974): 471–489.

McDermott, J. C. and R. F. Wescott. *Fiscal Reforms the Work*, Washington, DC: IMF Publications, 1996.

McKinsey Global Institute. *Employment Performance*. Washington, DC: McKinley & Co., 1994a.

McKinsey Global Institute. *The Global Capital Market: Supply, Demand, Pricing and Allocation*. Washington, DC: McKinley & Co., 1994b.

Mikesell, R. F. *Economic Development and the Environment*. New York: Mansell Publications Ltd., 1992.

Mill, J. S. "Of Poverty." In *Principles of Political Economy*. Book 2. New York: Appleton-Century-Crofts, 1881.

Mishan, E. J. *Twenty-One Popular Economic Fallacies*. London: Alcore, 1969.

Mishra, R. *The Welfare State Crisis*. Brighton: Wheatsheaf Books, 1984.

Morgenstern, O. "Professor Hicks on Value and Capital." *Journal of Political Economy* 49 (1941): 361–393.

Morrow, G. L. "Moralist and Philosopher." In *Adam Smith, 1776–1920*, edited by J. M. Clarke, Chicago: Chicago University Press, 1928.

Muth, J. F. "Rational Expectations and the Theory of Price Movements." *Econometrica* 29 (1961): 315–335.

Neumann, J. von. "A Model of General Equilibrium." *Review of Economic Studies* 13 (1945): 1–9.

Neumann, J. von and O. Morgenstern. *The Theory of Games and Economic Behavior*. Princeton, NJ: Princeton University Press, 1944.

Newhouse, J. P. "Medical Care Costs: How Much Welfare Loss." *Journal of Economic Perspectives* 6 (September 1992): 3–21.

Nordhaus, W. and J. Tobin. *Economic Growth*. New York: Columbia University Press, 1972.

Olson, M. "The Productivity Slowdown, the Oil Shocks, and the Real Cycle." *Journal of Economic Perspectives* 2 (Fall 1988): 43–69.

Organization of Economic Cooperation and Development. *Etudes économiques de l'OCDE, Etats-Unis*. Paris: OECD, 1996a.

Organization of Economic Cooperation and Development. *Études économiques de l'OCDE, Royaume-Uni*, Paris: OECD, 1996b.

Organization of Economic Cooperation and Development. *Politique scientifique et technologie: Bilan et perspectives*. Paris: OECD, 1991.

O'Riordan, T. "The Politics of Sustainability." In *Sustainable Environment Management: Principles and Practice*, edited by K. K. Turner, London: Belham Press, 1988.

Ormerod, P. *The Death of Economics.* London: Farber and Farber, 1994.

Otting, A. "Les normes internationales du travail, ossature de la sécurité sociale." *Revue internationale du travail* 132 (1993): 183.

Phillips, A. W. "The Relation Between Unemployment and the Change in Money Wage Rate in the United Kingdom, 1861–1957." *Economica* 25 (1958): 283–299.

Pigou, A. C. *The Economics of Welfare.* 4th ed. London: Macmillan, 1932.

Poincaré, H. *Leçons sur les hypothèses cosmologiques.* Paris: Hermann, 1911.

Poincaré, H. *La science et l'hypothèse.* Paris: Flammarion, 1968.

Poinsot, L. *Éléments de statistique suivis de quatre mémoires sur la composition des moments et des aires sur le plan.* Paris, 1842.

Polanyi, K. *The Great Transformation.* London: Beacon Press, 1957.

Polanyi, M. *Personal Knowledge.* Chicago: Chicago University Press, 1960.

Popper, K. *The Logic of Scientific Discovery.* New York: Harper & Row, 1959.

Pritchett, L. "Divergence Big Time." *The Journal of Economic Perspectives* 11 (Summer 1997): 3–17.

Quinzii, M. *Increasing Returns and Efficiency.* New York: Oxford University Press, 1988.

Rima, I. H. *Development of Economic Analysis.* Homewood, IL: Richard D. Irwin, 1967.

Rodrik, D. "Controversies, Institutions, and Economic Performance in East Asia." Working Paper No. 5914, National Bureau of Economic Research, August 1994.

Romer, P. "Increasing Returns and Long Run Growth." *Journal of Political Economy* 94 (October 1986): 1002–1037.

Roubini, N. and J. Sachs. "Political and Economic Determinants of Budget Deficits in Industrial Democracies." *European Economic Review* 33 (May 1989): 903–933.

Rowthorn, B. "Social Corporatism, Wage Dispersion and Labour Market Performance." In *Social Corporatism: A Superior Economic System*, edited by Pekkarinen, London: Clarendon Press, 1992.

Ruigrok, W. and R. van Tulder. *The Logic of International Restructuring.* London: Routledge, 1996.

Samuelson, P. A. "An Exact Consumption-Loan Model of Interest With or Without the Social Contrivance of Money." *Journal of Political Economy* 66 (December 1958): 467–482.

Samuelson, P. A. *Foundations of Economic Analysis.* Cambridge, MA: Harvard University Press, 1947.

Sayer, J. *Modelling the International Transmission Mechanism.* Amsterdam: North-Holland, 1979.

Scarf, H. *The Computation of Economic Equilibria.* New Haven, CT: Yale University Press, 1973.

Seater, J. "Ricardian Equivalence." *Journal of Economic Literature* 31 (1993): 142–190.

Shackleton, N. J. et al. *Initial Report of the Deep Sea Drilling Project.* Boston: Glomar Institute, 1976.

Shackleton, N. J. and N. D. Opdyke. *Memoir 145.* Washington, DC: American Geological Society, 1976.

Shanker, S. *Gödel's Theorem in Focus.* London: Croom & Helm, 1987.

Slovic, P. and S. Litchtenstein. "Preference Reversal: A Broader Perspective." *American Economic Review* 73 (1983): 596–605.

Smith, A. *An Inquiry into the Nature and Causes of the Wealth of Nations,* 5th ed., by Cannan (1776). Reprinted, London: Methuen, 1961.

Smith, A. *The Theory of Moral Sentiments* (1759). London: Bell and Sons, Ltd., 1911.

Solow, R. M. "A Contribution to the Theory of Economic Growth." *Quarterly Journal of Economics* 70 (February 1956): 65–94.

Solow, R. M. "Unemployment: Getting the Questions Right." *Economica* 53, No. 210 S (1986): S23–S34.

Spahn, P. S. "La taxe Tobin et la stabilité des taux de change." *Finances & Développement* 33 (June 1996): 24–27.

Squire, L. "Labor Force, Employment and Labour Markets in the Course of Economic Development." Working Paper No. 336, World Bank, Washington, DC, 1979.

Stern, E. "L'Asie en développement: un nouveau pôle de croissance." *Finances & Développement* 31 (June 1994): 18–20.

Tarski, A. *Introduction to Logic and to the Methodology of the Deductive Sciences*. London: Oxford University Press, 1941.

Tipler, F. J., C. Clarke and G. F. Ellis. "Singularities and Horizons: A Review Article." In *General Relativity and Gravitation*, edited by A. Held, New York: Plenum, 1980.

Thompson, L. H. "The Social Security Reform Debate." *Journal of Economic Literature* 21 (December 1983): 1425–1467.

Tobin, J. "A Proposal for International Monetary Reform." *Eastern Economic Journal*, 4 (July–October 1972): 153–159.

Tokman, V. E. and N. Garcia. *Dinamica del subempleo en America Latina*. Santiago, Chile: ILO, 1981.

Turner, J. A. and N. Watanabe. *Private Pension Policies in Industrial Countries*. Kalamazoo, MI: Upjohn Institute for Employment Research, 1995.

Ul Haq, M., P. Inge and I. Grunberg. *The Tobin Tax: Coping with Financial Volatility*. Oxford: Oxford University Press, 1996.

United Nations. *Etude sur l'économie mondiale, 1979–1980, 1980–1981, 1981–1982, 1991, 1993, 1994, 1995, 1996*. New York: Department of Social and Economic Affairs.

United Nations. *National Accounts Statistics: Analysis of Main Aggregates, 1988–1989*, E.91. XVII.17. New York: United Nations, 1991.

United Nations. *World Population Monitoring*. New York: United Nations, 1992.

United Nations Conference on Trade and Development. "Le développement à l'heure de la mondialisation et de la libéralisation," Rapport du Secrétaire général de la CNUCED, 9th Session, Geneva, 1996.

United Nations Development Programme. *Human Development Report, 1997*. New York: Oxford University Press, 1997.

United Nations Development Programme. *World Development Report, 1995*. New York: Oxford University Press, 1995.

United States Department of Commerce. *Long Term Economic Growth*. Washington, DC: Government Printing Office, 1966.

United States Department of Commerce. *Statistical Abstract of the United States, 1993*, Section 12. Washington, DC: Census Bureau, 1993.

United States Department of Commerce. *Statistical Abstract of the United States, 1995*. Washington, DC: Census Bureau, 1995.

Valdes-Prieto, S. "Administrative Charges in Pensions in Chile, Malaysia, Zambia and the United States." Working Paper No. 1372, World Bank, 1994.

Valdes-Prieto, S. "Vendedores de AFP: Producto del mercado o de regulaciones insuficientes." Working Paper No. 178, Unividad Catolica de Chile, 1995.

Varian, H. R. *Microeconomic Analysis*. New York: W. W. Norton, 1978.

Vickers, D. *The Tyranny of the Market: A Critique of Theoretical Foundations*. Lansing: Michigan University Press, 1997.

von Hagen, J. and B. Eichengreen. "Federalism, Fiscal Restraints and European Monetary Union." *Papers and Proceedings of the 180th Annual Meeting of the American Economic Association,* (May 1996): 134–138.

von Neumann, J. and O. Morgenstern. *The Theory of Games and Economic Behavior.* Princeton, NJ.: Princeton University Press, 1944.

Walras, L. *Éléments d'économie politique pure ou théorie de la richesse sociale,* (1874); 4th ed. Lausanne: Rouge, 1900. English translation, *Elements of Pure Economics,* edited by William Jaffe. London: Allen & Unwin, 1954.

Walras, L. "Principe d'une théorie mathématique de l'échange." *Compte-rendu des séances et travaux de l'Académie des Sciences Morales et Politiques* (August 16–23, 1873): 97–120.

Wang, H. *Reflections on Kurt Gödel.* Cambridge, MA: The MIT Press, 1987.

Watkins. K. "Globalization and Liberalization: Implication for Poverty, Distribution and Inequality." Background Paper for UNDP's *Human Development Report, 1997.* New York: Oxford University Tress, 1997.

Watkins, K., ed. *Oxfam Poverty Report.* Oxford: Oxfam, 1995.

Watson, M. "Asie de l'Est: L'enfant prodige devient adulte." *Finances & Développement* 34 (September 1997): 15–17.

Weinberg, S. *Gravitation and Cosmology.* New York: Wiley & Sons, 1980.

Whitehead, A. N. *Adventures of Ideas.* New York: Cambridge University Press, 1933.

World Bank. *Monitoring Environmental Progress: Expanding the Measure of Wealth.* Washington, DC: World Bank, 1995, 1996.

World Commission on Culture. *Our Creative Diversity.* Paris: UNESCO, 1995.

World Economic Forum. *The Global Competitiveness Report 1996.* Geneva, 1996.

World Economic Outlook (WEO). See International Monetary Fund.

World Health Organization. *Bridging the Gaps,* Report of the 98th World Health Assembly. Geneva: WHO, 1995.

Wright, G. H. von. "Preferences." In *The New Pelgrave,* 942–945, New York: Macmillan, 1987.

PERIODICALS

The Manchester Guardian (May 3, September 6, November 1, and November 15, 1992; September 6 and November 7, 1996; April 27, 1997; January 18 and January 25, 1998).

Le monde diplomatique (February and July, 1994; June and July, 1996; January, February, and April, 1997).

The New York Times (October 1, 1995; March 5, June 1, and December 8, 1996).

U.S. News and World Report (January 22 and November 25, 1996).

The Wall Street Journal Europe (May 15 and December 9, 1996).

INDEX

Administradoras de Fondos de Pensiones, 111, 185
Agent: economic, 5, 52
Analysis: economic, 5; variance, 148–52
Arbitrage opportunity, 41, 48, 64. *See also* Unrealized gain
Arrow, Kenneth, 5, 16, 32, 39, 49, 57, 61–62, 104
Arrow-Debreu Commodity (ADC): definition, 40, 52
Asymmetry: preference relation, 43
Athanasiou, Tom, 209
Austerity measures, 6, 96–97

Barrow, John D., 18
Beaudreau, Bernard, 129, 146
Beveridge Report, 90, 248 ch. 4, n. 1
Blank, Rebecca, 175, 186
Boulding, Kenneth, 193
Bourbakism, 39
Brahe, Tycho, 14, 29
Bretton Woods, 129, 140–41, 233
Broglie, Louis-Victor de, 9
Budget set: definition, 54
Bundle of Arrow-Debreu Commodity, 52

Carnot, Sadi, 27, 29
Casti, John, 21, 79
Chang, Anita, 178
Child workers, 177–78
Clausius, Rudolf, 27, 29
Cognitivism, 45
Comte, Auguste, 27
Conference of British Industry, 144
Conjecture: consumer rationality, 45–46; falling productivity growth, 129–31; Goldbach, 20–21; management of the public debt, 111–16
Connectedness: preference relation, 40, 43–44
Consciousness: false, 119; limited, 119
Consolidation: fiscal, 116, 142
Consumers preferences: definition, 43–47, 55
Consumption set, 44, 53–54
Convexity: strict, 55
Copernicus, Nicolas, 14, 29
Correspondence principle, 37
Cosmogony, 14–15, 27–29
Cosmology, 13–15, 23, 27–30
Cournot, Augustin, 33

Currency speculation, 134–41
Current account balance, 134, 157

Daly, Herman, 199, 207–9
Debreu, Gérard, 16, 32, 39, 49–50, 57–58, 61–62, 65
Debt to GDP ratio, 112–17; relation to economic performance, 149–51, *See also* Conjecture
Defensive expenditures, 205–6
Delphi experiment, 6
Demand: curve, 34; law of, 63; shock, 70
Derivatives, 139–40
Destutt de Tracy, Antoine Louis Claude, 117
Diffentiable potential, 64, 80–81
Dominique, C-René, 24, 45, 74–75, 202, 212–13
Douthwaite, Richard, 192–93, 197–99, 208
Downsizing and restructuring (D&R), 92–93, 96; impacts of, 142–46

Economic: development, 191–92; growth, 191–99 passim, 208–10; performance, 148–52
Economics: scientific status of, 16
Economy: political, 3–5. *See also* Regular economy
Eddington, Arthur, 28–29
Efficiency: markets, 90–91, 231–32; of decentralization, 55
Einstein, Albert, 9, 11, 15, 28–29; special relativity theory, 28; theory of gravitation, 11
Elasticity of demand, 71–72, 83. *See also* Demand
Empiricism. *See* Viewpoints of science
Employment index, 175–76
Endogenous growth theory, 193, 195–96
Endowment: initial, 40, 48, 53–54, 56

Entropy: 27, 191–92, 212. *See also* Thermodynamics
Epimenides paradox, 21
Excessive deficit procedure, 117
Exchange: corrected rate, 218; monetary rate of, 218; pure, 63–69
Externality, 42, 87, 102–4, 195

Falsification: criterion of, 11, 13
Forces of nature: electromagnetic, 11, 25–26, 28, 236–37; gravity, 25–26; strong, 25–26; weak, 25–26
Firm: definition of, 54
Fixed point, 58, 62; theorem, 58
Foreign debt: developing countries, 158
Formalist school of mathematics, 20, 38
Frictional unemployment. *See* Unemployment
Friedman, Milton, 110, 170, 172, 233
Friedmann, Aleksander, 15, 28–29

Gaia hypothesis, 202–3
Galbraith, James K., 173
Galbraith, John K., 164, 193
Galilei, Galileo, 15
Game theory, 49
Gamow, George, 15, 29
Gautier, Jean-François, 14–15, 22, 28
Geocentric universe, 14, 29
Georgescu-Roegen, Nicholas, 192, 202
Gini coefficient, 216, 226–27. *See also* Lorenz curve
Globalization, 92–101 passim; in Chile, 110, 146–47, 184–86; impacts of, 131–42 passim; in New Zealand, 146–47
Gödel, Kurt, 20; proof, 248 ch. 1, n. 11; theorem of, 20–22;
Golden period, 107, 142
Gore, Al, 93, 96, 105

Greenhouse gases, 213–14. *See also* Trace gases
Gross national product (GNP): deflator of, 123–24, 129; nominal, 123; real, 123;
Growth rates of countries in transition, 158. *See also* Economic growth

Hadamar matrix, 66
Hahn, Frank, 5
Heisenberg, Werner, 9, 248 ch. 1, n. 13
Heliocentric universe, 14, 29
Hicks, John, 16, 32, 36–37, 39, 207
Hidden unemployment. *See* Unemployment
Hilbert, David, 20, 38
Hubble, Edwin, 15, 28

Idealism. *See* Viewpoints of science
Ideology, 117–18, 121
Incompatibility, thesis, 89
Incompleteness of theoretical construct, 20
Inconsistency of theoritical constructs: definition, 20
Increasing returns to scale, 42, 87, 91, 102–4, 195
Indifference: curve, 43; subrelation, 43, 55
Inflation, 108–11, passim; definition, 123; expected rate of, 169–71; rate of, 153; role in economic performance, 128, 150–52; role in national income, 128–29
Ingrao, Bruna, 36, 50, 62
International Cross-Border Transactions, 115
Invariance: procedural, 44–46. *See also* Symmetry
Investment-output ratio, 194
Irreflexivity, 43
Israel, Giorgio, 36, 50, 62

Jacobian matrix, 65, 67, 82–83
Jorgenson, Dale, 107, 196

Kant, Emmanuel, 15
Kepler, Johannes, 14–15, 29
Keynes, John Maynard, 47–48, 95, 108–10, 113, 141
Kirman, Alan P., 48, 49
Krugman, Paul, 134, 179
Kuhn, Thomas, 42
Kuznets, Simon, 215–17, 220

Labor force: definition, 165–66; growth of, 187
Lane, Robert E., 91, 168
Laplace, Pierre Simon de, 15, 27, 29
Lemaitre, Georges, 15, 28
Lipsey, Robert, 109
Loan rates, 155
Lorenz curve, 216, 220–23
Lorenz-Poincaré equations, 28
Lotka-Volterra: prey-predator relationship, 74–75; process, 246
Lucas, Robert E., 49, 193–94

Maastricht criteria, 117, 145–46; Treaty of, 97, 117, 144
Mandeville, Bernard de, 4–5, 88
Market capitalization, 145; rates, 159
Market operations, 65–68
Marx, Karl, 118
Maxwell, James Clerk, 11; equations of, 45
McKenzie, Lionel, 36, 39
Meaningfulness of statements: definition, 11, 16
Menger, Carl, 36
Menger, Karl, 36, 38
Mercer Management, 143, 148
Metzler matrix, 66–67
Military expenditures: in G7 countries, 159
Miniparadigm, 7
Monotonicity: strong, 40, 55

Moody's criteria, 114–16

Morgenstern, Oscard, 32, 34, 38–39, 49

Multilateral Agreement on Investment (MAI), 119, 248 ch. 5, n. 1; impacts on Canada, 248 ch. 4, n. 8

Natural resource base, 205, 211

Neoclassical growth model, 193, 195

Neumann, John von, 16, 32, 38–39, 49

Newton, Isaac, 11, 15, 29, 61; theory of gravitation, 11

Non-accelerating inflationary rate of unemployment (NAIRU), 169–73

Nordhaus, William, 198, 250 ch. 7, n. 4

Occam, William, 22; principle of, 22, 70

Oil shocks-inflation, 92

Olson, Mancur, 106

Operationalism. *See* Viewpoints of science

Order: natural, 3–4

Ordering: definition, 44

Ormerod, Paul, 77–78

Output-capital ratio, 194

Pareto, Vilfrido, 36, 198; efficiency, 102–3; optimality, 91

Philosophy: moral, 4

Physics: atomic, 26; plasma, 26; quantum, 23–26

Physiocrats, 3–4, 101

Plank constant, 9

Poincaré, Henri, 27–29, 31, 247 ch. 1, n. 10

Poinsot, Louis, 33

Polanyi, K, 105

Polanyi, Michael, 7

Popper, Karl, 13

Poverty: absolute, 217, 223, 229; index, 224, 235; relative, 217, 224–29

Preference reversal, 26, 44–47

Price: definition, 54; well-determined, 56

Prigogine, Ilya, 29

Priors, 7–10, 12, 19

Privatization measures, 97

Production set, 54

Productivity: capital, 106–8; factors, 106; growth slowdown, 106–8, 121; labor, 106–8, 122–23, 194

Profit function, 55

Public debt, 111–16; definition, 112–13

Public good, 87, 102–4; definition, 42

Purchasing power parity (PPP), 218–19

Quantum object, 24

Quantum region, 26

Quantum theory. *See* Physics

Rationalism. *See* Viewpoints of science

Reagan, Ronald, 92

Regular economy, 58

Relativity theory: special, 11

Representative agent, 46–48, 61

Resources: accounting, 207; global, 200–204

Ricardian equivalence: principle of, 113

Ricardo, David, 102, 113, 174–75

Rodrick, Dani, 110, 125, 146

Romer, Paul, 193–94

Russell, Bertrand, 15

Sachs, Jeffrey, 112, 144

Samuelson, Paul A., 16, 32, 37, 39, 109, 118, 181

Scarf, Herbert, 58
Schrodinger, Erwin, 23; equation of, 23–24
Schockley, William, 13
Science: definition, 11–12; natural, 5, 8, 22–26; practioners of, 6, 8, 10, 13; social, 5, 8, 22–26, 51
Singh, Ajit, 134
Smith, Adam, 4–5, 16, 19, 50, 87–88, 90, 95, 101–2, 192; reference to de Mandeville, 247 ch. 1, n. 4
Smoot, George, 29
Social security system, 181–86; Chile, 184–85; the United States, 183–84
Society: ideal, 3
Solipsism, 8. *See also* Viewpoints of science
Solow, Robert, 109, 171–72, 179, 194, 195
Soros, George, 139–40, 249 ch. 5, n. 5
Span, Paul, 231–32
Speculative attack. *See* Currency speculation
Standard and Poor's criteria, 114–16
Stimulus-response framework (SRF), 45–46
Supply: law of, 63; shock, 70
Symmetry: definition, 17

Tarski, Alfred, 21
Tâtonnement: Walrasian, 35
Tequila effect, 100
Thatcher, Margaret, 92, 249 ch. 5, n. 3
Theorem: First Incomplete, 20–22; fixed-point, 58, 62; intermediate value, 58; meaningful, 37. *See also* Welfare theorems
Theory: economics, 52–59 passim; quantum (*see* Physics); scientific: definition, 10

Thermodynamics, 18, 23, 27; First Law of, 212; Second Law of, 27, 70, 212
Tobin, James, 198, 230, 233; tax, 19, 230–33, 250 ch. 7, n. 4
Trace gases, 213. *See also* Greenhouse gases
Trade diversitication, 134, 157
Transactions. *See* International Cross-Border Transactions

Uncertainty principle, 9
Unemployment, 164–77 passim; definition, 166; methods of measurement, 166–67, 243; rates of, 154, 187–88
Unit labor costs, 123
Unrealized gain, 41, 64
Utility function, 43, 46, 55, 63
Utility index, 43

Validity: scientific statements, 11–12
Variance test: between and within column analysis, 148–52, 249 ch. 5, n. 9
Vickers, Douglas, 172
Viewpoints of science, 7–10
Volatility. *See* Currency speculation

Wage-inflation theory, 122–29
Wage rate: definition, 123
Wald, Abraham, 16, 36, 39
Walras, Léon, 16, 31–37, 39, 62, 64; Law of, 58, 64
Ware-function, 23–24
Welfare theorems, 102–5
Whitehead, Alfred, 7
World Economic Forum, 98, 144
World inequality, 220–29
World real rate of GDP growth, 160
World trade pattern, 133, 157

About the Author

C-RENÉ DOMINIQUE is Professor of Economics at Canada's Laval University. He has worked in the private and public sectors and at the Office of Technical Cooperation at the United Nations. His areas of specialization include industrial studies, planning and policy analysis, microeconomics, and systems' dynamics. Professor Dominique has published extensively in *Industry and Development*, *Economics Letters*, *Journal of Economic Development*, and *Journal of International Economic Integration* among other publications.

ISBN 0-275-96378-0

HARDCOVER BAR CODE

DATE DUE

APR 0

DEMCO, INC. 38-2931

The American University

3 1194 006 780 187